M000315278

SHIPWRECKED

Appleton Oaksmith.
Courtesy of the David M. Rubenstein Rare Book and Manuscript Library, Duke University.

SHIPWRECKED

A True Civil War Story of Mutinies, Jailbreaks, Blockade-Running, and the Slave Trade

JONATHAN W. WHITE

ROWMAN & LITTLEFIELD
Lanham • Boulder • New York • London

Published by Rowman & Littlefield
An imprint of The Rowman & Littlefield Publishing Group, Inc.
4501 Forbes Boulevard, Suite 200, Lanham, Maryland 20706
www.rowman.com

86-90 Paul Street, London EC2A 4NE

Distributed by NATIONAL BOOK NETWORK

Copyright © 2023 by Jonathan W. White

All rights reserved. No part of this book may be reproduced in any form or
by any electronic or mechanical means, including information storage and
retrieval systems, without written permission from the publisher, except by
a reviewer who may quote passages in a review.

British Library Cataloguing in Publication Information Available

Library of Congress Cataloging-in-Publication Data

Names: White, Jonathan W., 1979– author.
Title: Shipwrecked : a true Civil War story of mutinies, jailbreaks,
    blockade-running, and the slave trade / Jonathan W. White.
Other titles: True Civil War story of mutinies, jailbreaks,
    blockade-running, and the slave trade
Description: Lanham, Maryland : Rowman & Littlefield Publishers, 2023. |
    Includes bibliographical references and index.
Identifiers: LCCN 2023001874 (print) | LCCN 2023001875 (ebook) | ISBN
    9781538175019 (cloth) | ISBN 9781538175026 (ebook)
Subjects: LCSH: Oaksmith, Appleton, 1827–1887. | Ship captains—United
    States—Biography. | Slave traders—New York (State)—New
    York—Biography. | Slave trade—United States—History—19th century. |
    Smith, Elizabeth Oakes Prince, 1806–1893—Family. |
    Escapes—Massachusetts—Boston. | United States—History—Civil War,
    1861–1865—Blockades. | Nicaragua—History—Filibuster War, 1855–1860. |
    New York (N.Y.)—Biography. | Carteret County (N.C.)—Biography.
Classification: LCC E340 .O257 2023 (print) | LCC E340 (ebook) | DDC
    973.6092 [B]—dc23/eng/20230201
LC record available at https://lccn.loc.gov/2023001874
LC ebook record available at https://lccn.loc.gov/2023001875

∞™ The paper used in this publication meets the minimum requirements of
American National Standard for Information Sciences—Permanence of Paper
for Printed Library Materials, ANSI/NISO Z39.48-1992.

For Ira Berlin, William Blair, Michael Burlingame, Matthew Gallman, Gary Gallagher, Allen Guelzo, Harold Holzer, Lewis Lehrman, Edna Medford, Lucas Morel, Mark Neely, Ron White, and Frank J. Williams—friends, mentors, and benefactors who have been so generous with me over the years, and who have taught me so much about Abraham Lincoln and the Civil War.

CONTENTS

ILLUSTRATIONS

ACKNOWLEDGMENTS

I owe an immense debt of gratitude to the archivists and librarians who facilitated my research, especially Trevor Plante and Haley Maynard of the National Archives in Washington, DC; Kevin Reilly of the National Archives at New York; Daniel Fleming, Joe Keefe, and Tracy Skrabut of the National Archives at Boston; Nathan Jordan and Sara Brewer of the National Archives at Atlanta; Sarah Waitz of the Center for Legislative Archives; Michelle Krowl of the Library of Congress; John Hannigan of the Massachusetts Archives; Marta Crilly of the Boston City Archives; Martha Gay Elmore of East Carolina University; Leslie Wilson of the Concord Free Public Library; Elizabeth Dunn of the Rubenstein Library at Duke University; Mark Procknik of the New Bedford Whaling Museum; Mary Ann Schneider of the Texas Heritage Museum; Jim Clipson of the HMS *Warrior*; Charles L. Miller of the National Archives at San Bruno, California; Tammy Kiter of the New-York Historical Society; Barbara Cahoon of the Register of Deeds' Office in Carteret County, North Carolina; and Jamie Wetter of the clerk's office in Adams County, Indiana.

My students at Christopher Newport University have been wonderful assistance. Daniel Glenn discovered Appleton Oaksmith during research on the slave trade during the summer of 2016; he and Emily Risko, Emily Munson, Hannah Broughton, Michael Sparks, Danielle Forand, and Reagan Connelly all tracked down newspaper articles and other materials that helped me flesh out this story. Jesse Spencer was able to locate hard-to-find items through Interlibrary Loan. Nancy Larcher, a student at the City University of New York, assisted me with research in New York City. And Caitlin Rosenthal of the University of California Berkeley very graciously had her student research assistant Wen Rui Liau assist me with materials at the Bancroft Library.

The Department of Leadership and American Studies, the College of Social Sciences, and the Office of the Provost supported research trips to

xi

the University of Virginia, Duke University, Boston, Washington, DC, New York City, and the Huntington Library in San Marino, California. Thanks to Ben Redekop, Lynn Shollen, Quentin Kidd, and Dave Doughty for providing this funding. An Andrew W. Mellon Fellowship at the Virginia Museum of History and Culture also supported this work.

Several scholars and friends read the entire manuscript, including Timothy Scherman of Northeastern Illinois University, the world's leading expert on Elizabeth Oakes Smith; Ron Soodalter, whose excellent study of Nathaniel Gordon was instrumental to my own thinking; Mark Neely of Penn State University, who has been a source of guidance and inspiration for almost twenty-five years; Bob May of Purdue University, who offered a very thorough and helpful review; and John Harris of Erskine University, who graciously read the entire book over a Christmas break. Robert Colby of the University of Mississippi read the introduction and discussed several aspects of the book. Timothy Scherman also answered innumerable emails about Oakes Smith, and Ann Gordon of Rutgers University graciously corresponded with me about Susan B. Anthony.

The historians to whom I am dedicating this book have guided and shaped my career. I am grateful to each of them for their friendship and wise counsel over the years. My parents, Bill and Eileen White, fostered my love of history when I was a child by taking me to historic sites and buying me books. They have always encouraged me in my vocation, and I owe them more than I could ever repay. My daughters, Charlotte and Clara, put a smile on my face every day . . . and sometimes still let me read them history books at bedtime. My wife Lauren, and mother-in-law Leigh, read an early version of the manuscript and offered helpful suggestions. For fifteen years (and counting!), Lauren has been the best companion I could have hoped for. She shares a birthday with Appleton Oaksmith, but none of his disreputable characteristics.

PROLOGUE

Today the Charles Street Jail is a luxury hotel. The main lobby, which was once the guard station at the center of the building, has a spectacular, high, vaulted ceiling. Over the years, the prison housed several notable inmates within its walls, including female suffragists who protested Woodrow Wilson's visit to Boston in 1919, Nazi POWs during World War II, and Frank Abagnale—the imposter-turned-FBI-consultant made famous by Leonardo DiCaprio in *Catch Me If You Can*. Malcolm X and Sacco and Vanzetti are also said to have spent time behind its bars.

The prison was established as a model penal institution in 1851, but by the 1960s it was dilapidated. In 1971, the inmates filed a lawsuit in federal court alleging that conditions in the jail violated their Eighth Amendment rights against cruel and unusual punishments. Rats, bugs, pigeons, and other critters infested the place, and the interior of the building was crumbling. As part of his research for the case, US district judge W. Arthur Garrity Jr. spent a night in the prison. He was appalled by the experience. In 1973, he ruled in favor of the prisoners, although the facility remained in use until 1990, when the final inmate was transferred to the new Suffolk County Jail.

In 1991, Massachusetts General Hospital acquired title to the abandoned stone structure. For a time, they used the prison yard as a parking lot. A decade later, workers began to convert the old jail into the Liberty Hotel, which opened to the public in 2007. Eighteen of the hotel's luxurious rooms are in old prison cells. On the ground floor, patrons can buy a drink at a bar called Alibi, in a cellblock that was once used as the "drunk tank cells" for boozers who were temporarily detained. On the south wing of the main floor is an upscale restaurant called Clink.[1] Diners who enjoy their meals at the first table on the left will be seated outside of what was known as Cell No. 9 during the Civil War.

In the summer of 1862, Cell No. 9 was occupied by Appleton Oaksmith, a thirty-four-year-old sailor from Maine who stood five feet, eight inches tall with a long, scraggly beard, piercing black eyes, dark brown hair, and a barrel chest. Oaksmith had just been convicted in the federal court in Boston of outfitting a whaling vessel for the slave trade. Now he was awaiting sentencing. He'd had several other run-ins with the law before this—at least one of which that cost him a small fortune. But never had he been in a situation like this. Had he followed the literary pursuits of his parents, he might have avoided this sort of trouble. His father and mother, Seba Smith and Elizabeth Oakes Smith, were nationally renowned writers and public speakers in the years before the war, and they had instilled in their children a love of literature, art, and poetry. But Appleton instead chose to follow the sea. From a young age, he displayed an adventurous spirit. At sixteen, he joined a long voyage to China. During the California Gold Rush he made his way around South America to San Francisco. From there he traveled to the Congo River, on the west coast of Africa, where he narrowly escaped death at the hands of three thousand African warriors. In the 1850s, he had continued pursuing the sea, taking a lead role in William Walker's filibustering campaign in Nicaragua, as well as the Cuban liberation movement. And then the war came. During the Secession Winter of 1861, Oaksmith tried to broker a peaceful maintenance of the Union. When that failed, he went into business with a fish oil factory owner in New York. The two decided that they needed a whaling vessel, but the whaling industry was in decline by 1861. And so, when he began purchasing old wooden sailing ships, federal authorities arrested him for slave trading. After spending several lonely weeks in Union military bastilles, he now sat in Cell No. 9—convicted, alone, and wondering what would happen next. Perhaps his days on the water had finally come to an inglorious end.

It may be that the saltwater of the ocean ran through Appleton Oaksmith's veins. His maternal grandfather, David Prince, had been the captain and part owner of a brig called the *Ranger*. But on March 26, 1809—during a voyage from Portland to Boston—he drowned off Gloucester, Massachusetts, when the boom of his ship swung and knocked him overboard. The young captain left behind a wife, Sophia, and two daughters (a third daughter had died earlier in the year). One of those children, Elizabeth Oakes Prince, was not yet three years old (she had been born on August 12, 1806). As an elderly woman in the 1880s, Elizabeth recalled a "distinct memory of feeling miserable in black, and seeing my mother's face all tears." As she and her mother and sister rode in a carriage to her paternal grandfather's house, they passed over the Piscataqua River. Sophia Prince stopped the carriage on the bridge and held young Elizabeth up to show her the water. She "told me my dear father was lying under water like that, and I clung to her neck in silent horror."[2] In 1845, Elizabeth would publish a poem titled "The Drowned Mariner," perhaps a cathartic exercise inspired by her father's death. The verses describe a fearless sailor in a storm who "swayed and rocked on the mast," until his "stout limbs" finally gave way, and he was swept overboard into a "watery grave." On the ocean floor, he joined countless others who "lightly sway" in this graveyard, "Away from decay, and away from the storm."[3] Perhaps, in death, her father finally found peace and rest.

On December 7, 1809, Sophia Prince married a widower named Lemuel Sawyer—also a sea captain—who had lost his wife six months earlier. Sawyer had two children from his previous marriage, a daughter named Eleanor (born August 3, 1806) and a son named Lemuel (born September 22, 1808). Elizabeth never said much about her stepfather, other than that he would bring her gifts from his trips abroad, including parrots, monkeys, and young alligators. Eleanor later remembered that Elizabeth "and I were brought up as sisters, and my father always treating her as his own daughter." Over the ensuing years, Sophia and Lemuel would have six more children together, one of whom, Benjamin Franklin Sawyer (born on January 5, 1813, and known as "Frank"), would go on to serve as his nephew Appleton's lawyer during the Civil War.[4]

With her father gone, Elizabeth grew close to her maternal grandfather, Seth Blanchard. Like her father and stepfather, he too went by "Captain." He had been a drummer boy during the Revolution, joining a company of Minute Men at the age of twelve in June 1775. As a young girl, Elizabeth would sit "with rapt attention, and childish awe" as he told stories of the "many and great perils" he had encountered at sea. Once he had barely escaped pirates in the Gulf of Mexico. On another occasion, during a long voyage to East India, Blanchard's hungry men started discussing cannibalism, but he exhorted them, "I fare with you, and will die with you, but so help me God, I will shoot the first man that attempts to kill one of you for this horrible purpose." Elizabeth remembered how these stories "used to thrill my nerves."[5]

On September 5, 1813, during the War of 1812, Elizabeth witnessed a naval battle between the American brig *Enterprise* and the HMS *Boxer*. Neighboring children, including a young Henry Wadsworth Longfellow, came home from school and with pale faces stood near their mothers to watch the fight. Cannons belched forth smoke as shells ripped holes through sails, masts, and men. Following the battle, the commanders of both vessels were laid to rest side by side in the cemetery in Portland. As a young girl, Elizabeth often visited the two gravesites.[6] She could not have known then—at age seven—that her life would continue to be upended by death at sea.

Shipwrecked had a serendipitous beginning. I was conducting research on the slave trade when one of my student research assistants asked me if I'd ever heard of Appleton Oaksmith. I hadn't, but the more I learned about his story the more I realized it was worth telling. A seafarer, poet, jailbird, convict, escapee, exile, and expat, Oaksmith led a life that touched some of the most important moments in nineteenth-century American history. During the 1850s, he became embroiled in several highly controversial international schemes—slave trading in Africa, filibustering in Nicaragua, and assisting Cuba in its fight for independence from Spain. And during the Civil War he found himself in prison, first charged with disloyalty and then with outfitting a slaving vessel. His—and his mother's—interactions with the Lincoln administration reveal the legal and illegal means that Lincoln would use to stamp out the transatlantic slave trade.

Oaksmith came of age during the era of Manifest Destiny—a time when Americans began moving westward over the Great Plains, and the world was embracing the Age of Steam. But he clung to the romantic Age of Sail. He was a man of the past in a quickly changing present. And the sea would be the downfall of his life.

Appleton's mother, Elizabeth Oakes Smith, was once something of a household name. She is largely forgotten today because of the tragic story in this book. Yet she and Appleton have one of the most remarkable family stories in American history. In her diary, she once remarked, "I hope Appleton will some day write his autobiography—it would be full of interest—full of adventure, hair-breadth escapes, and daring courage—yet he is gentle-hearted, courteous, and imaginative."[7] In like manner, when Elizabeth died in 1893, a local newspaper observed, "The history of the family would make a book of intense interest. Whatever their opinions of the character of the Madam every one agrees that intellectually she was the most remarkable woman they ever knew."[8] More than a century since her death, I have attempted to tell her family's story. Appleton is the central figure, and Elizabeth plays an important supporting role.

The family dynamics in Seba and Elizabeth's household were unusual—possibly unique—in early American history. In fact, they turned many social conventions on their heads. In many ways, Elizabeth Oakes

Smith defies categorization—especially on matters of race, politics, and gender. The matriarch of the family, she was an important feminist voice in the years leading up to the Civil War. Abolitionist leaders like Horace Greeley and William Lloyd Garrison ran in her social circles, and in her writing she praised the Haitian revolutionary Toussaint L'Ouverture and the enslaved poet Phyllis Wheatley. And yet she was the mother of a man convicted of slave trading, an ardent Democrat who grew to loathe Lincoln, and a carpetbagger in the postwar South who believed ex-slaves were lazy while their former enslavers were kind. She was a strong personality—a leader in her home, in American literary circles, and in first-wave feminist organizations (one modern writer likens her to Gloria Steinem). And yet the forces of a society at war were too much for her, ultimately leading to her psychological and emotional downfall. She was a loving wife who grew to resent her husband, and a devoted mother whose spirit was destroyed by the decisions of her sons. The arc of her life is a metaphor for the early women's rights movement—hopeful and prolific in the antebellum period, but "displaced and derailed" by the Civil War.[9]

While the Civil War may have stalled the momentum of the women's rights movement, it ultimately led to the destruction of the illegal international slave trade. And here, too, the Oaksmith story is central to one of the most important transformations in American history. Although it had been illegal for Americans to participate in the Atlantic slave trade since 1808, countless sea captains continued to do so, often with diplomats, judges, and juries turning a blind eye. Things began to change in 1861, when the Lincoln administration started to take strong and calculated steps to end America's involvement in the trade. As the story of Appleton Oaksmith reveals, Lincoln and his Republican allies used the war as an opportunity to expand federal power in this area, and they were willing to violate international law, if that was what it took.

Ultimately, this is the story of a sea captain whose life intersected with some of the most evocative moments and movements in American history—first-wave feminism, the California Gold Rush, the Atlantic slave trade, Southern schemes to seize Cuba and Nicaragua, the Northern push for peace during the secession crisis, four years of civil war, and the fight for racial equality during Reconstruction. Perhaps most poignantly, Oaksmith's story reveals how the Civil War could destroy a family that did not go near a battlefield.

I

YOUTH

And so I was married to a man much older than myself—very unlike—who does not fail to love me, but who would have been infinitely happier with a different woman. I was about sixteen, and never did any little creature more consciously forget the joys of girlhood, and lend herself to the yoke of married life. Then came my boys one after another. I have four, and to train them to virtue and manliness became the great aim of my life. They promise well, and only the great Father can know how deadly would be any blow coming upon me through them. But I hope and trust.

—Elizabeth Oakes Smith to Caroline May, ca. 1847

1

FAMILY

As an elderly woman, Elizabeth Oakes Smith recalled being jealous of the boys in her extended family who were able to go to college. She had always been a voracious reader, and at twelve years old she taught Sunday school for black children "who were by public feeling excluded from the white school." But she longed to expand her own intellectual horizons. One night in her teenage years, she timidly asked her mother if she could teach local students to earn money for college. She would then be able to open a school for girls, she explained. Sophia Prince Sawyer listened intently and then replied, "Go to sleep, child; no daughter of mine is going to be a school-ma'am." In her unpublished autobiography, Oakes Smith likened this experience to a sinking ship. She was forced to abandon her "dreams . . . and thus down the rapids inclined my little barque."[1]

Sophia wanted her daughters married off young, fearing they might become old maids. Years later, Elizabeth would complain that her early wedding "defrauded" her "of the sweet period of girlhood." On the evening of March 6, 1823, the sixteen-year-old Elizabeth married Seba Smith, who at the time was thirty-one. The wedding took place at the home of her parents, which was filled with friends and decked out "in the best style of the period." However, the weather that day was gloomy. Rain had fallen in torrents all night and it continued to come down during the day so that the streets of Portland, the capital of the new state of Maine, were flooded. The servants whispered among themselves, "A lowery day and a lowery bride." Elizabeth wore white satin with lace flounces, white silk hose and white kid slippers, long white gloves, and white flowers in her long golden-brown hair, which reached down to her waist. Conspicuously absent from the ceremony was Elizabeth's stepfather, Lemuel Sawyer. He'd wanted Elizabeth to marry Lemuel Jr., his son from his previous marriage, and refused to see her given away to someone else. Instead, he spent the day in Boston working on one of his ships.[2]

The groom was an up-and-coming journalist from Maine. Born in a log cabin in Buckfield, Maine, in 1792, Seba Smith enrolled at Bowdoin College in 1815, where he "had to study hard to supply the deficiencies of early education." Despite the obstacles inherent in his upbringing, he graduated in 1818 at the head of the class. A man of modest means, Seba had to borrow a gown from Portland minister Ichabod Nichols to deliver his valedictory address. Following graduation he traveled extensively, visiting many of the Mid-Atlantic states and also crossing the Atlantic Ocean to Liverpool. After returning to Portland in 1822, he became the editor of the *Eastern Argus*—a position he held until 1826. Initially, Smith took a highly partisan position as editor, but after being walloped on the head in broad daylight by a rival editor who wielded a club or a cane, Smith toned down the partisanship of his papers. In 1829, he founded the first daily newspaper in Maine—the Portland *Daily Courier*. Like his new bride, Seba would lose a loved one at sea. His brother Sewall died aboard the *Tamerlane* in 1827.

Years later, as an elderly woman, Elizabeth recollected the scene of her marriage with evident contempt. "Mr Smith was almost twice my age, wore spectacles, and was very bald," she wrote. Moreover, he offered little help in the home, "for he was naturally indolent, and his mind absorbed more or less in mathematics, which at length became the passion of his life."[3] Of course, this memory was colored by more than half a century of sorrow, and it is likely that she was not as down on her marriage as she later portrayed herself. Seba certainly did not share her negativity. In an 1839 poem titled, "To My Wife, Absent on a Visit," he called her "my bride" and "the morning light unto my eyes," though "sixteen years have fled . . . Since the day that saw us wed."[4]

Still a blossoming teenager when she was married, Elizabeth later claimed that she grew another two inches in the years following her wedding. She worked hard to learn the routine and responsibilities of a housewife, but she had her hands full, for not only did she acquire a husband, but she also took on six boarders who were apprentices in Seba's newspaper office. Despite her new workload, Elizabeth would rise from bed each morning several hours before Seba so that she could read and study the works of Rousseau, Voltaire, and Thomas Paine.[5]

In 1824, Elizabeth bore her first son, Benjamin, who died in infancy. For weeks she could do nothing but grieve and imagine his lifeless face and fingers. Over the ensuing nine years, she would bear five more sons: Rolvin (1825), Appleton (1828), Sidney (1830), Alvin (1833), and Edward (1834). Those who survived to adulthood, one family friend said, were "all manly, handsome and gifted." Sadly, Rolvin died from a scalding accident in 1832,

Elizabeth Oaksmith, ca. 1840s.
Thomas B. Read, *The Female Poets of America* (Philadelphia: E. H. Butler and Co., 1850).

when he was only seven years old. Elizabeth remembered him as "a most lovely boy—gentle, and intelligent in a high degree." The first time Rolvin saw a black man he stepped boldly up to him and said, "Dont you dare hurt my Mama." Without batting an eye, the man looked at four-year-old Rolvin and laughed heartily. Now, as he was dying a mere three years later, Rolvin asked his mother, "I have done some good, haven't I?" Seba placed those words on his little boy's headstone.[6]

Appleton was born on March 22, 1828—named after Jesse Appleton, the president of Bowdoin College when Seba had been a student there. His birthdate has been a matter of some confusion. At the time of this writing (July 4, 2022), Wikipedia and Find-A-Grave list his birthday as February 12, 1825. John Jay TePaske, Oaksmith's only other biographer, lists it as February 24, 1827. TePaske believed that Oaksmith had referred to himself as a "Valentine Child," but TePaske misread Oaksmith's journal. The "Valentine Child" was Appleton's younger brother, Sidney (born February 14, 1830). At any rate, Appleton became the center of his mother's world. "It was a warm lovely day when he was given to my arms," Elizabeth later remembered, "and he was a fine bright, handsome child." On the streets of Portland, strangers would stop "to look at" baby Appleton "and exclaim at his beauty." As a toddler, "App" seemed to know no fear. When he was only eleven months old, he climbed a ladder outside his parents' house to the second-story roof, and at three-and-a-half he crawled along the ridge of the roof while his family called out to him in fear from the earth below.[7]

Sometime in the late 1820s the family moved from Portland to Westbrook, into an old, dilapidated house with a leaky roof. The family had a nice garden, and old friends would occasionally come out to visit. But Elizabeth missed her social life in the city. Still, it was at this home that Seba would devise his most consequential literary creation: Major Jack Downing—a simple-minded yet ambitious fictional character who spoke in Yankee dialect and made astute and humorous political observations. Seba initially used Downing to satirize the excesses of partisanship in the state legislature. Eventually Downing walked his way to Washington where he became an informal advisor to President Andrew Jackson, thus offering Seba the opportunity to lampoon national political figures and the excesses of Jacksonian democracy.[8]

By the early 1830s, Seba was beginning to have a remarkable impact on American popular culture. Whigs and Democrats alike relished Downing's satire, and his words became part of the American vernacular. Many could quote him by heart, including Senator Stephen A. Douglas of Illinois, abolitionist Thomas Wentworth Higginson of New England, the western hero Davey Crockett, and Connecticut newspaperman Gideon Welles (who would later serve as Lincoln's secretary of the navy).[9] Once, when Andrew Jackson was ill, someone read the Downing letters to him. Novelist Washington Irving was so captivated by the Downing letters that he sent a bundle of them to Francis Lieber in 1834, telling the German political thinker that they contained "simple and blunt, yet forcible" commentary on national issues "at which nobody, of whatever party he may be, can help smiling." Even far away at sea, Downing's name could be heard over the rolling waves of the ocean. When Richard Henry Dana Jr. and his fellow sailors asked a passing ship who was president of the United States in 1836, the men aboard the other vessel sarcastically answered, "Jack Downing."[10]

As a young man studying law in the 1830s, Abraham Lincoln "took great pleasure in reading Jack Downings letters." Throughout his life, Lincoln told jokes and stories that he almost certainly learned from reading Seba Smith's creation. In fact, Lincoln's law partner William Henry Herndon later said that Lincoln "loved" reading Jack Downing, and that although "he was a terribly gloomy man, & Yet he loved mirth, because it gave vent to his gloom and his melancholy."[11] Later, as president, one correspondent would write to Lincoln, "You need no Jack Downing perpetually at your elbow," but then proceeded to offer advice anyway.[12]

Readers sent gifts to Seba Smith, including axes, baskets, and a gold-headed cane made from the timbers of the USS *Constitution*. Cartoonists depicted Downing in a top hat with a long-tailed coat and striped trousers—a popular forerunner to the national symbol, Uncle Sam. Soon imposters began printing their own "Jack Downing" letters, with one British observer noting that Jack Downings were as common in America as heads of John the Baptist were in Italian monasteries. In order to protect his own work, Seba gathered a collection of his original Downing letters and published them as a satirical campaign biography in 1833 (as if Downing were running for president).[13] Seba traveled to Boston to arrange for the publication and while he was away, he and Elizabeth wrote affectionately to one another. Never before had they been apart for more than twelve hours, and now he would be gone for several weeks. He wrote his wife of the "ardent undying affection which glows and burns in our bosems the more strongly the more we are separated," and he cherished the correspondence he received from her, telling her that he read one letter at the dinner table and that, "It served well for des[s]ert." In return, Elizabeth marked the spot where she had kissed one of her letters and wrote, "kiss this place because I have kissed it for you."

Sometimes Seba offered advice for his children—like telling Appleton not to chop wood with an axe if little Sidney was nearby. On other occasions he appended notes to his sons: "Dear Appleton," he wrote in one, "I hope you continue to be a good boy and do all you can to help your mother, so that she need not have to work so hard. And I hope you are very kind to your little brothers and dont do any thing to make you or them unhappy. I shall tell you about a great many things when I come home." Writing in the lisp that Sidney spoke with as a child, he wrote, "father thinks of you every night and every morning, and wants you to try to be as dood as ever you tan." The boys, in turn, wanted Seba to know how they were doing. On one occasion Elizabeth wrote, "Appleton says tell my Father I am a good boy." But as time passed, Elizabeth grew increasingly anxious for her husband to come home. She had taken responsibility for editing the newspaper in Seba's absence, and parenting on her own was not easy. "I am very sorry to write that dear Sidney is behaving rather naughty this morning. I told him I should write it down and he feels somewhat hurt."

On one occasion, Seba was invited to a party with the great Whig politician Henry Clay. Word began to circulate that "Jack Downing" was among the guests in the room, and the host took Seba by the arm and introduced him to Clay "as Major Downing." Seba "felt rather awkward," but Clay eagerly shook his hand and "remarked that he should be very happy to be introduced not only to Major Downing, but to the whole family."

Seba asked his wife to tell him every little detail of her days while he was gone, and called her "my dear companion," "my more than friend," "my dear E.," and other affectionate appellations. He signed his letters "with how much affection, I am sure I need not describe to *you*."[14] Historians have generally portrayed the Smith marriage in dour terms. "Unhappily married herself, she vehemently opposed divorce even as she campaigned for revolutionary changes in the marriage relation," writes one scholar.[15] But assessments like this are usually based on Oakes Smith's unpublished autobiography from the 1880s—a document that is colored by the bitter experiences of her later life. In her mind's eye in the 1880s, she envisioned her groom as "very bald," but his photograph, taken almost four decades after their wedding day, shows an even older man with a full head of hair. Indeed, their correspondence from the 1830s reveals a companionate marriage in which husband and wife missed one another.

Elizabeth adored her sons and took her parental responsibilities seriously. Once, in 1837, when it was time for the boys to receive a "smart whipping," she could not help but be amazed by how her sons reacted to the chastisement. "Appleton is a noble boy—I gave him his punishment first, and he, when it came Sidney's turn, begged me to whip him instead of Sidney, for he was most to blame." Elizabeth reported to Seba that Appleton did not "merely offer but begged, and intreated me to do it. Sidney, little scamp, I thought looked pleased at the suggestion, but I thought it best for each to suffer for his own sins. I then asked Appleton if he felt willing to

Seba Smith, ca. 1860.
Collections of the Maine Historical Society.

take a part of little Alvin's—he readily consented. I then asked Sidney if he would take the rest. No, I believe not said the little wag. I've had enough of it. And I dont want any, said Alvin, springing into bed."[16]

The Smith boys knew that their mother loved them with all her heart, and they adored her in return. One night when they were all in bed, one queried, "Have you seen any lady today, who, putting our love aside, is as handsome as our mother?" The boys lamented that "her lot in life" was "so hard and toilsome," and that she did not live in luxury. Years later Appleton recollected his childhood in Portland. He described his family as one "of moderate but ample fortune; but teeming with all of the simple elegancies of female taste." His mother, he said, "was a young and beautiful woman with flowing ringlets." "Never were children so happy," he rhapsodized, "never a Mother so proud, never a mother so loved. Happy, happy days were those, to the children if not to the Mother, which were passed in the city of their birth!"[17]

Unfortunately, the happiness would not last. Seba's publisher folded and he did not profit from his Jack Downing book like he thought he would. In the mid-1830s he got caught up in the land-speculating spirit of the age and invested large sums of money in a rural property in Maine known as "No. 8." This turned out to be a colossal mistake. When the Panic of 1837 touched off a major recession in the United States, the Smiths lost almost everything they owned. "My husband had staked our all, and lost," Elizabeth later recalled. Then, in a metaphor that was pregnant with meaning, she wrote, "I saw the shipwreck before us, but made the best of it."[18]

About this time, Seba's brother-in-law developed an invention for cleansing the fibers of Sea Island cotton in South Carolina. Knowing that Southern planters would pay a hefty sum for a machine that did this quickly and effectively, Seba invested the remainder of the family's savings into it. In early 1839, they packed up their belongings and, along with their white servant girl, made their way for Charleston. Elizabeth did not want to leave the "frosty air, rocky hills and mountain scenery" of her childhood home in Maine, but she dutifully gathered her family and the little belongings they could take with them and boarded the packet ship *King Philip*. The captain was a "bluff, kind-hearted Sailor." Along the way, Elizabeth taught him how to play chess and he taught her how to play whist. One night, the ship encountered a terrible storm that broke the cabin windows and flooded the room with water. As the waves rolled the ship and the rain poured down from the skies, "the children behaved like little heroes." After the boys finally, somehow, fell asleep, Elizabeth made her way toward the deck to look out at the storm. "Go down, Madam, go down," shouted the captain. "I won't," screamed Elizabeth, raising her voice above the sounds of the tempest. "You must, dear Madam," replied the captain, now with a gentler tone. "But, Capt. I want to see this terrible storm—I must see it."

Elizabeth did not say so, but she may have been thinking about the storm that killed her father so many years before. The captain realized that he would not be able to persuade this firm-minded woman, so he wrapped his pea coat around her and helped her up onto the deck. The wind howled and shrieked, and the ship heaved up and down upon the large swells. Elizabeth later recalled, "I needed just this tonic. . . . It was all terrible—but how much better than the dull, desponding hours of every day care! It was luxury to feel heroic even for a brief space of time. The rain came down in torrents and I was wet to the back-bone, but joyous." Eventually the captain screamed into her ear, "You have had enough of this," and carried her below decks.

In Charleston, the family mixed with wealthy planter families who came into the city for the winter. The sights of slavery were searing. One morning while walking along the city streets, Elizabeth passed a slave market. Her host walked faster and begged her to proceed without looking, but she refused. She let go of his arms and gazed upon "that most terrible of sights, human beings mounted upon a platform and sold with other cattle, and chattels and lumber of every kind!" Many years later she would recall that the scene "was terrifying to me, and I saw as it were in advance the terrible retribution that came with the Civil War."

Seba and his brother-in-law visited several large plantations, but the machine proved a dismal failure—it was too complicated, too slow, and, according to Elizabeth, required "more intelligence than would be at command by a negro workman." When the men returned to their boarding-house, they sat down next to Elizabeth and "wept like babies." The next morning, they took their trunks down to the docks and boarded the *Lafayette* for New York City. "Let us start again," Elizabeth assured her husband. "Things will come round all right, never give up the ship—there is no such word as failure for us."[19]

The *Lafayette* reached New York City amid a snowstorm near the end of 1839 and the family trudged "down-hearted, and worn" through the slushy streets. Seba and Elizabeth were "almost penniless, with four children to support." Initially they lived with Dr. Cyrus Weeks, the husband of one of Elizabeth's cousins. Weeks was a physician who supplemented his income by procuring corpses for anatomy classes at medical schools. One of the most frequent visitors to the Weeks home was Horace Greeley, a young—not yet thirty years old—outspoken editor who would go on to found the *New York Tribune* two years later in 1841. Toddling around the house along with the Smith boys was the Weeks's two-year-old son, Grenville, who would grow up to become the surgeon aboard the USS *Monitor* the night she sank off Cape Hatteras in December 1862.[20]

New York was still a small city in 1839. North of 30th Street "was a wilderness of rocks, bushes and cacti, with here and there a farm house."

Eventually the family settled into a humble, barely furnished home on Greenwich Street. Much of Elizabeth's time was spent reading and educating her boys. She would also take them on long walks through the city. Elizabeth relished the opportunity to cultivate her sons, teaching them their lessons as they all sat on moss-covered rocks that overlooked the Hudson River. At home, she and Seba taught them to play chess. As a young child, Appleton mastered French, Spanish, Latin, and Greek. But times were difficult. Seba went to meet with Horace Greeley to pursue a job in his office, but Greeley looked at him and without a second thought replied, "No, we want nothing from you. We want young men—not an old man." Seba recounted this rude rebuff in front of the children and they were "indignant." At the Church of the Messiah, Elizabeth and her boys would see Greeley "snore through sermon and prayer" in his pew, "but at the crash of the organ" he would "start up, as if shot, wide awake." During the 1850s and 1860s Elizabeth grew to loathe the wily editor. Years later, she wrote that he did not have "the capacity . . . for anything like what I should call friendship. I never knew a man so utterly *self-involved*."[21]

These years in New York City were difficult ones for the family. One Christmas Eve—about 1843—Appleton's little brother Edward fretted that "St. Nicholas will not come to us tonight; because we are poor!—is it true?—will he not come?" Elizabeth assured him that they had been "such good children that I trust and think he will not forget you!" She knew there would be gifts for the children on Christmas morning, albeit "simple" ones. After dinner she read a Christmas story. Then, after Edward and Alvin went to bed, Appleton and Sidney helped her wrap the gifts.[22]

To help make ends meet the family took in boarders, although they found it "an irksome and unprofitable business." In 1841, the celebrated poet and painter Thomas Buchanan Read rented a room. Read and Elizabeth appear to have grown fond of one another. He painted a large portrait of her, and published a sonnet in her honor. Later he would include her poetry in his anthology *The Female Poets of America*, in which he called her "one of our most brilliant writers."[23] In fact, Elizabeth had been writing for general audiences since the early 1820s, when she began writing pieces for Seba's newspapers on any number of subjects, including poetry and romance, politics, agriculture, and history. Her first novel, *Riches Without Wings* (1838), recounted the story of a family who was devastated by the Panic of 1837. She was pleased that this volume "touched a popular vein, and was selling very rapidly." Her ninety-page poem, "The Sinless Child," which first appeared serially in the *Southern Literary Messenger* in 1842, cemented her reputation as a literary figure in antebellum America. The main character in the poem—a perfect child named Eva—inspired the figures of the same name in Harriet Beecher Stowe's *Uncle Tom's Cabin* (1852) and Henry Wadsworth Longfellow's *Evangeline* (1847). But despite the critical acclaim and far-reaching influence, Elizabeth always regretted that she did not make more money from her writings. "The Sinless Child"—which was anthologized several times during her lifetime—only earned her $50.[24]

During the summer of 1842, the Smiths moved to Brooklyn. Both Seba and Elizabeth relied on their literary abilities to eke out a living. Throughout the 1840s Seba edited several short-lived magazines, wrote poetry and essays for newspapers, and published books. At various points he resurrected Jack Downing, a satire that became increasingly Whiggish in its politics. But making a living as a writer and editor was difficult. "I know it is rather a precarious business for a main dependence," wrote Seba privately; "it has been said it will do for a staff, but not for a crutch. However, since Mrs Smith and myself have each a staff, if we walk together I hope we may be able to keep from falling." Elizabeth kept writing—sometimes under the name "Mrs. Seba Smith" and sometimes under the masculine penname "Ernest Helfenstein." In the 1840s she published two more novels, three children's books, a play, a volume of collected verses, and any number of short stories, essays, and poems. Her second novel, *The Western Captive* (1842), which questioned the morality of westward expansion in the wake of the Trail of Tears, sold 2,500 copies in its first four days. By the mid-1840s she'd given up her earlier *noms de plume* and wrote under the name "Elizabeth Oakes Smith."[25]

Ironically, Seba's misfortunes—which necessitated their move to New York—created the opportunity for Elizabeth to shine. She made quite an impression in the literary community in New York in the 1840s. One acquaintance said her eyes "emit rays of light in the dark, which indicates great magnetism." Another literary insider wrote privately, "She stands head and shoulders above most of the female talent in our City—the only question is whether her constitution be strong enough for the necessary mechanical labor of triumphant authorship."[26] Soon she found herself invited to literary salons, the most famous of which were held at the home of the beautiful and vivacious Anne Charlotte Lynch. Born in Vermont in 1815 to an Irish immigrant who died in 1819, Lynch had a natural fondness for both literature and adventure. As a schoolgirl she wrote poetry, which she began to publish as early as 1835. After settling in Manhattan in 1845, she started a salon that gained a national reputation. The most famous writers and artists of the day visited her soirees, including Herman Melville, Margaret Fuller, and Horace Greeley. Lynch was tall, slender, with dark hair and eyes. Edgar Allan Poe described her "whole countenance" as "full of intelligent expression" and her demeanor as "dignified, graceful, and noticeable for repose." During her salons, Lynch encouraged guests to engage in conversations while she flitted about the room gracefully making witty and thoughtful remarks.[27]

To be invited to one of Lynch's salons was "evidence of distinction," for Lynch drew "the *moral* as well as intellectual line." The salons were simple yet elegant. Often the refreshments consisted of only tea and cookies. And yet the intelligentsia of New York flocked to Lynch's home. Sometimes the gatherings were so crowded that guests were forced to sit in the staircase. Melville captivated listeners with stories from the high seas, while Poe read "The Raven" one evening.[28] And on one occasion—with Elizabeth present at the gathering—Poe remarked that "*The Sinless Child* was one of the strongest long poems ever produced in America." Unfortunately, Seba was not present to hear such praise of his wife's work. Unlike most husbands, he chose not to attend the soirees with Elizabeth. Instead, Appleton and Sidney escorted their mother once they'd grown old enough to attend.[29]

Appleton and his brothers grew to adore their mother much more than their father. New York City artist David Edward Cronin later recalled that Seba "always appeared a genially kind old gentleman, though he seemed to accept a retired and almost obscure position in the household." Elizabeth, by contrast, "was almost worshiped. She was indeed a worshipful woman." Cronin surmised that Elizabeth's rising prominence in the literary world contributed to her sons' "estimation" of their parents. The "different estimates of their merits formed in the literary world, had penetrated the family domicile, and openly prevailed there." Seba often acted with a "sturdy, silent protest" against the way his sons viewed him. "It was, perhaps, the family skeleton, then closely hidden, but afterwards relentlessly exposed to the public."[30]

From a young age, Appleton seemed to have an insatiable appetite for adventure. In 1843, when he was sixteen years old, he went on a voyage to China on a ship owned by Grinnell, Minturn and Co., one of the leading international shipping firms of the era. "It was his first taste of the seafaring life to which he had become addicted in his early years in Portland and Charleston," recalled his mother. "On this voyage to China he learned the rudiments of navigation and sea lore that were to be so valuable to him in his later years." Elizabeth, Seba, and their other boys anxiously awaited Appleton's return in 1845, after a two-year voyage. One day back in New York, Appleton, now eighteen years old, took a rowboat from Manhattan to Staten Island with his mother and two other people on board. As the small party enjoyed the beauty of the water, a large steam-powered ferry veered into their path. The steamer nearly ran down the little boat, but Appleton jumped up and placed his hands on the side of the larger vessel. As his mother later recalled, "the row boat was shoved away from the wheels but the gallant boy went down in the whirl of waters—moments of horror and suspense intervened, when he sprung into the bow of the boat and shook himself like a young Lion. He said afterwards that he never lost his head but calculated without failure just where the row boat would be."[31]

In 1849, Appleton presented a petition to the New York state legislature to change his name from Appleton Smith to Appleton Oaksmith. His younger brothers eventually followed suit. Historians and literary critics have speculated as to why the family made this change. Some believe it was because Elizabeth thought "Smith" was too ordinary and uninteresting a name, while others see it as a purposeful assertion of her dominance over her husband. It may also have been an attempt to assert her own selfhood—a rejection of common law coverture in which a woman's identity was subsumed by her husband's. Whatever the reason, Elizabeth appears to have toyed with changing her name as well. She signed some of her correspondence "E. Oaksmith" that year.[32]

2

CALIFORNIA

As a teenager in the 1840s, Appleton Oaksmith kept a journal in which he recorded "the most pure and holy impulses of my heart." He delighted in confiding his inmost thoughts to its pages (which he considered a "kind of confessional"), including "the deep and true emotions of my first love." The identity of this "mistress" is unknown; in a later journal, he called her "L." Quite possibly she was Anne C. Lynch, the elegant, wealthy young woman whose soirees he attended with his mother.

When Appleton and "L" first met, their attraction was based largely on outward appearances. "She dressed with exquisite taste, her figure was faultless, her style attractive, her walk the personification of grace, and her beautiful eyes gave a brilliancy to her whole face, that was most enticing and loveable." The two would stroll along Broadway, laughing and talking, visiting theaters, balls, and "all fashionable places of amusement." Over time, he and "L" began to fall in love. "What had at first been commenced in sport, or for feelings of vanity in each of us, at length became a most bitter reality," he wrote. That "bitter reality" was that Oaksmith was poor and living beyond his means. He would have to go abroad to seek his fortune—although the thought of leaving "L" gave him a sensation of "utter desolation," for "we discovered that we loved each other deeply, passionately, and unchangeably."

When the couple decided to break things off, "L" did not cry. Oaksmith attributed her stoic resolve either to "womanly firmness or a tender regard for her lover that would not add to his grief by evincing her own." Either way, Appleton fell into "a period of deep and bitter grief" and "sad and hopeless disappointment." Yet he hid his emotions from his family and friends. In this state of despair, he threw his precious journal into a fire and watched the sparks fly into the air as the book turned into embers. A "bitter smile" creased his face. Then, "with an aching heart," he turned his attention to "the first duties of my life." He knew he had to make a way for himself in the world, so he boarded a vessel headed around South America for California. While standing on the deck he wrote "some bitter Byronic lines." This marked the beginning of a journey for San Francisco that generally took about 175 days.[1]

Appleton's heartbreak proved only temporary. One night in Panama City in May 1850, he found himself being mercilessly pursued by a throng of "rioters and assassins" (he never divulged the reason he was being chased). Running down the street, nearly out of breath, he saw that he was near the home of a young woman named Juanita, with whom he had a "slight acquaintance." He rushed to her door, knowing that it was his "only chance of escape." Much to his relief, she let him in before his pursuers could find him.

Appleton explained his predicament to Juanita, and when she heard "the tramping of feet outside the door" she knew he was telling the truth. He asked if he could sleep on a sofa in her room until morning, and she readily agreed. He lay down, exhausted, and closed his eyes as Juanita moved about the room preparing for bed. After a while he opened his eyes to see if she had put out the light. She was kneeling before an image of her saint, which stood on one side of her room. "With head bent reverently down and hands crossed upon her bosom she knelt for several minutes." Then she arose and slowly pulled a curtain across the image of the saint. "Why do you do that Juanita?" he asked. When she did not answer he repeated the question. "For fear that I should do something naughty and the good Saint should see me," she meekly replied.

"They have so many funny customs—things which amuse me," Oaksmith wrote in his journal when reflecting on this experience more than a year later. "Every good catholic has in his or her room an image of some particular saint to whom they repeat their prayers. Many a pretty girl of Panama after repeating her orisons before her saint will *cover him up* and then open her door to some favored lover. In the morning after the lover has gone the saint is again uncovered and kindly forgives the fair penitent for anything which may have been done wrong during the period when 'he was not watching over her.'" It is little wonder that Oaksmith would confide to his journal, "I like the place and I like the people" of Panama City. However, his mother would have almost certainly disapproved of his cavalier attitude toward women.[2]

About November 1850, Oaksmith arrived in San Francisco.[3] The city was a bustling, hilly landscape full of canvas tents, wooden houses, hotels, theaters, brothels, gaming establishments, crowds, carriages, horses, drunkenness, and debauchery. "Gambling here is an occupation, day or night, Sunday or any other time," wrote one gold seeker in 1850. "The grey-headed father and the beardless boy are seen side by side vying with each other who can win or lose the fastest, and even beautiful women engage in these games with the same earnestness of the sterner sex, betting their last ounce." Preachers were known to go directly from the pulpit to the gaming table. "Money here goes like dirt; everything costs a dollar or dollars. What is considered a fortune at home is here mere pocket money." Men would pay two ounces of gold just for a woman to sit next to them for an hour or two during dinner. They would pay upwards of fifteen to twenty ounces, wrote one French visitor, if they "wanted anything more from these nymphs."[4]

Almost completely penniless in this very expensive boomtown, Oaksmith worked full days, wrote for newspapers at night, and dabbled in shipping goods to mining towns, "sometimes losing and sometimes making." He wrote his brother, Sidney, "I have often been obliged to do things against my own judgment from want of money but never against my own principles, or my conscience." Within four months he had saved $300 to send to his mother. He had also been eating well and had put on weight. But he professed to want better things than the depraved life of the city. He hoped that he and his brothers could "all strive for the real and the true, the good, and the high" so that they could "build a monument that will stand" for generations, like the Washington Monument that was currently under construction in the nation's capital.[5]

On March 22, 1851—his twenty-third birthday—Oaksmith departed San Francisco on board the steamship *Gold Hunter*, a wooden-hulled passenger vessel that had been built in Westervelt, New York, in 1849. She measured 172 feet long, weighed 436 tons, and carried about sixty passengers for the Tehuantepec Railroad Company. The *Gold Hunter* arrived at Salina Cruz, near Tehuantepec, on April 6. There she discharged her passengers, who then proceeded to cross the Mexican countryside to Vera Cruz on the Atlantic Coast—a 145-mile journey by mule. From Salina Cruz the *Gold Hunter* traveled 359 miles back up the Mexican coastline to what Oaksmith described as "the old and crumbling City of Acapulco." Sitting in the steamer, on which he was the purser, Oaksmith decided to start keeping a new journal. He looked out at the city's fort where a Mexican flag waved "feebly" in the breeze, and he wondered when an American flag might again fly from the fortification, as it had during the Mexican War a decade earlier.[6]

On April 23, the *Gold Hunter* again got underway, heading back down the west coast of Mexico for Panama City, where the vessel would take on about one hundred passengers for California. Upon reaching their destination on May 5, Oaksmith saw old friends and acquaintances and conducted business for the steamer. "Almost all of the inhabitants knew me and I had to stop and shake hands with almost every one I met," he wrote. However, riding about the city one day he grew quiet and contemplative, thinking about "the many" others like him who had ridden through the city gate, never again to make it home. "I rode in silence for a time till my companions rolled me upon my loss of spirit and then I was App Oaksmith once more."[7]

The *Gold Hunter* left Panama City on the afternoon of May 15 with passengers bound for San Francisco. Heading back up the Pacific coastline, the sailors stopped at several port cities. At Realejo, on the west coast of Nicaragua, they met officers from an American ship. After supper at a fine hotel, the party enjoyed wine and conversation. "We told stories, we sang songs and had a grand time," Oaksmith wrote. One man played the guitar and sang "some very sweet songs" in both English and Spanish. After this, they "sallied out and serenaded all of the senoras and senoritas" in town.[8]

Back at sea a few days later, Oaksmith and the passengers spent the evenings on deck singing and talking. (The ship now carried about 160 passengers, including women and children.) When they stopped at Mazatlán, they learned that San Francisco had been "entirely destroyed by fire" on May 4. In fact, the fire destroyed about eighteen square blocks, or three-quarters of the city, including some 1,500 buildings. The *Gold Hunter* departed Mazatlán on June 2, "with considerable regret," Oaksmith wrote, "as I have made some most agreeable acquaintances there and it is a matter of extreme uncertainty whether I shall ever have the pleasure of seeing them again." But this was a common experience for travelers, he knew.[9]

The *Gold Hunter* stopped for water at San Jose, on the southern tip of Baja California. A few days later she reached San Diego, where the officers and crew went ashore for supplies. But Oaksmith was too sick to even sit up and look out the window to see the place. At first the doctor and passengers on board thought he had smallpox, which had infected at least one other passenger. But soon they realized it was just a fever. The doctor bled Oaksmith, putting him "through a severe course of medicine."[10]

On June 11, Oaksmith mustered all the energy he could to prepare the ship's papers for entrance at San Francisco. When he was finished, he "went to bed suffering much from my exertion." The next day the vessel arrived at the Golden Gate at 7:30 a.m. The rumors had been true—San Francisco had been destroyed by fire—"and many of my friends have been severe losers." Oaksmith had apparently left things behind with friends from his previous visit. "Among so many sufferers whose losses have been large, I should not even think of my own, but there were some things which I regret much. All of the curiosities (which were many) collected by me in my wanderings were destroyed; as well as a great many of my clothes and all of my writings, besides some papers of value." To make matters worse, the captain told Oaksmith that the *Gold Hunter* would have to be sold. "I feared as much," Oaksmith wrote in his journal. "I shall probably be 'adrift' once more then, and that very soon. I wonder what will come next! Let me but have my health, and with God's help, I care not."[11]

Oaksmith soon recovered his health and went ashore to tend to business and see friends. Deep sadness overtook him as he walked the familiar streets and saw "the havoc made by the fire. All the fine buildings on both sides of the Street which were the pride of the city are down." He looked for his favorite restaurant, Delmonico's, and found it "in a kind of one story wooden shed which stands on the spot where stood the elegant structure in which I used to so often meet my old circle of San Francisco friends." Locals now purchased "fireproof paint," and they eagerly read in the papers about implausible inventions like "the fire annihilator" that might be useful for preventing personal property loss. Oaksmith sensed that the merchants and other locals possessed "a stern unflinching spirit of determination . . . to mete out a severe and retributive justice" upon the arsonists who were wreaking such devastation upon the city.[12] Indeed, a Vigilance Committee had recently emerged as a body of local leaders intent on suppressing further lawlessness, even if it took harsh punishments to accomplish their ends.

Sitting in his room in the *Gold Hunter* on June 22, quietly reading a book, Oaksmith heard a fire alarm sound from the city. He sprang to his feet and hurried ashore as quickly as he could, hoping to help a friend who lived in the vicinity. But it was too late. Strong winds carried the blaze rapidly through the area, and by the time he arrived there was "nothing but the chimney left." Oaksmith found the plaza littered with furniture and other goods that people had managed to save from their burning homes. "It was a sad, a sickening sight," he wrote. "Women were there watching and weeping over the little remnants of their property, children who had got lost from their parents and knew not where else to go for safety, and men exhausted by their labors, or burned in their efforts to save the city." Corpses—"withered up by the fire"—were scattered in the streets. "Carts were driving furiously through the crowd laden with goods. Men were shot down *dead* detected in acts of plunder. The firemen were working manfully to arrest the flames which broke out in different places at the same time." The suffering, disease, destruction, and death were overwhelming.

The fire destroyed nearly a dozen blocks, including buildings that had escaped the May 4 inferno. The Jenny Lind Theater, which had been rapidly rebuilt over the previous six weeks, was destroyed a second time, just two days after reopening to the public. In the wake of the blaze, violence and hysteria overtook the people. Mobs beat at least two men to death while police shot and killed two looters. This was the sixth fire to destroy San Francisco in nineteen months. Tensions were high and frustrations grew. While Oaksmith stood in the street, gazing at the scene in disbelief, a friend saw him, and with a bitter smile said, "Well Oaksmith my house has gone for the third time and I shall not build it again until the scoundrels who caused its loss, this time, are hung. Come to the 'Vigilance Committee.' I am a member and you must be one too." Oaksmith decided to join "this powerful and well organized association." He signed the compact "by which I bound 'my life, my fortune, and my honor,'" and became chairman of the Visiting Committee to the County Prison.[13]

For the next few weeks Oaksmith was actively engaged in the work of the Vigilance Committee, often standing guard at the committee's offices and prison late at night. "Every member goes armed," he wrote. "We number now six hundred. Each with a revolver. By a resolution none but 'Colts' are allowed and every member must have one at least. Thus if all assembled we could fire *Three Thousand Shots* at a time." He saw all sorts of prisoners— murderers, adulterers, arsonists—brought in. On one evening the committee held a vigorous debate over whether to summarily execute a black man who had allegedly confessed to starting a house fire. "Many members were in favor of hanging the Negro at once," wrote Oaksmith, "and it required all of the eloquence of the calmer members to induce them to permit the Negro to remain in custody till we had used him sufficiently in discovering the others who instigated him to or aided him in the act." The lawlessness could be difficult to bear. "Men know not whom to trust," he wrote. "Truly, I think to myself this is a strange country. Where will it all end?"[14]

Work with the Vigilance Committee could be emotionally affecting. One trial led to the public execution of a murderer. Three thousand San Franciscans packed the Market Street wharf, while others watched from boats in the harbor. Oaksmith felt a sense of pity in his heart as he gazed at the well-dressed man standing on the gallows. "I will not say, as I looked upon his handsome features that I did not think of the time when a mothers kiss was imprinted upon that cheek, now so sunken and hollowed by suffering and crime, when a mothers hand played with those clustering locks, and when a mothers prayer went up to heaven for the future welfare of her darling boy."[15] As the product of a sentimental and romantic age, death and loneliness always made Appleton think of his mother's love.

San Francisco seemed to have lost all of its charms, and Oaksmith longed to leave. "Business was very dull," he wrote, "and the fire of 22nd June put a sudden damper upon everything." But he couldn't depart until he settled several lawsuits he had pending in the state and federal courts in the city (he and other crew members were suing the owners of the *Gold Hunter* for backpay). The lethargy of the legal system frustrated him, but finally in late July he won enough money to gain a financial interest in the *Mary Adeline*, a 185-ton brig that was originally out of Boston. On August 2, he penned a short note to the chairman of the Vigilance Committee announcing that "matters of business" would "render it necessary for me to be absent for a considerable length of time" and asking for a leave of absence until he could "again report myself for duty."[16] Four days later, he left gold country in command of the *Mary Adeline*, bound for San Juan del Sur in Nicaragua. "San Francisco, the city that I once thought was to be my home, I have left, and much it strikes me too, forever," he wrote. But he did not "feel the least shadow of regret at leaving it." Being the sentimentalist that he was, he penned a thirty-two–line poem that captured his feelings on the occasion. Much of its imagery focused on the death of young men at sea.[17]

Sketch of the Mary Adeline, *from Appleton Oaksmith's travel journal.*
Courtesy of the David M. Rubenstein Rare Book and Manuscript Library, Duke University.

Standing upon the deck at night, looking up at the stars as his vessel glided over the waves, Oaksmith wondered how long he would continue to follow the sea. He thought about the "Buccaneers of old" who "haunted" the waters below him, and he thought that he might need to find a new vocation—something other than sailing. "I like the romance of it, but alas there is too little of that left now." In truth, he missed his family and friends back home, and the solitude of the ocean made him ruminate on his past. In his mind's eye things were "ideal" back home. And he longed to see his mother. "Would that I had some one I could love, to talk with—My Mother, what would I not give if she were with me."[18]

His mother, in fact, would have coveted his comforting presence at this time. Back at home, Appleton's grandmother, Sophia Prince, had just died, and Elizabeth was heartbroken. In a letter to her other sons, she wrote, "My heart is full of anxiety for dear Appleton. I shall hope letters are on the way to me now from him. If not I shall faint with anxiety. Pray for him, my dears, and for your Mother also." Indeed, Elizabeth missed Appleton as much as he missed her. "We must send for Appleton to come home," she wrote. "Do not fail to write to dearly beloved, noble Appleton."[19]

On August 17, the *Mary Adeline* crossed the Tropic of Cancer. As the weather got warm, the crew passed the time catching fish, dolphin, and albacore. At night, Appleton had long conversations with his passengers—about God, astronomy, and weather. Whenever his ship passed a shipwreck, he ruminated on the "brave hearts" who once had "ploughed the ocean as gallantly as my own vessel did." But now those men and ships were gone. "Perhaps her commander was young in years like myself. He too might have had a Mother who kept within her mind his course over the Worlds great ocean and waited for the time when his Bark should homeward sail, and his form might gladden her eyes once more—Alas! how long may she not wait?—how long may she not hope?" But Oaksmith knew that death was something all sailors risked. And there were times "when experience and skill" might not be enough to save a sailor's life, "and there is but one thing left to us—To meet the fate that awaits us with a sailor's heart and a sailor's courage. To show till the very last a heroism that the world shall never know. Many as brave a heart has beat its last amid the roaring of the tempest and the surging of the billows, as ever went down on field of strife amid the clash of combat and the din of Battle."[20]

The *Mary Adeline* made a brief stop at Acapulco in early September and then returned to sea. After a terrible storm, the passengers began to get restless, complaining that the ship was traveling too slowly. "My passengers are gathered in little knots about the deck, and as is usual in such cases blaming me for adverse winds and calms, abusing my vessel and getting up quite a mutiny," wrote Oaksmith. "I leave them in disgust and retire to my room where I determine to let them have their own way as long as they do nothing but talk. When they undertake more I will have mine."[21]

The *Mary Adeline* arrived at San Juan del Sur on September 25. The passengers "felt very much ashamed of themselves" when they learned that they had beaten all of the other vessels that had departed San Francisco at the same time, and some that had left "ten days before I did." As soon as the sails were furled, Oaksmith informed the passengers that, "as they had expressed so much dissatisfaction at being obliged to remain on board my vessel so long, they now had an opportunity of leaving her and the sooner they did it the better." Before sunset they had all been kicked to the proverbial curb.[22]

Oaksmith spent the next two months at San Juan del Sur, daydreaming, watching alligators and sharks in the water near his boat, visiting friends, and trying to sell his cargo. He traipsed the countryside armed "with swords, Bowie-knives, and Revolvers" and wearing "mud-bespattered garments," unsuccessfully trying to find buyers for his goods. Finally, on November 18, he discharged the freight onto another ship at Salinas Bay. On November 30, he wrote in his journal, "Once more at Sea. Again on the wide, wide Ocean."[23]

Unfortunately, Oaksmith soon realized he had "a mutinous and treacherous crew" that obliged him "to be almost constantly on watch." Experienced sailors knew how easily quarrels could erupt on ships, and crews could turn against their commander. In his famous memoir *Two Years Before the Mast* (1840), Richard Henry Dana Jr. described how discontent and fatigue in the cramped quarters of a ship could lead to quarrels and far worse. "Many little things," Dana wrote, "daily and almost hourly occurring, which no one who has not himself been on a long and tedious voyage can conceive of or properly appreciate,—little wars and rumors of wars, reports of things said in the cabin, misunderstanding of words and looks, apparent abuses,—brought us into a condition in which everything seemed to go wrong."[24]

Oaksmith quickly found himself in a dire situation. At first his crew refused to do their duties on the ship, then they made "mutinous threats," and Oaksmith saw them suspiciously gathered together on the forecastle of the ship glancing about furtively. On December 3, he wrote in his journal, "The crisis is approaching. It now becomes a question of life or death." One of Oaksmith's mates overheard the crew planning their mutiny. They had determined to murder Oaksmith, the two mates, and the steward, believing that Oaksmith had $10,000 worth of personal effects on board. ("Liberal appraisers!" he wrote in his journal.) One crewman persuaded the others to spare one of the mates, who had children—"provided he offers no resistance and goes below *when he is ordered*." Another remembered a time when Oaksmith had been kind to him and thought they should spare him too, but the others persuaded him that Oaksmith was a harsh master and should be killed.

"Everything it seems is fixed, except the time," Oaksmith scrawled in his journal. "As near as we can understand they are waiting till we make land, as they do not know how to steer for the nearest shore." Two or three of the men had revolvers and Bowie knives. "This looks bad, and I must if possible get hold of them," Oaksmith wrote. "Now for a nap so that I shall not need to sleep to night."

The tension and anxiety on the ship were nearly unbearable, and the weather was thick and rainy. Oaksmith feared "that if I acted wrongly, inconsiderately, or rashly under the painful circumstances which exist, I should only be the means of hastening, instead of preventing, the catastrophe; and perhaps cause the shedding of blood that otherwise might have been avoided." Several plans percolated in his mind until finally he settled on one. He knew the two ringleaders were on separate nighttime watches. Although they sometimes went to the ship's wheel armed, Oaksmith believed that he could disarm them. The "worst man of all, the most desperate character on board," had the starboard watch on deck from midnight to 2 a.m. At 1:50 a.m., Oaksmith went on deck and stood on the weather side of the quarterdeck, while the second mate at the same time crossed over to the leeward. After about a minute, the mate walked toward the stern of the ship and looked into the binnacle, pretending to see what time it was. At that point Oaksmith approached the scoundrel at the wheel and put a pistol to his head. The mate came forward and placed the man in irons. Not a single word was spoken by any of the three men, but the man "flashed a glance at me from his eyes, and then instantly obeyed. But that glance! that single look!—how much did it betray to me. I have seen such looks before. It was as if he would look into my heart to see if I really possessed the cards of which I boasted. He seemed satisfied though in the instant and apparently did me the justice of believing that I would be as good as my word. He threw down the cards at once."

Oaksmith placed the shackled man in the captain's cabin and "told him what would be his fate if he opened his lips." The process began again two hours later. As the second man was waking up and crawling out of the longboat where he'd been sleeping, Oaksmith stepped forward and presented his pistol. "He at first seemed inclined to resist and looked around to see if any assistance was near, but a whispered word from me, and a cold pistol pressing slightly against his temple drove all such thoughts away."

Oaksmith confined the men separately and would not allow any communication with them. In the morning he told the crew what he had done and explained "what they might expect if I should observe, or hear of, anything at all suspicious in their words or actions." Over the ensuing days he became quite ill, but he "dare not have it known that I was suffering or at all enfeebled." His sleep became sporadic and inconsistent, and every noise aroused his suspicions. He kept a pistol under his pillow, which he pulled out and cocked several times in his sleep. Yet he was proud of himself—that he "could be thus vigilant in my slumbers. How finely strung must my nerves be, to permit me to handle so delicate a thing as a 'hair-trigger' in my sleep."[25]

Over the next few weeks, the weather became eerily still. "Nothing but calms, calms, calms," he wrote in his journal. Oaksmith believed that "if there is a Hell, the lowest spot in it to which the doubly-damned will be condemned, will be a great Sea, on which the Sun will never set and whose burning waves will never be fanned by a single breath." If such weather patterns continued much longer, he continued, "I feel that I should go mad."[26]

On Christmas Eve, Oaksmith saw visions of his family, scenes from his childhood and youth that brought back fond memories of his mother and brothers. Years rolled by like waves before him, and in his mind's eye his mother and brothers grew older. He saw Sidney, Alvin, and Edward. Each vision involved Christmas festivities—games, gift giving, and long, late-night conversations. He saw his mother writing, hunched over a table as he had seen her so many times as a child. In the final vision he saw four chairs, but one of them was empty. It was his own. He was away while the others were together at home. "A dreary, weary Christmas Eve," Oaksmith muttered as he threw himself onto a couch.

As Oaksmith slept that night, he had "pleasant dreams" about his past. He thought he was home again surrounded by "all of the thoughtful comforts that only a mother's hand can bestow." His brothers were wishing him a "Merry Christmas" when he was awakened by the second mate who had come in to say something about the weather. On Christmas Day he was in a foul mood. All he could do was read Shakespeare and wonder what those at home were doing.[27]

After weeks of bad winds and adverse currents, the *Mary Adeline* finally reached Payta, Peru, a small town with about four thousand inhabitants, frequently visited by whalers. On January 9, 1852, Oaksmith discharged his mutinous crew (some of whom had been in irons this entire time) and went into town to conduct business. At dinner one evening he explained to a local the difficulties he had procuring freights for the *Mary Adeline*. "If I were you Oaksmith I would rob a graveyard, and take home a cargo of *mummies*," said one man. "It would pay better than anything else!"

"Why. Have they mummies here?" Oaksmith inquired, more out of courtesy than genuine interest.

"To be sure they have! Put you under the sod and in six Months you would be a finer specimen of a mummy than was ever brought from Egypt." The man then explained that the ground was rich with saltpeter.

Oaksmith thanked him for this "information" but declined to take part in the venture. After dinner the men lit cigars and strolled through the desert town toward the beach.[28]

On January 14 the *Mary Adeline* departed Payta for Callao, near Lima. His crew were all "green hands"—Peruvians he had picked up at Payta who did not understand English and who hated cold weather. In about two weeks, they reached Callao, where the vessel would pick up water. There, Oaksmith stayed at the home of a customhouse official's wife. She welcomed him "affectionately" and mistook Oaksmith for one "Don Eduardito," a young American officer who had visited the place a few years before. "As I found myself so suddenly elevated in the lady's good graces I did not care to risk a fall by undeceiving her, so I continued to play the part of 'Don Eduardito,'" he wrote. He "must have looked and performed the character well," for several young ladies of the neighborhood who had had "some tender passages" with the original Don Eduardito "recalled to mind certain incidents in which he had borne a conspicuous part, and which I of course remembered perfectly—*upon being told by them*." They spent the evening laughing together about two little monkeys that Don Eduardito had taught to do funny tricks.

Oaksmith later admitted to his journal that he truly enjoyed the company of these two young women. "Like all true rovers of the deep, I had my heart assailed by two inamoratas at the same time, and finding it hard to make a choice 'I loved them both with equal fervor,'" he wrote. He wondered if they would ever figure out his deception. "Should they ever be informed of the counterfeit, I am certain, without egotism, that they will find it difficult to decide which of the two 'Don Eduarditos' they liked the best, the spurious or the genuine." When he departed a day or two later, he bade "a mournful and affecting farewell of all my *friends* in the place."[29]

Oaksmith reached Cape Horn about the second week of March and was thrilled to finally be "upon 'the Ocean of my home,' the Atlantic."[30] A month later he reached Rio de Janeiro. The Brazilians fired upon the *Mary Adeline* from a fort as she entered the harbor because she was a strange vessel. Once on land, several members of the crew deserted. Oaksmith toured the city and saw the emperor at an opera. Attending to business, he worked to find a cargo. "I had hoped that my next destination would be '*home*' (that dear place!) but it is not yet to be," he wrote in his journal. The only freight that he could find was bound for the coast of Africa "and I felt myself constrained by circumstances to accept it." He sent letters home, which is where his heart longed to be. But the need for financial success pushed him in other directions. "I am going still further from them, and nothing in the future looks clear," he wrote, wondering whether he would ever be happy again.[31]

While in Rio, Oaksmith met an American named George Marsden, who was known among foreign diplomats to be a "notorious slave-trader." It is unclear whether the two of them conducted any business together. Oaksmith wrote Marsden's name in the front cover of the master's log of the *Mary Adeline* but made no other mention of him. Later, Oaksmith stated under oath, "I was not connected with him in any kind of business in Rio Janeiro," although he may, of course, have been lying. Meanwhile, while on the women's rights lecture circuit in Philadelphia, Elizabeth Oakes Smith wrote to Seba of how "greatly anxious" she was "about dear Appleton—but I work, work, and try not to think."[32]

3

AFRICA

Oaksmith planned to depart Rio de Janeiro on Saturday, April 24, 1852, but he was "detained by a very mortifying search" by the Brazilian authorities who believed that his ship was going to be engaging in the slave trade. "Of course I offered no objection but could hardly keep my indignation from boiling over, as I walked the deck while the search was being made," he wrote in his journal the next day. "I determined to 'bide my time' and when I return (as I most probably shall) to Rio, to put them all to shame." He was particularly upset that the US consul in Rio, an old family friend, permitted the search to take place, because he believed it cast disgrace upon his entire family. "And I am only striving for *their* happiness and their comfort, and could I attain these through my own disgrace?"[1] In other words, Oaksmith would never dishonor his family by engaging in such a nefarious traffic.

Just two years earlier, in 1850, Brazil had almost entirely shut down the slave trade in and out of its ports, but high sugar prices continued to motivate unscrupulous sea captains to seek cargos of Africans. US minister to Brazil Robert C. Schenck opined, "A single cargo successfully landed and sold now would make the fortune of the adventurer." British, American, and Brazilian officials in Rio were suspicious of several ships seeking clearance to depart that spring. The *Camargo*, commanded by Nathaniel Gordon, a twenty-six-year-old captain from Portland, Maine, was slated to travel to Africa for a cargo of cattle and horses. These same officials believed that the *Mary Adeline*'s cargo "was precisely calculated" for the slave trade (it is unknown what Oaksmith's cargo actually was). Moreover, the British minister to Brazil claimed that George Marsden was "actively interested in getting up and aiding these speculations." Upon examining the ship's papers, government officials learned that one of the ship's investors was a "House that had been notoriously engaged in the traffic."[2] But the US consul reported back to Washington with "regret" that the *Camargo* and *Mary Adeline* had cleared the port. "The masters of these vessels both denied any such intention" to participate in the slave trade, he wrote, and "there was no sufficient proof exhibited at the time of sailing to justify a condemnation"—only "a strong suspicion and belief among those whose judgment in such matters is seldom at fault or mistaken . . . that these vessels, in some manner, will be used in carrying on this infamous traffic." In fact, the officials' suspicions regarding the *Camargo* proved correct. Captain Gordon picked up a cargo of 550 Africans, fifty of whom died during the return passage to Brazil. He landed them on an isolated beach about one hundred miles south of Rio and marched them through a dense forest so that they could avoid detection.[3]

The transatlantic slave trade had been illegal in the United States since 1808, and in 1820 Congress had declared that slavers would be treated like pirates.[4] The problem came with enforcement. Great Britain had similarly declared the Atlantic slave trade illegal in 1807, but the US government would not grant the British Navy permission to "visit and search" American ships—that is, the right to board vessels flying the American flag to inspect them for hidden cargos of human beings. Throughout the 1820s and 1830s, the British had been able to negotiate anti-slave-trade treaties with most European and Latin American nations. But without the cooperation of the United States, it was impossible to abolish the trade.[5] Some 272,000 Africans were forced aboard slavers between 1850 and the complete suppression in 1867—taken mostly to Cuba, but on a few occasions to places within the United States. Much of this illicit work was done by a group of slave traders known as the Portuguese Company who relocated from Rio to Manhattan after 1850.[6]

Although many Americans wanted to see the slave trade destroyed, US politicians were wary of granting the British "the rights of visit and search" during peacetime. They recalled the impressment of American sailors by the Royal Navy during the Napoleonic Wars, and they remembered how impressment had led to the War of 1812. Even a Northern leader like John Quincy Adams vehemently opposed granting the British this right. When asked if he could think of anything worse than the slave trade, he replied, "Yes. Admitting the right of search by foreign officers of our vessels upon the seas in time of peace; for that would be making slaves of ourselves."[7]

Under the Webster-Ashburton Treaty of 1842, England and the United States agreed to equip and maintain naval squadrons off the coast of Africa to suppress the slave trade. Notably, the treaty declared that the two nations would do this work "independent of each other" and that they would "enforce, separately and respectively, the laws, rights, and obligations, of each of the two countries, for the suppression of the slave trade." Because the treaty did not settle the matter of visit and search, British sailors still could not board and inspect vessels flying the American colors. A US diplomat in Brazil noted "how shamefully the flag of the United States is prostituted." An American officer in the Africa Squadron similarly observed, "Our flag has been lately much used in the slave trade, as none but an American man of war can capture it."[8]

Life in the Africa Squadron often proved frustrating for sailors, in large measure because the trade was so often conducted under the American flag. "The illegal slave trade as carried on by many of our own citizens is of a most distressing character," wrote Captain William McBlair. "They make arrangements to receive their slaves at certain places and should a man of war be discovered near at the time, the slaves are marched off perhaps to some other spot fifty miles distant & by signal from the shore or small boats kept for the purpose the slave dealer is notified of the change of arrangement." McBlair grimaced at the thought of "eight hundred of these poor persecuted creatures" having to subsist "upon only one plantain a day each" for the eight months that they would be kept in hiding. Making matters worse was that the American vessels were often powerless to stop the slavers when they flew a foreign flag. He was frustrated by the "inefficiency" of sailing vessels on the African coast, and the fact that many vessels would destroy their papers and flags to avoid trial for piracy in American courts. "We are mere scarecrows," McBlair concluded with irritation.[9]

Within this broader global context, the *Mary Adeline* finally departed Rio on Sunday, April 25. Heading across the sea, Oaksmith felt lonely yet again. Being master of a vessel was an isolating occupation. To pass the time he read *Ivan Hoe*, reminisced about his childhood, and wondered what his family was doing. When he saw another vessel in the distance, he would imagine the hopes and fears of the sailors aboard her. "And I think that perhaps these eyes which now look their last upon her, as she slowly disappears, may be the *last* that shall ever see her, that none shall see her more!" Indeed, death was an ever-present part of a mariner's life, just as it had been for his grandfather, Captian David Prince, who had perished at sea. Still, Oaksmith enjoyed being a sea captain. He wore a white suit, finding satisfaction in the way it looked. But he did not know how much longer he would remain a seafarer. "We shall see when this voyage is over," he mused. "Perhaps a happier or at least a more congenial career may open for me."[10]

After a mere thirty-eight days, Oaksmith made it to Loango, on the west coast of Africa, on June 6. He was surprised at the beauty of Africa, as he had expected "something desolate and wild; but the country about Loango is beautifully interspersed with shady hills and smooth unbroken lawns." From his ship he could not see any habitations, but he did spot two old slave factories—places of embarkation for captured Africans to be put aboard ships.

Each day small groups of Africans paddled some five or six miles from the mouth of the Congo River to trade. Barter with European and American merchants was a common form of legitimate trade for Africans who lived near the Congo River. In the morning they would load up their canoes with goods. After a long day's work, they would paddle back to the shoreline, their canoes filled with new objects. Oaksmith was astounded and "much amused at the ridiculous bargains which have been made." The "Natives" would exert enormous energy "for the purpose of disposing of *one* pumpkin and *one* duck, for these they will receive an empty junk bottle or some other equally useless thing and go away contented," he wrote. Then, repeating a commonly held and bigoted view, he added, "For a common old musket, I have been told, a son would sell his Father or Mother!" Soon the deck of the *Mary Adeline* looked, sounded, and smelled like a barnyard, with ducks, chickens, sheep, goats, and pigs making a cacophonous noise.

Oaksmith's agreement with the merchants back in Rio was to visit two ports in Africa, although he did not yet know which those would be. So he continued to sit offshore "waiting for orders" and hoping that this was the place he would discharge his cargo. During this time, he encountered British warships patrolling the African coast. Surely he knew that only American naval vessels could legally search his ship for evidence of slaving. He nevertheless invited the British aboard. His loneliness made him eager for interaction with other English-speaking sailors. At 9 p.m. on June 6, a British officer named Kiddle of the HMS *Fire Fly*, a five-gun British warship built in 1832, boarded the *Mary Adeline*. "It was quite refreshing to see one who comes so near a countryman as does an Englishman," wrote Oaksmith in his journal, "and we chatted together for half an hour or more when he took his leave promising to see me again."[11] Under the Webster-Ashburton Treaty of 1842, Oaksmith did not have to permit Kiddle to board his ship (and if Kiddle had done so against Oaksmith's will, it would have provoked an international incident). But Oaksmith appears to have had nothing to hide. And if he had had something to conceal, Kiddle might have discovered it, for the *Fire Fly* had captured a vessel outfitted for the slave trade just a week earlier, on May 30.[12]

On June 7, Kiddle returned to the *Mary Adeline* with the commander of the *Fire Fly*, George Alexander Seymour. Perhaps Seymour wanted to confirm that the *Mary Adeline* was not a slaver. Then the *Fire Fly* went out to sea. Finally, on June 10, Oaksmith spotted a launch heading toward him from the African coastline. When it reached him, he was boarded by a Portuguese consignee, or agent, of his cargo. The man instructed Oaksmith to go into the Congo River, which he "foolishly consented" to do. He worried, though, because he had encountered the strength of the current far out at sea and he knew "the difficulties of its ascension must be immense." At 9 a.m., Oaksmith and his crew "hove up" for the Congo River. As he feared, his ship struggled against the strong current. "Words cannot tell how disgusted I feel!" he scrawled in his journal. "I had hoped to have discharged my cargo at Loango and then there would have been some chance to getting home before the bad months come on. Deeply do I regret now that I did not peremptorily refuse to go to this infernal River." Oaksmith now believed that he had "been deceived by my charter-party through my ignorance of their language, as when they refused to designate the two Ports, for which they stipulated, they assured me that they would be as easy to access as Rio de Janeiro." But he had consented to go "and must make the best of it."[13]

On June 17, Oaksmith reached Shark's Point, a bend near the mouth of the river that served as one of the principal slave trading posts in the area.[14] Around the bend sat the HMS *Dolphin*, a three-gun, 318-ton British warship searching for slavers. Built in 1836, one contemporary described her as "a very fine sea boat, sails like a witch, and is very easy." The *Dolphin* fired a warning shot and then ran up an English ensign. Oaksmith answered by raising the Stars and Stripes. At 4 p.m. Second Master H. P. Ward, the master of the *Dolphin*, boarded the *Mary Adeline* and "kindly volunteered to assist me round the Point."[15] Ward also may have wished to see if there was anything suspicious aboard the vessel, such as extra lumber for building a slave deck.

The current flowing out to sea carried tremendous force, often running six miles per hour. One American sailor observed, "The Congo . . . sweeps into the Atlantic with a heavy current carrying with it large floating islands of grass, trees, bamboo, etc., which are sometimes met over a hundred miles at sea." Another remarked that the surf crashing onto the shoreline was so loud that it could be heard twenty miles inland, "reminding one of the sound of Niagara."[16] As the *Mary Adeline* struggled against this current, a "crowd" of about eight Portuguese men who worked for the consignee joined Oaksmith's boat. He was tempted to make them place their cargo onto their launches, which could be much more easily managed on the river, but knew that his contract bound him to go further up the river to an actual port.[17]

For several days Oaksmith kept trying to take the *Mary Adeline* around the bend at Shark's Point, but he could not overcome the force of the current. On Saturday, June 19, at about noon he again tried to pass Shark's Point. After about an hour, he was "pretty-well up with it" when he got stuck on the bank. Oaksmith signaled the *Dolphin* for assistance, which sent small boats with anchors, hawsers, and other equipment to help. The *Dolphin*'s boats reached the *Mary Adeline* about 4:30 p.m. and the crews of both ships worked with "utmost exertion" to free the American vessel, but the tide quickly receded and, as darkness approached, the *Mary Adeline* was still stuck in the mud. Second Master Ward of the *Dolphin* said that he could do no more that day and started preparing to take his leave. The Portuguese men on the ship began to exhibit "great anxiety and tribulation" and begged Oaksmith to ask Ward to leave a guard on the *Mary Adeline* because they feared that they would be attacked by a large group of Africans that was assembling on the shore. Oaksmith paid little attention to this request, believing that the Portuguese possessed a "natural cowardice," but he asked Ward whether "any thing need be apprehended from the Natives." Ward replied that "he thought not" but that if Oaksmith saw "anything threatening or suspicious in the night to fire a musket or two and they would either send assistance to us or throw some 'grape and canister' upon the point."

Oaksmith went into his room and loaded his pistols, "more for the purpose of keeping order on board of my own vessel than anything else— for I really did not much fear an attack from the Natives." But he began to feel some anxiety when he saw the Africans' movements on the beach. Oaksmith and his two mates kept watch all night, while some of the Portuguese slept in their launch—too afraid to stay aboard the *Mary Adeline*. Meanwhile, the Africans built fires along the shoreline, and Oaksmith and his mates "could occasionally hear their voices in loud altercation" as they sat in circles around the fires.

At 4 a.m. on Sunday, June 20, the *Dolphin* hauled up next to Oaksmith's vessel with anchors and warps, but the current was so strong, and the river's swell so heavy, that the work was "not only very difficult but hazardous." The men toiled away until 8 a.m., when it became apparent that the Africans were preparing to attack. Oaksmith "cast my eyes upon the shore" and saw an "unusual numbers of the Natives were gathered in close proximity to the vessel; many of them armed with muskets." The weather was perfectly calm, which meant that the current would make it difficult for the *Dolphin* to position herself to protect the *Mary Adeline*. Ward and Oaksmith conferred together for a moment, and both agreed that the Africans would hardly dare to attack the stranded vessel while the *Dolphin* was so near. If an attack did come, however, Oaksmith would run up his ensign upside down, at which point the *Dolphin* would immediately open fire upon the shoreline. "If it comes to the worst," Oaksmith said to Ward, "and I am boarded, I shall take to that house [the ship's cabin] and maintain it if possible till you can get to my assistance. In which case as you can see it from your mast heads, do not fail to fire directly upon my vessel." Ward and his men then departed on several small boats.

Oaksmith called his mates into the captain's cabin to load their meager arsenal of six muskets and two rifles. "If we are attacked and they get on board of us, the only chance for our lives will be this cabin," Oaksmith said. "We must keep together, for I have no one else on board on whom I rely except you." The men went to the galley and started to boil water.

The Portuguese quickly began to pack their baggage onto a launch so that they could escape before the attack came. In truth, Oaksmith would rather have had them gone, but he also knew that their departure at this moment would expose the ship's weakness to the Africans. "I told them, through one who could understand, that over the side they should not go, and they apparently seemed to understand me for they remained on board. It would have been my duty to have shot the first man who attempted to leave." And so the Portuguese hid below decks "*in* berths and some of them *underneath* them, some of them behind bulkheads and some of them *missing*." Oaksmith was frustrated by these "rascally Portuguese," but he also knew that men who "have to be sought, under such circumstances, are far better out of the way." The ship's steward—who had been with Oaksmith since California—was sick, but he "crawled up out of the lower cabin" to join Oaksmith's "little band." He would go on to prove himself "a brave fellow through the whole fight."

The *Dolphin*'s boats were hardly out of sight when about three thousand African warriors gathered on the beach, close under the brig's stern. At least half had muskets and several carried hooks and poles for scaling the side of the ship. On the shoreline they danced and "howled and capered about in the most hideous manner, making signs of how they would cut and tear the poor 'Mary Adeline' to pieces when they got possession of her." They also acted out "some not very pleasant little ceremonies as to how we were to be treated when they had taken us prisoners." Oaksmith and his tiny band gathered upon the starboard quarter with their weapons hidden, "looking down as unconcernedly as we could upon this fearful assemblage and at the same time watching most warily every movement." In truth, Oaksmith feared that the *Dolphin* might not be able to help him as she would need a moderate breeze to fight the current to reach the *Mary Adeline*, and at that moment the wind was "dead calm."

Some of the Africans seemed to recognize the Portuguese men on board. They pointed and shouted, "me sabey you Point Elena!—me sabey you Pointee Elena!" which Oaksmith believed meant that they had seen them at the slave factories at Point Elena. One of the Portuguese men ran to the side of the boat and pounded his chest, retorting, "yes me Point Elena me Point Elena!" But Oaksmith "silenced him upon the instant." The Africans "made signs to the Portuguese to come down and go away and they would spare them," and Oaksmith could see in their faces that they longed to go. But Oaksmith left no doubt how he felt in the expression on his face. "Perhaps they read in mine something else!"

Looking around the bend, Oaksmith could see that the mast headman on the *Dolphin* was watching intently and reporting what he could see to the officers on deck. Still, he felt anxious, for he knew that "if the Savages were resolute, without a breeze, her assistance might come *too late*." Not more than ten minutes had elapsed since the last of the *Dolphin*'s boats disappeared around Shark's Point when the steward shouted, "Look out Captain there's one of them cocking his musket!" Oaksmith looked in that direction and saw three or four hundred muskets leveled at the ship as the Africans let out a "fiendish yell." "Down!" Oaksmith cried, "down every body!" They all got their heads below the bulwarks just before "the whole volley came crashing over and around us."

Oaksmith and his men sat up and fired several rounds while the *Dolphin* sent a shell hurtling through the air toward the beach. The "Savages with wild yells turned and fled," Oaksmith wrote. Lieutenant Commander William Wood of the *Dolphin* later wrote, "At this time I might have destroyed them all, as we were not more than a quarter of a mile from the shore. But not liking to take so much life, I merely frightened them with a shell or two, which had the desired effect." But the fight was far from over. The Africans returned in groups of between ten and twenty to fire at the vessel from the cover of the bushes. "We had to be very careful therefor as to how we exposed ourselves for we knew that a dozen muskets which *we* could not see, were constantly on the alert to 'pick us off,'" recalled Oaksmith. "At the same time every black head that showed itself through the bushes was sure to be saluted by us: and I felt certain before long that they entertained more respect for us than they did at first."

Looking through his glass at about 11:30 a.m., Oaksmith saw a crowd gathering in the distance, and he became "convinced that a large body of the devils were again approaching for another combined attack." Oaksmith and his men braced themselves, but the mast headman on the *Dolphin* had also spotted the mass of men, and the British warship sent a round of grapeshot into the shoreline. "In an instant the woods seemed alive with black forms which had gradually been creeping down nearer and nearer to us with all the stealthiness of tigers. Wildly they fled along the beach and we soon saw them gathering in immense numbers in a little bay just below us, and out of the reach of the 'Dolphin's' guns."

The commander of the *Dolphin* took this opportunity to send a six-pound cannon and some grape shot to the *Mary Adeline*, which Oaksmith mounted on the top of the quarterdeck house "in a position to sweep the beach." Oaksmith sat down by the gun carriage and looked out at the bushes through his glass. Occasionally a bullet whistled by him, but he felt confident that he was too far away from them to be hit except by "a chance shot."

At about 2 p.m., a light breeze sprung up and the *Dolphin* weighed anchor and began to head toward the *Mary Adeline*, but before she could get there the current caught her and swept her a long distance into the river, where she was forced to lay her anchor before getting carried even further away. With the *Dolphin* stuck further away, Oaksmith knew that he was vulnerable, and looking through his glass, he saw "a large crowd creeping through the bushes" toward the shoreline. Oaksmith decided to hold his fire so that they would not know that he had seen them. He lay down on top of the house and, with the assistance of his mates, brought the gun to bear upon them. He then stood up and shouted, "Fire!" Oaksmith watched the Africans through his glass as they turned and ran "howling away, dragging some of their companions with them." The *Dolphin* also sent more shots.

For the duration of the afternoon, the Africans moved stealthily down toward the shoreline in small groups of three or four, undetected by Oaksmith and his men. "The first notice that we would have of their proximity would be the whistling of their bullets," Oaksmith wrote later in an official report of the action. These "light skirmishes" continued all afternoon and into the evening. About 5 p.m., the *Fire Fly* arrived and came to Oaksmith's assistance (although she too got temporarily grounded). At 9 p.m. Oaksmith discovered another crowd of Africans along the shoreline. He "threw some 'grape' among them," causing them to retreat from their final attack of the day. Oaksmith thought it "a most extraordinary thing" that none of his men were hit by the gunfire considering how many shots had been fired at his ship. He also felt relieved because the Africans were firing nails, pieces of iron and copper, flints and other stones, and chunks of lead, instead of bullets. Such projectiles, Oaksmith knew, would have caused "very dangerous wounds."

Early on Monday morning, June 21, the Portuguese consignees started for the other side of the river to get launches to retrieve their cargo since they believed the *Mary Adeline* would be lost. But the currents proved too strong for them. During the day, three of the *Dolphin*'s men were "severely" injured while trying to help Oaksmith when their cutter was overturned in the surf and thrown against the beach. On Tuesday the 22nd it was decided to move Oaksmith's cargo over to the *Dolphin*. The crew of the *Dolphin* assisted from 10 a.m. to 5 p.m., moving about three-quarters of the cargo, working to the tune of the sea shanty, "Cheerly, Man." As the weight of the vessel decreased, the *Mary Adeline* again started to float. By 7 p.m. Oaksmith had anchored the brig in deep water. The men cheered. "A wild, fierce, tiger-like yell of disappointment broke upon our ears from the fiends upon the shore in answer to the hearty cheer of the seamen," wrote Oaksmith in his journal. That night the *Mary Adeline*'s captain slept soundly in his berth for a full eight hours. "This was the first time that I had closed my eyes since the night of the previous Friday," he wrote. Meanwhile, the *Dolphin* hovered in the distance to keep "the Natives" in check.

The next morning Oaksmith awoke refreshed. He went on board the *Fire Fly* to thank Captain Seymour, for the *Fire Fly* was supposed to have left the vicinity the previous day, but Seymour "with great kindness consented to wait for the purpose of getting the [*Mary Adeline*] off." Soon Lieutenant Commander Wood of the *Dolphin* joined them, and the three men sat down for breakfast. Wood insisted that Oaksmith stay on the *Dolphin* until he had recovered from the fatigue of the previous few days. Oaksmith gladly and gratefully accepted the invitation, and he looked forward to the companionship of the Englishmen. "Never have I met a pleasanter companion than Wood and my only regret is that I must so soon lose him." Oaksmith decided to stay with Wood until his cargo was fully turned over to the Portuguese, at which point he would return to Brazil "and from then I trust to 'home'"—with his family in New York City.

On June 24, Oaksmith sat in Wood's cabin writing out a lengthy account of the previous few days. He felt "a just and a high sense of the mercies of a great Providence which has so ordained and directed these events, that I am left in health and safety to recount them."[18] He also penned a letter to Kiddle, thanking him for all that he and his men had done. "I cannot take leave of you after the important services which you have rendered me, without acknowledging the extent of my indebtedness," he wrote, "and I feel confident that without the timely assistance which you rendered me in so efficient a manner, I should not now be in possession of my vessel."[19] Oaksmith might have added that he might not be alive, either.

Oaksmith spent the next few days aboard the *Dolphin*. "To a poor devil who has but just escaped the double horrors of being shipwrecked and murdered, perhaps tortured, by Savages, the cordial and genuine hospitality, with which I am treated on all sides on board of this vessel, is a most grateful thing," he wrote. He and Commander Wood became "bosom friends," and all of the British officers showed kindness to the beleaguered American sailor. At dinner in the gun room on June 26, the Englishmen toasted, "The President," and Oaksmith reciprocated by toasting, "The Queen." On deck at night the men sang songs, including "Yankee Doodle" and "God Save the Queen." But the highlight for Oaksmith came when one "jolly tar, in pure sailor style" belted out "The Ditty of the Mary Adeline," or "The Battle of the Congo," which had been composed by the gunner's mate and set to music by the corporal of Marines. Oaksmith was so touched that he requested a copy of the verses.[20]

Oaksmith delivered the last of his cargo on Tuesday, June 29. Of the $30,000 worth of goods, he gave one-third to the *Dolphin* and the *Fire Fly* as salvage for the work they had done in rescuing him. He also presented a seven-stanza poem, titled "Farewell Lines," to the men of the *Dolphin* and a six-stanza poem by the same title to Lieutenant Wood. The first poem praised the men of the *Dolphin* for saving the *Mary Adeline* and her men, recounting the battle in rhyme.

> All honor to the "Dolphin's" crew, and to their country's name!
> When pulseless lies my heart in earth, they both shall live in Fame!
> And ye, who did such fellowship, kindly to me extend,
> Must feel that in America, ye have at least a friend.

The second poem praised Wood's friendship, which "burn[ed] with stronger flames than love." He marveled at the circumstances of their meeting— "that wild time when first we met upon the Congo's tide"—and cherished the thought that he had gained "that rarest thing, a friend!"[21]

Oaksmith bade farewell to his British friends and made his way toward the Atlantic. Lieutenant Wood later stated that Oaksmith "was very grateful, and was a very superior, gentlemanly man." The breeze and current took the *Mary Adeline* swiftly out the mouth of the river. July 4, 1852, was an Independence Day like none other in Oaksmith's life to that point. "At Sea!!!" he wrote with exhilaration in his journal.[22]

The Battle of the Congo River received press attention throughout the Atlantic World. The *New York Times* described how Oaksmith and his crew "most bravely and gallantly defended" their ship from "a furious and savage assault." Meanwhile, a nautical magazine in London wrote, "Every credit is due to Mr. Oaksmith, master of the *Mary Adeline*, for his constant exertions, correct judgment, and cool determined conduct under these trying and dangerous circumstances."[23] But soon the story began to morph. Legends of Oaksmith as a vicious slaver emerged in the late nineteenth century. More than thirty years later, one man who had sailed with Oaksmith in the 1860s recalled that he "was a stout, well-built man, . . . with a swarthy complexion." "They used to tell some terrible things about him on the ship. One of them was that when coming across from the west coast of Africa with a load of 'blackbirds,' he was chased by a man-of-war, when he fastened the negroes to a long chain cable and dumped 'em overboard, so in case he was captured there would be no evidence against him." The old salt admitted, "I don't know that this is true, but I do know that he was a determined and desperate man."[24]

Oaksmith's journal suggests that he did not go to the Congo River on a slaving voyage. He had, after all, gone from port to port in South America looking for a cargo to pick up that might take him back to New York. Historians have nevertheless presumed that he had nefarious intentions. Historian John Jay TePaske writes, "Despite Oaksmith's protestations in Rio de Janeiro concerning the rumors that his vessel was a slaver, it seems certain that the *Mary Adeline* was fitted out as a slave ship. Oaksmith was strangely quiet about the identity of his cargo, and there can be little doubt that he made the voyage to Africa to secure slaves."[25] But this evidence is not really persuasive since Oaksmith never discussed any of his cargoes, from Acapulco to San Francisco and then back around South America before heading to Africa. In fact, he wrote home in late 1851, as his father explained in a letter to Elizabeth Oakes Smith, that "he was going to some port on the west coast of South America to look for freight, he could not tell where it might be, perhaps to Europe, perhaps to some of these eastern states, perhaps back to California."[26] If Oaksmith was entering the slaving business during his voyage to Africa, that was not what he'd set out to do.

The news reports out of Rio in April that Appleton was "bound to Africa" came as quite a surprise to his family members back in New York.

"This was quite unexpected and makes me feel anxious for him," wrote Seba to Sidney. "I don't know what kind of voyage he is to make [and I] am afraid it will be [a] hazardous one."[27] Hazardous indeed. But not necessarily illegal. Imports from Africa increased dramatically in the decades leading up to the Civil War. Trade in ivory, gum, palm oil, and copper ore increased steadily throughout the decades. In 1827, Americans purchased 4,700 tons of legal African products. By the 1850s, that number had grown to more than forty thousand tons per year. Exports to Africa also increased. The US Treasury Department kept a record of all the commerce from the United States to foreign ports around the world. The reports list nothing more specific than "Africa generally" (meaning that it is impossible to know how much went to the Congo River as opposed to other African ports), but the statistics are instructive. For instance, in the fiscal year that ended on June 30, 1852, American merchants exported small amounts of some items to Africa, such as pickled fish (valued at $3,899), wood and timber for ships ($11,810), cheese and butter ($7,664), pork products ($13,774), flour and various grains ($72,740), alcohol ($92,871), tobacco ($60,217), gunpowder ($60,906), billiards tables ($225), umbrellas ($45), and cotton products ($570,688). To be sure, the total exports to Africa represented less than 1 percent of American exports around the world.[28] But it is not beyond the realm of possibility that Oaksmith intended to make a lawful voyage to Africa. Legal traders regularly entered the Congo River. As one historian has written, "vessels employed in the legal trade in palm oil between Africa and the United States went to many of the same places that slave ships embarked captives, making the efforts of US authorities extremely delicate."[29] This was a region in which both licit and illicit trade thrived.

We will also never know why the Africans attacked Oaksmith's ship— whether it was an act of war against a man they believed to be a slave trader (which seems most likely), or simply an attempt to plunder his ship and cargo. Nevertheless, it appears that Oaksmith's experiences on the Congo River may not have been wholly unusual. After spending time near Shark's Point, another American sailor observed, "The natives, near the mouth of the river, have been rendered treacherous and cruel by the slave-trade; but a short distance in the interior, they are represented as being civil and inoffensive, disposed to trade in elephants'-teeth and palm-oil."[30] This assessment aligns with Oaksmith's experience, although he never got far enough upriver to unload his freight.

Whatever his purpose for having gone to Africa, Oaksmith was now finally on his way back to the Western Hemisphere. Sailing across the Atlantic Ocean, the *Mary Adeline* was shorthanded, owing to sickness and desertion over the previous few weeks. Indeed, Oaksmith found himself doing the duty or two or three men. On July 14, he had to bury a sailor at sea. "A seaman's lot is cast always among strangers—for them he toils—among them he lives—and among them he dies," he wrote in his journal. This man had likely sailed under an alias, so his family would never know his fate. "Many a poor tar I expect is sleeping quietly beneath the bosom of the ocean whose friends are still waiting for his return."[31]

On July 21 Oaksmith anchored at Bahia, Brazil, after a very quick passage from Africa. He was quarantined on account of the death on his ship, but the consul, John S. Gillmer, got the quarantine lifted after a few days. Oaksmith informed Gillmer that if the *Dolphin* had not intervened in the situation, "not one who was on board my vessel would ever have been heard of again," and he asked Gillmer to see that the US government properly acknowledge the gallant and generous actions of the British sailors. He also provided Gillmer with an account of what had happened from the British naval officers "in order that you may be convinced that nothing discreditable was entertained in relation to myself or my flag in connexion with the affair." In other words, Oaksmith wanted the US government to know that he was not a slaver—and that the British Navy would attest to that fact. Gillmer passed the message along to Secretary of State Daniel Webster, and President Millard Fillmore subsequently extended his thanks to the British government "for this kind and important service to an American vessel."[32]

Oaksmith stayed with the Gillmers for a week but could not find any freights bound for home, so he went to Rio de Janeiro, where he arrived on August 9 after a "toilsome and weary passage." He remained in the Brazilian capital, seeing many friends, until October 6, at which point he sailed for Martha's Vineyard with the cargo of the whaler *Henry Clay*, which had been condemned at Rio. Oaksmith reflected on how he had left his home two years earlier "to seek my fortune in the great El dorado of the West," but that he was "now returning to that home; a wiser, if not a better man than when I left. Of happiness I may not speak; and yet I sincerely believe, the greatest that I have enjoyed during my long pilgrimage is that which comes to me now in the thought that I am bound home."[33]

Only a few pages remained to be filled in Oaksmith's journal. He thought that the worst of his journey had passed, but one last dreadful incident still lay ahead. In mid-November, the ship endured several days of terrible storms near Bermuda. The weather finally cleared up on November 23. Standing on the deck, Oaksmith gave some instructions to his mate, Alexander E. Allinson. After dinner Allinson went to work, while

Oaksmith went into his cabin. After a short while, Allinson came to ask a question, which Oaksmith answered quickly. "Those were the last words he ever spoke to me or I to him," Oaksmith wrote in his journal, "and I remember him now with pain and sorrow that my reply was too impatient for the kind, respectful manner in which he addressed me." From his room, Oaksmith could hear Allinson talking cheerfully with the other men when, all of the sudden, he "heard something heavily strike the deck." Oaksmith was ready to shout "an angry word," imagining that someone had thrown something carelessly down onto the deck. But when he came outside, he saw Allinson lying motionless. Oaksmith ran to him and lifted him in his arms as blood poured like "a living stream from his mouth and nostrils, and every muscle of his body seemed relaxed." Oaksmith placed a mattress on the cabin table and lay Allinson down upon it. He never showed any sign of consciousness. "My God! what tears I shed when it dawned upon me that he was dying," Oaksmith later wrote. "How I reproached myself for every harsh word I had spoken to him!" Visions of Allinson's kind and devoted demeanor poured through Oaksmith's mind, causing him to cling "more strongly to that crushed and bleeding form, which Death was bearing away from my very arms."

The weather had been beautiful all day, but now, as Allinson lay dying, a storm began to emerge. Oaksmith ordered the crew to take the sail while Oaksmith clung to Allinson's "nearly lifeless form." After a few minutes more, it "all was over." Oaksmith took "the poor, crushed, bleeding body" and "straightened and composed [it] upon the sofa," and then went to command the ship. "Throughout all the long dreary night that followed the winds howled and moaned through the rigging and the Brig plunged and tossed as though frightened through the Sea." All night long Oaksmith walked the deck, periodically looking through his cabin window at Allinson's lifeless body.

In the early morning hours of November 24, Oaksmith called his steward to assist in preparing the body for burial. They laid an ensign over the corpse, and Oaksmith called, "Strike eight bells!" and "Call all hands to bury the dead!" The crewmen came over to perform this solemn duty. Oaksmith read the funeral service with tears welling in his eyes, and saw "many a rough cheek moistened, among those to whom death is but too frequently a by-word and a jest." After pitching the dead man into the sea, Oaksmith watched the waves close over Allinson's body. He then turned away, unable to contain his grief. Allinson had been with him since San Francisco—had helped suppress the mutiny and fight off the African warriors. His death had come so suddenly, so unexpectedly. "It all seemed like a dream!" Oaksmith wrote. And indeed, for several days the incident tortured Oaksmith's dreams at night and kept him in a melancholy mood by day.[34] Oaksmith would always have a heart for those who perished at sea, or who lost a loved one to the waves. A few years later he sent a short note to his mother introducing a young man who had just lost his mother at sea: "I have taken the liberty to offer him the use of some of my wardrobe," he wrote, so that the young man could go see his sister. Oaksmith allowed the man to take almost any clothes that he wanted.[35]

Monday, December 6, 1852. "In sight of Martha's Vineyard." Oaksmith had been traveling for three years. He hastily took up his pen to close out his journal, thinking about "the many things that have happened to me" since he began writing in the book. "This is finished. My Native land is in sight. I close the covers of this misère upon an Era of my life. A new one is dawning upon me! I know not what it may be! but wherever it closes may I feel as I do now that I am a better and a wiser man than when it commenced."[36]

4

DIPLOMACY

Seba Smith was relieved to have his son nearing home. On December 8, 1852, he wrote to Appleton, "I have this moment received and read your very welcome and heart-rejoicing letter of the 6th, on your arrival at Edgartown [Martha's Vineyard]. Most devoutly do I feel thankful to our heavenly father for the mercy and protection that have kept you in your long and perilous wanderings, and brought you at last in safety so near to us. May you soon be with us."[1]

Appleton's adventures had brought him fully into adulthood. One observer noted that he "favors his mother in features; and, with his flowing beard, grown in foreign countries, he makes up a marked person." At twenty-four years old, he was thick set, stood five feet, eight inches tall, had broad shoulders, a square neck, tan skin, and a "full round head." Another acquaintance thought he had the "sharpest, most penetrating eyes I ever saw,—quick, darting, black eyes, on which the whites seemed to stand out clear all around the ball." Now an experienced world traveler who was fluent in Spanish, he hoped to become the US consul at Rio de Janeiro. Perhaps it hurt his chances that Portuguese was the language of Brazil, for nothing ever came of this.[2]

While Appleton had been away, Elizabeth emerged as a leader in the women's rights movement. Even in the 1840s, her literary works offered pointed commentary about social inequalities and the place of women in society. She made a different sort of name for herself when she climbed Mount Katahdin in 1849—reportedly the first white woman to do so.[3] But she really flashed into the limelight when she published a series of editorials in Horace Greeley's *New York Tribune* between November 1850 and June 1851. Oakes Smith urged readers to view women as individuals, rather than as a monolithic class—and she maintained that women who used their intelligence should not be viewed as unfeminine. She recognized that nature had designed men and women differently, but this did not mean that women were inferior. Nor should women be denied "human rights" or equal opportunities for intellectual development. Oakes Smith lamented that girls were too often "defrauded" of their "girlhood" by being made "baby wives"—an experience she knew all too well. And once married, a woman lost her legal personhood, was confined to her home, and lost her ability to gain financial independence.

Inequality between husbands and wives led to unhappy marriages and a rise in the divorce rate, she continued. If Americans wished to guard against divorce, they could eliminate its seeds by granting women more equality in society. "Were women allowed the exercise of their best faculties, and remunerated equally with the other sex," she maintained, "they might often escape the desire for divorce by a knowledge that the avenues to wealth or distinction were open to them, and thus they might fill up the desert of their life." In other words, women needed real equality of opportunity—including the right to vote.[4]

Oakes Smith had her critics, and Horace Greeley allowed hostile responses to appear in his columns.[5] She determined that women needed a newspaper of their own to push for women's rights, and she hoped to enlist leading suffragists like Elizabeth Cady Stanton in the enterprise.[6] In late 1851, Oakes Smith asked Greeley for financial backing for such a paper, but he declined. In response, she sent him a private note with little attempt to mask her frustration and disappointment. "No, I do not like your answer," she wrote, "it is neither kind nor enlightened. You see I do not flatter you any more than you did me. But I am not angry. I do think there is a want of sight in right on your part—and I do not think your vision as to human requirements is growing clear. On the contrary—I fear success has blinded you much." She supported a paper, she told him, "because Women need it, and should have it," especially since most newspapers were hostile toward "the true spirit of reform." And she wished to edit it because she needed the financial support. She'd received no pay for her essays for the *Tribune* even though she'd asked Greeley for compensation. "Now are men treated in this way," she asked. No, of course not. And part of the reason

that Women suffer as they do, in matters of labor is because men do not see into their position—they take it for granted that a married woman is supported—she is alive, and they do not ask, nor care how she lives. She may labor ten fold harder than men will labor to keep their families together, and then they must take their chance to find bread for them, their families after men are served. No, my Friend, I do not, and did not ask flattery at your hand, I have enough of that always to starve upon—I asked you in the true spirit of one who claims to look into the heart of humanity—I asked you to see me into this matter and lend it a helping hand—The Tribune is prosperous—what is a few hundred of dollars to a man who is earning his tens of thousands.

Oakes Smith informed Greeley that she was "no one Idea woman" and that the "paper I wish to establish could never be a one idea paper. The one Idea papers all belong to your sex, and are almost nauseating." She concluded, "No my good friend, or enemy, which you will, the laborer cannot work without implements. I may write and lecture, and I have my subjects so near at heart, that I do this with little or no pay, but I must live. . . . We are on equal terms now friend Greeley. . . . You decline aiding us—I regret this—but you have a right to do what you will with your own. I only think your practice does not well accord with your preaching."[7]

Greeley, for his part, was outraged by Oakes Smith's letter. The very next day he sent her a hasty note. "Now there are already fifty papers (I think) edited by women," he informed her. And if she needed to make a living she should write "for the most widely circulated periodicals to which you can gain access and being thus made known as an intellectual champion of Reform, you would be invited to Lecture, either to mixed audiences or to women only." He had grown weary, he explained, of reformers asking for his money. "Perhaps I am not liberal—I certainly do not boast of being so," he wrote, "but were my income twice what it is, it would not satisfy the demands made upon it by claimants who think they know better what I ought to do than I can, and who tell me that the sincerity of my *professions* (!?) of Philanthropy, Benevolence, &c. will be tested by my compliance with or refusal of their demands." He then closed by quoting Elizabeth's words about friends and enemies back to her. "Your 'friend' I fear I cannot be, since the practical condition seems to be a surrender of my judgment and my purse to your requirements. If I were capable of such submission, I should not profane the name of friendship by applying it to the result. No, since we cannot be friends and have no reasons and no wish to be enemies, let us be former acquaintances who have chosen our several paths and will walk them to the end." Upon receiving this letter, Elizabeth wrote at the top, "full of conceited assumptions by no means warranted by my communication to him."[8] There would be no further contact between her family and Greeley for more than ten years.

In her effort to attain rights and equality for women, Elizabeth took to the lecture circuit. She delivered lectures in New York, Boston, Cincinnati, Cleveland, and Philadelphia, among other cities and towns. Audiences paid twenty-five cents to hear her speak on "Manhood," "Womanhood," and "Humanity." Many spectators expected to find a "brazen-faced woman with masculine airs" upon the stage but instead encountered "a pure-minded and highly womanly woman" and someone who was "lady-like, refined, dignified, and intellectual." At New Bedford, Massachusetts, one man who listened to her speak on "Womanhood" thought, "She treated the subject very ably." A journalist who heard the same lecture noted that her "manner was easy and self-possessed, and she has a voice of such sweetness and purity." She could be easily heard throughout the hall and even managed to capture the attention of "the rude and ungainly boys" who had been brought to the lecture by their mothers. "If we are to have lectures by ladies at all," the reporter concluded, "we hope it will be by such ladies as Mrs. Smith."[9]

In her speeches, Oakes Smith hoped to rouse conservative women "from sloth and imbecility, from pettiness and discontent, into some sphere of true nobleness." She found herself "happier in being thus a voice to my kind than I ever could be in any mere Artistic effort." Later reformers praised Oakes Smith for opening the lyceum circuit to women. Oakes Smith also became a prominent member of women's rights conventions in the 1850s where she articulated more radical positions. At the Syracuse Convention in 1852, she declared that "we aim at nothing less than the entire subversion of the existing order of society, a dissolution of the whole existing social compact. . . . Let us protest against Law in which we have no voice; against Legislation in which we are not represented; against a Democracy in which half of the people are denied the rights of Citizenship. I call upon every woman here to enter her solemn protest against a country claiming to be free, and yet denying to her the rights of a citizen."[10]

Oakes Smith made a positive impression on many who saw her. Henry Clay described her as "the perfect model of the American matron, and a decided ornament to the country that gave her birth. Seldom has a woman of any age acquired such ascendancy by the mere force of a powerful intellect. Her smile is the play of a sunlit fountain." Another man thought her "bearing was majestically grand, her manners refined and dignified, yet cordial, and taking her all in all, she looked, acted, and moved the born patrician." But her professional demeanor did not stop her from being lampooned. Beginning in 1853, Wood's Minstrels performed a song titled "Lecture on Woman's Rights" in which a black-faced minstrel, William W. Newcomb, appeared in Puritan or Pilgrim attire and an old-fashioned woman's bonnet. Another parody song performed by Wood's Minstrels was "Dedicated (Without Permission) to Mrs. Oakwood Smith and Mrs. Amelia Bloomer." One verse went:

> 'Tis "woman's Right" a home to have
> as perfect as can be,
> But "Not her right" to make that home
> to ev'ry lover free;
> 'Tis "woman's Right" to rule the house
> And petty troubles brave,
> But "not her right" to rule the head
> and treat him as her slave

Adding racism to their misogyny, Wood's Minstrels published a print of Newcomb portraying Oakes Smith as an elderly black woman at a podium singing this song.[11]

PLANTATION MELODIES.   33

Mr. Wm. Newcomb, as he delivers his celebrated Burlesque Lecture on " Woman's Rights." By Mrs. Oak Woods Smith, at Wood's Minstrel Hall, 444 Broadway.

"Mr. Wm. Newcomb."

M. C. Campbell, *Wood's New Plantation Melodies* (New York: Garrett, 1859), 33.

Courtesy of the New York State Library.

In some ways it should be unsurprising that Oakes Smith was the recipient of racist barbs. She and Seba had been enemies of slavery for many years. He had been a founding member of the Maine Anti-Slavery Society in 1833, and she had been horrified by the slave marts she saw during her family's brief sojourn in Charleston in 1839. But her priority in the 1850s was women's rights. "I am with you heart and soul in the anti slavery movement," she wrote to Wendell Phillips. "I shall not forget that I owe my best recognition to the friends of that reform, and hereafter I hope both in my paper, pulpit or Lecture room to speak boldly the truth in that field of action." But that time had not yet come. To the abolitionist William Lloyd Garrison she wrote, "My sympathies have always been with you, and God willing, when I am stronger, and our course better established, I shall be able to speak out boldly in aid of your righteous work." She was grateful for the positive coverage her lectures received in Garrison's newspaper, *The Liberator,* but she told Gerrit Smith, "I believe the abolitionists blame me for not advocating their reform more heartily, but they have enough in the field already, while this one of Women has comparatively few."[12]

Scholars have routinely suggested that Seba disapproved of his wife's ideas and work on the lecture circuit, but if that was the case, he did not say as much to her.[13] In fact, Seba encouraged her success as a public speaker, even as he missed her during the cold winter months. He also gave her advice for public speaking. In one letter, he offered "two slight criticisms" of a recent lecture she'd given. "The first was, a little too much of smile once or twice upon the features at some of the sarcastic sentences." Second, he said, "was what appears to me rather too much gesticulation" when she spoke. "Good oratory in a *man* will not allow a gesture to have the appearance of being made to enforce the sentiment," he wrote. "A gesture, to be effective, must have the appearance of being the involuntary result of the sentiment." Seba conceded that there may be double standards in how men and women were perceived on the stage. He quickly added that he made "these remarks because I feel that you will be glad to have me do so" and from "a desire to promote the welfare of those whom God has made dear to me."[14]

But for all his emotional support, Seba did very little to actually support his family. Throughout the 1840s and 1850s he served short stints editing several newspapers and magazines, but he never attained much permanence or success. Periodically, from 1847 until 1856, he contributed Jack Downing stories to Washington's Whig newspaper, the *National Intelligencer,* and he published a number of other works. But beginning about 1847, he became obsessed with "some special problems in mathematics" that culminated in a book entitled *New Elements of Geometry* (1850). Seba worked tirelessly to promote the volume among college faculty in both the United States and England, but with little success.[15] Between their financial hardships of the past decade and Seba's obsession with geometry, the Smith–Oakes Smith marriage underwent some difficult strains. When Elizabeth's mother died in 1851, she wrote a heartbreaking letter to her sons describing their grandmother's death. But of Seba she simply wrote, "Tell your father I had thought to see him here before now. Is he well?"[16] Elizabeth must have been frustrated with her family's financial position, for in 1852 she wrote to Seba, "God knows I have had a hard toilsome life, and I have a right to expect better things."[17]

Although things were difficult at home, Elizabeth could be proud of how her sons were moving up in the world. Sidney had recently been appointed US commercial agent and then the US consul at Aux Cayes, Haiti. He now stood five and a half feet tall with brown hair, gray eyes, ruddy complexion, an oval face, a round chin, and a prominent forehead. In support of his son's appointment, Seba had informed the Whig secretary of state, Daniel Webster, "that I am sure Major Downing and the inhabitants of Downingville generally would regard the appointment as a special compliment to that primitive village." Seba also informed the secretary that these fictional characters "pray night and morning that God will preserve the life and health of Daniel Webster" so that he could be nominated for president in four years. In her own recommendation letter, Elizabeth Oakes Smith downplayed partisan politics and hoped Webster would consider her request regardless of the "Babel of masculine voices, all clamorous for office as Washington must necessarily present." Elizabeth and her sons' true political colors were revealed after Franklin Pierce assumed office in 1853. Now the family had to appeal to a Democratic administration for Sidney to retain his post. Appleton sent a letter to the State Department calling Sidney "a good Democrat" while his mother followed suit, writing that while Sidney "is too young to meddle much with politics but has cast his first vote as a good Democrat." She added, "he was appointed by the late administration without reference to party."[18]

Upon his return from Africa, Appleton took up work as a shipping and commission merchant with an office on Pearl Street in Manhattan. His younger brother, Alvin, worked for him as a clerk. One night in 1854, Alvin had a dream that a great storm arose and shipwrecked a boat he was on, but he was saved and taken aboard another vessel. He woke up the next morning exhausted and depressed. At breakfast Alvin told his family about the dream, and Seba, Elizabeth, Appleton, and Edward listened with rapt attention. A short while later, Appleton instructed Alvin to take the brig *Sophia* to Aux Cayes, Haiti, for a cargo of lumber. Before leaving, Alvin told one of his cousins, "Good-bye, Nellie; I am going to be wrecked." Her face turned pale, but she tried to cheer him before he departed. After several days at sea, the *Sophia* encountered the wreck of the *Royal Southwick* out of New Bedford, Massachusetts, floating in the ocean. Alvin went aboard the ship and found her completely abandoned and stripped of all valuables. A few days later an immense hurricane battered the *Sophia*. The eight men on board chopped down their mast to keep the ship from capsizing, and for three days and nights they pumped water out of the hull. With their provisions gone and the men nearly spent, they were finally picked up by a passing vessel. Curiously, the ship and its sailors seemed familiar to Alvin. After a meal he exclaimed to the commander, "Captain, I have been aboard you before in a dream." Alvin and the seven other sailors eventually made their way to Aux Cayes, only to find that Sidney had given up his post and left the consulate two weeks earlier. Upon finally returning to New York, Alvin recounted the entire story to Appleton, who replied, "You see, Alvin, how the old adage is verified, 'truth is stranger than fiction.'"[19]

Appleton continued to escort his mother to literary soirees in New York City, and at these gatherings he met several revolutionary figures from Europe and Latin America. Among these was General Domingo de Goicouria, a short, handsome Castilian nobleman who had "fine presaging eyes, and swarthy complexion," and who gesticulated noticeably when he spoke. Goicouria owned large estates in both Cuba and Spain, and because of his strong antislavery sentiments, he had once transported fifteen hundred Spanish peasants to Cuba to work on his plantations rather than use slave labor. But this move upset authorities in both Spain and Cuba and made them suspicious of him. Goicouria subsequently joined various movements to liberate Cuba from Spain, and even though he was antislavery, he was willing to work with proslavery white Southerners who wanted to annex Cuba. "The old Spanish blood is bad," he would say. "A free people must not be selfish in their freedom—God over-rules all."[20]

White Southerners, for their part, were anxious to conquer parts of Latin America because they wanted more territory in which to expand slavery. Since 1848 they had been looking to Cuba. The admission of California as a free state in 1850 only increased their sense of urgency. In 1854, three American diplomats—including future president James Buchanan—issued the Ostend Manifesto, which hyperbolically declared that the safety, security, and survival of the United States required the annexation of Cuba.

When Spain refused to sell, however, some Americans came to believe that they should seize the island nation on their own. Goicouria joined one of the most prominent groups, the Cuban *junta* in New York, which had secured former Mississippi governor John A. Quitman to lead the expedition. While the *junta*'s stated purpose was to liberate Cuba, Quitman's goal since at least mid-1853 was annexation.

Appleton had shown sympathy for the Cuban liberation movement since at least 1851, and at the literary soirees, he was captivated by Goicouria's stories. It is little wonder that when Goicouria asked him to fit out ships to assist the *junta*, he was eager to join in the adventure. In late 1854, he worked as agent for the *Massachusetts*, a boat owned by the "notorious slave-trader" George Marsden, whom Oaksmith had first met in Rio de Janeiro in 1852. Marsden allegedly wanted the *Massachusetts* fitted out for filibustering in Cuba, but she was captured off the coast of New Jersey in January 1855, before she got underway.[21] Oaksmith also procured two other ships, the *Amelia* and the *Magnolia*. He placed on board the *Magnolia* two hundred cases of rifles, two cases of pistols, two pieces of field artillery, and thousands of other items needed to equip an army, including clothes, shovels, fifes and drums, ammunition, cooking utensils, and canteens. The *Amelia* received a similar cargo.[22]

The ships departed New York on March 5, 1855, claiming to be loaded only with ballast and bound for Georgia, when in fact they were headed for St. Joseph Bay, Florida, where they would transfer their military cargoes over to Quitman's ships. Unbeknownst to Oaksmith, however, Quitman resigned his connection to the *junta* in April, and the captain general of Cuba learned of the expedition and was preparing to oppose it. An even more immediate concern was that the Pierce administration had set itself strongly against filibustering. So as Oaksmith's two vessels cruised around the coast of Florida laden with $150,000 worth of cargo, the US government had revenue cutters chasing them down.[23]

In early May, Oaksmith traveled to Philadelphia to testify in a slave trading case in the US circuit court. Although Oaksmith was not personally implicated in the case (he appeared as a witness for the prosecution), George Marsden was one of the men suspected of owning the ship involved, the *Grey Eagle*. A commission merchant who had sold things to Marsden testified, "We were paid by the account being charged to Mr. Oaksmith; we had an open account with Mr. Oaksmith at the time, and it was charged to his account." When the prosecutor asked by whose direction he had paid Oaksmith, the witness replied, "I do not recollect to a certainty, but I suppose it was understood between Mr. Marsden and

Mr. Oaksmith; I sold the goods to Mr. Marsden and the bill was paid by being charged to the open account of Mr. Oaksmith." Later in the trial, Oaksmith testified that when Marsden came to New York in the autumn of 1853, he was in a "somewhat embarrassed" position (meaning without money), "and I offered him the use of a desk in my office." Oaksmith then testified that he had made purchases for Marsden and that Marsden had reimbursed him. All of those transactions were recorded in Marsden's checkbook, which was in evidence. The trial ultimately led to an acquittal—not because the defendant, James G. Darnaud, was innocent, but because the prosecution was not able to prove that Darnaud was an American citizen and that the vessel was owned by Americans.[24]

A few weeks later, on May 26, Oaksmith left New York to try to communicate with his vessels before federal ships captured them. When he arrived in Macon, Georgia, on June 11, however, he found a letter informing him that the *Magnolia* had already been seized and sent to Mobile on June 1. Oaksmith dashed off a disingenuous letter to Secretary of State William L. Marcy, writing, "Believing that the administration entertains a wrong impression in regard to the ultimate destination of certain of my property, which has lately I am lead [*sic*] to believe in a measure attracted their attention, I here solemnly declare that it is my only intention to dispose of the same in an honorable and legal manner at the earliest possible moment, so that I may save myself from any further loss: and that I have no knowledge, acquaintance, or connection with General Quitman or Colonel [Henry L.] Kinney or any of such affairs as they are said to be connected with." Oaksmith stated further that he planned to sell part of the property to the Venezuelan government and "cannot be held responsible for any *false* reports to which may be circulated prejudicial to myself."

Oaksmith next sent a letter to the captain of the *Amelia* instructing him to cruise for thirty days within a certain area of the sea. "While cruizing you will be as near as possible to the above Lattitude and Longitude every Wednesday and Sunday at 2 P.M.," Oaksmith instructed the captain, hoping he would be able to locate the *Amelia* before she was captured by a revenue cutter. Oaksmith continued:

> Under no circumstances whatever will you ever acknowledge to any one where your cargo came from. Simply say that it belongs to me, that you are responsible to me and no one else—that you believe I have sold it to the Venezuelan Government and that you are waiting for my further orders.

I shall not be able to sell the cargo to the parties I expected to—So that you can say with a clear conscience, that you are engaged in a perfectly legal business. Don't let any one frighten you, and stick to the property at all hazards and protest against any interference.

Answer no questions, simply tell whoever troubles you, that you would advise them to let you alone. That I am a man well known, the owner of the vessel and cargo, and they can see me if they want any information.

Oaksmith traveled to Mobile on June 14 and began gathering information about the seizure. On June 23 he learned that federal authorities in Washington—wanting to squelch attempts by American civilians to freelance in foreign affairs—had ordered his ship to be prosecuted. He was livid and wrote angrily about the government. But he had to prepare for trial, so he retained a lawyer and studied case law. Upon reading reports in the newspapers, he wrote in his journal with dismay, "The papers of the day are full of all kinds of absurd reports concerning the 'Magnolia' which are quite amusing to me. Very few have any coloring of truth."

July 1 was a rainy day in Mobile, and Appleton stayed in his room at the Battle House Hotel writing "Maggie Bell," a long poem about a lost lover. Although he published it anonymously, "Maggie Bell" gained national attention almost immediately and within a year had been quoted in newspapers and periodicals throughout the United States and Europe. The *New Orleans Daily Crescent* observed, "We are sure no one old or young can read it without having the finer elements of his nature awakened or a tear brought to the eye in sympathy for Maggie's fate."[25]

On July 2, Oaksmith learned that the US fleet in the Gulf of Mexico was searching for the *Amelia*. He also made his first appearance in court, but the US attorney asked for a postponement, which was granted. "I wish 'the Government' was a man so that I might deal with him as he deserved," wrote Oaksmith in his journal, "but this multitudinous, chimerical unity, is hard to fight." On July 6, Oaksmith met with his brother Sidney and General Goicouria. They agreed that Appleton would own the property on the ships and that if he could sell it, he could keep what was owed him and turn the balance over to one of Goicouria's associates. The trial then commenced ten days later, on July 16. For two days the prosecutor focused on the Cuban liberation movement, General Quitman, "the secret manner in which these vessels left New York," and "their long sojourn in St. Josephs Bay." On July 17 and 18, Oaksmith presented his defense. His lawyer argued that he had not violated the federal Neutrality Act of 1818 because the law prohibited committing hostilities (i.e., arming vessels to fight); it said nothing about merchant vessels transporting arms to the people of another nation.

With the arguments closed, Appleton and Sidney departed Mobile on July 19 to search for the *Amelia*. After three weeks at sea, they finally located her on August 8. The two brothers went on board—Sidney with his luggage—and for several hours they carried stores and water onto the *Amelia*. Finally, at 8 p.m., Appleton bade his brother farewell. He returned to his boat and sailed for Mobile. In the gloom, Appleton heard Sidney's voice one last time carrying over the water: "Good bye App." Appleton responded "with a heartfelt earnestness and watched the Bark with peculiar emotion as the black night slowly enshrouded her and bore her from my sight."[26]

Upon returning to Mobile, Appleton learned that he had won the *Magnolia* case. The judge believed that the vessel had left New York "under very suspicious circumstances" and he was certain that the "large quantity of arms and munitions" aboard her was headed for Cuba. But, according to the judge, "the whole case rests on the single question, whether the Barque Magnolia has been armed and equiped [*sic*] to cruise and commit hostilities against the Island of Cuba." The judge concluded, "The evidence shows beyond dispute, that the Magnolia was an ordinary freight vessel, somewhat inferior, as such, and had been altogether employed for the transportation of merchandise." Appleton had expected this result. But, unfortunately for him, the government appealed the ruling.[27]

On August 14, Appleton left for New York City. Then in September he traveled to Portland, Maine, to recoup "in some little degree my mental health." In the city of his birth, he met a young Italian woman named Isotta Rebecchini, who was known for her "musical talent and culture." (By some accounts she was twenty, by others younger than eighteen.) In town she taught music and modern languages, and one local newspaper reported that she "has a powerful mezzo-soprano voice . . . and is pronounced by those who have heard her in private here as capable of rendering the highest order of Italian music with great excellence." Very beautiful and slender, Isotta stood five feet tall, had a high forehead, grey eyes, a large mouth, dark brown hair, dark complexion, and a flat chin. The two must have been immediately enamored with one another, for they married after only ten days' acquaintance. Unfortunately, there was no time for a honeymoon. Just three days after the wedding Appleton traveled to Washington to inquire about his ships.[28]

At the Willard Hotel on October 5, just a few blocks from the White House, Appleton penned a letter to Secretary of the Treasury James Guthrie, claiming that he was innocent of any wrongdoing and that the *Mag-*

nolia was losing value while she sat in the possession of the US marshal in Mobile. Guthrie replied the next day that this matter was not within his power, so Oaksmith headed back to Alabama to take care of his affairs.[29] Meanwhile, the *Amelia* had been under Sidney's command since August. Sidney steered her for Haiti, where he had been US consul just a few years earlier, and obtained permission from the emperor to keep her at Port-au-Prince without having to go through customs. Sidney and the Haitian government entered into a negotiation over the sale of the arms, but they could not come to an agreement. Then on October 15, Haitian soldiers boarded the vessel, seized it, and ran it aground. Sidney became convinced that the new US consul had persuaded the emperor to seize the ship and turn it over to the United States. The *Amelia* was sent to New York, where she was sold by the US marshal.[30]

It is hard to fathom that Seba Smith could have been unaware of his sons' involvement in the Cuban liberation movement. Regardless, he used his final Jack Downing letters to lampoon Americans who wanted to seize Cuba. "We must have Cuba or our whole country would go to rack and ruin," states the fictional hillbilly-turned-statesman. Downing decides to become a filibusterer himself and takes a vessel called the *Two Pollies* to Cuba. Unfortunately, he finds that the Pierce administration will not "help me take Cuba—not a single war-vessel, nor a steamer, nor a private filibuster, nor even so much as Bill Johnson on a pine-log with a fowlin'-piece." Despite these obstacles, the men aboard the *Two Pollies* never lose their enthusiasm and they sing a patriotic song to the tune of "Yankee Doodle." The song, with a pun for a title—"Captain Robb"—pilloried white American imperialists who believed they could forcefully claim any land they wanted. The third verse went:

> Aye, Cobb, but something whispers me—
>   A sort of inspiration—
> That I've a *right* to every farm
>   Not under cultivation.
> I'm of the "Anglo-Saxon race,"
>   A people known to fame, sir;
> But you, what right have you to land?
>   Who ever heard your name, sir?

According to Seba's satirical verses, the land of Cuba belonged to Captain Robb "Simply because—*I will it.* . . . I've plenty more of arguments / To which I can resort, sir— / Six-shooters, rifles, bowie-knives, / Will indicate the sort, sir."

While Seba criticized the violence and sheer arrogance of the filibusterers, he also took aim at the government for seizing and condemning private vessels caught up in the schemes. This was being done, he said, "all along the coast, and making them suffer the delay and expense of lawsuits to prove that they had no notion of going to Cuba." But Downing vowed to resist any attempts to seize the *Two Pollies*.[31]

In the closing lines of his final Downing letter, dated January 21, 1856, Seba noted that "we've got a quarrel brewin', too, with Colonel Walker, out there in Nicaragua."[32] He chose not to continue the Downing series, however—perhaps because of Appleton's very public involvement in this notorious affair.

William Walker was one of the most peculiar figures in nineteenth-century America. One acquaintance described him as "a little, white-haired, white-eyebrowed, boyish-looking man, with cold, icy-gray eyes, a quiet, passionless manner, which renders him exceedingly mysterious and enigmatical, even to his most intimate friends." A graduate of the University of Pennsylvania medical school, Walker had spent time in San Francisco in 1850 and 1851, but it is unclear whether he and Oaksmith met there. (In the 1950s one of Oaksmith's daughters claimed they had.) As early as 1853, Walker sought to use private military forces to establish American colonies in Mexico. When this venture failed, he set his sights on Nicaragua, a Central American nation bitterly divided by civil war. In 1855, Walker sailed for Nicaragua and the following year established himself as president. The US government officially recognized his regime.[33]

Having failed to liberate Cuba, General Goicouria began working with Walker in Nicaragua (Walker promised to help liberate Cuba once he had settled matters in Nicaragua). Goicouria approached Oaksmith in March 1856 to assist in the venture. In May, Oaksmith helped organize two mass meetings and parades in New York City where fifteen thousand onlookers excitedly cheered the Walker cause as one hundred cannons boomed in their ears. In June he traveled to Granada for Walker's inauguration as president. One New York newspaper reported that Oaksmith and several other gentlemen stood on the roof of the hurricane deck as their vessel departed New York harbor. They "waved their handkerchiefs and smoked their segars in a perfect halo of present satisfaction and prospective glory." Walker placed significant responsibilities upon Oaksmith, making him Minister Plenipotentiary to the United States and an agent of the Nicaraguan government. Among his duties were recruiting men for Walker's army as well as raising arms, munitions, and supplies.

In August, Oaksmith traveled to Washington, DC, where he met with John Quitman, who was now a member of the House of Representatives from Mississippi. Quitman arranged a meeting with President Franklin Pierce to discuss Oaksmith's credentials as the Nicaraguan minister to the United States. The three men met on August 3, but Pierce refused to make a decision. For about a month Oaksmith's credentials were in a state of uncertainty, until mid-September when the Pierce administration decided against recognition, a decision that had much to do with larger diplomatic affairs involving England and other Central American nations. From August until November, Oaksmith worked diligently to raise recruits and supplies for Walker's cause, but financial constraints and lack of organization hampered his efforts. When he finally defected from Walker at the end of the year, he was in a tenuous financial situation.[34]

Walker's efforts to seize and govern Nicaragua proved a disaster. The nation was caught in a civil war, and he found his government under attack from neighboring Central American nations. Walker believed that he needed to attempt a desperate measure in order to try to save his administration—something that might appeal to new recruits and gain him new political backers. In September 1856, he issued a proclamation reinstating slavery in Nicaragua. (This action went against the antislavery sentiments he had held for most of his life.) "It was a calculated gamble to arouse a new enthusiasm in the southern United States to compensate for his decline in influence elsewhere," writes one historian. "To the extent that the filibuster now became the darling of southern slave expansionists, it worked." Indeed, white Southerners became enthusiastic for Walker's cause, but the proclamation did little to salvage Walker's regime. Fifteen years later Oaksmith disavowed having supported Walker for proslavery reasons, claiming instead that "the proof exists that I resigned my connection with the Nicaraguan movement because Walker . . . issued what was called the Slavery Proclamation reopening that traffic to Nicaragua." He further added that "it was at my instance and on that ground that General Quitman abandoned it at the same time." It is unclear what proof he meant. It is possible—even likely—that Oaksmith had not joined Walker for proslavery reasons since he'd joined the cause well before Walker's proslavery proclamation. However, Oaksmith's explanation of Quitman's resignation makes little sense since Quitman supported Walker until the end of his life.[35]

Back in Brooklyn, Elizabeth Oakes Smith was heartbroken when Sidney lost "a beautiful child" in September 1856. To help dull the pain, she and Seba toiled "indefatigably" at their work editing the *United States*

Magazine.[36] Appleton and Isotta had three children before the Civil War. Buchanan, born in 1857 and named after the current Democratic president, died in infancy. A grief-stricken Appleton turned to poetry, writing verses titled "My Little Boy and I" and "Gone."[37] Next came two girls, Bessie in 1858 and Corinne in 1860.

Despite the joys that came with fatherhood, Appleton's hasty marriage to Isotta would become one of his greatest regrets. Elizabeth noted how miserable her son was with his new wife. "Alas! my Poet, my beautiful boy is sadly unhappy with Isotta, who has little or nothing [in] common with him—jealous, violent and weak in intellect she is unfit for the position she holds." In fact, Oakes Smith grew to loathe her daughter-in-law. She complained in her diary of the "discordant life of Isotta, who has a wonderful faculty of extracting the bitter even from the sweets." Even the family dogs refused to show affection for her. Despite her strong views regarding the sanctity of marriage and her public opposition to divorce, Elizabeth wished that her son would seek one.[38]

In 1859, Appleton and his parents began publishing a new monthly magazine called *The Great Republic.* They promised that it would be "superior in every respect to anything ever issued before in this country" and then added, "IT WILL BE THOROUGHLY NATIONAL—IN NO WISE SECTIONAL OR SECTARIAN, AND WHOLLY IMPERSONAL." The prospectus claimed that distinguished writers, including Orestes A. Brownson, George D. Prentice, Anna C. (Lynch) Botta, and Matthew Fontaine Maury, would be contributors. One advertisement promoted a future article by Calhoun McKenzie titled "The Slaver of the Coast; or, the African Trader." Although the article never appeared, McKenzie was almost certainly a pseudonym for Appleton (he had previously written under other pennames, such as Derrick de Roos). Unfortunately, within one year the magazine folded and Appleton went into bankruptcy. Elizabeth's half-brother, Benjamin F. Sawyer, served as his attorney.[39]

Times were hard. In 1859, Appleton was found guilty in a city court of assault and battery upon one of his creditors, who, according to a news report, "had the impudence to address him with some asperity upon the subject of his neglect to settle a small bill." At issue was an eight-dollar engraving Appleton had ordered for *The Great Republic.* The judge presiding over the case, however, believed that the victim had "acted wrong in the first place" and let Appleton go. (Appleton had previously had the victim arrested for libel.)[40] Some of the family's friends believed that Elizabeth wished to relocate to Virginia, but instead she and Seba moved to a home they called "The Willows" in the small fishing village of Patchogue, on Long Island. Appleton and Sidney's families also moved into the home. Having so many children, parents, and grandparents in one place inevitably led to quarrels, but the problems seemed to be exacerbated by the tensions between Elizabeth and Isotta. Elizabeth claimed that once when Isotta was in a terrible "rage" she caused her oldest daughter,

Bessie Oaksmith.
Courtesy of the David M. Rubenstein Rare Book and Manuscript Library, Duke University.

Bessie, to faint. "I had offered to take care of the darling but she refused. Seeing the child had stopped crying, I ran out of the room and begged Appleton to come—he took Bessie and laid her on the bed to all appearance dead. It was a long time before she revived, and he then laid her in my arms and gave her to me. God only can know how dearly I love that child, who has been to me as my own."[41]

Now bankrupt, Appleton did anything he could to make ends meet, even working at a cotton factory in New York and investing in a paper factory in Virginia.[42] One friend noted that he "is full of projects, & I am sure I hope he may realize all his expectations." Calling him by the title of his most famous poem, she concluded, "Maggie Bell grows stout, & would seem to be losing somewhat of grace & comeliness." His health, too, appeared to be failing. About this time, he was "prostrated by a serious attack of '*brain fever*' brought on by great domestic affliction" and as a consequence "was compelled to entirely change his occupation and pursuits, and relinquish every kind of mental effort or labor."[43]

5

SECESSION

Sometime about 1859, Elizabeth Oakes Smith had a terrible vision. Although the nation was at peace, she saw "the immense camps of a vast soldiery—slaughter and demolition—sights to harrow up the soul—and then predicted—'there will be war—very soon war will come upon us—a terrible strife, which will last twenty years—twenty years.'" Oakes Smith thought often of that vision, praying, "God avert such a protracted calamity."

About this same time, Oakes Smith had another vision of a clear, calm, beautiful ocean with bright lights that were "flashing with rays." She saw a ship with its sails unfurled and "men thronging the deck trying by a thousand nautical maneuvers to catch every breath of air," but there was no wind to move the vessel. In the distance she saw an immense iceberg "rolling—surging down in the wake of the ship . . . towering in light—with turrets and battlements like a vast moving citidel steadily advancing upon the fated denizen of the deep." Closer and closer the iceberg came as Elizabeth watched "breathless with horror." She saw the terrified faces of the sailors and "felt the agony of their poor hearts." "I thrilled with their dread, and felt the certainty of doom in my own blood," she wrote. "On, on came the iceburg—it now cast a great black shadow over the ship—the sea began to boil—I heard the rushing wave." But suddenly "the wind roared and surged." The canvas of the sails filled with air and the ship leapt forward. Her heart "beat with hope" as the iceberg suddenly toppled over and sank into the sea. The sound was like thunder and the waves roared. The danger was gone, and "there was nothing left but the great sea." Without realizing what she was doing she cried aloud, "God have mercy upon the dear souls."

The vision of the ocean passed away quickly, and Elizabeth was relieved to find that it did not affect her health. But years later—in the middle of the Civil War—she still thought about what she'd seen, wondering, "Did this . . . vision portend the wreck of the Constitution—was it a portent of the wreck that came upon my family?"[1] Indeed, in the 1860s and 1870s her family would be struck by terrible calamities at sea as if by a giant force of nature.

Oakes Smith's vision also reflected something about the United States at the end of the 1850s. The nation was engulfed in political crises, with slavery ripping at the fabric of society. White Southerners claimed that slave owners should be able to take their "property" anywhere they pleased—including into the western territories—while Republicans countered that Congress could prohibit slavery from spreading into the federal territories. The Southern viewpoint won a significant victory in 1857 when the US Supreme Court held in *Dred Scott v. Sandford* that the right to own slaves was a fundamental right protected by the Constitution and that Congress could not prohibit slavery in the territories. Dark clouds, indeed, were on the national horizon. In 1858, Senator William Henry Seward of New York declared, "It is an irrepressible conflict between opposing and enduring forces, and it means that the United States must and will, sooner or later, become either entirely a slave-holding nation, or entirely a free-labor nation."[2]

The political crisis of the 1850s came to a head on Tuesday, November 6, 1860. Voters throughout the nation—except in South Carolina, which did not yet have a popular election for president—went to the polls and cast their ballots in one of the most consequential elections in American history. The vote was split between four major candidates, and although he captured less than 40 percent of the popular vote, Abraham Lincoln won almost 60 percent of the Electoral College. Almost immediately, Southern "Fire-Eaters" began calling for secession. South Carolinians acted first, formally withdrawing from the Union on December 20. Mississippi followed a few weeks later, on January 9, 1861, then Florida on the tenth and Alabama on the eleventh.

By now, most Northerners were alarmed by the course of events. For a variety of differing reasons, some Northerners thought that the South should be allowed to go in peace. Abolitionists like William Lloyd Garrison believed the Union would be better off without the immoral blight of slavery. Others, like Horace Greeley, thought that Southerners would eventually see the folly of their action and return to the Union within a matter of months or years. Finally, pro-slavery Northerners believed that the South was justified in seceding. The Northern states, in their view, had not fulfilled their obligations to the people of the South and therefore should consent to Southern secession.

Some Northerners and Upper South statesmen sought to broker a compromise that might stave off war. Senator John J. Crittenden of Kentucky introduced a series of constitutional amendments and congressional resolutions that would offer extra protections for slavery, but Congress rejected Crittenden's proposal. National leaders also met in Washington, DC, while earnest "Union-saving meetings" convened throughout the North.[3]

By the time of the Secession Winter of 1860–1861, Appleton Oaksmith was "an active member" of Tammany Hall, New York City's powerful Democratic political machine. Oaksmith had probably risen to this position of prominence because of his public speeches and administrative roles during William Walker's crusade in Nicaragua. The leadership of Tammany Hall consisted primarily of white Protestants, but its main constituency was Irish Catholic immigrants who came to America in the 1840s and 1850s to escape the potato famine in their homeland. Although the political machine was sympathetic toward white Southerners and slavery, it was ardently pro-Union.[4] As a leader of Tammany's "Union League," Oaksmith therefore hoped to help broker a peaceful resolution of the sectional conflict. On January 4, he sent a "Confidential" letter to Senator Seward, a leading Republican who would soon become Lincoln's secretary of state. Oaksmith invited Seward to address "a meeting of the Citizens of New York . . . upon the issues of the moment." He hoped that in his lecture Seward would state *"how far* . . . you will be prepared to advocate" four resolutions. The first and fourth were certainly things that Seward could endorse:

> 1st. The Constitution is a perpetual Charter, granted to their posterity, by *the People* of the *Nation* brought into existence by the Confederation. Consequently no right exists for any State or portion of our people to pretend to a separate Nationality within our borders. . . .
> 4th. That "this Union *must* and *shall be preserved.*"

But the middle two resolutions were anathema to Republicans. Oaksmith asked Seward if he agreed that a "strict construction of the *spirit* of the Constitution would, and does entitle Slavery to protection in the Territories *as property*, upon the same basis that other property is admitted and protected there." This view—which had been articulated by Chief Justice Taney in the *Dred Scott* case—was one of the ideas Republicans most staunchly opposed. (Republicans like Lincoln pointed out that the Constitution referred to slaves as "persons" not "property.") Oaksmith also asked Seward whether he could adhere to the creation of a "geographic line through the Territories to the Pacific, south of which Slavery will be protected," and to the "right of protection to Slaves in all the Territories, *as property*; *without* representation." Finally, Oaksmith inquired whether Seward would "make every honorable concession to the South, to protect their interests, and to grant a general amnesty for the past."[5]

Oaksmith had drawn these resolutions from the series of compromises put forth by Senator Crittenden. But these views ran counter to the Republican platform, which held that Congress constitutionally could—and should—ban slavery from the territories. Lincoln, as president-elect, had stated that he would accept "no compromise on the question of *extending* slavery." And Massachusetts attorney Richard Henry Dana Jr. spoke for many Northerners when he declared that the North would not "buy the right to carry on the government, by any concession to slavery."[6]

Knowing that Seward had come out publicly in favor of some sort of sectional amelioration, Oaksmith wrongly believed that Seward was closer to his views than to Lincoln's. His concluding language, therefore, must have seemed patronizing to Seward—if the senator ever actually read it:

> A large portion of your fellow citizens, including thousands who have differed with you politically, believe that you occupy a position which, if you can square your convictions to the basis of the foregoing propositions, will enable you to do *substantial service* to your Country.
>
> If, my dear Sir, you can bring yourself fully to the endorsement of the above views *an opportunity will be given to you*, of writing a page in the history of the World, which may never occur again. A true Patriot will sacrifice "all save his honor" for his country, and I *truly believe* there is nothing in your record which need or should deter you from adopting these views.

Oaksmith closed by admonishing Seward, "A man belongs more to his *country* than to his party," and, "The party lines of 1860 are swept to the winds!"[7]

In some ways Oaksmith was prophetic. Republicans would seize the banner of antiparty "Unionism" throughout the Civil War, seeking to bring pro-war Democrats into their fold on election days. (In fact, in 1864 the Republican Party jettisoned their name and ran as the Union Party.) But conservative, pro-slavery Democrats like Oaksmith would tend to be left out of this new political coalition. By the second year of the war, Republicans were roundly castigating Democrats of Oaksmith's stripe as disloyal "Copperheads."

Although Oaksmith asked for "an *immediate* reply" (he underlined the word "immediate" twice), he never received one. A week later Oaksmith again wrote to Seward asking whether he had received the first letter. "From the position which you occupy it would seem that more good would be likely to result if we could offer the 'olive branch' through your hand—We who have mainly been opposed to you in Politics can give you an opportunity of doing a service to your Country which your own Party cannot. I speak in the *past* not the present, for we know *no party* in this 'League.'"[8]

Seward was not likely to respond to letters like these. He would have certainly sympathized with Oaksmith's desire to compromise—in December 1860, Seward had advised young New York Republicans "to show

William H. Seward.
Courtesy of the Library of Congress.

the greater virtue of moderation in triumph" to avoid civil war. But he had more important things to do than to address Tammany Democrats. In December, he had gone to Washington to try to broker a sectional compromise. And at the time that Oaksmith wrote his letters, Seward was busy preparing a major address to be delivered in the US Senate. In that speech, Seward offered a series of compromises to the South but also unequivocally declared that he would adhere "to the Union in its integrity and with all its parts . . . in any event, whether of peace or war, with every consequence of honor or dishonor, of life or death."[9]

While Oaksmith waited in vain for a reply from Seward, he and his Tammany Hall associates went to work to save the Union. On January 14, 1861, they sent out invitations for a "private meeting of the conservative men of New York" to be held at 7:30 p.m. the following night at the Union League's committee rooms at Musical Hall, 765 Broadway. Invitees were "earnestly" requested to attend "to discuss certain proposed measures to arrest the threatened calamity of civil war." They were required to bring their invitations to gain admittance. When the meeting convened, Oaksmith stated that his object was to organize a mass meeting so that the citizens of New York could emphatically express their feelings "irrespective of party interest or feeling, and by such expression to sustain the [Buchanan] Administration in maintaining the Constitution by enforcing its law." Oaksmith then read letters from Democratic congressman John Cochrane of New York and Senator John J. Crittenden of Kentucky, which stated that if New Yorkers would unanimously proclaim themselves for the Union that it "would go very far toward removing the obstacles now in the way of tranquilizing the country." Oaksmith asked the other members present to state their candid opinions of the crisis, urging that the organizers of the meeting had taken all possible means to protect the confidentiality of the gathering and to keep it from being reported in the press.

Several people stated that the time had come "when party distinctions should be merged in the general good, and even obliterated, to perpetuate the integrity of the Union." Moreover, they were for "the Constitution inviolate, under which we had so long lived happily." Some worried about the Democrats "in our very midst" who were "inclined to sedition" and "were using every effort to stimulate rebellion, and to give aid and comfort to those engaged in this course." At the end of the discussion, Oaksmith offered a resolution calling for a mass meeting "to express their sentiments in favor of *union* or *disunion*," but the gathering rejected Oaksmith's resolution because they believed it would tend "to aggravate instead of subduing impending evils." A committee was then appointed to draft resolutions to preserve the Union and sustain the laws while also holding out "the olive branch of peace."[10] The next day, January 16, Oaksmith sent out a second invitation to a smaller number of people to attend a private meeting on January 19 "to take the preliminary steps for a strong expression of public opinion by the PEOPLE of the city of New York in favor of this Union and the enforcement of the laws." Again, the meeting was to be "a private one" and invitees were required to present their invitations to gain admittance.[11]

When the meeting convened at Musical Hall on Saturday, January 19, Oaksmith made a brief speech stating that he "did not want coercion, but wanted the laws maintained." An ex–prize fighter and former Democratic alderman named William "Billy" Wilson spoke up, asking why he had received the invitation, who had called the meeting, and why there were not more prominent persons present. Oaksmith "blandly" asked, "How would it be if I had a letter from the President?" "Oh, that would do very well," replied Wilson. "If you have one I would like to see it." Wilson had called Oaksmith's bluff. "I have a letter, gentlemen, from a very influential man, a member of Congress," continued Oaksmith. He then held up a "scrap of paper" which he claimed was a letter from John Cochrane—presumably the one he'd read to the other meeting a few nights earlier. "That is very well as far as it goes, but let me see the letter from the President," retorted Wilson. Of course, Oaksmith could not produce such a letter.

Oaksmith offered a "long series of resolutions" calling on President Buchanan to enforce the laws, declaring secession unlawful, and urging Congress to devise some sort of compromise that could avert civil war. Wilson responded with a long speech of his own in favor of maintaining the Union. He also criticized Southerners for hating Northerners. Two men sitting toward the front of the room remarked with upturned noses, "He talks like Beecher." Oaksmith's resolutions were voted down. Wilson then offered a "short resolution" that stated that the people of New York supported the Constitution and the Union, that they opposed secession, and that Buchanan ought to enforce the laws. This resolution was adopted.

Several men began making speeches and the meeting quickly degenerated into a discussion of where "yaller people" came from. "They were nigger and white blood mixed," said one man, "and . . . Congress ought to pass a law to stop it." Finally the meeting was called back to order and Oaksmith produced "a voluminous document" to establish a Union League on the basis of a pro-slavery platform. Oaksmith asked all men present to sign the document, but only a few did. A committee of nine was then appointed "to take the whole matter in hand" and the meeting then adjourned. The committee of nine met on Monday, January 21, and this time Oaksmith defeated Wilson when they argued over whose resolutions to adopt. A subcommittee was appointed to raise money for future activities. If they succeeded then they would call a mass Union meeting, but if they did not then the whole matter would be dropped.[12]

On January 22, the subcommittee met to plan a mass meeting to be held at the Cooper Institute in New York City on the evening of January 28; however, they could not secure high-profile speakers for the event. One person declined "to be a party to any movement to recommend the adoption of the Crittenden Resolutions" because "the present laws, under the Constitution as it is, are quite sufficient to meet the present emergency." In this person's view, the only way to show true devotion to the Union was to vigorously enforce the law and refuse to compromise with Southern traitors.[13] Nevertheless, a large and enthusiastic crowd met at the Cooper Institute on the night of January 28. The *New York Times* reported that it was "one of the largest meetings ever assembled in that oft-crowded edifice, while outside of the building a separate meeting was also organized, bonfires burned, and guns fired, and all in honor of the Union." As the audience waited for the evening program to begin, a brass band played "deafening" patriotic music from the stage. (The *Times* added in parentheses that the band "persisted in playing throughout the evening at most inopportune moments.") The first speaker called on "every man to lay aside partisan feelings and rally round the standard of his country. . . . the Union as it was, as it is, as it shall be." But the next speaker criticized Republican Party policies, stating that the Union could not be "maintained unless we recognise Slavery as it existed at the time of the formation of the Government, and maintain and preserve it."

One of the meeting's organizers, James T. Brady, offered a long, rambling series of resolutions that purported to declare the voice of the people of New York. The resolutions opposed secession but simultane-ously defended slavery and offered concessions to the South. Brady ac-cepted the Southern viewpoint that slave owners should be allowed to take their "property" into "all the Territories" and that slavery should be fully protected in the states where it already existed, but he also declared that Southerners ought to seek redress for their grievances through the normal legal and political channels provided in the Constitution. One resolution bizarrely urged abolitionists to focus their attention on developing techno-logical innovations that "may in the course of time be fitted to perform the functions now exacted from slave labor alone." Finally, after offering "every honorable concession" to the South, the resolutions stated that Lincoln ought to be sustained as president, "laying aside all party differences," so long as he abided by his constitutional obligations.

Most of Brady's resolutions were well received by the audience, except for the one that declared support for Lincoln. This one was met by a mix of hisses and cheers. And when some people tried to hiss at the closing part of the resolutions—which called for patient negotiation and conciliation of the South—the band played "The Star-Spangled Banner," which brought the crowd to their feet in enthusiastic cheers.

After a few more speeches—some of which were highly conciliatory toward the South—Oaksmith offered a resolution that three commissioners from the city be appointed to visit the Southern secession conventions "and confer with the delegates of the people in regard to the peace and integrity of this Union, and report the result of their visit to the people of this City at the earliest practicable moment." The resolution was adopted "with great applause" and Oaksmith was among the men selected. The meeting then closed with a "highly partisan" speech that was "greeted with mingled applause and hisses," while the band played "The Star-Spangled Banner."[14]

From Oaksmith's perspective, the event had been a triumph. The following day, he sent a telegram to Robert N. Gourdin, a wealthy, pro-secession Charleston merchant who was heading a correspondence effort with other Southern leaders, to ask whether the New York commissioners— "all friends of the South"—would be "fairly received" if they traveled to South Carolina to discuss the sectional crisis. Gourdin replied that his state's convention and legislature were not in session, but that the governor had seen Oaksmith's letter and that he would "cordially and kindly" receive the commissioners if they came.[15]

Oaksmith sent letters to other Southern state officials as well. According to the *Brooklyn Evening Star*, he and the other commissioners hoped to "undeceive the people [of the South] as to the designs of the North."[16] But as might be expected, nothing significant came of this correspondence. Southern states continued to leave the Union. Georgia departed on January 19, then Louisiana on January 26, and Texas on February 1. By the time Lincoln took the oath of office on March 4, 1861, seven Deep South states had all left the Union and the nation was careening toward civil war.

In the midst of this crisis, Oaksmith penned a patriotic poem titled "The Union Marseillaise." He called on the "sons of the Union [to] wake to duty" for "the Union must be saved." If "Liberty herself lie[s] bleeding" by assaults from "erring brothers," then

God keep us firm and brave—
The Union must be saved—
March on, March on, all hearts resolved
On Union, Peace, or Death.

In many ways, Oaksmith's poem was a call for Northern restraint. "Though madness, erring brothers leading, / May seek to desolate the land, / We will not raise a single hand / Till Liberty herself lies bleeding." But if the nation should be brought to ruins,

We then will for this Union rise:
And like the mountain torrent rolling,
As irresistible, our band—
Will sweep for-ever from our land
The curse its greatness now controlling.[17]

On April 12, any further discussion of compromise was rendered moot. Before dawn, Confederates in Charleston opened fire on Union-held Fort Sumter. After the fort surrendered thirty-four hours later, Lincoln called for seventy-five thousand volunteers to defend the national capital. This action caused the Upper South to secede—Virginia on April 17, Arkansas on May 6, North Carolina on May 20, and Tennessee on June 8. Now the battle lines were drawn.

Lincoln quickly began to take drastic actions to protect the national capital and subdue the rebellion. One of his first steps was to suspend the privilege of the writ of habeas corpus along the "military line" between New York City and Washington, DC. This controversial decision enabled military officers to arrest civilians suspected of disloyalty and to detain them without charges if "public safety" required it.[18] Many abolitionists also wanted the president to strike an immediate blow against slavery. But while Lincoln believed that slavery was morally wrong, he did not think that he could attack it in the seceded states because he believed the Constitution still protected slavery there (Lincoln refused to acknowledge the Confederate states as out of the Union). Nevertheless, Lincoln could attack slavery on the periphery. He fully committed his administration to destroying the illegal transatlantic slave trade, much of which now centered on Cuba. "We are a powerful nation," Seward had declared shortly before becoming secretary of state, "and it is simply a point of duty to apply our power to bring this evil to an end."[19]

II

WAR

I look upon myself sometimes with a sort of doubt *as to my own identity*—when I reflect upon this case and all I have seen in the papers. Am I *myself?* But when I remember the days of *Salem witchcraft*, and the spirit that actuated her people then— as well as the *loyalty* they showed in the *Hartford Convention* days—I say "*anything* is possible in Massachusetts."

—Appleton Oaksmith, September 8, 1871

6

THE *AUGUSTA*

Abraham Lincoln was elected to the presidency on a platform that called the African slave trade "a crime against humanity and a burning shame to our country and age." The Republican platform further called for "the total and final suppression of that execrable traffic."[1] Very early in his presidency, on May 2, 1861, Lincoln placed the Department of the Interior in charge of suppressing the illegal transatlantic slave trade. Much of this work would have to be accomplished in New England and New York—areas that had been hubs for slave trading. Indeed, one pro-slavery but anti–slave trade Virginian complained that slave traders "are all from North of Balt[imore]" and that one slaver "was owned by a Quaker of Delaware who would not even eat slave sugar," while another ship was chartered by a trader who "is also the owner of an abolitionist newspaper in Bangor, Maine." This Virginian continued, "The very lands in the Old and in the New World . . . where abolition petitions flow, are the lands where . . . there are owners of vessels to be 'chartered and sold deliverable on the coast of Africa.'"[2]

On August 15, Secretary of the Interior Caleb B. Smith assembled the US marshals from along the Eastern Seaboard for a "convention" to discuss measures for catching and successfully prosecuting slave traders. They met at the Manhattan office of the marshal of the Southern District of New York, Robert Murray. George C. Whiting, the Interior Department official responsible for overseeing federal anti–slave trade activities, also attended. Murray explained to his colleagues the surreptitious means that slavers used to evade detection. Among the suspicious features of a "slaver incognito," Murray told them to look out for large numbers of water casks, great quantities of rice and white beans, lumber for building a slave deck, jerked beef, rum, a "very heavy list of fine ship stores for cabin use," and a medicine chest that was much larger than would typically be needed for a ship of its size. Whiting pledged to the marshals "the heartiest co-operation" of the Interior Department "and assistance in all laudable efforts to suppress the slave trade." After this discussion, Murray took his colleagues to the docks in Brooklyn and showed them several vessels that had been seized for involvement in the traffic. The marshals boarded and inspected each ship, examining the cargo holds, the slave decks, and the storehouses. They then returned to Murray's office where they unanimously agreed that they would need to hire "discreet secret agents" if they were to effectively operate against slave traders. Secretary of the Interior Caleb Smith had already permitted Murray to use secret agents in New York. From this point forward the other marshals would utilize them as well.[3]

Robert Murray would develop a reputation for having "set his face against" the slave trade and for bringing "confusion and shame and terror into the ranks of those engaged in it."[4] He assembled a team of secret agents to watch the docks by day and by night for suspicious activities, even sending them to track slave traders all over the world. On one occasion, Murray himself stayed out from 11 p.m. to 3 a.m. watching the dockworkers. On other occasions he traveled to ports in other states, including the old whaling town of New Bedford, Massachusetts.[5] Back at his New York City office, Murray ruminated on the ways that slave traders were able to skirt the law. In January 1862, he drafted a bill "for the more effectual suppression of the African Slave Trade," which he presented to several members of Lincoln's cabinet.[6]

Murray was proud of his accomplishments, and though he never felt that he got the credit he deserved, he made sure his superiors knew what he had done. "Since entering upon the duties of this office, I have made an earnest effort, at least, to check the Slave Trade from this Port," he wrote to Interior Secretary Caleb Smith in June 1861. "The seizures and arrests thus made have had the effect of stopping, at least temporarily the fitting out of slavers in this Port." In January 1862, Murray further described how he had "pursued those iniquitous dealers in human flesh night and day, with all the vigor and determination I possessed; not only in this District but through all the ports of the United States and in foreign countries where they have been accustomed to fit out their vessels with impunity." So successful were his efforts—and so above reproach was he—that the slave traders of New York "held a meeting, and, unanimously decided to abandon the idea of influencing me, as they had exhausted every conceivable mode to do so—either through persuasion of political friends, or through bribery—without avail."[7]

For his part, Caleb Smith praised Murray for "the very commendable zeal which [he] has manifested in his efforts to break up the horrible slave traffic which has heretofore disgraced our government." Indeed, Smith was proud of the work his department was doing, writing to an American agent in Liberia that "the most vigorous measures are being put into execution for the suppression of this odious trade, and to bring those who may be found in it to condign punishment." George Whiting agreed, telling US Marshal John S. Keyes in Boston that the Lincoln administration was "giving the slave trade some good knocks." Of course, Murray's targets had other impressions. One political prisoner would later call him "a common and vulgar-looking man, exhibiting the shy subserviency which became the office he had to discharge."[8]

Throughout the Civil War, Murray worked closely with E. Delafield Smith, the US attorney in the Southern District of New York. A prominent mercantile lawyer in the city before the war, Delafield Smith would go on to secure several convictions of slave traders as well as the condemnation of five ships suspected of being slavers. Smith was appalled by

E. Delafield Smith.
Courtesy of the Library of Congress.

the wealthy families of New York who built mansions "with the gains of adventures which involve the transportation of human beings from their homes in Africa to the strange coast of Cuba, in stifling pens, beneath tropic suns, with the actual calculation, founded upon terrible experience, that if two thirds die and one third land, the venture is a fair success!" He wondered, "Ought it not to have been plain to his intelligence, that the carved columns, the expanded arches, the dizzy domes of a palace so erected, would, in a future guilty imagination, rest, for their caryatides, upon the shoulders of slave men, the breasts of slave women, and the bodies of slave children? Oh God! How many costly stone structures raise their ornamented fronts impudently to heaven, while their foundations are laid—literally laid—in hell."[9]

Delafield Smith and Robert Murray showed more respect to African Americans than most whites of the era ever would. In July 1861, Murray played host to a young black man who had mutinied on a captured ship and killed several Confederate sailors who had tried to enslave him. Murray asked the brave sailor, "Did they beg, any of them?" And Smith joked, "We will have to run you for President yet."[10] It was within this legal and political context that Appleton Oaksmith would come under the watchful eyes of Murray and Smith, the most active and ambitious federal officers engaged in destroying the slave trade.

Despite his minor prominence in New York's Democratic circles during the secession crisis, Appleton Oaksmith was still facing difficult life circumstances. The shuttering of *The Great Republic* in 1859 and his filing for bankruptcy in 1860 had made him desperate. Now living with his parents, his family, and his brother Sidney's family at "The Willows" in Patchogue, Oaksmith needed to find a way to regain his footing.[11] Somehow, he managed to connect with a wealthy Long Island businessman named Jacob Appley. At forty-six years old, Appley had amassed a sizeable fortune (reputed to be worth half a million dollars), including more than sixty houses in Manhattan, a flour store, a vessel, and a large fish oil factory on Long Island. Oaksmith "pleaded poverty & want of employment," stated one man who was familiar with their acquaintance, and "Mr. Appley being a man of wealth and of benevolent disposition advanced him money & started him in the ship chandling business at Greenport L.I." (A ship chandler deals in maritime supplies and equipment.) About this same time Appley became convinced that he needed whale oil to mix with the fish oil he was producing, so he hired Oaksmith to purchase and fit out a vessel for "a short whaling voyage on the North Atlantic Ocean."[12] This was a curious decision, as stockpiles of whale oil could be purchased at bargain prices in old whaling towns like New Bedford.

In May, Oaksmith began negotiating with Gilbert H. Cooper of Sag Harbor to purchase a 399-ton vessel called the *Augusta*. Cooper had owned the ship since 1857 and had sailed her in the Pacific Ocean from July 1857 until January 1861, hunting for whales. Several other people were interested in the vessel, but on May 30 Oaksmith and Cooper finally negotiated terms, agreeing on a price of $4,900 cash for the ship and many of the articles on board. Within ten days of the sale, Jacob Appley used his steamboat to tow the *Augusta* to Greenport. A few days later Oaksmith hired Captain Isaac M. Case to serve as master of the *Augusta*. Case was "an experienced whaling Capt. [and] a man in good standing" who'd entered the whaling business in 1832 and in that three-decade period had only been home three winters.[13]

Oaksmith contracted with Case to go on a fifteen-month whaling voyage—a much shorter time than the typical three-to-four years that whalers went to sea. Oaksmith's plan seemed suspicious because the whaling industry had become far less profitable since the discovery of petroleum in Titusville, Pennsylvania, in 1859. It is little wonder, then, that several of the men who owned an interest in the *Augusta* doubted Oaksmith's stated reason for purchasing the ship. One of them, George M. Clearman of the firm Sturges, Clearman and Co., told US Marshal Robert Murray that Oaksmith was probably purchasing the *Augusta* for a slaving expedition. Once the sale was complete, Murray immediately detailed two deputies, Luther Horton and John H. Smith, to watch what cargo was taken aboard the vessel. They reported to him daily.[14]

Murray gathered information over the next three weeks, and on June 19, US Attorney E. Delafield Smith obtained a libel from the federal court in New York City to seize the ship. The language of the libel was vague. It alleged that a "certain citizen or certain citizens of the United States or a certain foreigner or some other person coming into or residing within the same, whose names are as yet to the said attorney unknown did for himself or for themselves or some other person or persons . . . on the tenth day of June . . . fit, equip, load and otherwise prepare the aforesaid vessel being a Bark called 'Augusta' within a Port or Place of the said United States . . . for the purpose of carrying on a trade and traffic in slaves to some foreign country." Four days later, on June 23, Marshal Murray ordered Deputy Marshal Horton to seize the *Augusta* at Greenport, Long Island. When Horton reached the ship, Oaksmith greeted him and introduced him to Captain Case. Horton asked whether the vessel was fully loaded. Horton later recalled that Oaksmith replied that he "had everything on board except a few small cabin stores," but Oaksmith denied having said that. "I did not tell Horton that we were ready for sea except a few cabin stores,"

Oaksmith would later testify in court. "I might have stated that she was nearly ready for sea, except some whaling gear and some cabin stores." Either way, Horton then handed Oaksmith the libel, which authorized the seizure of the ship. Oaksmith read it and asked for a copy for his own records. He maintained that *"she was going on a legitimate voyage, was going Whaling."* Clearly agitated, Oaksmith said he "would not resist that authority." It appears that he did not yet know why his vessel was being seized.[15]

Horace Greeley's *New York Tribune* reported that "a species of black fish" had been "caught" in the waters nearby. Some reporters feared that the seizure might have been premature—that the ship had been seized before ample evidence of a slaving voyage had been placed upon her.[16] In court on July 2, Jacob Appley claimed that he was the "sole owner" of the *Augusta* and denied that she was to be used as a slaver.[17] But federal authorities were not convinced. On July 3, Murray informed Secretary of the Interior Caleb Smith about the *Augusta*. "Her ostensible voyage was a whaling one," wrote Murray, "but from the quantity of water casks on board, and other articles not connected with a whaling voyage, but especially adapted for a slaver, and from admissions made by parties in interest that she was going to the coast of Africa for a cargo of negroes, I have little hesitation in coming to the conclusion that such was her purpose and destination."[18]

The trial of the *Augusta* began in August. Presiding over the case was US district judge William D. Shipman. In previous slave trading cases in New York, the federal judges Samuel R. Betts and Samuel Nelson had interpreted the anti–slave trade laws so narrowly (and with such contorted logic) that the city had become, according to one historian, "a haven for the outfitting of slavers." But now, sitting in for Betts and Nelson was Shipman, the federal district judge from Connecticut. (It was not uncommon in the nineteenth century for a federal judge in Connecticut to help lighten the busy caseloads in New York.) As a US attorney in Connecticut in 1859, Shipman had prosecuted the whaler *Laurens* for preparing to engage in the slave trade. He lost the case, and the federal judge in that case issued so a strong denunciation of Shipman's arguments that Shipman began to doubt whether he had been right to bring the prosecution. "I am in great doubt whether to appeal this case," he later wrote. "The Judge's opinion is so decided, not to say fervid, in vindication of the ship, that it is calculated to inspire me with distrust of my own opinion, which may be biased."[19] That judge died in 1860, however, and President Buchanan placed Shipman in his seat. As a federal judge, Shipman would now be the final arbiter in these cases, and he would handle them much differently than his predecessor.

William D. Shipman.

Proceedings, December 9, 1929, Being on the Occasion of the Presentation to the United States District Court for the District of Connecticut of a Portrait of William Davis Shipman, a Judge of Said Court 1860 to 1873 (n.p., [1929]).

Shipman strove to be impartial and fair-minded on the bench. And although he was a Democrat who had been placed on the court by the pro-slavery James Buchanan, he used his position to go after Northern slave traders. One admirer observed that "he scrupulously avoided politics" as a judge and that "none of his judicial decisions were colored by partisanship." Shipman himself was proud of his deportment as a federal judge. After the war, he wrote, "No one will know what I went through during the war. . . . By some Democrats I was regarded in full sympathy with the [Lincoln] administration and its party henchmen. By some Republicans I was considered a secessionist and anxious for the success of the confederacy." One acquaintance later recalled Shipman as "a man's man" who enjoyed "good company, good wine and good stories." He dressed nicely, was average in height but "rather thick set." And although he could come off as "gruff," those who knew him personally knew he had "a most kindly nature." US Attorney Delafield Smith praised Shipman for his "unsparing thoroughness, justice and intelligence in the discharge of the duty."[20]

Marshal Murray wanted the trial postponed, but Benjamin F. Sawyer, Appleton's uncle and lawyer, pressed for it to begin quickly. US Attorney E. Delafield Smith was sick and confined to his bed when the trial began on August 13, so Assistant US Attorney Stewart L. Woodford argued the government's case. Woodford was a young lawyer and ardent Republican who had been part of the convention that nominated Lincoln for president in 1860. In April 1861 Lincoln had appointed Woodford assistant US attorney for the Southern District of New York, where he oversaw a bureau that prosecuted naval captures. One observer wrote that he "combines, with an agreeable appearance and pleasing address, the graces and polish of a gentleman. He is a cultivated scholar, and a close and logical lawyer. His eloquence is of the highest order, and his presence before an audience is strangely magnetic, as thousands can testify who have heard him from the political rostrum and in the court-room."[21]

Woodford called numerous expert witnesses to prove that the *Augusta* was not preparing for a whaling voyage. One witness testified, "The whaling business has stopped at Greenport. It is some 3 or 4 yrs since the business was abandoned there, or since any vessel has sailed from there for whaling. . . . The business ceased in Greenport because it was not . . . as profitable to fit out a vessel at Greenport as at New Bedford." But, this witness added (undercutting the prosecution's position), it could be "a little cheaper" to fit out the *Augusta* "where several vessels are fitted out [at the] same port. I shd not regard it as suspicious for a person to come to Greenport to fit out a whaler."[22] Most of the prosecution's witnesses testified

Stewart L. Woodford.
Courtesy of the Civil War Museum of Philadelphia and the Union League Legacy Foundation.

regarding the stores, equipment, and cargo aboard the ship. The purpose of this testimony was to prove that the *Augusta* was not fitting out for a long whaling voyage but instead for a short trip to Africa.

After the government rested its case, Oaksmith testified about why and how he had acquired the ship. He admitted, "I am somewhat familiar with whalers but not fully. I was agent for fitting out the Augusta. Mr. Appley said the Augusta was for sale cheap, and had a good many things and he thot she could be bot low enough and sent on a short voyage on a small capital, so as to make it profitable. I bot her." He insisted that the ship was only to go on a fifteen-month voyage, "not 3 or 4 yrs." And he defended the vessel's inventory, saying that the beef *"was in good condition"* when he placed it on board and that he acquired the provisions that Captain Case had requested.[23]

The other main defense witness, Captain Case, recounted how Oaksmith had hired him to go on a fifteen-month voyage. "I had a conversation with Oaksmith about what would be wanted. We made a memorandum of what was wanted. I considered it sufficient. The Augusta was in suitable condition to perform the voyage." Case insisted that he had not agreed to go on a slaving voyage. "Nothing was s[ai]d about the Augusta going on a Slaving voyage till it was noised around the village, about the time of the seizure." He then recollected a conversation he'd had with Deputy Marshal Horton, about the time that the ship was seized. "Now look here," Horton had said, "if that Ship is condemned do you know in what position it is going to place you in." When Case said he did not know, Horton replied that "if she was condemned" that Case would "be indicted same as an owner." Case told Horton that "I did not see how that could be, that I did not see how they could indict a man for shipping to go whaling." Case further testified that he'd told Horton that Oaksmith had engaged him to go as the master of the *Augusta* for "whaling and for no other purpose. *I had not heard the name of slave, negroe or anything of the kind mentioned until it was noised around outside.*" Case then added that he had engaged a former mate of his who had been on his last whaling voyage, and that "I have had a great many come & want to go with me. *I had offers made from all the experienced whalemen I shd need.*"[24]

The trial closed on August 19, and several weeks passed before Shipman rendered his decision. During that period Oaksmith continued to work as a shipping agent, fitting out a ship in New Bedford, Massachusetts (to be discussed in subsequent chapters). On September 4, while traveling on a vessel from Boston to New York City, he encountered his prosecutor, Stewart L. Woodford, in a saloon on the ship. This was the first time they'd met since the trial. The two men ate dinner together, and when Oaksmith learned that Woodford did not have a stateroom, he replied that he had two berths in his room and that Woodford was welcome to sleep there. They spent most of the evening together in "general" conversation. Only once did the *Augusta* come up. Oaksmith asked when Judge Shipman would decide the case. Woodford replied that he did not know. Oaksmith added, "I have no fear of the result, for it cannot help being in our favor." To this Woodford suggested "that we had had our fight in court, and while receiving [your] kindness, [I do] not wish to discuss it again." They dropped the matter and returned to other topics. Upon reaching New York City, they parted ways.[25]

On Friday, September 20, Shipman filed his opinion in the case, ruling against Oaksmith and Appley. In his mind, Oaksmith's arguments just did not add up. The *Augusta* "was a much larger vessel" than was needed for a fifteen-month voyage, and he was not persuaded that someone new to the whaling business would buy such a large vessel at this time when whaling was not as profitable. One of the benefits of such a large ship, Shipman pointed out, was that there would be no need to build a slave deck, as other illegal slavers had to do. "It is quite obvious that this vessel was well adapted, as to size and construction, to carry a slave cargo. She had two permanent decks, which dispensed with the necessity of a temporary slave deck. The large fry works [for processing blubber into oil] were admirably fitted for cooking the slaves' food, and were ample in size for the necessity of a large number of negroes."

Of greater significance, Shipman did not think that the *Augusta* was really fitted out for a whaling voyage. "She was materially wanting in tow lines, whale irons, iron poles, knives, axes, hoop iron, and grindstones," he wrote. "She was also greatly deficient in flour, molasses, and vinegar, and considerably in the quantity of beef and pork." Shipman pointed out that some of the beef on board was "good and sweet, and suitable for the crew to eat," while "the greater portion was more or less tainted"—most likely to be fed to African captives. Shipman was not persuaded that this tainted beef had been fine when Oaksmith purchased and inspected it, as Oaksmith had claimed in court. Similarly, the judge noted that much of the water was tainted from being stored in oil casks. Such nasty fluid might be offered to slaves, but it would not have been consumed by white sailors.

Other evidence also led Shipman to believe that the *Augusta* was preparing for a slaving voyage. There was too much food for a fifteen-month voyage, and Oaksmith and Captain Case had not yet pulled together an experienced whaling crew, even though they were only a few weeks away from departure. All this evidence, and the dropping price of whale oil, led him to his conclusion: "I am therefore of the opinion . . . that the Augusta was not fitted for a whaler, but that what was done ostensibly for that purpose was merely colorable, and to conceal the real enterprise contemplated. What was that enterprise? That it was a guilty one, there can be no doubt, assuming the concealment to have been proved. . . . Concealment implies guilt, and what other guilty traffic demanded such an outfit?" Shipman therefore concluded that the ship was being fitted out as a slaver, and he ordered her condemned and forfeited to the United States.[26]

Delafield Smith was pleased with how Woodford had handled the prosecution, and he later recalled that Marshal Murray and Deputy Marshal Horton "expressed at the time great gratification at the decision, and at the manner in which Mr. Woodford had conducted the case." Shipman's opinion gained some attention in the newspapers. The New York *Evening Post* praised it, claiming that it would help lead to the end of the illegal slave trade: "This forfeiture, with others recently announced, will do much toward exterminating this traffic at this port and its vicinity." But Oaksmith and Appley would not accept Shipman's decision without a fight.[27] Oaksmith and his lawyer called on Woodford at his office several times in late September. On September 25, Oaksmith asked Woodford if he'd had lunch yet. They went to Delmonico's at the corner of Broadway and Chambers Street, in New York City's financial district near the courthouse. The two men sat by a window overlooking Broadway. Oaksmith asked Woodford something about the case, to which Woodford replied that Oaksmith would have to ask his lawyer. While they were eating, Deputy Marshal Horton came in and walked up to the table. He leaned over and whispered something into Oaksmith's ear that was inaudible to Woodford. Then he quickly left the restaurant. After they were finished, Oaksmith paid for the meal.[28]

In early October, Benjamin F. Sawyer filed the paperwork to appeal the case. Soon thereafter, Oaksmith went to Woodford's office. As Woodford recalled the conversation,

> Oaksmith said he had had very hard luck; no matter what he touched or how innocent it was, he got jerked up, and lost everything. He spoke a few moments of his past life, and said he had a wife and children who were with his mother, who were dependent on him; that Appley, who was rich, had taken him into business at Greenport; that Appley was very angry about this Augusta matter, and he was afraid he would lose this, about his last chance for an honest living. He said law costs so much

that Appley had got tired of paying costs and fees, though his vessel was innocent, he thought they would rather pay the government something if Uncle Sam would let up, than to keep on with the fight.

Woodford replied that if Oaksmith had any propositions he would relay them to Delafield Smith. Oaksmith said that Appley would give $1,500 if the government would release the vessel. Woodford replied that Smith would not accept any compromise until it was first approved by the Treasury Department. Woodford then visited Smith, who was still home sick and confined in bed. He told Smith that he thought Oaksmith would pay $2,000 to have the ship returned, but Smith said that was "too small, but he did not see as there was anything objectionable if they would pay into court somewhere near the value of the vessel and cargo" if the secretary of the interior approved.

About dinnertime on October 3—the same day that Sawyer filed the petition of appeal—Oaksmith went to the courthouse and told Woodford he had a private matter to discuss. Woodford replied that if it didn't concern Appley or the *Augusta* that he would be happy to chat. Oaksmith said "it was a long matter, and as we were both busy we could save time by going to dinner and talking it over there." They went to their usual spot at Delmonico's. The matter had to do with a Cuban friend whose ship, the *Ardennes*, had been seized in New York, and who had lost a substantial amount of money in a lawsuit. Woodford said he could not take a retainer in that case until the *Augusta* business was concluded. When they finished eating, Woodford picked up the check since Oaksmith had paid for the last.[29]

On October 7, Sawyer made an application to bond the vessel, and he argued the motion in court on October 8. Judge Samuel R. Betts ordered an appraisal and asked Woodford and Sawyer to name the appraisers. They agreed that each party would select one. Sawyer named Thomas Stack, a shipbuilder from Williamsburg in Brooklyn. Woodford named Henry T. Capen, a merchant who also happened to be Woodford's father-in-law and in whose home Woodford lived. On October 9, Oaksmith informed Woodford and Capen that Stack was in Washington, DC, on government business, and that Capen could proceed alone. He then invited Woodford to go to Delmonico's again to discuss the *Ardennes* matter. At dinner Woodford said he was convinced the *Ardennes* was a slaver but he would do his best to help. Oaksmith paid for the meal.

For obvious reasons, Oaksmith wanted to get the lowest possible appraisal of the *Augusta*. "You will please bear in mind that the vessel is over twenty-five years old," he wrote in a short note to Capen. The appraiser assured Oaksmith that he "wanted to do justice by the owners and the government both." Oaksmith hoped to get the vessel for somewhere in the neighborhood of $2,000, but Murray sent him word that "if the vessel was bonded for anything less than her value I would seize her again immediately."

On the morning of October 10, Capen appraised the *Augusta* at $2,200. At noon that day, Sawyer and Oaksmith arrived at Woodford's office to discuss the appraisal. Sawyer wanted the appraisal filed immediately so that Oaksmith could regain possession of the ship, but Deputy Marshal Horton joined the conversation and informed them that the government had received another offer of $3,500. Hearing this—and believing that the vessel was worth considerably more than what Capen had appraised it for—Woodford told Sawyer that the appraisal would not be filed. Sawyer said, "Keep cool, come in the court-room, and let us talk it over." They sat down on a bench in the public section of the courtroom, and Horton also joined them. Sawyer tried to persuade Woodford that the appraisal was correct. "Right or wrong," Woodford replied, "it shall not be filed. Mr. Capen is a connexion of mine, and such an appraisement would put me in a false position." Horton remarked, "Mr. Woodford is right, and if Mr. Capen is his father-in-law he does right in having it appraised again by somebody else."

Woodford walked out of the courtroom and asked Capen how he came to the value of $2,000. Capen replied that that was what the ship was worth. "How much do you appraise her outfit and stores?" asked Woodford. Capen responded that he did not know of any except her rigging. Capen turned to Oaksmith and said, "You did not tell me there was any outfit." "I know I did not," said Oaksmith, "but I am willing you should call them five hundred dollars." Capen said he could not appraise them without seeing them. "Let us try to arrange it peacefully," interjected Sawyer, at which Woodford turned to his father-in-law and said, "Colonel Capen, you will oblige me by filing no appraisal today. I want you to resign to-night, and we will have this thing all done over again."

Capen seemed upset by this turn of events but agreed to resign. Sawyer and Woodford then got into a heated exchange, in which Woodford said that he did not care whether Sawyer liked it or not. The next day, Woodford appointed Thomas P. Stanton in Capen's place. On October 16, Stanton told Woodford that he and Stack had agreed on a value of $3,250 for the vessel and $1,000 for the cargo. A few days later Sawyer provided sureties, and on October 28 the vessel was bonded and discharged for $4,250.[30] Oaksmith and Appley could now reclaim their ship and fit her out for her voyage. Oaksmith later claimed that he and Appley planned to go on their original whaling voyage "with the view of *proving by performance her original intent.*"[31]

October 28 was a significant day for Appleton's mother as well. On Sunday, October 27, Elizabeth had visited the officer in charge of military recruitment in their village and promised to bring India rubber cloaks for the men. The next morning she and her two daughters-in-law—Isotta, and Sidney's wife, Fanny—"dressed . . . with some bravery," putting on silks, velvet, lace, pearls, diamonds, and large red, white, and blue hats that looked like turbans. "The effect was really fine and tasteful," Oakes Smith wrote in her diary. "I wished to show some marks of honor to the young soldiers of our town starting for the war." The three women, along with Fanny's daughter Eva, and Appleton's daughter, Bessie, made it to the observatory, which was streaming with American flags and festooned with red, white, and blue bunting. Martial music welcomed the young recruits, "who appeared in handsome style followed by a large concourse of people of all ages and both sexes from the village." Oakes Smith stood under an archway with her daughters-in-law at her side. When the music stopped she stepped forward and waved an American flag before the cheering crowd. She then "addressed them from my very heart for I do not recall many words of what I said, though many were melted to tears." The crowd interrupted her several times with applause. When she finished speaking, she turned to the commander and told him she hoped the cloaks would be useful and comfortable for his men. The soldiers then filed past, each "bowing and taking his gift from the pile." Oakes Smith found it "an affecting sight" and when one of the boys said, "God bless you," she was "moved to tears."[32]

Over the ensuing weeks, Oakes Smith worried about the "suffering Country" and felt "ashamed of my comforts while men are shedding their blood that we may be secure." She looked to the heavens and prayed for the Union soldiers, confessing, "there is little else I can do." In mid-November she was pleased to hear Sidney say, "This crisis in our country has shown us our great men, and we have them, men true to principle, and brave, as well as capable."[33] About this same time she sent a four-stanza poem to Lincoln entitled "Hymn for our Country," which called for blessing on "our Country," "our Councils," and "the Banner of our Land!" "Let Justice reign, and Truth arise / To guide our steps alway[s]. / Upheld by His almighty hand! / God bless the rulers of our Land." Lincoln replied on November 14, thanking her for the "strikingly beautiful and original poem."[34]

But there was some foreboding within the Oaksmith family. One night Alvin, who was now living in South America, had a "very vivid and terrible dream" about Appleton. "I saw my poor, dear Brother in a sort of dungeon—all stone—there was a small table and pitcher upon it," he wrote. "I saw two or three men, perhaps more all around and disputing and threatening him. App had a knife in his hand which he seemed unwilling to use even in self defence. They were too many for him and he was forced to submit. I saw my Brother's face flushed and excited and the tears streaming from his eyes." At this, Alvin sprung out of bed and cried, "Great God deliver him from evil," starting his wife, Delfina, awake.[35]

Trouble, indeed, was brewing. Marshal Murray began feeding articles to the *New York Tribune* that praised his own work and raised the question of whether there had been fraud in the *Augusta* case. Murray was convinced that Oaksmith and Woodford were conspiring to enrich themselves by bonding the *Augusta* below her actual value so that they could send her on a profitable slaving voyage. Woodford, he believed, had attempted "a deliberate and wicked fraud upon the Government."[36]

When Woodford learned that Murray suspected him of collusion, he called at the marshal's office to protest his innocence. On Wednesday, November 6, Woodford told Murray that he was indebted to the marshal for his help over the years, but that Murray had wronged him in charging him with impropriety without speaking to him first. Their conversation quickly became heated. Murray told Woodford that he thought highly of him but that "his connexion with the bark Augusta looked very black, and that unless it could be explained I did not wish to have anything more to do with him." Murray asked how Woodford had come to dine at Delmonico's for two successive days with Oaksmith. Woodford said "that Oaksmith had come to him and told him he was ruined, and cried, and worked upon his feelings, and that he had believed him." Murray replied that "if a man like Oaksmith had worked upon his feelings it was evidence to my mind" that Woodford was "unfit" for his position as a prosecutor.

Woodford was taken aback. He said that Murray's deputy, Luther Horton, had proposed the $2,000 bond because "it would be a good deal better for the government and all to settle the case by paying some decent amount into court." At this, Murray became enraged. He slammed his fist on his desk, called the situation a "perfect outrage," and said he would dismiss Horton. Woodford "begged" Murray not to fire his deputy, saying that Horton had not done anything wrong. But Murray said, "No. I shall do it the moment he comes in. I will not have a man of that character around me."

As Woodford prepared to leave, he said, "I hope I have satisfied you that I have done nothing wrong." Murray "told him he had not; that the statements he had made . . . satisfied me that there was collusion somewhere, and that I was determined to probe to the bottom." As Woodford remembered the conversation, "Before I left the marshal expressed himself entirely satisfied with my explanation; we shook hands, and, I supposed, parted good friends."

When Murray confronted his deputy, Horton claimed that Woodford had been the one to propose the $2,000 bond and that he (Horton) had said the ship was worth $4,500. Murray fired him anyway.[37] Judge Shipman eventually investigated the situation and absolved Woodford of any wrongdoing. Delafield Smith and Secretary of the Interior Caleb Smith concurred in Shipman's assessment. Nevertheless, the accusation that Woodford colluded with a slave trader became a major impediment to his political career.[38] The following year, in 1862, he left his position as a federal prosecutor to join the Union army.

On that same day—Wednesday, November 6—Murray sent a letter to Secretary of the Interior Caleb Smith, informing him that the *Augusta* had been bonded "at what I consider less than her value" and that she was about to "proceed on the same illegal voyage with the same cargo." Smith replied the next day that Murray and Delafield Smith could use their "sound discretion" to determine whether Oaksmith had committed a new offence and the ship should be detained again. Murray immediately sent a detective to the Atlantic Dock to see what was being loaded onto the *Augusta*. He next asked Hiram Barney, the collector of the port, not to permit the ship to clear the port if she carried the same cargo. Murray then asked Woodford to issue a libel, granting him authority to seize the ship. For some reason Woodford did not produce the libel for several days, and during that intervening period Barney forgot to inform the coastwise clearance department not to permit the *Augusta* to sail. So at 3 p.m. on Saturday, November 9, the *Augusta* departed New York City for Greenport, near the eastern tip of Long Island.[39]

The coastwise inspector at Greenport alerted Murray to the presence of the *Augusta*. "I know Appley, Oaksmith, Israel Peck, and Captain Isaac M. Case very well. I know their view with regard to secession and slavery, especially the African slave trade," he wrote. "I am ashamed that she should get away from this place they are a damnable set, the whole of them; I know them all. If there is any way under heaven that I can be of any service to you in this matter, or others of a similar kind, I am at your service at any cost." A few days later he asked again, "What will you do, and what shall I do?" And another official telegraphed Murray, "Shall we seize?"[40] Before sunrise on the morning of November 17, Oaksmith prepared to take the *Augusta* to sea. But a strong gale arose. Despite his best efforts, the wind and waves forced him back to Fire Island, where his ship was grounded. Murray regarded the storm as "a special interposition of Providence."[41]

7

FORT LAFAYETTE

Robert Murray was livid. He believed that the *Augusta*'s sailing from New York City on Sunday, November 17, was "a direct fraud upon the Government."[1] That night, while he was waiting at the New York harbor police station to escort two captured Confederate agents, James Mason and John Slidell, to prison at Fort Warren in Boston, Murray received a dispatch stating that a sloop had arrived at Fire Island with sixteen or eighteen men on board—"evidently sailors, and supposed to be the crew of a privateer, or, perhaps, a crew which had murdered their officers and escaped." Murray telegraphed the sheriff of Suffolk County to arrest and detain them. On Monday morning, November 18, the sheriff replied that these were Oaksmith's men—including Appleton's brother, Sidney. Murray then telegraphed Secretary of State William H. Seward—whose State Department oversaw the arrest of political prisoners early in the war—for permission to detain Oaksmith and Appley at Fort Lafayette.[2] Murray assured Seward that Oaksmith "is one of the most expert scoundrels engaged in this nefarious business, highly educated, and possessing talents that would grace almost any position in social or civil life, if honestly applied. He has been engaged in this illegal traffic for a number of years, and has given me more trouble in my operations, against the Slave Trade, than all other men engaged in it."[3]

The staff in Delafield Smith's office were concerned that they did not have proper legal authority to detain the men. Smith told one of his subordinates that he "must find a way; that the men must be held, if possible, until the marshal's return" from Boston. Meanwhile, a lawyer named Welcome R. Beebe petitioned the federal court in New York for a writ of habeas corpus to have the crewmembers released. A clerk in the US attorney's office explained what they did in response: "We got one of the officers to make an affidavit against the men for aiding and abetting the fitting out of the Augusta as a slaver, although we were well aware that we then had little or no evidence to support this particular charge. But this was the best we could do. We then got a warrant from the commissioner, and had the men formally arrested. We (the district attorney [Delafield Smith] and myself) that day attended before Judge [Daniel P.] Ingraham, on the return of the *habeas corpus*, and got it dismissed." On Friday, November 22, federal prosecutors began examining the men. "The district attorney said we *must*, by all means, keep them till the marshal returned," while their counsel, Beebe, insisted on their release. The government prevailed, and the men were held until Murray's return from Boston on Monday, November 25. Murray then assumed custody of the men and imprisoned them at Fort Lafayette—a military installation where they would be beyond the reach of civil law.[4]

On November 29, federal authorities also arrested Jacob Appley at New York City. The deputy marshal who conveyed Appley to Fort Lafayette remembered the trip: "I had a conversation with him on the way down. He told me he intended the Augusta to go on a whaling voyage; that since the last seizure of the Augusta and the arrest of the man he had begun to change his mind, and begun to think that Oaksmith was trying to cheat him." Appley claimed that Oaksmith had tried to prevent him from boarding the *Augusta* and he "got disgusted with the way Oaksmith was acting, and he left there and went about his business."[5]

Fort Lafayette was, according to one contemporary newspaper report, "a low, diamond-shaped structure, sitting squat upon a little pile of rocks, a few hundred feet from the shore, unattractive, dismal and gloomy with no redemptive sign, save the beautiful flag which floats ever, from sunrise to sunset." Its imposing walls stood forty or fifty feet tall with powerful heavy guns facing the channel.[6] The political prisoners were housed in four small casemates and two larger battery rooms. Oaksmith found himself in Casemate No. 2—a stone chamber about fourteen by twenty-four feet with an arched ceiling that was about eight and a half feet high at the highest point of the arc, a single fireplace, and a plank floor.

Joining Oaksmith in his cell were three Californians who had been arrested for disloyalty during a trip to the East: William M. Gwin, a Mississippi slave owner who had served as a US senator from California for the past decade and who had a son in the Confederate army; Calhoun Benham, a former federal prosecutor in San Francisco who had been a second in one of the most infamous duels in American history; and Joseph L. Brent, a San Diego Democrat and longtime associate of Gwin's. Also in the cell were two men suspected of illegally corresponding with the South: William P.

Fort Lafayette.
Courtesy of the Library of Congress.

"Prison in Casemate No. 2, Fort Lafayette, New York Harbor."
Harper's Weekly, April 15, 1865.

Converse of Brooklyn, and Ruston Maury, a Liverpool merchant who had been living in the South for many years. Together these six men shared a mess, pooling their money to procure items from New York City. They were allowed one hour of outdoor "exercise" each morning and each evening. And each inmate took a day to clean their cell. "This," Oaksmith wrote, "gives each one a hard days work once a week."[7]

Shortly before Oaksmith arrived, eighty political prisoners—many of whom were members of the Maryland legislature—complained to President Lincoln about their conditions at the fort: "In one of the small casemates, twenty three prisoners are confined, two thirds of them in irons, without beds, bedding, or any of the commonest necessaries. Their condition could hardly be worse, if they were in a slave-ship, on the middle passage." Because the men were kept in such cramped conditions with very little ventilation—and without any opportunity to bathe—they grumbled that "it is barely possible to sleep, in the foul and unwholesome air." The atmosphere of these rooms was "offensive & almost stifling," they continued. Contagious diseases were spreading. Fresh water was lacking. And the food was "of the commonest and coarsest soldiers' rations, almost invariably ill-prepared & ill-cooked."[8]

Upon seeing a complaint from a recently released prisoner in the newspapers in late October, Lieutenant Colonel Martin Burke, the military officer in command of Fort Lafayette, griped to Robert Murray, "You and I both know how hard the Government has striven to make those Prisoners comfortable, and if in the whirlpool of business, they may have apparently been neglected, we can both testify as to the present ample preparations which are being made, not only to render them comfortable, but even to put it beyond the complaint of some who *would* be unreasonable." Burke further wondered whether such "improper and false" public complaints from prisoners who had been released might "invalidate the parole or the person or persons making them." In other words, if prisoners publicly protested, they should be rearrested. For his part, Murray informed Secretary of State Seward that he had "not been inattentive to their wants and I have in every instance responded promptly to all the requisitions made upon me by the Commanders of Forts Lafayette & Columbus."[9]

Little appears to have improved at Fort Lafayette by the time Oaksmith arrived in November. In prison, he claimed that he was subjected to "shameful indignities" and "inhuman barbarity" that, "through my body, have trampled the sacred Constitution in the dust." For a time, he was kept in solitary confinement and had his mail searched. "I was in the position of a man *bound hand and foot*, and subjected to the vindictive stabs of merciless enemies and assassins." Oaksmith sent several letters to Seward, arguing that he was innocent and that his case was "of greater moment to the entire people of the North than it is to me" since it was "*one of the most danger-ous precedents* sought to be established" to detain a man without a warrant or any charges. "I am, by birth, education, and instinct, a gentleman," he told Seward, "and it is unnecessary for me to say with *what feelings I have experienced this barbarous treatment.*"[10]

Sitting in a damp, dark room, Oaksmith turned to poetry, just as he had during so many other sad or solitary moments in his life. Writing by firelight, he penned "A Dream of the Bastile," a two-hundred-line poem in which his soul flew out "through the grated bars" to seek wisdom from "the heavenly stars." His lines expressed his anger with leaders in Washington, who were "mad with lust of power" and driven by "greed of fame" but who would never be "ranked among the great." Further in the distance, he saw "Two armies of *brothers*" locked in combat, and he thought of the wives and mothers who would weep when so many were "Lying in heaps of dead." Oaksmith had previously "thought that our Age was brighter," more enlightened, "than any the world had seen." But no. The war had proved otherwise. Brothers and fathers and sons were now "Met in a deadly strife." Mothers and widows at home wept as the corpses of soldiers were flung "Into the trenches. . . . Anywhere out of sight" with "None to pray for them there!" Still, in the end, the poet hoped he could turn to his pillow in faith that "GOD WILL DEFEND THE RIGHT."[11]

While Appleton sat in prison, Robert Murray was determined to get to the bottom of the *Augusta* affair. "It is conclusive to my mind, that a great fraud has been practised [*sic*] upon the Government in the case of the bark 'Augusta,'" he wrote to Martin Burke, "and I am exceedingly anxious to prove it to the bottom and expose the guilty parties whoever they may be and I confidently rely on your cooperation and assistance in procur-ing this important testimony."[12] After some pressure, one of the *Augusta*'s crewmen, Edward Myers, "expressed a strong desire" to meet with Marshal Murray. He informed Murray that he'd shipped on the vessel thinking it was going on a whaling voyage, but that "Oaksmith called the sailors to-gether and swore them not to divulge in relation to the voyage, which was to be the coast of Africa for a cargo of slaves." According to Myers, Oak-smith had told the men that they would be paid $2,000 apiece for the trip, after which rum "was passed round and they had a jolly time of it." Myers knew that he took a great risk when he shared this story with the marshal. Indeed, as he left Fort Lafayette that day, one of the other sailors said to him, "You son of a ——, if you say anything we will cut your G—d d—d heart out."[13] Oaksmith later explained away Myers's decision to turn state's witness: "Being in irons, deprived of counsel, subject to close confinement and meager diet, it is not unnatural that some one or more of them, under the fear of greater hardships and torture, should have announced himself as ready to swear by any statement his inquisitors might dictate, provided he could thereby gain his liberty." Oaksmith claimed that "the majority" of Myers's statement was "absolutely false." Elizabeth Oakes Smith later recorded in her diary that Myers "afterwards filled with remorse, recanted the atrocious lie. I understand he is now in a dying state at the hospital."[14]

Newspapers throughout the nation speculated about Oaksmith's activities and fate. The *Brooklyn Daily Eagle* remarked that he "has been instrumental in fitting out more slavers than any man in the country. Whether he will succeed in getting out of his present difficulties remains to be seen." The San Francisco *Evening Bulletin* similarly surmised that he was "now almost sure of getting his deserts" for his participation in "the ebony trade."[15]

On November 25, shortly after arriving at Fort Lafayette, Oaksmith penned a long letter to Seward, reminding him of his two letters from January, during the secession crisis. "I was . . . one of the first Democrats to take ground in favor of an uncompromising maintenance of the Union," he wrote. He advised Seward that the power to confine political prisoners ought to be "used with caution and judgement. It should never be permitted to be used as an instrument for the gratification of personal or political vindictiveness and malice." He then assured the secretary that "whatever the allegations" against him may be, "they are *utterly and entirely false*" and that the man who made them—Robert Murray—was "a traitor inasmuch as he has prostituted a power which you unquestionably feel is not only a delicate but a dangerous one." Oaksmith therefore urged that the best course of action was his "immediate release."[16]

In his private correspondence, Oaksmith tried to encourage those at home who were worried about his fate. In a letter to his mother, dated November 29—a letter that she never received because it was confiscated by prison authorities—he thanked her for the "bountiful supplies" she had sent, telling her that he would share them with his cellmates and other "less fortunate fellow prisoners." Oaksmith wanted her to believe that he was living in "quite a comfortable room with a fire" and that he was a member of "the best mess in the Fort." Indeed, he wanted to offer her comfort during this time of great distress. "Taking everything into consideration we are as comfortable and happy as we could be under the circumstances," he told her. But the core of his letter was a reflection on the constitutional crisis in the North during the Civil War. "There is a very serious question at stake in my incarceration, one involving the very existence of this Republic; and I shall not deal with it lightly," he wrote. "When men can be taken by force of arms, manacled, and confined in a Prison, cut off from communication with the World, without warrant or process of law, and without even a distinct accusation, and entirely without cause, it is time for people to begin to think on the Fate which awaits them."

Oaksmith acknowledged that the Confederate rebellion "is unquestionably a great evil," but he worried that those who remained in the Union were "falling upon a greater one. Personal liberty, and the right to a speedy trial are among the strongest guarantees of our Constitution, and without these there can be nothing like 'Liberty,' and no Government can be permanently maintained which strikes at these." From Oaksmith's perspective, the Lincoln administration was usurping power intended "to crush Rebellion" and instead was diverting it "from its original intention" so that "designing and wicked persons" could "gratify their every hatred and malice." And he had a point. After all, the Constitution permitted the privilege of the writ of habeas corpus to be suspended "when in Cases of Rebellion or Invasion the public Safety may require it." In other words, the government could not detain just anyone—they had to be suspected of aiding the rebellion—and their arrest had to be related to public safety.

Oaksmith believed he was situated to judge these developments "calmly and dispassionately," although he was surely deluded in so thinking. He admitted that it would be impossible to predict what the future would hold, but he was adamant that Lincoln's suspension of habeas corpus and declaration of martial law were unconstitutional. "In a government of opinions and principles and popular suffrage the adoption of the iron rule of the sword can have but one result," he wrote solemnly. He continued:

> There never can be *Liberty* so long as the Military power is placed above the Judiciary.
>
> My labors in behalf of the Union are well known to some. My imprisonment is entirely without parallel, and I intend to take the *stump* against this unconstitutional exercise of power, as soon as I can do so with propriety.
>
> At present there is nothing [that] can be done against the fanaticism so to speak, of the Republicans. I fear the Revolution here more than I do the one at the South. That will only lose us territory which can be recovered, this will lose us *principles* which may never be restored.[17]

Oaksmith received no response to his letter to Seward of November 25, so he tried again on November 30 and December 3. (Oaksmith later claimed that before sending these letters he showed them to someone who knew Seward who replied, "*If I sent them he would send me to Fort Warren, and keep me there till the end of the war.*") The first letter recounted the events surrounding his arrest and insisted that Edward Myers's statement was the result of multiple "offers of liberty and pecuniary reward [that] have been repeatedly addressed to them, to induce them '*to confess*' and 'turn State's evidence.'" The other sailors had "all utterly refused, because they have nothing to confess." Myers, however, had finally caved "under the combined forces of the *Inquisition*, and offers of liberty and reward . . . [and] has consented to obey the Marshal's orders, *and swear as he directs.*" In the second letter Oaksmith again professed innocence, claiming that he had never had any interest in a slaving vessel. He again rejected Myers's statement as "*entirely false,*" reiterating that it had been given to avoid further imprisonment "*in irons*" and "*on bread and water.*" Even more important, Oaksmith pleaded with Seward to abide by the Constitution, insisting that persons accused of a crime had certain rights and protections that were guaranteed in the nation's fundamental law.[18]

If Oaksmith and the other prisoners believed that their constitutional rights were being violated, they soon learned that they had little legal recourse to seek any vindication. On December 3, the commanding officer at Fort Lafayette came into the prisoners' quarters and informed them that the State Department "will not recognize any one as an attorney for political prisoners, and will look with distrust upon all applications for release through such channels, and that such applications will be regarded as additional reasons for declining to release the prisoners." Furthermore, the prisoners were informed that if they wished "to make any communication to Government they are at liberty and requested to make it directly to the State Department."[19] In other words, the prisoners would be penalized for attempting to exercise their rights under the Fifth Amendment, and only the executive branch of the federal government would determine who could be released and when. The message bore the name of Seth C. Hawley, a New York police clerk and longtime associate of Seward's who had been hired by the State Department to investigate the cases of political prisoners.

If that were not enough, military authorities seized any of Oaksmith's correspondence that might help him alleviate his circumstances. Previous to hearing Hawley's edict, he had tried writing to lawyers, but he came to believe that the letters "never were received" because they had been confiscated by prison authorities. So now he stopped trying. Unbeknownst to Oaksmith, military authorities also seized a letter addressed to him by

Seth C. Hawley.
Courtesy of Trudy B. Hawley, Hawley Society genealogist.

New York attorney Algernon Sydney Sullivan in which Sullivan offered to serve as Oaksmith's counsel. (Earlier in the fall Sullivan had been arrested for defending Confederate privateers on trial for piracy. He found himself in Fort Lafayette based on nothing more than a one-sentence telegram from Seward.) In taking these actions, federal authorities were determined to prevent Oaksmith from effectively defending himself.[20] Seward seemed to see no constitutional improprieties in these actions. His view was to win the war first and settle legal disputes later. "Let us save the country," he told a friend, "and then cast ourselves upon the judgment of the people, if we have in any case, acted without legal authority."[21]

Some of the seizures hit Oaksmith particularly hard. On December 7, Delafield Smith, the US attorney in New York City, sent Oaksmith a letter (the contents of which remain unknown) that came to the attention of Marshal Murray. Murray immediately sent Martin Burke an order, informing him, "It is important for the ends of public justice, that I should have possession of that letter. Will you do me the favor to cause an examination to be made of Oaksmith's person and baggage, for the purpose of obtaining it?" Oaksmith refused to turn over the letter to Burke until, on December 13, he was placed "under the intimidation of physical force," at which point he relented. He then protested this seizure of "my private property" in a letter to Burke. A few days later the letter was returned to him, although he would not retain it for long.[22]

Oaksmith's family was likely unaware of Seth Hawley's December 3 edict, so they continued to work to secure his release from prison. December 9 was a busy letter-writing day at "The Willows." Isotta and Elizabeth both sent letters to Lincoln, with the two women almost certainly collaborating even though they despised one another. Isotta informed Lincoln that her husband was "confined in Fort Lafayette on the false charge, as I understand, of disloyalty to the Union." She assured the president, "There is no more loyal citizen in the country than he is," and she urged him to read Appleton's poetry. Elizabeth sent Lincoln a copy of Oaksmith's poem, "The Union Marseillaise." Curiously, Isotta's letter found its way into Oaksmith's disloyalty case file, which is now housed in the records of the State Department at the National Archives. Elizabeth's letter, by contrast, is held in Lincoln's personal collection of correspondence at the Library of Congress, indicating that the president had likely seen the letter and poem, recognized the author's name, and chosen to keep them.[23]

Elizabeth also wrote to US senator John P. Hale, a New Hampshire Republican, asking for his intervention with the Lincoln administration. She told him that if he trusted what was in the newspapers "you would suppose my Son a desperado, and a low carouser, instead of what he really is, a man of dignity and refinement, a Poet, and a most affectionate and devoted Son." She concluded, "I need not say to you, that I am suffering inexpressible anguish at these events; you are a tender father and may form some idea of what a Mother must feel situated as I now am." To underscore the point of her son's noble character, she enclosed a copy of Appleton's poem, "The Union Marseillaise."

That same day she also wrote a long letter to Seward. She reminded the secretary of state of Appleton's efforts on behalf of the Union earlier that year, and let him know of her own grief. "I do assure you he is not guilty of any wrong, as time and opportunity will abundantly prove," she wrote. "I need not say that his family have been plunged into the depths of distress by this unhappy event. Indeed so paralyzed have I been by the greatness of the blow, that I have been unable to take these steps to procure his release, which a Mother's affection would dictate." She informed Seward that Appleton's doctor had recently diagnosed him with "an enlargement of the heart," and that Sidney's health had been declining since his brief imprisonment at Fort Lafayette. "You are in power, and prosperous," she wrote, "my family is a wreck—surely there is a God in Heaven, who ruleth in the affairs of men—to Him I leave my cause." She asked Seward for a pass to visit Appleton "at suitable hours, daily if possible." If Seward could "have any sympathy with the anguish a Mother must feel" under such circumstances, she begged him to grant this request.[24]

Elizabeth's family recognized the serious emotional strain she was enduring. Writing from Italy on December 14, Edward Oaksmith sought to encourage his mother by reminding her of the providential wisdom and love of God. "God permits that we be afflicted in this wor[l]d undoubtedly for His own great and perfect views," he wrote. "Knowing what is best for us; and though sore trials seem thrust upon us, it is better to believe that these very trials are means to raise us more intimately into relation with 'Our Father in heaven.'" Then Edward added, "*I have read the papers*—I shall be at home shortly."[25]

Elizabeth tucked Edward's letter away, perhaps finding some encouragement in it. But she knew that what she really needed was an interview with the secretary of state. Unfortunately she did not know him, so she turned to James Cephas Derby—a prominent New York publisher who had released several of her works in the 1850s as well as a number of other important books, including Solomon Northup's *Twelve Years a Slave* (1853). Derby's brother, had, in fact, been an admirer of Appleton's poem, "Maggie Bell," and years later Derby would publish Frederick W. Seward's memoir of his father. Derby helped arrange an interview between Elizabeth and the powerful cigar-puffing secretary of state.

On December 16, Oakes Smith traveled to Washington, DC, to meet with Seward, whom she described in her diary as having "neither a human soul nor vestige of moral conscience." From all she could gather, Seward and his subordinates were greedy, corrupt, power-hungry, and cruel, using their positions in government to "ensnare . . . political opponents." Upon entering Seward's office, she told him, "The Administration is not responsible for all the bad acts of its officials; but, when it has made a mistake in an appointment and the office is abused, it is its duty to investigate the matter, and remove the unworthy incumbent."

"Whom do you refer to Madam?" he asked.

"I refer to the Marshall [*sic*] of New York, Sir, who to my certain knowledge is an ignorant man, a lying man, and a malignant man."

Seward arose from his chair and walked to the corner of the room, showing "both sprite and excitement in his face." Then he turned to her and replied, "I suppose I shall be called just such names—I suppose the same kind of epithets will be applied to me."

Oakes Smith "certainly thought he deserved them" but she was wise enough not to say so. Instead, she quietly replied, "*I*, Sir, never presumed to couple your name and that of Marshall Murray together." At this, Seward sat back down "with the air of a man conscious that he was acting a very undignified part." The meeting apparently ended with Seward telling her that he was awaiting a report on the case from Seth C. Hawley and that "*when that report was received, if it was favorable,* [Appleton] *would be immediately released.*"

Throughout the conversation, Oakes Smith thought "Seward was insolent, imperious and petty. I would hardly have anticipated to find a public functionary for whom I should feel so little respect."[26] Three years later, she remembered the experience in her diary, remarking that she'd "witnessed his automatic use of a bell suspended over his table. At a moment the door opened, and the dispatch was ordered. The whole New York Police were at his call; and Marshall Murray the most obsequious, and most unprincipled of tools ready to do his behest." While this recollection may have been influenced by things she'd read in the newspapers in the three years after her actual encounter with Seward, it aligns with an anecdote about Seward's "little bell" that circulated widely during the Civil War. Seward was reputed to have told the British minister in Washington, "My lord, I can touch a bell on my right hand and order the arrest of a citizen in Ohio. I can touch the bell again and order the imprisonment of a citizen of New

York; and no power on earth but that of the President can release them. Can the Queen of England in her dominions do as much?"[27]

Upon returning to New York, Oakes Smith called upon Hawley "with the natural solicitude of a Mother, preferring to know the worst, rather than endure this terrible suspense." To her pleasant surprise she found that Hawley's report had already been sent to Washington a few days earlier "and that the report *was favorable*—he could make out no *charge against* him." Upon learning this wonderful news, she wrote to Derby pleading with him to help. "At this critical juncture of the country, I am aware that the Department is overwhelmed with work, and the case of my Son must have been thus delayed. Now will you, my kind, excellent friend, try to have the matter looked into? It seems very simple now, and will probably occupy the Officials of the Secretary but a brief space. Will you ask that the release may be transmitted at once?" If the order for release was going to be delayed further, Oakes Smith asked Derby to procure for her a pass so that she could at least visit her son in prison.[28]

Elizabeth likely never saw the report that Hawley produced. In fact, Hawley had already written his report three days earlier, and it was damning. Hawley opened with a statement about Oaksmith's loyalty—probably with words to the effect that he had shared with Oakes Smith. "There is no evidence to establish any charge of disloyalty against Mr. Oaksmith," he wrote. "He is perhaps as Loyal to the United States as to any Government." But from that point forward, Hawley reported that Oaksmith had embarked on "a man stealing expedition" to Africa and that he could be convicted in New York, but that he would be more likely to be convicted in Boston. In fact, Hawley believed that "this is a case when the Prisoner ought not to escape the ordeal of a trial for slave dealing before the courts of Boston." (The reason for transferring Oaksmith to Boston will be discussed in greater detail in the next few chapters.) Hawley thus "strongly recommend[ed]"—after having a "full consultation" with Murray—that Oaksmith be sent there "immediately."[29]

On December 17, Oaksmith learned that Jacob Appley had been released from prison. He was incredulous. "I had a natural right to suppose that my release might accompany his," he wrote to Seward. "It has not." When this letter to the secretary was returned to him, undelivered, the following day, Oaksmith penned a postscript to Seward again calling his "particular attention to the fact that *Mr. Appley has been released*" while he had not.[30] There were reasons for this difference in treatment, however. Unlike Oaksmith, Appley had come to be seen as a sympathetic figure. The Hartford *Daily Courant* surmised that Appley was an eccentric, irresponsible spendthrift who "is a prey to sharpers of every kind and degree. If anybody has anything to sell which nobody else will buy at any price, a customer is always to be found in him. . . . When the news was given of his arrest and imprisonment, no one believed that he was really guilty. He was only the tool and victim of Oaksmith, and others who were at the bottom of the undertaking." Judge Shipman similarly believed him "the stupid or the pliant tool of others."[31]

When Elizabeth Oakes Smith went to Washington, she was furnished with a pass "to make a single visit, in presence of a proper officer."[32] A story appeared many years later that when she visited Fort Lafayette, Lieutenant Colonel Burke lost patience with her claims of Appleton's innocence. "Well madam if you don't believe it look at the positive proof in those papers," he said while handing her a stack of materials. She allegedly threw them into the fire, saying, "Well, general, if these papers are proofs we will burn them."[33] It makes for a nice story, but Burke would not have had that sort of evidence in his possession at the fort.

In fact, during her visit on December 18, Elizabeth informed Appleton about her conversations with Seward and Hawley. Mother and son were hopeful, and Appleton "looked forward confidently to my release." When, on December 19, an order from Seward arrived at the fort, he was sure the day of his salvation had come.

8

FORT WARREN

Unbeknownst to Oaksmith and his family, federal authorities in three cities had been working together for about a week to ensure that his imprisonment would end with a conviction in a federal court. On December 10, a warrant had been issued in Boston for Oaksmith's arrest. The following day, Robert Murray informed Seward that Oaksmith was under indictment in Boston for outfitting a slaving vessel at New Bedford, Massachusetts, and he asked the secretary to discharge Oaksmith from Fort Lafayette if he (Murray) determined there was enough evidence in Boston to secure a conviction. On the evening of Friday, December 13, Murray traveled to Boston to ascertain "the nature of the testimony against him" before surrendering him to civil authorities there, for Murray was "determined that he shall not cheat the law this time." In the meantime, Assistant Secretary of State Frederick W. Seward replied to Murray on December 13 with an order for Oaksmith's release, "unless in your judgment there are well founded reasons for his further detention."[1]

The US marshal in Boston, John S. Keyes, was also pressing Seward to send Oaksmith to his city. On December 14, Keyes informed Seward that Oaksmith had been indicted in the federal court in Boston for fitting out a whaling vessel called the *Margaret Scott* for the slave trade. "The evidence against him is conclusive, and his conviction morally certain," wrote Keyes. "I wish you would issue an order to the U.S. Marshal at N.Y. to transfer him to Fort Warren, so that he may be within this District and then he can be arrested and brought to justice on this charge." Keyes then got to the crux of the issue: "There is so much difficulty thrown in the way of the removal of slave traders from New York where they have counsel & friends to help them, that in this case of such a notorious offender it would be very desirable to resort to a more summary process." If federal civil authorities in

Boston could only "get hold of the defendant we can proceed at once with his trial. His conviction would tend materially to put a stop to this nefarious traffic in both New York & Massachusetts."[2]

Frederick W. Seward replied to Keyes on December 17, informing him that an order had been issued to release Oaksmith from Fort Lafayette.[3] When, on December 19, Oaksmith learned that an order pertaining to him

John Shepard Keyes.
Courtesy of the Concord Free Public Library.

had reached Fort Lafayette, he was relieved, thinking he would soon taste freedom. (Again, the day before he had met with his mother and learned that Seth C. Hawley was going to report positively about him to Seward.) So he proceeded to Colonel Burke's office carrying with him a valise full of letters—mostly from his mother, wife, and others, but also containing the letter from E. Delafield Smith. Instead of being released, however, Colonel Burke informed him that he was being transferred to nearby Fort Hamilton. He was rowed to the dock at Fort Hamilton, then placed into the cabin of a small police steamboat (Murray's order had said to "take a receipt for him"). The only other people aboard the boat were a few policemen, the crew, and three of Murray's deputy marshals, all of whom were armed with revolvers.

Soon the steamboat departed Fort Hamilton for Manhattan. "Shortly after the boat left the dock, and after she had got *out of hearing from the shore*, those three persons entered the cabin and forcibly searched my person and effects, and, with force and violence, took from me every paper and document which I then had about me or under my control," remembered Oaksmith. Once they reached the New York City wharfs the prisoner was then conveyed onto the Fall River Steamboat, while one of the deputies "carried my papers away with him" and the other two showed Oaksmith the order signed by Seward instructing Murray to take the prisoner to Fort Warren. Oaksmith was devastated. "Sick in body and mind, worn out with the indignities from which I had suffered, defenseless and deeply impressed with the conviction that the people were too much under the control of the '*terror*' to dare even to aid me in my efforts, if I had availed myself of what the law and Constitution gave me a perfect right to do—I suffered myself to be conveyed through three separate Judicial Districts, upon no higher authority than Wm. H. Seward's *individual order*, to Fort Warren." Oaksmith would later lament, "I blush when I think of my cowardice. I reproach myself for the shame, that I should have proved *myself* so false to the Constitution, as to have permitted these armed myrmidons of Murray thus to violate its sacred obligations through their treatment of me. Better by far to have put the question to the test, and have awakened the people of this country to a sense of their peril and impending degradation, by falling beneath the murderous bullets of these creatures of tyranny in the vindication of my liberty and manhood!"[4]

Murray's deputies carried with them a letter from Marshal Murray to Marshal Keyes, which began: "I send by Deputies Sheehan and McKay your particular friend Appleton Oaksmith and trust that you will see that justice is done him at the hands of a Boston Jury." Murray advised Keyes that bail be fixed at $15,000 but that "if there is any chance for him to obtain that amount I would suggest that you land him in Fort Warren for safety." Murray then closed with a line about another prisoner: "In relation to Pierce my impression is, that he will be bailed here, however, the manner in which I have handed Oaksmith over to you may change the programme."[5] Murray, in short, appeared to be increasingly willing to skirt normal judicial process when federal prisoners attempted to avail themselves of constitutional protections.

On Friday, December 20, Oaksmith arrived at Fort Warren—another large stone fortification meant to protect an American harbor but that now was being used as a prison. One Marylander who had arrived there shortly before Oaksmith wrote that "a more desolate place could not be imagined anywhere this side of the Arctic regions." Federal civil authorities were taking every precaution to make sure that Oaksmith could not somehow slip through the cracks. Marshal Keyes and US Attorney Richard Henry Dana Jr. met to discuss the matter, and then both wrote to Seward about how the transfer of authority should take place. "To prevent any accident or mistake," Keyes advised Seward, "I would suggest that the order of discharge should be enclosed to me, so that I may be at the Fort when it takes effect." Similarly, Dana told the secretary, "It will be better that the order be sent to the Marshal, than directly to Col. Dimmick [the commander at Fort Warren], lest there be some mistake or slip." Dana then added, "I am much obliged to you for your assistance to us in getting so important a man under control of law."[6]

At this point Oaksmith had no idea why he had been transferred to Fort Warren. His thoughts were with his family. On December 22 he wrote a short poem titled, "One Void," which spoke of the pain he felt at the thought of his son, Buchanan, who had died in infancy a few years before. The next day he penned a note to Seward. "I respectfully request to be 'paroled' for thirty days—solely for the purpose of attending to family matters which are suffering very seriously," he wrote. "Upon the expiration of my parole I will return to this Post, and await whatever '*the Power greater than Kings*' has in store for me, and in whose Justice I have a perfect faith." He then signed it, "Appleton Oaksmith, Prisoner of State."[7] As with his other correspondence with Seward, Oaksmith received no reply.

In some ways, Fort Warren was an improvement over Fort Lafayette. Political prisoners—like the Maryland prisoners, who'd been transferred here shortly before Oaksmith—were housed in the officers' quarters, unlike in the casemates at Fort Lafayette. These quarters consisted of two two-story buildings, each with one floor above ground and one below. Prisoners in the front of the buildings faced the parade ground and had well-lighted rooms, while those in the back faced the embankment of the fort's walls and had significantly less light. Whether above or below the ground level, these rooms were all dry and offered protection from the frigid Boston winter. One Maryland prisoner wrote home, "Tell Sister that I am more comfortable here than she would suppose. I occupy a very good room furnished nicely and intended for an officer of the Fort."

The prisoners were to be "treated with all kindness" and were permitted to purchase "such comforts as they require, if they have the pecuniary means." In other words, men with financial resources could make themselves comfortable. From the fort the prisoners could see ships in the harbor, church steeples, and the Bunker Hill Monument in the distance. Men with means fared well within the prison walls, with one writing, "money will enable you to live anywhere, especially where there is a Yankee near and he wants it, as he usually does." The prisoners even regularly enjoyed drinking wine and spirits. "Indeed we have a better daily table than any hotel affords; and whatever wine or luxuries we choose," wrote one inmate.

For leisure, the prisoners regularly engaged in religious worship, singing, playing cards and backgammon, smoking cigars, and giving speeches. One man wrote home to a friend in Maryland, "We have eight in one room, where we sit, sleep, read and write, play whist, play the guitar & fiddle, sing Dixie, sing the Star Spangled banner, dance, sing hymns, study the lives of the saints and the character of the martyrs . . . and have a great time generally." For outdoor exercise they played football. According to one observer, they "went at it like boys" as the parade ground became "a scene of merriment" among the distinguished state legislators and other political prisoners. Often, they socialized with their guards, and relations between the prisoners and the guards seemed unusually friendly.[8]

The commander at the fort, Colonel Justin Dimick, also seemed to have a more empathetic view of his role as commandant over the prisoners than had Martin Burke at Fort Lafayette. Nearing retirement (he was sixty-one years old), Dimick was highly regarded by the prisoners for his kindness, generosity, Christian faith, and military professionalism. One prisoner noted that he "will always make courtesy and humanity consist with his military duty," while another called him "a gentleman of the old school." In fact, the very same prisoners from Maryland who had protested their treatment in New York spoke highly of Dimick. George William Brown, the ex-mayor of Baltimore, later recollected "the warm feelings of respect and friendship with which he was regarded by the prisoners who knew him best, for the unvarying kindness and humanity with which he performed the difficult and painful duties of his office. As far as he was permitted to do so, he promoted the comfort and convenience of all."[9]

Of course, some in the State Department were not pleased with Dimick's lax treatment of the prisoners. Seth C. Hawley warned Seward that Dimick's watch over the political and military prisoners "is conducted too loosely" and that it might be best to put someone in charge of the prison "who will feel that this is a business of life and death." Of great concern to Hawley was that the political prisoners and POWs could mingle together. Hawley feared that the prisoners might easily escape or overtake the guards. Not wanting to be known as the source of this criticism, though, Hawley added, "I would not like to have it known to the military gentlemen that I have made these suggestions as I know nothing of war, &c."[10]

Despite Hawley's attempt to separate the political and military prisoners, a special camaraderie seems to have developed among the prisoners at Fort Warren that did not exist at other Civil War prisons. Autograph books still survive in archival institutions around the United States, filled with signatures, sentiments, dates of capture, and home addresses.[11] While imprisoned, Oaksmith signed a number of these, usually writing an impromptu verse to accompany his signature. These lines often suggested that the future would judge the nation's present leaders for their actions.

> Time writes his verdicts in eternal thought;
> The future sits in judgment on the past;
> The wrongs of men, by whomsoever wrought,
> Are not ordained perpetual to last:
>> The verdict soon or late will set them right
>> Whose motto is "For Truth to brunt the fight!"

Oaksmith hoped that others "may learn the worth of lessons taught us here." In another autograph book he wrote:

> Nations may fall and flags be swept away,
> The idle dreams of fame fade one by one,
> The light of unknown heroes of to-day
> Go down to-morrow in a glorious sun:
>> But one great principle will never die,
>> *A people's right to choose its destiny.*

And to yet another prisoner, he dedicated these lines:

> When other years have brought their full return
> Of peace, throughout this desolated land,
> May we who in these walls in bondage yearn,
> Strangers, but yet a sympathetic band,
>> Find in the world and in each heart the test
>> *That what we did and thought was for the best.*[12]

When Oaksmith first arrived at Fort Warren he brought news to some of the Marylanders about their friends who remained at Fort Lafayette. Nevertheless, Oaksmith quickly became a pariah in this new bastille. One Maryland legislator noted that he "was a man of fine personal appearance, intelligent and polished in his manners." But the Maryland legislators "did not desire the company of a slave trader" and also "suspected him of being a spy," so they refused to allow him to join their mess. The legislators wrongly believed that Oaksmith had been "a prominent and active member of the Black Republican party" during the election of 1860. One day when Oaksmith sat down at the mess-table "uninvited," the other prisoners took "no notice" of him, which Oaksmith took "very hard."[13]

Christmas Day 1861 was a time of great celebration at Fort Warren. Citizens from Boston, Baltimore, and elsewhere sent loads of food and presents to the prisoners at the fort, and the men feasted on turkey, ham, beef, venison, lobster, cranberries, pastries, iced fruit cakes, and other delicacies. They also drank large quantities of wine, brandy, eggnog, and apple toddies. According to one Marylander, "We were enabled to dispense the good things to all."[14] It is unknown whether Oaksmith joined in the revelry. Sitting in his cell, he could hear the distant chimes of church bells in Boston. Saddened, he wrote a short poem called "Footprints" that took him back to childhood memories of Christmastime.

> Alone, within my silent cell,
> I hear the Christmas chimes
> The dear old chimes I loved so well
> In far-off happier times.
> But ah! where is the joy that lent
> Such music to their tone,
> Which lit the brow too early bent
> By sorrows not its own?
>
> Within these walls their echoes ring
> Most mockingly to me;
> They serve but memories to bring
> Of things I may not see:
> They garner up the sheaves of thought
> From all the furrowed plain,
> O'er which from childhood I have wrought,
> And bring them back again.

Oaksmith "trace[d] the footprints of my life," thinking back to more innocent times and "memories of the past," hoping he might learn something by "looking calmly back."

And so these holy days may bring
New faith to such as I,
Who yet may see the hopes of spring
Shine through the wintry sky;
And as my footsteps onward tend
Through the long vale of Time,
My heart with childhood's faith shall bend
To hear the Christmas chime.[15]

That evening, about fifty prisoners gathered in one of the underground quarters near the sally port to hold "the trial and execution of Wm. H. Seward for treason, in having abolished the Constitution and the Laws and usurped the Government." A "stuffed figure . . . representing the culprit" sat in a makeshift criminal box, while a "judge" presided, twelve jurymen were selected, and "the prisoner [Seward] was assigned counsel." The prosecuting attorney made an opening statement. Both lawyers then examined witnesses and made speeches. Once the case was closed the jury deliberated for a short period before finding "Seward" guilty. The "judge" then made a speech about "the enormity of his crimes and the justness of his condemnation" and then sentenced the effigy to be executed, which was "immediately" done. One of the prison guards was present for the entire proceeding, "and between the trial and a bucket of egg-nog on the table in the corner of the room where he stood, seemed to enjoy it very much." The prisoners were confident that when he awoke the next morning he would find "his recollection of the doings of the previous night very much impaired." At least they hoped so, for some worried that they might get in trouble for what they'd done. Wrote one prisoner to his mother, "What jokes we cracked, what songs we sang, and the name of the obnoxious individual whose effigy we sentenced to an ignominious fate, after a solemn trial, verdict found & sentenced rendered—these are secrets not to be communicated now or here."[16]

If Oaksmith attended the mock trial of Seward that Christmas night, he undoubtedly enjoyed it. The Christmas chimes he'd heard earlier in the day may have also increased his faith that he would soon be released from Dimick's charge. But it would not be for the reason that he hoped. On December 23, Seward issued an order for Oaksmith to be released from Fort Warren. He also instructed Keyes to "cause a police examination to be made, in some cases, of the persons and baggage of prisoners discharged from custody, to the end that no correspondences or other improper papers, be conveyed by them to persons outside the Fort."[17]

On December 27, Oaksmith signed one final autograph book, opening with the line, "Hope springs eternal in the human breast."[18] Shortly thereafter he was summoned to Dimick's office where the colonel told him "that an order had come for his release." Oaksmith asked to see the order and then realized the awful truth—that he was to be turned over to Marshal Keyes and subjected to a police examination. He was released in Boston and then immediately rearrested by civilian authorities. According to one news report, Marshal Keyes "pounced upon him with a warrant" for his arrest for outfitting the slaver *Margaret Scott*.[19] At 11 a.m. the following morning, Saturday, December 28, Oaksmith appeared before US district judge Peleg Sprague for a bail hearing. The *Boston Herald* reported, "He is a man apparently about 35 to 40 years of age, nearly six feet high, rather fleshy, and of very fine general appearance. He has a full beard, dark and very long, dark brown hair, exceedingly keen eyes, and physiognomy exhibiting great coolness, caution and intelligence."

Federal prosecutor Richard Henry Dana Jr.—a maritime law expert whose own career at sea had become famous in *Two Years Before the Mast*—made an opening statement in which he described Oaksmith as "the recognized head and agent" of "an immense [slave trading] organization in New York." Oaksmith, according to Dana, "has been a main actor in fitting out slave ships, and vast amounts of money have slipped through his hands. . . . It has been suspected that in almost every department of this government this gold has been used to prevent the triumph of justice." One of Oaksmith's recent dupes had been Samuel P. Skinner, whom Dana called "a poor man" and Oaksmith's "tool." Dana told the court that it had been "almost impossible" to get Oaksmith "here, and his arrest at last was due to accident." Fortunately, Secretary of State Seward had gotten involved so that he might be tried in Boston, although Dana pointed out that Oaksmith was also under indictment in New York for fitting out a slaver.

"No, sir; that is not so," interjected Oaksmith. "I was never indicted in my life before." (Oaksmith was technically correct, although he would soon be under indictment in New York.)

"I think I am right," continued Dana. "I think there is an indictment against him in New York."

Because he believed Oaksmith was such a major player in the slave trade, Dana maintained that "a small amount of bail would be useless" since Oaksmith "must have a great amount of capital at his command." Moreover, "he had been asked to employ counsel, and afforded every opportunity to do so." So Dana suggested $20,000 so that "there might be no escape from justice by means of straw bail or low bail."

When Oaksmith stood to address the bench, he told the judge that "this is the first time I have ever been before a court in this capacity. It will

Richard Henry Dana Jr., ca. 1870.
Courtesy of the National Portrait Gallery, Smithsonian Institution.

be useless for me to say it at the present time, but as God Almighty is my judge, I never, in any way, shape or manner, have been interested in the slave traffic. If any circumstances of my life have given the District Attorney good cause to think I am as guilty as he says, it is my misfortune. He has stated many circumstances I never heard of before." Oaksmith pointed out that Dana now seemed to think that Skinner was innocent. "The time may come when he may think me fully as innocent."

Oaksmith challenged Dana's assumption that he had had an opportunity to hire counsel. In fact, just the opposite was true. Although Oaksmith did not say so, he could have pointed out that, during his imprisonment, military authorities and State Department officials had explicitly prevented him and the other political prisoners from finding legal representation. "I clearly am a victim of persecution," he continued, recounting his recent ordeal of being "torn from home, and thrown into a dungeon" and searched and rearrested. In light of all the violations of his constitutional rights, Oaksmith wondered aloud, "it seems useless to employ counsel."

Oaksmith wanted the court to know that he was not the wealthy man the prosecutor supposed. "I am not worth one single farthing in the world," he told the court. "I think it will be an utter impossibility for me to raise one thousand dollars by going among all my relatives and friends." He pointed out that his mother had some property she might be able to sell to help make bail, but "I could not hope to raise one-fourth part of the sum the District Attorney has named." Oaksmith conceded that "there must have been some suspicious circumstances, or honest men would never have got the foundation for so long an indictment as this one. But there are two sides to every question, and the learned counsel for the government will find there is a very different one to this case from that which he now sees."

Again, Dana read the statute under which Oaksmith was being charged and suggested that bail be set at $20,000. At this Oaksmith made a curious reply, revealing that he must have been following other slave trading cases in the press. "Your Honor," he began, "I have always endeavored to keep posted in the current literature of the times, and I have never heard of a case where a person charged with this offence has been required to give more than $5,000 bonds." Judge Sprague admitted that he had seen no evidence other than the claims in the indictment, and so he must balance the competing interests of the government and the defendant. He therefore set the amount at $5,000.

Dana stated that he wanted Oaksmith to be required to appear in court "from day to day," but Oaksmith replied, "I don't think I can get that amount of bail; I don't think you need have any uneasiness." "I don't know about that," retorted Dana. Judge Sprague then reminded Dana that the whole purpose of bail was to ensure that the prisoner appeared when his trial began during the March term of the court. Oaksmith was returned to jail, unable to procure the $5,000.

On January 4, 1862, Oaksmith again appeared in court—this time to ask for a reduction in bail. He read affidavits from six persons who confirmed that he was insolvent, could barely support his family, could not pay his debts, and was "not in a position to procure large Bail." Two of the deponents testified that Oaksmith could not have been involved in the slave trade without their knowledge; one pointed out that he had declared bankruptcy in July 1861; several stated that his arrest had destroyed his ship brokerage business; and Elizabeth Oakes Smith stated that her son's young family had been staying with her since his arrest since they could not support themselves.

In court, Oaksmith recounted the details of his arrest, maintaining that he had been "brought into the jurisdiction of this Honorable Court by fraud and violence on the part of the United States Government and its officers, in direct violation of all law, justice, or precedent." He stated that he had not owned a vessel "in whole or in part, of any kind" for more than three years, and that he *"has never been engaged in the Slave trade,* and has never had any interest in any vessel engaged in or fitted out for that traffic." Moreover, Oaksmith argued that the indictment upon which he had been arrested had been obtained while he *"was illegally and unconstitutionally deprived of his liberty"* and that "all of the allegations contained" in the indictment "are wholly false, malicious and untrue."

Taking all of this into account, Judge Sprague reduced the bail to $4,000. A San Francisco paper remarked, "When brought up for examination, Oaksmith played the persecuted, poverty-stricken saint to perfection, calling God to witness that he had never in any way or shape been interested in the slave-trade."[20] Perhaps it was a ruse, but he truly had no way of obtaining that kind of money.

9

CHARLES STREET JAIL

Appleton Oaksmith's new home was a cell in the county jail in Boston. Built between 1848 and 1851, this "new" Boston penitentiary— known as the Suffolk County Jail or the Charles Street Jail—was a model of prison ingenuity, combining the idea of an "inside cellblock" with a "cruciform" configuration, which was popular among European asylums. Prisons modeled in the cruciform style had a central structure that served as the jailor's residence and guardroom, or observatory, with four wings. This design had become widely used by the second quarter of the nineteenth century because it gave prison guards clear lines of sight down every corridor of cells. Inside each cellblock the cells were arranged back-to-back, and corridors separated the cells from the exterior walls (creating the "inside cellblock"). Each cell measured eight feet by eleven feet with a ten-foot-high ceiling (much more spacious than the cells at Auburn Prison in New York, which were three and a half feet by seven feet with seven-foot ceilings). The north and south wings had fifty cells each, and the long east wing had 120 cells. Each wing housed different classes of inmates: debtors and witnesses were held in the south wing; women and juveniles in the north; and criminals—either pre- or post-trial—in the east. Separating out these various classes of inmates enabled state authorities to use architecture to promote morality, "preventing, as it does," reported physician Solomon D. Townsend, "the communication of the experience of those hardened in guilt to those just entering the threshold."[1]

The center of the "cross" design was an octagonal, roughly 4,900-square-foot "great central guard and inspection room." The prison's designers noted that all four aboveground floors of the four wings of the prison "are easy of access, and under control and supervision from one central position, viz., the large octagon Guard Room."[2] (Of great significance, the prisoners could not see the guards from their cells.) The prison had room for instruction, religious observance, and work. Prisoners who demonstrated good con-

Charles Street Jail.
Courtesy of the Library of Congress.

duct could even have access to "privilege rooms," which were much larger cells at the end of the north and south wings—"well and agreeably lighted, with room for exercise, and furnished with good and clean bedding, the lofty areas giving sufficient and healthful ventilation"—that served the purpose of "*encouragement.*"[3]

The prison's architect boasted of the institution's security features. From the guardroom, "the *supervision* extends outside and inside, to all the principal walls, windows, corridors, staircases, galleries, cells, doors, fastenings; so that one sentinel on duty in the guard room can see more, know more, exercise more control, prevent more escapes, than many men on duty in an ordinary Prison." He continued:

> The *security* against escape is also seen in the plan of building in this respect: it is a Prison within a Prison, so that, if a prisoner breaks the wall of his cell, he is still in Prison, and has another wall to break, while at the same time he is in sight and hearing of the sentinel in the guard room.
>
> This *security* is increased by the construction in this, also—that it admits of an entire separation of the prisoners, thus placing the responsibility of breaking a cell on the individual occupying that cell, and on him alone.

The cells being as numerous as any probable number of prisoners, the prisoners can be separated entirely, especially at night, one from another, and, so far as is necessary, by day and by night.[4]

One early visitor to the Suffolk County Jail remarked that "perfect security against escape has been furnished, the keepers having a supervision of the whole edifice, not only from the centre area, but from their private rooms." If the lines of vision were not enough, the ability to hear sounds from all parts of the prison also contributed to the security of the jail. "But the most happy effect of the arrangement in management of such an institution is the perfect silence which reigns throughout," continued this observer. "Standing in the centre area, where all the cells can be overlooked, no one would be sensible that a human being was confined there."[5]

Whereas some early nineteenth-century prisons, such as Eastern State Penitentiary in Philadelphia, had dark, foreboding exteriors to "exhibit as much as possible the great strength and convey to the mind a cheerless blank indicative of the misery that awaits the unhappy being who enters within its walls," the Charles Street Jail's exterior, according to one contemporary, was "perfectly simple, unadorned and substantial." By the 1840s, some American penologists had been pushing for less frightening prison exteriors. "I do not like the appearance of these dark, funeral pall galleries," wrote one prison official. "A prison is never more likely to reform man by being made dark, gloomy, and dismal. The confinement is punishment enough, without adding to it by darkness and blackness. The lighter, the whiter, and the purer, the more likely to answer the benevolent purpose of a penitentiary."[6]

The Charles Street Jail appears to have been built on this idea—constructed with expensive Quincy granite, and in a "new and dignified North Italian mode of the Renaissance Revival" that one historian describes as "unadorned" yet "quite sophisticated." The prison boasted thirty enormous windows—ten feet wide by thirty-three feet high—in the walls of the wings and in the central guardroom, providing significantly more daylight to the interior of the building than other penal institutions. In addition, each of these windows had beneath it other windows that were ten feet wide and nine feet high. When the prison opened in 1851, visitors came from throughout the United States to marvel. "This is beautiful," remarked an astonished Kentucky jurist in 1852. "This is justice and humanity combined. The crime is punished, but the man himself is respected." A year later, a Missouri minister called it "the model prison of the age."[7]

Oaksmith found himself in Cell No. 9—on the west side of the south wing on the main floor (which was actually the second story). This corridor had four cells plus a fifth that was attached to a privilege room. It is unclear why he was not placed among the criminals in the east wing. It may have been because he was a federal prisoner, or because he stood accused of a nonviolent crime. Inside the cell, Oaksmith had a bed with extra blankets, a chair, a kerosene lamp, and a table on which he kept books, newspapers, a pen, ink, and paper. Soon after moving in, he covered his window and door with newspapers. "Visitors, coming in, would want to know where Oakes Smith's cell was, & of course they had a curiosity to see him, & I suppose they looked in," recalled one turnkey (this was a term used for jailers). These "curtains" gave Oaksmith some semblance of privacy. "I suppose he put them up to prevent people from looking into his room," recalled another prison employee. "Anybody coming in to the door could look right into his room."

Throughout his time in prison, Oaksmith entertained visitors. His mother occasionally made the trek from New York. "She was there in the spring often; I think she has not been there since his trial," recalled one prison official. "I won't be certain but she was there once since the trial." Other visitors included his brother Edward, a store clerk named G. Bacon who was about thirty-five or forty years old, a Mrs. Beers, a Miss Bennett (one of these ladies claimed to be a cousin), a Warren Appleton, a young boy (whose identity is unknown, possibly Mrs. Beers's son), and a Mr. Phelps who knew Elizabeth and had previously served on the governor's council.

In the summer, Oaksmith "complained of being sick" to Dr. Solomon D. Townsend, the physician tasked with caring for federal prisoners. As a result, Oaksmith "was allowed to come out & exercise in the guard-room" after the other prisoners were locked up in their cells. The doctor had not ordered this exercise, but it had been done in the past for other prisoners, so the guards thought nothing of letting Oaksmith do the same. After all, the guardroom was essentially a "prison within a prison" and not even the guards had keys to let themselves out. Often in the evenings, Oaksmith would sit at the desk in the guardroom reading or writing. The guards were probably captivated by what one acquaintance described as his "winning features and mild, suave and polished manners." Occasionally he chatted with them. "He sat reading the newspapers, talking politics, & telling stories," recalled one officer at the jail. "He is a man who has travelled a good deal, and used to interest us by telling of his travels."[8]

On January 18, 1862, Oaksmith sent a petition to the federal court asking for a further reduction in bail. He claimed that the prosecutors had made "many statements" that were "entirely false and untrue, and which uncontradicted were of a nature to prejudice the interests of this deponent before this Honorable Court." And in cryptic language, Oaksmith alleged that since his last hearing on January 4, "an Act of Providence" had "placed it within [my] power . . . to have left the jurisdiction of this Court without Bail or hindrance." To do so, however, would have been "inconsistent" with his "honor" and so he "did not avail [myself] of such opportunity and did not sustain any idea of so doing." But Oaksmith wanted the court to know that he'd had this opportunity—whatever it was—as "corroboration" of his "repeated assertions" that he had "no desire or intent to avoid this trial or do anything contrary to Law and right."[9] The court, nevertheless, refused to reduce bail any further.

On January 31, Oaksmith penned a long letter "To the Public" describing the ordeal he had endured since the previous summer and decrying the accusations against him that had been circulating in the press. With "sorrow and indignation" he told his readers that "every allegation which has been paraded before the public regarding me" was rooted in "utter untruthfulness and malice." In justice to his family, the public, and himself, he now needed to reveal the truth.

Oaksmith claimed that his accuser, US Marshal Robert Murray, was "an unscrupulous and bad man" who was abusing his "very extraordinary powers." He claimed that Murray knew that he was innocent "and is actuated only by base and cowardly motives." Oaksmith pointed out that every article in the press about him "invariably closes with an elaborate encomium of the wonderful skill, ability, fidelity and zeal of the incorruptible Marshal Murray." He wondered, "*Would it require a very penetrating mind to guess at the source of all these things! Let the public* THINK!" (In this, Oaksmith was correct—Murray regularly fed self-aggrandizing stories to the *Tribune*.)

Throughout the long ordeal, Oaksmith claimed that Murray "has endeavored, by the most unscrupulous means, to blacken my name, and PREJUDICE MY CASE, and he has succeeded in so far that I find it impossible to procure bail in this city for even the moderate sum of four thousand dollars." Had Oaksmith made as much money in slave trading as he was accused, then why did he "*find it impossible to raise four thousand dollars' bail, and am lying sick and suffering in prison from an utter inability on the part of myself and family to get it.*"

Horace Greeley published Oaksmith's "manifesto" in the *New York Tribune* with a comment that the prisoner deserved "a hearing" since the accusations against him had been circulating so widely in the press. "If he has spoken wisely and well, so be it," concluded Greeley; "if not, the error and the damage are his own."[10] It is unclear how the manifesto was received among the public, but it certainly resonated with families of political prisoners. The son of a Maryland legislator kept a handwritten excerpt from it with his father's letters, remarking that his father had been "imprisoned, without cause or charge, by order of that Arch-fiend William H. Seward, in 'Fortress Monroe,' 'Fort Lafayette,' and 'Fort Warren.'"[11]

On February 1, Oaksmith penned a poem called "Unrecognized" that expressed how it felt to be in jail, accused of a heinous crime, and bound to "breast alone Life's overwhelming sea." It began:

> I am content,
> Unrecognized by all the world, to wait
> And do, with uncomplaining lips, my stent
> Of human fate.

Sitting in prison, "severed" from his loved ones, he knew that "friends prove / False" and that "human praise" was little more than "vanity." He now had "To stand alone, / And have men deem us worse than we have been." Unable to turn to friends or loved ones, he instead knelt to God in prayer, "And in my isolation every grief of mine / To Him reveal."

> Without a sigh
> I'll stand and meet my woes as best I can;
> Feeling, to bravely face one's destiny,
> Becomes the man.

Despite his efforts to bear his imprisonment with fortitude, loneliness and despair continued to creep in. Later in February he penned a sonnet entitled "Deserted" about how "Friendship and Love . . . fail us in misfortunes night."[12] He likely thought a great deal about his two little daughters, and his wife, who was pregnant. On March 18, Isotta delivered a baby boy—Peyton Randolph Oaksmith, who would be known by his middle name.[13]

But Oaksmith had not been completely forgotten by the outside world. One correspondent told him, "We were speaking of you last night & all had the same impression that you would be with us soon, God grant it may be so." At home, Oaksmith was "thought of, with the kindest remembrances. . . . All join in love to you, & prayers for your deliverance." Oaksmith also corresponded with at least one of his former cellmates from Fort Lafayette, Ruston Maury, who assured him that the crew of the *Augusta* had been "well cared for" after Oaksmith's transfer to Boston. Oaksmith had apparently asked Maury for assistance in procuring money

for bail, but Maury replied, "I have no future, no money, & few friends.
. . . I would gladly help you out with Bail if in my power, but my dear
fellow I am not able."[14]

In late March, Oaksmith sent an urgent note to Horace Greeley. "Will
you please come to me without loss of time," he wrote. "The reasons which
impel me to this request are not alone of a selfish or cowardly nature, and
that they have been duly considered must be perfectly apparent to you."
His reasons for needing to see Greeley, he said, were of "sufficient weight
to justify the request." And he warned Greeley, "Do not go near *any of the
United States officials* here, but take a carriage directly for the Cambridge St.
Jail and ask for *me, at* any hour between 9 A.M. & 9 P.M., and you will be
permitted to see me *privately.* I await your coming."[15] Nothing appears to
have come of this message, but the letter does indicate that Oaksmith may
have gained the trust or friendship of some of the prison officials, who were
county, not federal, employees.

At some point during this incarceration, Elizabeth Oakes Smith
relayed an offer of release to her son, but it was on terms that he would
never accept (this may be what Oaksmith was referring to in January
when he asked for his bail to be lowered). She later described it in some
detail in her diary:

> I could not till these great trials came upon us, have believed that any
> human being would be so willfully, deliberately, and indignantly given
> to lying, as this same man [Marshal Murray]. Atrocious falsehoods have
> been told by him and he has induced others to perjure themselves by
> swearing to them, only that he might break down Appleton, and render
> my whole family odious. He does this because we are of the Democratic
> party, and it is a part of the system of this wicked Administration.
>
> Appleton was offered a good office, his freedom, and all proceed-
> ings to be quashed, provided he would perjure himself and denounce
> Mr. Andrews, who has an office in the Custom house, and is in the
> way of W. H. Seward. Appleton refused indignantly. The offer was
> made through me—I said I would rather see him in his grave. I had
> full confidence in him. I wrote him all that passed at the interview,
> but gave no advice.
>
> Language cannot describe the amount of perjury daily practiced—the
> bribes offered and taken—my heart is sick at the record—and I, who
> have lived in an atmosphere so different, find it often difficult to believe
> what I hear, and see.[16]

Several years later, Oakes Smith gave a more detailed account of what
had happened. According to this later recollection, she received a message

requesting her to travel to New York City *"upon important business."* She went with her son Edward and was escorted by Jeremiah G. Hamilton to the office of a Mr. James B. Taylor, whom Hamilton represented as an owner of the *New York Times* and a confidante of Secretary Seward. Oakes Smith observed "a door slightly ajar, and knew that our astute Secretary of State was *honorably* ensconced in the adjoining room," silently eaves dropping on their conversation.

After some small talk, Taylor made a list of proposals to Oakes Smith, which she was to communicate to Appleton:

> First. Mr Oaksmith's debts should be paid up to the amount of ten thousand dollars.
> Second. He should be appointed to an office in the Custom House.
> Third. All legal proceedings against Mr Oaksmith should be quashed.
> In return for all this, Mr Oaksmith was to denounce a certain person in the Office of the District Attorney [Stewart L. Woodford], *as having received a certain sum of money in return for services connected with the slave trade*, the said person being then politically prominent.

Oakes Smith "listened with indignation" and, rising partially from her chair, exclaimed, "I would see him in his grave first." She was "humiliated at the insult we had received, distressed upon every side, ruined in name and fortune," but eventually concluded, "If he will do this he is past praying for. But I must know of what metal he is made." She wrote her son a letter revealing the offer from these "Bribers, and abettors of Perjury," but did not state any of her own thoughts about the offer. Appleton soon replied in a letter, "If they want a perjured scoundrel they must look somewhere else for him. I am not their man." Elizabeth fell on her knees and thanked God that her son was so honorable. She claimed that other similar offers had been made on other occasions but that Appleton finally told her, "Do not tell me of these humiliating overtures." Oakes Smith was disgusted by Seward. She believed he had become Appleton's "mortal enemy" because of the manifesto Oaksmith wrote from prison in which he disclosed to the public how Seward abused *"that little bell."* She concluded, "Shame on such vile exercise of power! Shame on the men, who seek to build up themselves and party on the ruin of all that should be dear and honorable to manhood."[17]

Throughout this ordeal, Elizabeth carried herself in public as well as she could. One family friend noted that "her eyes are brilliant, complexion clear, her appetite good & she appears full of life animation & good courage for the future," apparently still exuding confidence that the charges against her son would be dropped.[18] But in her heart she was suffering deeply. She asked famous friends and acquaintances to help secure Appleton's release. She knew the Catholic theologian Orestes A. Brownson was well connected in Washington, and she asked him to "say a good word for us when it may do us some good, with Mr Lincoln, who is, I am sure, a well disposed, kindly hearted man."[19] She also implored her old friend and fellow writer, Sarah H. Whitman, to write to Secretary of the Interior Caleb B. Smith on Appleton's behalf. Whitman was "surprised & touched & deeply pained" by the "sorrowful letter from Eva." "My heart aches for her," she continued. "It is all very very sad."

Whitman did as Oakes Smith requested. She asked Secretary Smith "to spare [Appleton] all unnecessary rigor & restriction while awaiting his trial" on behalf of his mother, "one of our most loyal & honored American women who has for many years been known to the public, through her various literary productions, as a woman of great genius & culture. She is struck down by the blow which falls upon her son." But Whitman refused to say anything about Appleton's guilt or innocence. Years later she explained to a friend, "I said to the authorities what [Oakes Smith] *wished* me to say, with the exception of giving my own testimony to [Appleton's] character as an honorable gentleman, which *I could not do* with truth, as my acquaintance with him was slight." This omission caused a great rift in the friendship between Whitman and Oakes Smith (Whitman's letter was made public in official US Senate records and was likely then seen by Oakes Smith). "After that our correspondence, which had been friendly & affectionate (for I sincerely loved her), ceased altogether," wrote Whitman in 1874. (In her autobiography, Oakes Smith accounted for the split in the friendship simply by saying, "A series of events had suspended for awhile our correspondence.") In reality, it made little difference what Whitman wrote, for Caleb Smith replied bluntly that his department had no authority over these matters.[20]

That Elizabeth Oakes Smith would forsake a dear friend in this way reveals just how severely she had been struck down by the blow of her son's arrest. "I have trodden the vine-press alone," she confided to her diary. "I have been dragged in the dust of humiliation and sorrow. So sudden and unexpected was the calamity upon our household, that for a time we could not comprehend its nature. Now we begin to unravel the threads of malignity which some secret enemy has been winding around us."[21]

10

EXECUTION

While Appleton Oaksmith wallowed in his cell at the Charles Street Jail, a drama involving the Atlantic slave trade was coming to a climax back in New York City. An ugly scene had unfolded on August 7, 1860, on the coast of West Africa. As the sun beat down on the mouth of the Congo River that day, 897 African men, women, and children were shoved aboard a slaving vessel called the *Erie*. Nearly half of them were children, with one an infant of just six months old. None appeared much older than forty. Captain Nathaniel Gordon had purchased these captives with whiskey. Now, as they boarded his vessel, the heartless slave trader separated the men from the women and used a knife to cut any remnants of their clothes from their bodies so that they were totally naked. It took only about forty-five minutes to load the unfortunate cargo. Clearly an expert in the trade, Gordon packed "the Negroes . . . wonderfully close, [so] that their sufferings were really agonizing, and that the stench arising from their unchecked filthiness was absolutely startling." Indeed, one witness later stated that the "filth and dirt upon their persons [was] indescribably offensive" as the slaves had been detained belowdecks with little ventilation, ridden with open sores, and in their own excrement and vomit.[1]

Gordon set sail out of the mouth of the Congo River the following morning, August 8. One of his crewmen later testified that Gordon promised the sailors "$1 per head for every negro he landed alive on the coast of Cuba." As the voyage got underway, Gordon spotted a ship in the distance. Mistakenly supposing that she was a British warship, he ran up the American flag at which point the unknown vessel fired a warning shot at the *Erie*. Gordon had made a fatal error, for the ship that had hauled up next to him was the USS *Mohican*, a steam-powered sloop of war that had recently joined the Africa Squadron.[2] Gordon's entire voyage was over in only a few hours.

This was Gordon's fourth and final slaving venture. He'd had the *Erie* fitted out and provisioned in Havana, Cuba, in the spring of 1860. He "solemnly" swore to the American consul there that his ship was "chartered for a legal voyage to the coast of Africa." Gordon also promised the crew that this was a "legitimate voyage." The consul was "morally convinced" that the vessel was a slaving ship but believed he had "no right, under the law, to detain her."[3] So Gordon was on his way to Africa and his fateful encounter with the *Mohican*.

The commander of the *Mohican*, Sylvanus W. Godon, found a number of foreigners on board the *Erie* "claiming to be passengers." Even more, "there was no acknowledged Captain or mate, and no Ships papers to be found." He did locate a clearance from Havana dated January 20, 1860, that listed Gordon as the captain, but Gordon told Godon that "he sold the vessel up the Congo, and is now a passenger on board." Not believing this excuse, Godon arrested Gordon "and two persons believed to be mates." Commander Godon placed a prize crew on the *Erie* and ordered them to sail to Liberia, where the captives would be set free. Godon also placed Gordon and the two mates aboard and ordered the prize crew to then "proceed to New York" so that the ship could be condemned and sold, and the slave traders could face prosecution. (The *Erie* would be sold at auction on February 5, 1861, for $7,823.25.) He sent four of Gordon's crew—Thomas Nelson, Samuel Sleeper, Thomas Savage, and John McCafferty—aboard another vessel, the *Marion*, to Portsmouth, New Hampshire, for trial.[4]

As the *Erie* made the two-week, 1,500-mile journey to Monrovia, some three dozen Africans died of disease. One official in Liberia noted that the captives were "poor, nude, emaciated, enfeebled and dying creatures, hundreds of them Boys and Girls." Despite attaining freedom, they would still be far from their homes, and among strangers and in the Western culture in Liberia. In fact, in Liberia some were exploited as cheap labor.[5]

Gordon would eventually arrive in New York City on October 3, 1860 (the same day that his four crewmen arrived in Portsmouth). On October 25, US Attorney James J. Roosevelt (Delafield Smith's predecessor) indicted Gordon for piracy and engaging in the slave trade. He also indicted Gordon's two mates, William Warren and David Hall, for voluntarily serving on a slaver. But Roosevelt then offered Gordon a plea bargain. If Gordon would identify his financial backers in New York, the prosecutor would drop the piracy charge—which was a capital offense. Under this agreement, Gordon would face no more than two years imprisonment and a $2,000 fine. Roosevelt offered this deal because New

York was "the head and front of the slave trade" and Gordon's testimony would be "of much more use to the government than by hanging [him]." Feeling overconfident—since no American had ever been executed for slave trading—Gordon rejected the offer. Soon, however, Roosevelt was pilloried in the press. The *New York Times* blasted the plea deal, headlining, "Punishment for the Slave Trade to be Abolished." Roosevelt quickly relented and rescinded the offer, much to Gordon's dismay, since he had changed his mind about the deal. Even still, it does not appear that Roosevelt did much to prepare for the trial.[6]

On November 22, Gordon's crewmembers—Thomas Nelson, Samuel Sleeper, Thomas Savage, and John McCafferty—were convicted in the US circuit court in Portsmouth, New Hampshire, of serving aboard a slaver. They were sentenced to pay a one-dollar fine and imprisonment at the common jail in Portsmouth until September 15, 1861. On May 9, 1861, they were tried for piracy but were acquitted.[7] On May 11, two days after their acquittal, the four men penned a letter to Lincoln asking for pardon for their earlier conviction. They claimed to have joined Gordon's ship in Havana, Cuba, in the spring of 1860 without knowing the real purpose of the voyage. They thought it was a "trading voyage," they said, but after they discharged the cargo in Africa and took on the captive Africans, they realized they had been deceived. The four men claimed that Gordon gave them the opportunity to remain in Africa instead of serving on the return voyage, but they knew they could not have done that. "If we had gone on shore and remained, it would have been certain death. If we had manifested any opposition to the objects of the voyage, our lives would have been taken," they told the president. So they chose to remain on board the *Erie*. They pleaded, "We were entirely ignorant of the character of the voyage, until after we had been some time at sea. After this time we were in duress."

The four prisoners told Lincoln that "some of us served in the United States Navy" and that "we are innocent of the offence, for which we are suffering punishment." They promised that if Lincoln would remit their sentence they would "be glad" to enlist in the Union navy. The local sheriff, the prosecuting attorney, and the judge who convicted them all signed the letter saying that they thought Lincoln should agree to these terms; however, Lincoln chose not to interfere with their sentences.[8] They would have to serve out their time in prison.

Initially Gordon was imprisoned in the Eldridge Street Jail, a minimum-security prison where he was "dined and wined to an almost unlimited extent," and, for a $50 bribe to the jailor, was even allowed to leave and walk around the city "on his parole" that he would return. In earlier cases, some accused slave traders had made their escape from the United States under such circumstances, but Gordon was not particularly worried at this point about his fate. The US marshal later wrote that Gordon considered himself "not as a felon, but a gentleman temporarily out of his latitude." But in April 1861, Lincoln appointed Robert Murray US marshal for the Southern District of New York. Murray quickly moved Gordon and his two mates to the New York City Hall of Justice, also known as "the Tombs"—a large, granite structure built in the Egyptian style in 1838. One New York City guidebook stated that "the melancholy aspect of the building makes one give an involuntary shiver as he passes." An early history of the city added that it was the place "where the worst felons and murderers are confined."[9]

The warden at the Tombs observed that Gordon and his mates initially "felt but little concern at their arrest and imprisonment—there never having been as yet anyone hanged for their offence." But when the Lincoln administration took control of the federal government, the prisoners "became greatly alarmed at their position."[10] Delafield Smith's appointment as US attorney for the Southern District of New York on April 4, 1861, gave Gordon a reason to be concerned. A prominent New York Republican, Smith received bipartisan support from the bench and bar of the state. One judge of the Supreme Court of New York noted that in court he "is a ready speaker and examines witnesses searchingly and well."[11]

The trial commenced on June 18, 1861—about the same time that Oaksmith was beginning to fight to regain control of the *Augusta*. Throughout the proceedings, Delafield Smith made a strong case for execution. He tried to persuade the jury that "the slave traffic has no connection whatever with slavery" so that conservative jurors might not allow their racial prejudices to hang the jury. The defense argued that Gordon had been born outside of the United States, and that he had sold the *Erie* to foreigners in Cuba—that, in fact, Gordon was "merely an idle spectator" on the vessel. First Mate William Warren, who himself was under indictment for his role in the venture, testified that the *Erie* was under the command of a Spanish captain, not Gordon.

Judge William D. Shipman, the same judge who presided over the *Augusta* case, thought the defense's claims stretched the bounds of credulity. If Gordon "was the master-spirit of the enterprise" who directed the kidnapping of the African captives and "if the Spanish Captain was only a cover and the defendant was really the man," then the jury should find him guilty. Shipman reminded the jury that "the presumption, of course, is in favor of his innocence," and that for the jury to convict they must find that he was "proved guilty beyond a reasonable doubt." "If on considering this case, you can say that you feel an abiding conviction to a moral certainty that the charge is proved, it will be your duty to bring in a verdict of guilty. If you have a reasonable doubt, you will find the accused not guilty." The trial had taken three days. The jury deliberated for twenty hours but could not reach a verdict. Seven voted to convict while five voted for acquittal. On June 21, Judge Shipman declared a mistrial.[12]

The Republican press reacted with anger. Horace Greeley's *New York Tribune* remarked that "the failure of the jury to agree is disgraceful, especially to themselves." For too long the slave traders in the city "almost invariably manage to elude the meshes of the law," either by bribing jurors, "spirit[ing] away" vital witnesses, or escaping before they can be arrested or tried. Democratic officeholders, the *Tribune* alleged, "have become thoroughly corrupt." But now the Republican Party would put a stop "to this iniquitous complicity with crime." The Lincoln administration was "determined to break up the African slave-trade, and it will accomplish it." But first it would be necessary to "purge" the courts and other federal offices "of these pimps of piracy."[13]

Delafield Smith filed for a retrial, which, due to a series of delays, did not take place until November 6, 1861. For this trial, Smith was able to secure additional witnesses against Gordon, and he reported to Washington that he was "confident, with the new evidence" that the trial would "result in a capital conviction, to the infinite honor of [the government] and of humanity." The defense tried the same tactics as in the first trial, this time having both First Mate William Warren and Second Mate David Hall testify that Gordon had not been in charge of the ship. But now their testimony was challenged by a new witness for the prosecution, who testified that Gordon had been in command of the vessel during the entire voyage. Perhaps most importantly, Smith had the jury sequestered during this trial so that they might not be bribed.[14]

This time the jury took less than thirty minutes to deliberate, and they returned with a verdict of guilty. The *New York Times* rejoiced, "The Slave-trade has experienced a blow from which, it may be hoped, it cannot recover." Meanwhile, the public crowded into Delafield Smith's office the next morning to ask if it was really true. Smith triumphantly telegraphed Washington, DC, "No fitter example [than Gordon] could be made. The cruelty exhibited by the evidence in these cases surpasses the common belief in respect to the atrocities of this trade." In contemplating his fate, Gordon would do well to "think of the agonies of the dying in his ship's hold, where sores and death appeared within a few hours after the living cargo was taken on board."[15]

Gordon's counsel moved for a mistrial, but Judge Shipman denied the motion. Back in the courtroom on November 30, Gordon was asked to stand. "He did so," wrote one observer, "the expression of his countenance rapidly changing." When asked if he had anything to say, he forced a smile and replied, "I have nothing to say whatever." Shipman then delivered a long, heartfelt address during the sentencing. After recounting the facts of the case, Shipman told Gordon, "You are soon to be confronted with the terrible consequences of your crime, and it is proper that I should call to your mind the duty of preparing for that event which will soon terminate your mortal existence and usher you into the presence of the Supreme Judge." The judge therefore implored the pirate "to seek religious guidance . . . and let your repentance be as humble and thorough as your crime was great. Do not attempt to hide its enormity from yourself; think of the cruelty and wickedness of seizing nearly a thousand fellow-beings, who never did you harm, and thrusting them beneath the decks of a small ship, beneath a burning tropical sun, to die of disease or suffocation, or be transported to distant lands, and be consigned, they and their posterity, to a fate far more cruel than death."[16]

Judge Shipman further implored Gordon to "think of the sufferings of the unhappy beings" who, in "helpless agony and terror" had been ripped from their homes and families. "Remember that you showed mercy to none, carrying off as you did not only those of your own sex, but women and helpless children." He continued with surprisingly egalitarian language for a Democrat:

> Do not flatter yourself that, because they belonged to a different race from yourself, that your guilt is therefore lessened—rather fear that it is increased. In the just and generous heart the humble and the weak inspire compassion and call for pity and forbearance, and as you are soon to pass into the presence of that God of the black man as well as the white man, who is no respecter of persons, do not indulge for a moment the thought that He hears with indifference the cry of the humblest of his children. Do not imagine that, because others shared in the guilt of this enterprise, yours is thereby diminished, but remember the awful admonition of your Bible, "Though hand join in hand the wicked shall not go unpunished." Turn your thoughts toward Him who alone can pardon—who is not deaf to the supplications of those who seek His mercy.

Shipman then declared that Gordon would be hanged by the neck on February 7, 1862, at some point between noon and 3 p.m. Gordon stood stoically as Shipman read his statement, only flinching for a moment when the judge uttered the words, "hanged by the neck until you are dead." Upon returning to the Tombs, Gordon's wife Elizabeth "was overwhelmed with grief."[17]

The Republican press rejoiced at the news of Gordon's sentence. "For once, when no doubt exists as to guilt, a terrible example should be made," editorialized the *New York Times*. "It will do more to stop the slave trade than a dozen war vessels on the African Coast." Indeed, Gordon's death would be an incredible deterrent to future slave trading, whereas a pardon would only encourage more of the evil commerce. The editors of a Baptist newspaper similarly opined that they were "influenced neither by personal feeling, nor general bloodthirstiness" in calling for Gordon's execution, but by the belief that when he was hanged "that system" by which "he hoped to enrich himself, not caring for the blood and tears of his victims . . . will receive a blow, in this country, which will not need to be many times repeated." At the White House, Republican senator Charles Sumner of Massachusetts told Lincoln "that though I am against capital punishment, I am yet for hanging that slave-trader" in order to deter other slavers, "to give notice to the world of a change of policy," and to demonstrate "that the Govt. can hang a man."[18]

Others pushed for clemency. The *New York Herald* argued "that the punishment of death is too severe a penalty to attach, to what is, in this point of view, the *mere violation of a commercial law*" (emphasis added). Nearly 180 citizens of Gordon's hometown in Maine signed a printed petition asking for mercy "in behalf of a young and devoted Wife and infant Son, for a most excellent and highly respectable Mother, for fond Sisters, and an extensive circle of the most respectable connections." A New York Republican urged Lincoln not to execute Gordon because the crime of slave trading had "become obsolete" during the war. "Whatever other result may ensue from the present contest with the Southern States the absolute and total abolition of the Slave trade has been effectually accomplished." Others maintained that Gordon should not be executed because he could not have expected a death sentence for the crime. The letters and petitions poured in, so much so that the New York *World* reported that every "possible social, professional and other interested influence has been brought to bear upon Mr. Lincoln, and it is stated that never before has a President been so thoroughly and persistently approached for official interference as in this case."[19]

Gordon's lawyers, one of whom was now a Union soldier, traveled to Washington to meet with the president. According to news reports, Lincoln "gave the subject his earnest and careful attention. At length he decided that he could not find it to be his duty to interfere. He admitted that it was hard for a man to lose his life for violating the law, which had been a dead letter for forty years, but did not see that that fact would warrant him in overruling the courts, or setting aside a law in Congress."[20]

Meanwhile, Delafield Smith also traveled to Washington to make sure that Lincoln would not undo his hard work. According to Smith's own account of the meeting, Lincoln had already prepared a reprieve for Gordon. He sat listening to Smith while holding the reprieve and a pen in his hand, listening "very patiently and with a sort of wail of despair," flourished the pen over the document and said, "Mr. Smith, you do not know how hard it is to have a human being die when you know that a stroke of your pen may save him." Some have believed this story is apocryphal, and yet corroborating evidence survives. Lincoln told his family physician that he did not want to execute slave traders "but that he did not wish to be announced as having pardoned them, lest it might be thought at Richmond that he feared the consequences of such action and then he might be compelled to hang fifty such men."[21]

While the account of Smith's visit to the White House is likely exaggerated, if not untrue, (it was published as a secondhand account well after Smith had died), some observers did worry that the president would cave to the pressure. Indeed, Smith published a public letter in the *New York Times* arguing that Gordon's execution was necessary for stopping the slave trade. Others similarly feared that the president's kindheartedness would get in the way of justice. "We hope the President's good nature will not overcome his duty as guardian of the laws," wrote William Cullen Bryant's New York *Evening Post*, adding that Gordon "deserves to die a thousand" deaths. If Gordon was not hanged, "it will be said that we administer justice on the slave-trader in the same hesitating, procrastinating spirit that we are making war on the rebels."[22]

Some evidence, in addition to Smith's account, suggests that Lincoln may not have fully made up his mind by the beginning of February. Ralph Waldo Emerson visited the White House with Senator Sumner and wrote that Lincoln "argued to Sumner the whole case of Gordon, the slave-trader, point by point, and added that he was not quite satisfied yet, and meant to refresh his memory by looking again at the evidence." Emerson concluded in his diary, "All this showed a fidelity and conscientiousness very honorable to him."[23]

Lincoln brought the Gordon case before his cabinet on Tuesday, February 4, 1862—three days before the scheduled execution. Attorney General Edward Bates was at home sick, so Lincoln sent him a note asking for his legal opinion on a very important matter: could a president "lawfully grant to the convict a respite of his sentence, without relieving him altogether of the death penalty?" Knowing the urgency of the matter, Bates replied that night: "I have no doubt that you can" because the Constitution gives the president the power to grant both pardons and reprieves. Bates explained the difference: "A reprieve does not annul the sentence, as a pardon does. It only prolongs the time, & fixes a day for execution, different from & more distant than the day fixed by the Court." In his note, Bates took no position on "the justice or expediency of using the power" because Lincoln had not asked him; however, the following day the attorney general verbally told Lincoln "that I did not see any good reason for interfering at all unless he meant to pardon or commute—that there were men watching opportunities against him, and that by interfering at all he might give them a handle." Lincoln replied that "he had no intention to pardon Gordon but was willing to give him a short respite." The cabinet, Lincoln told Bates, had concurred with this plan.[24]

And that is precisely what Lincoln did. On February 4, Lincoln issued a proclamation granting Gordon a two-week stay so that Gordon might make "the necessary preparation for the awful change which awaits him." Lincoln's rationale was simple. Since such "a large number of respectable citizens" had "earnestly" sought Gordon's pardon, and since no one had ever been hanged for the crime, Gordon likely believed that he would be released, and had not prepared himself to meet his maker. Lincoln would give him that time. The hanging would now take place on Friday, February 21, 1862, between the hours of noon and 3 p.m. Lincoln concluded, "In granting this respite, it becomes my painful duty to admonish the prisoner that, relinquishing all expectation of pardon by Human Authority, he refer himself alone to the mercy of the common God and Father of all men."[25] This last line reminded Gordon that all people were created equal and endowed by their Creator with certain unalienable rights—even those who had been crammed below the decks of a slave ship off the coast of Africa.[26]

Gordon's attorneys used this extra time to petition the US Supreme Court on February 14, asking the court to restrain any further proceedings in the case. But on February 17, Chief Justice Roger B. Taney handed down a decision denying the appeal, saying that the Supreme Court did not have the jurisdiction to do what Gordon's lawyers were asking.[27]

Meanwhile, back at the White House, life had become a whirlwind for Lincoln. Since late January, he had been pushing Major General George B. McClellan to move against Richmond by George Washington's birthday, February 22. Despite all of the president's efforts, McClellan simply would not budge, bringing Lincoln great emotional distress. On a personal level, the Lincoln family was facing an excruciating trial. The Lincolns' two younger sons, Willie and Tad, fell ill in early February, probably of typhoid. According to Attorney General Bates, the president was "nearly worn out, with grief and watching." Willie eventually succumbed, dying on February 20 at the age of eleven. Mary Lincoln's black seamstress, Elizabeth Keckly, later recalled the scene. "I never saw a man so bowed with grief," she wrote. "He came to the bed, lifted the cover from the face of his child, gazed at it long and earnestly, murmuring, 'My poor boy, he was too good for this earth. God has called him home. I know that he is much better off in heaven, but then we loved him so. It is hard, hard to have him die!'" Keckly continued, "Great sobs choked his utterance. He buried his head in his hands, and his tall frame was convulsed with emotion." Standing at the foot of the bed, Keckly's eyes also welled up with tears.[28]

It was within this context—both military and personal—that Lincoln faced a barrage of appeals for Gordon's life. In addition to the flood of petitions, Gordon's wife and mother arrived at the White House on February 18 with a petition signed by "over eleven thousand of our citizens of New York who are warm and earnest upholders of the Government," asking for Gordon's life to be spared. They traveled with the wife of a New York City judge who pleaded with Lincoln, "I would not intrude upon the sanctity of your sick room and upon your hours of grief but for the sake of Mercy, and for the sake of an afflicted Mother and wife who are bowed down with sorrow and look to God and to you to lift the heavy burden they are suffering under." But Lincoln refused to see them. Instead, the three women met with Mary Lincoln. Elizabeth Gordon gave Mary a poem pleading for her husband's life. Mary, in turn, tried to persuade her husband to act in the case, but Lincoln "would not allow his wife to broach the subject, and poor Mrs. Gordon returned to New York heartbroken and disconsolate."[29]

Next, Gordon's lawyer pressed Lincoln with a long letter on February 18, arguing that for various reasons Gordon ought to be spared the gallows. In conclusion, he urged Lincoln not to allow the celebrations surrounding George Washington's birthday on February 22 to be "marred by the creaking of the gallows—or saddened by the report of the dying groans and struggles of a human being sacrificed to appease the spasmodic virtue of men, who are loudest in their demand for the abolition of the death penalty, as more barbarous than the slave trade and more vindictive than murder." Lincoln asked Attorney General Bates to give his opinion on the matter. Bates replied that same night: "I see nothing in the papers, as presented to me, to make it proper for you to interfere, to stop the course of law"[30]

Trying one last gambit, another of Gordon's attorneys traveled to Albany and persuaded Edwin D. Morgan, the Republican governor of New York, to telegraph Lincoln. "I think it important that Gordon should be respited a few days longer," wrote the governor. "I therefore recommend it & desire that you communicate by telegraph to the marshal at NY." Lincoln assured Marshal Murray that "no change in the sentence would be extended by him." Murray, in turn, informed the superintendent of government telegraphs not to let any more messages regarding Gordon to come through "unless delivered to him personally by the President or Secretary Seward."[31]

Large swaths of the population in Manhattan continued to protest the looming execution. Posters reading "Citizens of New York to come to the Rescue" and "Judicial Murder" appeared throughout the city. A gathering of citizens at the New York Merchants' Exchange sent Lincoln a telegram asking him "to commute the sentence of Nathaniel Gordon in the full belief that it will substantially justify the requirements of the law and do more to suppress the trade that it is the policy of the government to prevent than would his execution." But Lincoln would not be swayed. While these sorts of decisions placed tremendous distress on his mind, the president would later say, Gordon "must be an example. . . . It had to be done; I couldn't help him."[32]

The final twenty hours of Gordon's life were heart wrenching. His mother, wife, and little son arrived at the Tombs in the afternoon. His mother sought to get him to clear his conscience before God. After she left, his wife, Elizabeth, "bore a haggard look," having "evidently eat[en] but little, for a long time," reported the New York *Journal of Commerce.* "As she entered the cell of her husband, she fell fainting on the floor, and had to be carried out into the reception room, where, by the assistance of the prison physician, she soon recovered, when her husband was brought out to her." During their conversation, Mrs. Gordon fainted again. When their time was up, "she with one shriek fell headlong at her husband's feet." Gordon picked her up and kissed her. He then hugged his son "and kissed and kissed [him] until the keeper was compelled to remove [him]; and then, with a trembling step, he returned to his cell in company of his spiritual advisors." Alone with his guards, Gordon told Robert Murray that he had more anxiety "for the future welfare of his family" than for his own fate. When Murray informed him that his family "should be well taken care of," Gordon "expressed heartfelt satisfaction" and said he "was prepared to die like a man."

Four guards were assigned to Gordon's cell for the night. He was moved to a new cell, stripped of his clothing, and provided with a new suit, consisting of "a loose business coat, black pantaloons, white shirt, and coarse, heavy boots." These were the clothes he would be hanged in, although the primary reason for the change was to prevent suicide. In his new cell he requested cigars and materials for writings. He penned letters to his two mates, William Warren and David Hall, who were also imprisoned at the Tombs, and also one to his wife. Later reports stated that he wrote "no less than a dozen letters," including one to his son to be opened "when he arrived at the age of discretion."

Gordon expressed no desire to sleep that night. Between 3 and 4 a.m., his guards "heard a moaning sound" coming from his cell. When they arrived they found him "laboring with convulsions" and "in great agony and suffering intense pain." They immediately called for the prison physicians who administered antidotes and pumped his stomach. They would not allow him to cheat the gallows. Once resuscitated, Gordon admitted to having taken strychnine, a highly toxic, colorless alkaloid often used as a pesticide, which a friend had smuggled into the prison in a cigar. According to one report, "watching his opportunity he bit the end of it off and swallowed it all, and threw himself upon his bed to die. He had not taken the poison over five minutes when discovered." According to another report, Gordon "passed the remainder of the night in physical agony, half dead and half alive, and repeatedly expressed his wish to die."

The execution had been set for 2 p.m., but the prisoner had become so weak from his attempted suicide that the prison doctors now feared that he would not survive until the appointed time. The morning passed by quickly. At 10 a.m. Gordon gave his gold ring to his guards and asked them to clip a lock of his hair to give to his wife. Several ministers also attended him, although he clearly had no interest in their services. At 11 a.m. a clerk from one of Gordon's lawyers rushed to the Tombs with a dispatch from Albany, "The Governor has telegraphed to the President to respite Gordon. See Murray." But when no further news arrived, the proceedings moved forward as planned.

At noon, Murray informed Gordon that the time had come. The prisoner "expressed great surprise," thinking he had two more hours to live. Again the clergy entered the room to pray for him, and the guards gave him whiskey as a stimulant. With his arms tied and a black cap on one side of his head, Gordon was carried "on the Deputy's shoulders" to a chair in the hallway. The *New York Times* reported that he "was not sober—that is, so powerful had been the effect of the poison that, in order to keep him alive till the necessary moment, they had been obliged to give him whiskey enough to make an ordinary man drunk three times over."

Gordon sat "lollingly in the chair, gazing listlessly around," while the marshal read the death warrant. Apparently thinking there might be some hope yet, Gordon asked him to read Lincoln's reprieve twice, which the marshal did. He then asked for more whiskey. At that point, Gordon said, "I have a word to say." His words reflected his mistaken—if not delusional—belief that the prosecutor, Delafield Smith, had promised to seek his pardon after conviction (which was not an uncommon practice in nineteenth-century criminal cases). "I die with the clear conscience of a man who has done, intentionally, no wrong," Gordon continued. "When a man gets up in Court, and says to the jury that if they will only convict a man for him, he will do everything to get that man pardoned, and then goes to the President and begs him to hang the man, it's very mean and contemptible. Such a man would do anything to promote his own ends. He is a mean fellow." Gordon then "looked around with a senseless smile" and asked for some more whiskey, which was given to him.

The procession formed and headed for the gallows. "The sight was sickening," remarked the *Brooklyn Daily Eagle*. "The poor man was so weak that he could not stand on his legs. Two stout men on each side supported him, and in fact carried him along. His legs quivered, his face was the picture of despair—he was to all appearances as nearly dead as mortal could be." At the scaffold, Gordon said, "Well, a man can't die but once. I'm not afraid." The hangman, Bill Isaacs, pulled the cap over Gordon's face and adjusted the rope around his neck.[33] Gordon turned to the executioner and said, "Bill, I'm an old salt. This sort of death is hard lines. Make the knot run easy, and fix it on the right side." He then reminded the marshal, "Don't forget your promise." And back to the executioner: "Make short work of it now, Bill. I'm ready."[34]

Bill Isaacs was a small, dark-complexioned man "with hair black as a raven's wing, and eyes that seem to emit sparks of fire when their owner is excited." He went by the *nom de plume* Henry Isaacs to protect his family and, according to one account, was a man who "does not take pride in his calling." He had been serving as executioner in New York since 1853, lifting "his fellow beings out of existence by means of a half in rope." In fact, he often used the same noose on different convicts—the noose that he would use on Gordon had recently been used to hang an infamous murderer and pirate.[35]

Estimates vary as to how many people were present at the execution, ranging as high as four hundred to as low as fifty (plus a contingent of about forty Marines from the Navy Yard stationed there as guards). One eager witness was US Marshal John S. Keyes, who hurried down from Boston to see it. At some point during the morning, Delafield Smith arrived to inspect the gallows, but he left "saying that it was too much for him—he could not stand it." Gordon's body "swayed hither and thither for a few moments, and all was quiet," reported the *New York Times*. "No twitchings, no convulsions, no throes, no agonies. His legs opened once, but closed again, and he hung a lump of dishonored clay." Afterward his body was taken to a room to be examined. "The neck was broken, and the same meaningless smile sat on the blanched lip, while the same glassy look stared from the half-closed eyes."[36]

Newspaper reaction to the Gordon execution was swift. The *New York Times* declared that "the majesty of law has been vindicated, and the stamp of the gallows has been set upon the crime of slave-trading in so forcible a way that it will not soon be forgotten. And it was time. That crime has been far too lightly thought of among us of late." While the editors of the *Times* "are sorry for his family and friends," they "cannot but rejoice that the Slave-trade has received a heavy blow. Our City has been disgraced by it long enough. Our whole country has shared that disgrace." The *Anglo-African*, a black newspaper in Manhattan, rejoiced, "The firmness of President Lincoln in this affair is the most solid indication of character he has yet manifested." In Connecticut, the *Hartford Courant* opined that the execution "will do more to put a stop to the fitting out of slavers from American ports than all other influences combined." Meanwhile, a Baptist paper in Manhattan reminded its readers, "Four times had he subjected some hundreds of innocent men, women and children to the terrible horrors of the middle passage; and once, to avoid capture, he had caused 600 human beings, with souls as valuable as his, to be flung alive into the deep." If someone was executed for murdering just one person, then surely Gordon deserved to die. Further west in Indiana, one newspaper simply stated, "Verily, the world moves."[37]

Massachusetts senator Charles Sumner approved of the execution, for, he said, "the Slave-trade is treason to man." In like manner, New York City diarist George Templeton Strong praised Lincoln for his decision not to intervene. "He deserves credit for his firmness," wrote Strong on the day following the hanging. "The Executive has no harder duty, ordinarily, than the denial of mercy and grace asked by wives and friends and philanthropes." Indeed, the execution "served him [Gordon] right," and Strong hoped the law might "promptly exterminate every man who imports niggers into this continent."[38]

11

TRIAL

Sitting in his cell at the Charles Street Jail, Appleton Oaksmith was having difficulty finding a lawyer willing to take his case. One friend recommended Charles L. Woodbury, Dana's predecessor as US attorney in Massachusetts and the son of former Supreme Court justice Levi Woodbury, saying he had "resided in *Georgia*, and his feelings are I think friendly to that quarter—at all events I dont think he has any abolition about him." But Woodbury declined to take the case. By the summer of 1862, Oaksmith had come to believe that "nothing but the direct interposition of God, could successfully defend" him. If this was true, then one friend advised, "you will find few men if any of ability to undertake to carry you through the courts, and I, therefore, were I in your position would not ask counsel to defend." Only if Oaksmith could offer "*any* testimony . . . which presents a favorable feature" did this friend think it was worthwhile to hire an attorney. Ultimately, he told Oaksmith, "You are essentially in the grasp of madmen in reform, and they will crush you if possible."[1]

The efforts of men like Murray and Keyes to keep Oaksmith away from lawyers had almost worked. In the final few weeks before the trial, Benjamin F. Sawyer stepped forward to represent his nephew, just as he had done (and in fact was still doing) in the *Augusta* case.[2] Sawyer believed that Oaksmith's arrest and imprisonment had "been brought about, by the misrepresentations of parties in official position in this City," and that the case against him was "actuated by motives of malice and vindictive feelings toward . . . Oaksmith, rather than from any sense of justice or regard for the public good."[3] But Sawyer would have a difficult time proving Oaksmith's innocence in court. Indeed, he had his work cut out for him.

Oaksmith could have been tried in New York City. In fact, he was indicted there on February 18, 1862, for outfitting the *Wells* for the slave trade. And Murray believed that he could procure even more indictments against him.[4] But New York had deep ties to the slave trade, and too many acquittals, mistrials, and hung juries had occurred there over the years. Union authorities thus wanted to move Oaksmith to another jurisdiction. In Boston, they believed the juries were "not as shakey" as juries in New York.[5]

Fortunately for federal prosecutors, Oaksmith had been implicated in an important slave trading case in Massachusetts. On November 14, 1861, Samuel P. Skinner, a career sailor in his mid-fifties, had been convicted of procuring and fitting out an old whaler called the *Margaret Scott* at New Bedford for a slaving expedition. The *Margaret Scott* had presumably been fitted out for a whaling voyage—which typically lasted three years—but she was lacking in basic tools like compasses, hoops for casks to fill with whale oil, or boat knives, and "her fitment was in every respect insufficient for catching or securing whales, or taking in blubber." In addition, she had an insufficient crew for whaling, 1,200 barrels of fresh water, which was much more than a whaler would need, as well as twice as much bread and only nine barrels of "good beef, while there were forty barrels of what is known as 'shank beef'"—poor quality meat presumably intended for the African captives. The court sentenced Skinner to five years at hard labor and a $1,000 fine. This case was extraordinarily significant in that it was the first conviction for slaving where the vessel had not actually gone to Africa. Immediately after his conviction, Skinner and the ship's master, Captain Ambrose Landre, a forty-nine-year-old sailor who was under indictment but had not yet been tried, both offered to turn state's evidence to testify against Oaksmith. US Attorney Richard Henry Dana Jr. learned a great deal from Landre's disclosures, but thought Skinner's were "not of much use, if of any." It was Landre's sworn statements—in which he said "we were going to the Coast of Africa for a cargo of slaves, we were not going a whaling"—that led to Oaksmith being "discovered and arrested."[6]

In preparing for the trial, members of the prosecution made multiple trips to New York City and New Bedford to gather evidence, determining that "no pains or expense should be spared on my part to obtain convictions."[7] Indeed, federal authorities in Boston wanted no stone left unturned as they prepared for trial. US Marshal John S. Keyes believed "this is no common or ordinary case but one of the highest importance to the suppression of this infernal traffic."[8]

New Bedford, the site of the alleged crime, was a unique community in mid-nineteenth-century America. The whaling capital of the world, New Bedford boasted a vibrant and politically active black community, among whom were several hundred escaped slaves. (Frederick Douglass had first gone there when he fled from slavery in the 1830s.) In the 1850s, New Bedford had been a boomtown. With the price of whale oil surging, evidence of wealth could be seen throughout the city. "The town itself is perhaps the dearest place to live in, in New England," wrote Herman Melville in *Moby Dick*. "Nowhere in America can you find more patrician-like houses; parks and gardens more opulent, than in New Bedford." Just before the war, *Harper's New Monthly Magazine* described the bustling seaport as the "Mecca, or Holy City of the whale-hunters," where the docks and streets were "covered with anchors, rusty cables, harpoons, hoops, and lances; staves and empty oil-casks sounding the blows of the cooper." Banks, insurance offices, dance halls, hotels, bars, brothels, and other businesses lined the streets near the wharves, inviting sailors and merchants to find respite after long and perilous periods at sea. But by the end of the 1850s, things had taken a dramatic turn for the worse. The Panic of 1857, in conjunction with the discovery of petroleum in 1859, had all but destroyed the whaling industry. "Business is extremely dull," wrote one prominent citizen in his journal in January 1862. While some whalers continued to go to sea during the war—in 1862, New Bedford fitted out sixty whaling ships, of which fifty-seven sailed—the numbers revealed a declining market. Between 1861 and 1862, the number of barrels of whale oil and pounds of whalebones brought into New Bedford decreased by more than 50 percent. To make matters worse, Confederate privateers and commerce raiders caused maritime insurance premiums to skyrocket, making it more difficult for voyages to be profitable. By the end of the war, things in the city looked bleak. "Our idle wharves were fringed with dismantled ships," wrote one local observer. "Cargoes of oil covered with seaweed were stowed in sheds and along the river front, waiting for a satisfactory market that never came."[9] It was within this context that the fitting out of vessels like the *Margaret Scott* looked so suspicious. If whaling was undergoing such a steady decline, federal authorities wondered why someone like Oaksmith would choose to enter the industry now.

On May 8, US Attorney Richard Henry Dana Jr. asked the court to postpone the trial until the next term. A few weeks later, on May 26, Oaksmith was arraigned in court on ten counts of violating the federal slave trade act of 1818. In drafting the charges, Dana made sure to cover any and every possible illegal action. In fact, he charged Oaksmith with crimes that were inconsistent with one another. The first four counts charged Oaksmith with acting as "owner" of the *Margaret Scott*, the second four charged him with acting as "factor" (meaning either as agent or financier), while the final two charged him simply with aiding and abetting. Those charging him with being "owner" (counts 1–4) and "factor" (counts 5–8) were identical, other than his relationship to the vessel. Counts 1 and 5 charged him with fitting, equipping, loading, and otherwise preparing the *Margaret Scott* for a slaving voyage from Africa to Cuba; counts 2 and 6 charged him with causing the ship to be fitted out for a slaving voyage from Africa to Cuba; counts 3 and 7 charged him with sailing the vessel from New Bedford for a slaving voyage; and counts 4 and 8 charged him with fitting out the vessel for a slaving voyage in order to acquire slaves from an unknown foreign country and to sell them at an unknown place. Count 9 charged Oaksmith with aiding and abetting a slaving voyage from Africa to Cuba, while count 10 charged him with aiding and abetting a slaving voyage from an unknown place to an unknown place.

Oaksmith pleaded not guilty to all ten charges. Three days later he petitioned the court for a postponement, explaining that he could not get bail and that because of a "former sickness" he was not "at the present moment . . . in a fit state of health to undergo the mental labor of a trial." Oaksmith also pointed out that the witnesses who could exonerate him were all out of the country and he had no way of reaching them, although he expected them to return to the United States by the fall. He believed he could prove his innocence of all charges and that a man named Stewart (Oaksmith could not remember his first name) "was the equitable owner" of the *Margaret Scott* and had been the source of the money for her purchase.[10] In other words, if he could only get his witnesses, he could prove that he was neither owner nor factor but merely a broker—an agent acting on behalf of a purchaser.

The court rejected Oaksmith's motions, and the trial commenced on Monday, June 9, with Supreme Court justice Nathan Clifford presiding as a circuit judge. A native of Maine—with a specialty in maritime law—Clifford had served as a Democrat in Congress and as US attorney general in the Pierce administration. Because of Clifford's strong Southern sympathies, Horace Greeley's *New York Tribune* had strongly opposed his nomination to the Supreme Court in 1857, crowing, "Thus the process of deterioration goes on, and the Supreme Court is gradually becoming a mere party machine, to do the bidding of the dominant faction and to supply places to reward party hacks." Now, in 1862, Elizabeth Oakes Smith complained that Clifford was "an *old enemy*" of her husband's from when they lived in Maine, and she did not believe that her son would get a fair trial.[11]

In the weeks leading up to the trial, Elizabeth Oakes Smith had been too distressed to even read the newspapers for fear of what she would see printed

Nathan Clifford.
Courtesy of the Library of Congress.

about Appleton and Sidney.[12] But on the first day of the trial, she joined six other women, as well as a three- or four-year-old girl, in the courtroom. One of the women—Sidney's wife, Fanny—sat on a settee on Oaksmith's right, while Elizabeth sat to his left. The child, Appleton's daughter Bessie, rested at his feet, one journalist calling her "a silent spectator of the scene about her." "The dramatic effect was perfect," reported one newspaper, "but upon the hard-fisted, stern-faced New England jury it was entirely lost."[13]

The first day of the trial did not involve much more than the opening statements. Oaksmith complained that his mail had been opened and read while he was in prison, but Justice Clifford concluded that "there was no reason for any action in the matter." Witnesses began to appear the next day. John F. Tucker, a clerk at the Merchants' Bank in New Bedford, testified that $7,275 had been deposited in that bank "in the name of Oaksmith, or by him" sometime between August 1 and September 9, 1861, and then had been withdrawn before September 12. Thomas E. Borden, a stevedore who had unloaded the *Margaret Scott* at New Bedford after she had been seized, testified that "she was not fitted out as whalers usually are"—that she had more fresh water and too few provisions for a whaling expedition. Others testified about the sale price of the vessel, that her sails and rigging were insufficient for a long whaling voyage (which could last upwards of three or four years), and that the whaling industry was depressed at this time. A reporter for the *New York Herald* noted that Oaksmith "appeared much interested in the evidence elicited from the witnesses, taking copious notes of the questions and answers."

The next witness to appear was Ambrose Landre, the captain of the *Margaret Scott*. Upon seeing the witness, one newspaper reported, Oaksmith "turned pale, and stroked his beard a little nervously."[14] Sawyer asked whether Landre's testimony was valid if he was under indictment in that same federal court for his role in the alleged slaving voyage. Justice Clifford replied that his testimony was admissible.

Landre testified that he had met Oaksmith in July 1861 at the wharf in New Bedford and that they had talked for thirty minutes about purchasing a ship to send to Africa on a slaving voyage, although they would try to make it appear like a whaler. They agreed to meet again at 10 p.m. that night at the Parker House in New Bedford, where they decided that Landre should find and purchase a vessel for the voyage and that, after the successful trip, Oaksmith would pay him $5,000, each officer would receive $1,500, and each member of the crew $500. Landre told Oaksmith that $1,500 was not enough for the officers, so Oaksmith agreed that they would be "satisfactorily compensated." Landre was "to use every endeavor to make her pass as a whaler," and the officers and crew would be kept in the dark as to the real purpose of the voyage until after they were at sea. Over the ensuing few weeks, the two men corresponded and finally they agreed to purchase the *Margaret Scott* for $2,400 in the name of Samuel P. Skinner. The vessel was supposed to be cleared on Saturday, September 7, but before she could get underway, she was detained by a revenue steam tug and both Landre and Skinner were arrested. Throughout his three-and-a-half-hour testimony Landre called Oaksmith "Morris," for throughout their alleged dealings Oaksmith had gone by the name "A. Morris." But he confirmed in court that Oaksmith was the man he knew as "Morris."

After a five-minute recess, Sawyer subjected the witness "to a most rigid cross examination" that lasted about an hour and a half. Sawyer got Landre to concede that "there were several boat companies in the cargo of the *Margaret Scott*, such as are used in whale boats," and that Landre was under two or three indictments for outfitting vessels for slaving voyages. Still, Landre insisted that no inducements had been held out to him to testify against Oaksmith. (It is worth noting, however, that after Oaksmith's trial, Dana dismissed the charges against Landre.)[15]

Next to the stand was Western Rowland, a New Bedford merchant who testified that Oaksmith had been the purchaser of the *Margaret Scott*. A New York City postal clerk then told how Oaksmith had a post office box that corresponded to the one that Landre had used to address "A. Morris." A New Bedford hackman described how he had driven Oaksmith from the city depot to the Parker House and that he had seen Oaksmith write his name, "A. Morris." The court then adjourned until the following morning at 9:30 a.m. According to one reporter, "The testimony was conclusive, and to the point. The prisoner evidently felt that it was all up with him, and when the court was dismissed for the day, broke down under the weight of his feelings."[16]

When the court reconvened for the third day of the trial, on June 11, Sawyer continued his cross-examination of Landre. Mrs. Landre then testified that "a man named Morris" had come to her home in New Bedford "and that man was the defendant now in court, under the name of Oaksmith." She "supposed" that the *Margaret Scott* "was to go on a whaling voyage" and she was planning to join her husband. She had "no idea . . . that the voyage was to be for slaves." Most of the rest of the day was consumed by testimony from expert witnesses that Marshal Murray had brought from New York, such as one who had been a US official on the coast of Africa for thirty-four months and showed "the tricks and devices resorted to by slavers to obtain a cargo of slaves on the coast." The prosecution also summoned "the two best experts in handwriting accessible here," paying them fifteen dollars each to testify. Again, throughout this testimony Oaksmith was joined by his mother, the six women, and the little girl. "The ladies were dressed in most elegant taste," reported the *New York Herald*, "and two or three of them were of remarkable beauty. They were, of course, objects of interest to all present."[17]

On day four the defense called twenty-two witnesses, although only seven took the stand (under federal law at the time, defendants were not permitted to testify in their own defense). Edward Oaksmith claimed that his brother had recently been engaged as "a shipping and commission merchant, publisher of a magazine, ship broker, and engaged in various other branches of business, more or less prosperous." The defense also sought to prove that "A. Morris" and Appleton Oaksmith were two different people.[18]

The most daring if not farcical strategy for the defense involved calling the many women who had been sitting with Oaksmith—now fourteen strong—to the stand. Fanny Oaksmith, Appleton's sister-in-law, was first to testify. In appearance, she was "about the medium height, elegantly and tastily dressed, a rather stern-looking, but finely expressive and intellectual face, and a sharp, keen eye that looked as though it would not quail before the gaze of hundreds turned upon her." But after only two questions from Sawyer "she broke down and stepped from the stand as if faint." Appleton, according to one reporter, leapt from his seat and "caught her in his arms, and a most affecting scene ensued.—She was led out among a perfect ovation of smelling salts, perfumed handkerchiefs, ice water, and other restoratives."

Next to the stand was Elizabeth Oakes Smith. When asked about a particular date, she "alluded, in feeling terms, to a little child [Buchanan], belonging to [the] prisoner, which was removed at this time by the hand of death." At this, the witness became too choked up to continue speaking and broke down in tears. Oaksmith, showing similar emotion, covered his face with his handkerchief, "while the fourteen ladies, as in duty bound, drew their handkerchiefs in a body, and cried in a solid column." One Brooklyn reporter thought "the dramatic effect would have been fearful had it not been overdone." Hoping not to get caught up in the emotion, the twelve men of the jury stared at the ceiling, "as if suddenly interested in centre-pieces and stucco work."

A few other women took the stand for the defense but their testimony was largely immaterial. When the court instructed the prosecution to cross examine one of them, Dana replied, "I have not the slightest desire, your honor," while throwing up his hands with a broad smile on his face. "I have no objections," stated the witness with her own smile. "O, I dare say it would be very agreeable to you," snickered Dana, "but, may it please the Court, we don't insist."[19]

Robert Murray thought "the defense was exceedingly lame."[20] According to the *New York Herald*'s reporter, "The evidence [presented by the defense] was not material enough to alter the complexion of the case

Fanny Oaksmith.
Courtesy of the David M. Rubenstein Rare Book and Manuscript Library, Duke University.

as previously reported." In fact, the defense's main strategy appears to have been to appeal to the jury's emotions and sympathy. "Not less than sixteen ladies were in the court room during the progress of the trial," continued the *Herald*. "Fourteen of these were grouped about the defendant, in apparent sympathy with him, and seemingly deeply interested in the progress of the evidence." Meanwhile Captain and Mrs. Landre sat in the back of the courtroom near the door to the witnesses' room. Clearly, they had an interest in the outcome of this case.

After the defense rested, the prosecution called Samuel P. Skinner, who had just been brought from prison. Skinner stated that a few days earlier four men had brought him a letter from Oaksmith that read, "The trial is going on nicely. Pursue the same course all the way through as you have done." But Skinner claimed that they had taken the letter back after he had read it. Skinner recounted having met Oaksmith the previous summer, corresponded with him (with telegrams signed "A. Morris"), and received money from him for the purchase of the *Margaret Scott*. Skinner further claimed that Oaksmith had come to his house and told him and his wife "that he should go by the name of A. Morris while there, . . . explaining that he was insolvent and could not do business in his own name." But at the same time, Skinner said, Oaksmith gave him a business card "written by Oaksmith, in the handwriting of the latter"—meaning Morris.

Dana showed Skinner a great deal of respect during his questioning. One newspaperman reported, "He appeared on the stand direct from the prison-yard, and the hard labor to which the law had consigned him, an honest-looking, earnest-faced man, gray-haired and gray-bearded, a sufferer at this advanced period of life for the guilt and sins of others." But when Dana addressed him "mildly, but respectfully, gave him the old title, by which he had been known for more than twenty years at home—'Captain Skinner'—the blood rushed to his face and head, he stood erect, and his eyes flashed as if conscious innocence was in his heart. In a moment he remembered his present condition and the purpose for which he had once more been brought among his fellows, and proceeded to give his testimony, while tears coursed down his careworn face."[21]

Skinner's testimony concluded at about noon and Justice Clifford called for a thirty-minute recess. At about 12:40 p.m. the court reconvened for Sawyer's closing argument. Ten women sat between Oaksmith and the jury, while "several other ladies, fashionably dressed and apparently deeply interested, were scattered about the room." The lobby of the courtroom was filled with spectators, while inside the bar sat many of Boston's most distinguished lawyers.

Sawyer addressed the jury for three and a half hours, restating the evidence from the defense's perspective and briefly touching on the testimony of each one of the fifty witnesses. He claimed that the *Margaret Scott* had been seized based on suspicion—"in accordance with a feeling of general distrust that had obtained throughout the country since the breaking out of the present unholy rebellion." He acknowledged that federal authorities rightfully wanted to prevent ships from going out as pirates, privateers, or slavers, but maintained that "many were suspected for no possible cause whatever." The *Margaret Scott*, he contended, "was one of this class." Sawyer then sought to destroy the credibility of the two star witnesses—Landre and Skinner—calling them "low, miserable, degraded wretches, whose testimony should not be received." He concluded by recommending his client "to the merciful consideration of the jury."

After Sawyer's remarks, the court adjourned until Saturday morning, June 14, at 9:30 a.m., when Dana presented the closing argument for the prosecution. His remarks "were of the most eloquent and forcible character," reported the *Herald*. "He stated the evidence briefly, dwelling upon the more important facts that pointed not only circumstantially but directly to the prisoner as the guilty party. His remarks were brief, but pertinent, and produced a marked effect upon the jury." Justice Clifford then summed up the case for the jury, reminding them of the significance of the charges against Oaksmith. "If the prisoner was guilty of the crime with which he stands charged, he should receive the proper verdict at their hands." It was now left to them to determine.[22]

Robert Murray had invested a great deal of time, energy, and resources into seeing Oaksmith brought to trial, and he watched the events unfold with a keen eye. His motivation in so strongly pursuing Oaksmith seems to have been rooted in Oaksmith's attempt to take the *Augusta* to sea back in November 1861. From Murray's perspective, Oaksmith was a "shrewd" character who had tried to defraud the government. And he had tried to pull off this great scheme through one of the vilest ways possible—the slave trade. Murray was now finally close to exacting his revenge. In a private letter he praised Dana and Keyes for exhibiting "considerable zeal and talent" and said that Justice Clifford "summed up in the cleverest and most impressive style." He also took note of how Oaksmith's demeanor had changed throughout the five-day trial. According to Murray, Oaksmith had looked "quite insolent to the witnesses and his keepers" when the trial began, but after hearing Landre and Skinner testify, "he seemed to recognise the utter hopelessness of his case, and assumed a dejected air."[23]

The jury deliberated a mere thirty minutes before finding Oaksmith guilty of eight of the ten counts. The only two charges he was acquitted of—counts 3 and 7—involved him sailing the vessel from New Bedford, which he clearly had not done. Oaksmith had stood up to hear the verdict. When the foreman spoke the word "guilty," he "sank to his seat and gave way to the deepest emotion." Murray hoped that Oaksmith "will receive the utmost penalty of the law, for he is one of the most unscrupulous, bare-faced scoundrels ever let loose upon society, whose laws he has for a long time wantonly and boldly defied."[24] Officials at the Interior Department agreed. "I hope the Judge will put him up for the longest time and the largest am[oun]t," wrote George C. Whiting to Murray. "The conviction of a person of his social standing and intelligence and one who was head devil, must have a good effect upon the inhuman crew."[25]

Oaksmith returned to prison to await sentencing. Journalists speculated that he would be sentenced to five years' imprisonment and a $5,000 fine, plus another year of imprisonment for every $1,000 of the fine that he could not pay. Based on his personal financial situation, this could turn into a ten-year sentence. The *New York Independent* rejoiced, "The vigorous and honest administration of President Lincoln has struck another powerful blow at the slave trade. . . . The sentence is quite as significant as that of Gordon, recently executed in New York." Indeed, "Oaksmith's sentence shows that the Government is resolute to mete out to high and low alike, without respect to persons, the righteous penalties of the law against this infernal traffic. No healthier or more hopeful sign could be given of the spirit in which our wholesome laws are to be administered."[26] The British consul in Boston similarly reported back to London, "The vigilance of the United States' Government's legal officers will have the best effect for furtherance of repression of this horrible Traffic."[27]

Federal authorities were overjoyed at the result of the trial. Robert Murray exulted that Oaksmith's conviction was "a greater triumph in the cause of the suppression of the Slave trade than the execution of Gordon the slaver captain" and he praised the US officials in Boston, saying they "deserve the highest credit for the manner in which they conducted the prosecution."[28] George C. Whiting, in turn, praised Murray for all he had done, telling him that Oaksmith's conviction "vindicates triumphantly, the boldness and energy of your action in the premises and more than ever proves your sagacity in such matters."[29]

Years later, John S. Keyes would write in an unpublished memoir, "Then I caught and convicted Appleton Oaksmith the chief confederate slave trader and had much connection with Murray of New York over this case and Gordons." Keyes rejoiced that this work "made life full and interesting" and "was useful to the government and doing good service to the Union." Indeed, 1862 marked a turning point in America's relationship with the slave trade. The convictions of Gordon, Skinner, and Oaksmith occurred about the same time that Secretary of State Seward negotiated a new treaty with Great Britain that permitted British sailors to search American vessels suspected of slaving. Seward would tell Lincoln that the Lyons-Seward Treaty was "the most important act of your life and of mine." In like manner, in early 1862 a New York Republican wrote: "Whatever other result may ensue from the present contest with the Southern States the absolute and total abolition of the Slave trade has been effectually accomplished." Lincoln himself came to a similar conclusion, telling Congress in 1863 that, "so far as American ports and American citizens are concerned, that inhuman and odious traffic has been brought to an end."[30]

And what of the *Margaret Scott*? The government had purchased her for $4,000 on November 30, 1861, and sent her off to Charleston Harbor, where she was sunk as part of the famous "Stone Fleet" that blocked the waterways into the city. By the time of Oaksmith's trial in June 1862, she had been submerged in South Carolinian waters for nearly six months—a "righteous retribution," said the *New York Times*.[31] If the *Margaret Scott* had been intended to bring Africans to Cuba in contravention of Spanish and American law, she now would instead be used to strangle the Confederacy by inhibiting blockade-running traffic in and out of the South's most violently pro-slavery city.

Benjamin F. Sawyer immediately filed a motion for a retrial, saying that his client's conviction was "against law" and "against the evidence and *weight* of *evidence*." Sawyer criticized Justice Clifford for charging the jury "that they might convict upon the testimony of the accomplice alone *uncorroborated*." He also believed that Clifford should have included several other points—more favorable to the defense—in his jury charge, such as that Oaksmith's "intent should be clearly established."

But larger events conspired to prevent Sawyer from being able to represent Oaksmith at the appointed time to argue the motion for a retrial. After Oaksmith's conviction, Sawyer hurried back to New York, where he appeared before Judge Shipman to ask for a postponement of the *Augusta* case, which was set to be argued June 20 to 27. Sawyer explained that he had not had time to prepare for the case since he had been handling matters in Boston. But US Attorney Delafield Smith opposed the request, and

Shipman sided with the prosecution. Meanwhile, Justice Clifford had set Monday, June 23, as the day to argue the motion for a retrial. Sawyer sent a deposition to Clifford stating that it would be "impossible" for him to return to Boston to argue the motion, as the *Augusta* case would still be going in New York. He simply could not be in two different cities at the same time.

It is unknown whether the prosecutors and judges worked behind the scenes to create this impossible situation for Oaksmith's attorney. Regardless, neither judge would grant Sawyer's motion for a postponement. Oaksmith's motion for a new trial thus went nowhere.[32] He would have to wallow in the Charles Street Jail awaiting sentencing.

III

ISOLATION

Since Death is a part of the economy of human existence, it is merciful to us that our precious groups are broken up—separated we are each able to face our own calamities and perhaps to think the more calmly of those that come to our friends, while were we permitted to grow old together we should be unlikely to form other relations, and one affliction after another would harrow up the soul till at last the survivor would stand in the midst of the graves—solitary, bleeding, disconsolate. God is great—God is merciful even in the sorrows that are inevitable to life.

—Diary of Elizabeth Oakes Smith, November 10, 1861

12

ESCAPE

Following the trial, Elizabeth Oakes Smith was in such a dire financial position that she could not afford to travel from New York to Boston to see her son. (Seba was bringing in little, if any, income by now.) And eight months in the Charles Street Jail took its toll on Appleton. With ample time for quiet reflection, he continued to write poetry—which his mother characterized as "full of pother and tenderness"—as well as letters to loved ones. In early September he wrote a poem titled, "My Little Daughter's Prayer," which he dedicated to his four-year-old daughter, Bessie, asking God to bring "Peace upon the Earth." Prison life may also have made him more altruistic. On September 6, 1862, he wrote his mother, "From my stand-point of life, I say, one should make sacrifices of time, of money, of comfort for a friend."[1]

At some point in the summer or fall of 1862, Oaksmith decided that he would take his chances on a jailbreak. Sometime late at night on Wednesday, September 10, or perhaps in the wee hours of the morning of the eleventh, he seized his opportunity.

In the north end of the jail yard stood a separate building where workmen were installing new boilers. A door had not yet been built for the boiler room—the door was going to be constructed in place of one of the kitchen windows. Oaksmith's cell was at the head of a flight of stairs that led down to the kitchen. One widely circulated newspaper report stated, "It is believed that he took advantage of the absence of the workmen from the kitchen, and of the fact that his door had been carelessly left unfastened by the officer in charge on Thursday morning, to steal quietly down stairs into the kitchen and thence through the window into the yard." He then scaled the wall of the prison with a ladder "which had been either accidentally or purposefully left for his use." His absence was not discovered until 10 a.m. on September 11, at which point, the *Boston Transcript* reported, "the astonished officers found the bird had flown."[2]

So reported the newspapers.

The details of Oaksmith's escape are murky, full of conflicting evidence. In a letter addressed to US Marshal John S. Keyes—that Oaksmith left in his cell on the morning of his escape—he wrote:

> In regard to the *means* of my escape, I feel it my duty to say that *no officer or person*, directly or indirectly, connected with this jail has had the slightest knowledge or suspicion of the matter, and, it is needless to add, no person in any way responsible for my safe keeping has directly or indirectly connived at, or even suspected such a thing. And further, from the nature of the arrangements, unless they had positive knowledge, or a very strong suspicion of such an intent it would have been impossible to have prevented it.
>
> I also desire to say in justice to myself, that in no single instance have I in any way directly or indirectly taken advantage of any kindness which I have ever received from any person connected with this establishment to aid, prepare for, or further my escape; and that *no relative whatever*, and no friend who has openly visited me has had the slightest knowledge or even suspicion of such an intent.[3]

And yet years later, Oaksmith's daughters claimed that the escape had not been at his initiative at all. According to them, he found a note on his breakfast tray one morning in July telling him that he "should be ready to escape at any time but to be sure to continue in his usual habits." For more than a month he heard nothing else, they claimed, but then on that fateful September morning at 4 a.m. he was "awakened by a man standing over him with a bundle of woman's clothes." The prisoner put on the disguise "and walked out of the prison on the man's arm without a hand being laid on him." One writer concluded from this account, "It seems certain that Oaksmith's friends had bribed the guards, thus making the escape possible."[4]

Without an account in Oaksmith's own hand, it may never be known with certainty how he managed to escape. Could he have walked out dressed as a woman even with his full beard? Perhaps, since it was in the dead of night. Would it have even been possible to bribe the guards? Again, perhaps. Everyone—and everything—has a price. But to accomplish such an escape from the prison, several different persons would have had to be in on the deal.

As described in chapter 9, the Charles Street Jail was a "prison within a prison." Only three men—the sheriff and the two turnkeys—had access to the prison's keys. For the most part, these three officers' duties were outside of the prison, in the lower office and at the entrance to the jail.

Every evening around sunset, one of the turnkeys walked by each cell to make sure that they were locked. Once he had finished his rounds, he would lock the keys in the safe in the office, which was located outside of the prison. At that point, only the turnkey or the sheriff had access to the cell keys because they were the only ones who had access to the safe. At about 8 p.m.—when the keys were locked into the safe—the guardroom was then locked with a large spring lock. "The guard is just as much a prisoner as though he were locked into a cell," explained one of the turnkeys. "He is locked into the guard-room, & has to remain there until the turnkey opens the door in the morning."

Every morning, a little before sunrise, a turnkey would give a key to one of the guards to unlock several prisoners who were responsible for starting fires and making breakfast in the kitchen in the cellar. The kitchen was "ordinarily a strong room with grated windows and an outside door which is locked" (although at this time one of the windows was no longer grated). The officer of the jail would leave the kitchen door unlocked for about fifteen or twenty minutes. The prisoner who started the fires, Daniel White, had been in on "a bastardy warrant" since July 21. The other six or seven cooks "were rather a docile class of men . . . rather stupid kind of men," recalled one prison official, "men in for fines, for drunkenness," or crimes like arson. While the prisoners were in the basement cooking, one guard would stay in the guardroom and another would tend to the prisoners.

About 6 a.m. each morning, George Booth, one of the turnkeys, would then open every cell and "take a gang to empty the night buckets & change them." Booth later claimed that he would lock the doors after the buckets had been cleaned, but other evidence suggests that the doors were typically left unlocked so that breakfast could be dropped off within each cell. About 8 a.m. the prisoners would be brought out of their cells to do work, such as cleaning floors or whitewashing.

The evening of Wednesday, September 10, had gone just like any other. The prisoners were locked into their cells about 6 p.m.—that is, all except for Oaksmith. For several weeks he had been allowed to read and write in the guardroom. The guards put Oaksmith in his cell, but they left the door ajar so that all he had to do was push it open to walk out.

About 6:30 or 7 p.m., Oaksmith walked the short distance down the corridor to the guardroom and sat at the table, where he read a recent issue of the Boston *Traveler*. Oaksmith talked a little while with Darius F. Bradley, one of the officers at the jail, about how Senator Henry Wilson of Massachusetts had fled from the battlefield along with other picnickers at Bull Run in July 1861. Bradley then went to bed until his 1 a.m. shift began. Benjamin Richardson, the other officer on duty that night, later recalled that Oaksmith "was extra jovial that night" as he told stories and talked politics.

After about fifteen or twenty minutes, Oaksmith went into his cell and then returned with a basket of pears. He asked Richardson to take some. "I would not take any at first, because I thought it was difficult for him to get them," Richardson later recalled, "but he urged me so hard that I took two or three." After a few more minutes, a female prisoner called for the guard to come assist her. Her cell was on an upper corridor on the north wing, on the opposite side of the prison from Oaksmith's cell. Richardson climbed the three flights of stairs to her cell and found her sick and in need of medicine. He returned to the guardroom and went to the medicine dispensary, which was a bookcase near the stove. He gave her a dose of "black-drop" in an apothecary glass—"a common medicine which we give to any of them, no matter what ails them." Richardson estimated that this errand took twenty or thirty minutes. When he returned to the guardroom, he found that Oaksmith was no longer there, so "I then went & locked his door," which closed with a loud clank. Richardson later recalled that the kerosene lamp was out in Oaksmith's cell. "I concluded he had gone to bed & locked the door. If I had opened the door & looked in, I should have concluded he had gone to bed, the way he left it, for his shoes & stockings were left there as usual, & the bed rigged up in that way. Anybody would have thought there was somebody there." Richardson then returned to the guardroom and read an evening newspaper. Twice during the night, he walked through the entire prison, checking the doors and peering down the corridors. Back in the guardroom he quietly read a newspaper or book. Then at 1 a.m. he awoke Bradley and went to bed.

At about 5:45 a.m., Officer Bradley unlocked the cells of the men on the kitchen detail. He then unlocked the kitchen door. "I left it open while I was in the kitchen, some 15 or 20 minutes, giving directions about breakfast that morning," he later recalled. "I came back & locked the door after me."

About that same time—at 6 a.m.—George Booth, a turnkey, made his rounds of the prison to change the buckets. There were four cells in Oaksmith's wing, but only two of them were occupied. First he unlocked Oaksmith's door, then the other. Booth looked into Oaksmith's cell and thought he saw the prisoner asleep on his bed (he could not really get a good view since Oaksmith had newspapers hanging over his door and window). He then claimed to have locked the cell door.

An African American prisoner named William Thompson, who was in for having a "noisey [*sic*] house," delivered Oaksmith's breakfast around 8 a.m. Thompson returned about 11 a.m. to collect the tray and found the food still on it. As Oaksmith often slept late, he did not think it unusual enough to go into the cell. Thompson reported back to Officer Daniel Jones, and Jones told Thompson to go in and wake up Oaksmith and "tell him to eat his breakfast." Thompson returned to the cell and found the bed stuffed with things like Oaksmith's extra blankets to make it appear as though a man was asleep in it. He quickly returned to Jones and informed him, "There's no Oakes Smith there."

Officer Jones rushed to the cell. "I found his bed had the appearance of having a man in it," he later recalled. "There was a small carpet bag fixed at the head, & another little below, & a blanket turned down on the pillow to look like a man's head. I turned the blankets down, & saw that he was not there." Jones immediately notified George Booth, the turnkey, and then "started right up to the Court House to notify the sheriff." While waiting for the sheriff to arrive, Booth examined the cellar underneath the kitchen as well as some of the cells on the lower floor of the prison. "I didn't know what to do," he later admitted. Outside in the yard, prison officials found a tall ladder leaning against the interior of the prison wall.

Several of the prison officials questioned the prisoners, but none knew anything of Oaksmith's escape. Officer Bradley went to the Providence Depot "to keep a lookout" from 1 p.m. until midnight. US Marshal John S. Keyes went to Oaksmith's hometown of Portland, Maine, hoping he might find him there. As another precaution he even telegraphed authorities in Canada "in the event of his reaching there."[5]

Inside the cell were two notes, one to John M. Clark, the sheriff of Suffolk County, and one to US Marshal John S. Keyes (the note to Clark does not appear to survive). Oaksmith intimated to Keyes that he had been negotiating terms for release with US Attorney Richard Henry Dana Jr., but that he had come to the conclusion that their negotiations were not being done in "good faith." Under these circumstances, his only option was to escape. "It is a very painful alternative to me," he continued, "but I see no other way of obtaining that vindication which is my right." Moreover, "I cannot endure a further prolongation of my *useless*, *unmerited*, and cruel imprisonment."

Oaksmith warned Keyes that if word of his escape was leaked to the press, it "will shut the door to any and all arrangement, and will compel me in self defense to publish to the world what had much better be buried in oblivion. *My* sole desire and aim is to *end* this matter in such a way that my honor and good name may be left untarnished. The cruelty of these proceedings was greater to my family than to me." He then advised Keyes that he would be "far beyond your jurisdiction" by the time Keyes read the letter. "I do not wish to expatriate myself, or rather be *forced* to expatriation," he wrote, "but if no other resource is left to me, so be it—and the wrong be upon the heads of those who have caused it."[6]

Sheriff Clark quickly issued a $300 reward for Oaksmith's "arrest and delivery at Boston Jail, or . . . at any place from which he can with safety be returned to said jail." The physical description of the escapee bordered on comical.

> ESCAPED FROM BOSTON JAIL on the morning of September 11, 1862, APPLETON OAKSMITH; height 5 feet 8 inches; dark swarthy complexion; sharp, full, hazel eyes; Roman nose; very dark brown hair, slightly thin on the top of his head; had long, full beard, probably trimmed or shaved off since his escape; stout built, weight about 160 pounds; genteel address; air of shrewdness; soft, white hands; handsome teeth; fine looking; age 34 years; in appearance, with full beard, about 40 years; likely to disguise himself as a woman or a sailor.[7]

Clark's description of Oaksmith as possibly dressed as a woman is curious, especially in light of Oaksmith's daughters' later claim that he made his escape in women's attire.

On September 13, Marshal Keyes informed authorities in Washington of Oaksmith's escape. "He has been in close custody since his conviction, in the safest cell of the jail," wrote Keyes, "and I have within ten days and at various previous times impressed on Sheriff Clark the jailer, and my officers on his subordinates, the necessity of the utmost vigilance as he would probably attempt an escape as the time drew near for his sentence." Keyes explained that "the only theory that can be devised of the manner of his escape, unless there was collusion on the part of some of the officers of the jail," was that Oaksmith had escaped through the open kitchen window sometime after 6 a.m., when the turnkey unlocked the cells in each corridor to change the buckets. While this was happening, "Oaksmith might have slipped from his cell round the corner of it, & down the stairs into the kitchen, & thence into the yard and over the wall 16 ft high by means of a ladder which was in use in building the addition, & was found standing against the wall when the escape was discovered." There was "no sign & we have no clue" how he got down on the other side. "He probably had

John M. Clark.
Biographical Encyclopedia of Massachusetts of the Nineteenth Century (New York: Metropolitan, 1879).

confederates outside in waiting for him, who helped him off, as a thorough search for him in the city and telegrams to every point where he would be likely to go, a close guard of the water front, and all the railroad routes have failed to throw any signs of him. . . . He left a letter to the sheriff and another to me written in his usual inflated style." Keyes explained the steps he was taking to try to recapture Oaksmith, and then concluded, "If he had no outside assistance he showed so much sagacity & skill in getting away that his probable recapture is very doubtful."[8]

A month after the escape—on October 13—a federal grand jury convened to hear testimony regarding the escape. The officers of the prison recounted their daily routines, their experiences with Oaksmith the night before his escape, and their initial reactions upon discovering that his cell was empty. Officer Bradley surmised that some of Oaksmith's female visitors "might some how or other have procured him a key to the kitchen door," but when asked how they could have procured a key, he replied, "They couldn't. I don't think they ever went to the door. At this time, they were repairing, and the outside door was open, & the kitchen door could easily have been reached by parties from the outside. But that is all suspicion, as I have said. That has been the suspicion of all of us—that he was aided by parties outside who had access to him & by other means which we know nothing about."

Officer Richardson told the grand jury, "We concluded he must have slipped out when the door was opened in the morning. Mr. Bradley opens the door to let the boys in to make the fires in the kitchen & cook. He could have slipped out at that time." When asked how Oaksmith got out of his cell, Richardson guessed that "he must have been locked out" and "passed the night well enough by keeping away from me" as Richardson did his rounds through the prison corridors.

The grand jury concluded that the privileges that had been extended to Oaksmith "seem unwise and unusual" and that "there was a want of proper restraint & neglect of reasonable precautions, and an absence of due care and vigilance on the part of the sheriff and those having Oaksmith in custody, in their conduct towards him, which in every way facilitated his escape."[9]

How Oaksmith accomplished this feat remains a mystery.[10]

In October, Edward Oaksmith was arrested and briefly imprisoned in Boston so that he could be questioned about his brother's whereabouts. Edward was a tall, handsome, polite, eccentric, and artistic young man with an exquisite tenor voice and talent for acting. (He was known to walk around Broadway in a beautifully embroidered Mexican sombrero and concho.) He probably had no information for his inquisitors.

Edward Oaksmith.
Courtesy of the David M. Rubenstein Rare Book and Manuscript Library, Duke University.

Elizabeth Oakes Smith had her own theory about how her son escaped from prison. While ruminating on it more than two years later, she wrote in her diary, "I have no doubt that the door was left open by orders of Marshall Murray, who visited Boston on Saturday and Sunday before. Appleton had become acquainted with a transaction of his involving a large amount of money, and Murray knew that it would involve him seriously with Seward, who had been deceived by him. Edward told this to Murray, and told him that *we should make use of it*; he turned very pale, and replied, 'I will go on to Boston, on Saturday'—and he did go, and this I believe to be the result."[11] No corroborating evidence for this theory appears to survive.

13

EXILE

Appleton Oaksmith's descendants claimed that upon escaping from jail he went to Portland, Maine, where he hid at his grandmother's home for more than a year. At Portland he met his beautiful young cousin, Augusta Mason, who apparently "on first sight of the stranger . . . broke into tears and rushed from the room." Occasionally he traveled from Maine to New York City to get money. Eventually in late 1863 or early 1864, he left the United States for England, taking his eldest daughter, Bessie. In England he became a ship captain and Confederate blockade-runner, smuggling cotton from Galveston, Texas, to Liverpool.[1]

The problem with family lore is that it is seldom accurate. In fact, Oaksmith himself later denied ever having gone "to Portland or anywhere else in disguise."[2] Instead, he arrived at Havana on a sailing vessel on October 20, 1862—just over a month after he escaped from prison. It is unknown where he went immediately after escaping from prison, but it was not likely his grandmother's home since both of his grandmothers had died in the 1850s. Upon announcing his arrival in Cuba, early news reports stated that "his health is said to be much shattered, and he is at present residing on a plantation, under medical treatment. He will probably be heard of again before long." He joined his brother Sidney who had been in Havana since February 1862.[3] It is unclear why Sidney had gone to Cuba, but it may have been to avoid an arrest and prosecution like his brother's.

When word reached Boston of Oaksmith's whereabouts, Marshal Keyes asked Secretary of State Seward to seek Oaksmith's extradition. Considering the overwhelming proof of Oaksmith's guilt and the importance of this case in leading to an end to the slave trade, Keyes wrote, "I take the liberty of bringing it to your notice in the hope that you may find some method of inducing the Spanish Government to surrender this convicted felon to the authority of the law." Keyes also informed Seward that "should there be any expectation of a favorable result and a surrender

171

of him to American authority," that Sheriff Clark "will personally assume any expense attendant on his removal from Havana to this District without charge to the United States."[4] The problem for Keyes and Clark and Seward was that the United States did not have an extradition treaty with Spain, so such an effort would be illegal.

Much of Oaksmith's time in Cuba is shrouded in mystery. He gathered affidavits and other records to try to prove his innocence. He also wrote semi-frequently to his mother, but she appears to have destroyed this correspondence. Clues remain in her diary, such as this notation from May 24, 1863: "Received a letter from Appleton—he writes resolutely—manfully—but continues very ill. Nerves and health greatly shattered. He suffers also from his strong desire to see his children. Letter dated Cuba May 1st." Back in Patchogue, Oakes Smith tried to keep her home, "The Willows," beautiful, with the garden well maintained. "This is Appleton's room," she wrote one day in July 1863, "and I strive to make it lovely—waiting his return."[5]

In Cuba, Oaksmith continued writing poetry. On February 27, 1864, *Harper's Weekly* published a sentimental unsigned poem entitled "Forget-Me-Not," which was in the voice of a young woman walking in a garden, bidding her lover farewell as he prepares to go off to war. She stoops and picks up a forget-me-not, and "twined it softly in his vest" as the two lovers embraced. The man—wearing his uniform and sword—promises to bring back the little flower and then slowly rides away. She never hears his voice again, for she soon receives word that he has been killed.

> This little casket that I wear
>   The rest can better tell—
> A withered flower, a lock of hair,
>   A blood-stained word, "Farewell!"
> They buried him upon the field,
>   Upon the battle-plain;
> And life to me can never yield
>   A comfort to my pain
>
> I often, at the twilight hour,
>   Steal down the garden-walk,
> Where once I plucked the little flower
>   Beneath the roses' stalk;
> And when I reach the wicker-gate,
>   And no one else is nigh,
> I almost think I see him wait,
>   As then, to say "Good-by."

And sometimes, when the shadows creep
        Along the garden-wall,
I hear a voice which makes me weep
        Out of the darkness call.
It seems to say—as still I stand
        Upon the same old spot—
"I'm waiting for that little hand—
        My dear, FORGET-ME-NOT!"

Readers of *Harper's* would have presumed that "Forget-Me-Not" had been written by a woman who'd lost her lover in the war. The visual imagery on the page above the poem appeared to validate that assumption. It featured

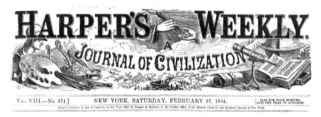

"Forget-Me-Not."
Harper's Weekly, February 27, 1864.

angels standing in grief around a scroll that read, "In Memory of our Soldiers and Sailors who On Land or at Sea, Have Fallen Martyrs for Liberty and Law. Peace be with Them. Amen."[6] Appleton expressed themes and ideas that were almost universally experienced during the war. Perhaps he saw some similarities between others' loneliness and his own.

Oaksmith earned ten dollars for this composition. Ironically, his mother had difficulty placing her own work during this time. When *Harper's Magazine* rejected an article she'd written, she groused in her diary, "The literary press is entirely in the hands of Black Republicans, who ostracize all of a Democratic stamp—and all who do not submit to their dogmatism. I see little hope for a high-toned literature—or hope for our poor lost Union, while the power remains in the hands of these demagogues."[7]

Throughout Appleton's exile, Elizabeth cared for her three grandchildren—Bessie, Corinne, and Randolph. She adored them and doted on them, and the children loved being with their grandparents. Bessie and Corinne formed memories during that time that would stay with them for the rest of their lives—helping with the cow, picking buttercups along the path to the meadow, and enjoying warm summer days on the swing beneath the Willow tree. But sometimes Elizabeth looked "sadly . . . upon these little ones" and wondered what their futures would hold. "They are bright handsome children," she wrote, and she thought Bessie "spirituelle and beautiful." But caring for the children could be difficult with Isotta around. "Here I am month after month rearing these young children, who are very dear to me" but "the violent temper of their mother makes it necessary for me to protect them from her out-bursts of irritation. It does seem unaccountable to me how any human being can be subject to such paroxisms, which are humiliating if nothing worse."[8]

Oakes Smith could do little more than wait and hope that something might bring about a change. "My great sorrow is that my beloved children cannot be with me, and most especially Appleton, who has done so much to procure it, and to embellish it," she wrote in her diary on June 5, 1863. "My heart aches for him. The victim of a conspiracy, which in other times would be traced home and punished—he was a Democrat, young, ardent, popular—hundreds less known have been arrested, and by threats of fines and imprisonment have been terrified into inaction."[9]

Indeed, knowing that she could do little to help her son, Elizabeth turned her attention to the war. She was, in a practical sense, an exile within her own country, a prisoner in her own home. She regretted "bearing so patiently and in silence the persecutions of my family." Had she publicly "shown the falsity of the charges—the perjuries of the witnesses,

I should have at least commanded respect, whereas now I have merely invited their cruelty by my silence."[10] Many a day she would sit in solitude reading old letters from family and friends before burning them. Her attention was particularly attuned to the Lincoln administration's policies regarding civil liberties and the excesses of Union generals who overzealously used their authority to arrest and detain civilians. For two years now, Lincoln had suspended the privilege of the writ of habeas corpus, which essentially gave the State and War Departments the authority to arrest and indefinitely detain civilians without charges. Article I of the Constitution permits the privilege of the writ to be suspended "when in Cases of Rebellion or Invasion the public Safety may require it," but Democrats claimed that Lincoln was abusing this power. (Most of Article I of the Constitution deals with the powers of Congress, so Democrats, and some Republicans, claimed that Lincoln was exercising a power not delegated to him.) Indeed, many believed that Lincoln was using it to go after political opponents instead of individuals who offered aid and support to the Confederacy.[11] Lincoln's suspension had been the legal basis for Appleton's arrest in 1861 even though he had done nothing pro-Confederate at that time.

The most notorious arrest of the Civil War occurred in Dayton, Ohio, at 2 a.m. on May 5, 1863, when Union soldiers arrested former congressman and antiwar firebrand Clement L. Vallandigham for "disloyal speech." Vallandigham had publicly criticized the recently adopted Conscription Act as well as Republican efforts to silence antiwar Democratic views. The draft law was particularly onerous to rural farmers and working-class Americans because it permitted conscripts to pay a $300 commutation fee to avoid service—something that made the Civil War seem like "a rich man's war but a poor man's fight." But from the stump, Vallandigham was careful not to counsel unlawful resistance to the laws. No, "the remedy" for these "evils," according to Vallandigham, was for Democratic voters to use ballots to cast "King Lincoln" from his throne. For these sentiments, Vallandigham found himself arrested by the military in the dead of night, arraigned before a military tribunal, and ultimately exiled to the Confederacy.[12]

Oakes Smith read about these proceedings in the newspapers and noted in her diary that the "whole Country [is] in a ferment because of the arrest" and "mock" trial of Vallandigham. "It is a high handed pill of oppression in keeping with other acts of this imbecile and tyrannical Administration," she continued. "It is no worse than many other arrests no worse, nor so bad as the way in which Appleton has been treated—but then Appleton had incurred the personal malignity of Seward, a man incapable of integrity, and Seward, our Secretary of State, can only be reached through a bribe, and we had no money if we had been willing to accept the offers made, through his agents and emissaries. The world is infinitely worse than I had imagined!"[13]

A few weeks after Vallandigham's arrest, Confederate general Robert E. Lee marched his Army of Northern Virginia into Pennsylvania—a movement that would culminate in the Battle of Gettysburg on the first three days of July 1863. Oakes Smith's diary became a record of the panic that seized the North. "So disgusted have the people become with the present Administration that they seem rather disposed to receive, than repel the invaders," she wrote. "Many say openly that the prospect of restoring the Constitution would be better under Jefferson Davis, than under Abraham Lincoln. Immense Peace Meetings prevail through the country, and resistance to the enrollment [conscription] is the common sentiment." In fact, Oakes Smith had become convinced—quite irrationally—that Lincoln had such "treacherous . . . designs" to allow Lee to capture Washington.

The Fourth of July was no celebration for Oakes Smith. "A sad day to me," she confided to her diary, "crowded with reminiscences of the days when my children were about me—however we made it a bright day for the little ones." The next day, after praying for "our unhappy country," she noted, "The people are sick of the war—the soldiers must fight or be shot down as mutineers—they have no faith in our rulers nor in their military leaders." Then on July 6 the news arrived in her village: "A terrible battle has been fought at Gettysburg. The Union army is said to be triumphant, with a loss of twenty thousand men—Good God! what horrible carnage—I am sick at the record—my whole soul revolts at this sanguinary conflict. Such a victory is as ruinous as defeat. There must be a compromise—for neither party will yield and each seems as equal to the other in point of courage and persistency."[14]

Many in the North rejoiced at the Union's triumph at Gettysburg. Writing from New York City, Delafield Smith congratulated Lincoln on the victory at Gettysburg as well as the capture of Vicksburg, Mississippi, on July 4. "Your friends in New York gratefully congratulate you on the Glorious results of your plans & labors for your Country. You have had the Blessing of God. You will have the Support of the people," he wrote.[15] But a hideous tragedy was about to overtake the North's largest metropolitan area.

On Monday, July 13, Oakes Smith took an early train for New York City "where the most appalling scenes awaited me." The draft had just commenced in the city, and thousands of people now crowded the streets in a state of unrest. She found a working-class woman "threading her way through the living mass, as I was doing myself, and found it convenient

Elizabeth Oakes Smith, ca. 1860.
Courtesy of the David M. Rubenstein Rare Book and Manuscript Library, Duke University.

to use her and her basket as an entering wedge. Sometimes it would cross my mind, that if paving stones should take wing my position would be a dangerous one—but I had little anxiety for myself."

Oakes Smith felt like she was "intoxicated—drunk with excitement." She could sympathize with the grievances of the mob. Poor Irish immigrants could not afford to hire a substitute if they were drafted, or pay the $300 commutation fee to avoid the draft if their name was selected.

> I had seen the people submit to so many arbitrary measures—seen them go like sheep to the slaughter in this stupidly managed war—seen them die without a word for measures repugnant to them—seen the encroachments upon our liberties made daily by this corrupt Administration, and yet the people were silent—bitter—cursing deep, not loud, and I began to lose all hope—I wished I could do or say something to rouse them—but nothing seemed able to do this—the people tamely cowered under oppression—the radical Editors lied and deceived them as did the rulers at Washington, and I despaired for American freedom. I knew the draft was repugnant to the genius of the country—I knew that the whole burden of war fell upon our working men, and the clause of exempting those who were able to pay the $300 threw all the burden upon the poor men, still it seemed as if the people would submit.

But now there was "a perfect howl of rage and indignation from the masses." Oakes Smith asked her "pioneer" with the basket, "What is the matter? what are the people about?" The woman turned and with a fierce expression on her face, replied, "They wont be carried off to the war—that's what is the matter."

"Well, would you have your husband carried off in this way?" she asked.

"If they do, they ve got to fight me first," was the prompt reply. Then looking at Oakes Smith, she made a "sneering" laugh: "Eh! you ladies can pay the $300 and keep your men to home."

Oakes Smith turned and went up Broadway, where the shops were now nearly all closed. She saw several policemen who looked "haggard, dusty—exhausted." In her view, they were finally receiving a reaction from the people they had trodden upon. "I grew ruthless in my indignation," wrote Oakes Smith, "for their insolence and cruelty had become a public cry."

At 3 p.m. she joined someone for dinner at Delmonico's, the elegant, upscale restaurant that had recently opened in a three-story brick mansion on the northeast corner of 5th Avenue and East 14th Street. But as soon as they were seated the waiters rushed into the room, barring the doors and closing the windows, for they could hear "that great sound as of the sea—the tumult of the people." The riot quickly turned from anti-draft to anti-black as well, and the furious mob killed any African American they could lay their hands on. "There goes a nigger," Oakes Smith heard someone cry, "and the cruel, remorseless multitude, three thousand strong were in pursuit of the unhappy fugitive. He was without doubt torn in pieces."

Oakes Smith and her companion made their way up 36th Street. All was "dire confusion—mad uproar," she wrote. As policemen, soldiers, and rioters clashed in the streets, she was dismayed to hear the wealthy of the neighborhood calling on the soldiers to fire into the crowd. "There was no expression of pity," she wrote, "no sympathy for the poor laborer, who in his mad vengeance sought a sort of justice—a wild revenge one most true." Later that night and a few blocks away, the mob threw stones through the windows of Horace Greeley's *New York Tribune* office while shouting, "*Them* are the niggers up there." The crowd broke into the ground floor of the building and smashed some furniture, shattered some windows, and started small fires, but quickly dispersed when a police officer fired a shot into the air. Overnight the building was placed under martial law by Union general John E. Wool, and was stocked with firearms and cannons loaded and ready to fire. Greeley was incensed that his building was being used as an arsenal, but in the end, the military presence saved his office.

Early the next morning, Tuesday, July 14, Oakes Smith went down to Wall Street, but she found all business suspended. The stages and cars were not running "and the frequent discharges of the military told that hot work was in progress." She tried to make her way uptown to catch a train for home but she could not get through the city streets. Fortunately, as she was "struggling onward" and "nearly exhausted," a carriage stopped in front of her. Its owner, Jeremiah G. Hamilton, asked if she would like to go back to his house to rest. How well Oakes Smith knew Hamilton is unclear, but they had met at least once in 1862, when he had escorted her to a meeting to discuss Appleton's arrest. Hamilton was a prominent businessman in the city (she gave him the appellation "Esquire" in her diary). At fifty-six years old, he had become a millionaire on Wall Street, which was a remarkable accomplishment—for he was a black man in a city awash in racial prejudice. Oakes Smith described Hamilton as "I think an eastern Indian—his complexion is darker than that of a mulatto, but his features are Caucassian [*sic*]—and he is a highly cultivated man." His dark skin notwithstanding, Oakes Smith eagerly climbed into the carriage and went back to Hamilton's home at 68 East 29th Street. While sitting inside with Hamilton's family, two of his children stepped out upon the balcony facing 29th Street to watch the crowds passing by. Hamilton "sprang from his chair," brought the children back inside and closed the window. Oakes Smith wrote, "*He* understood the hazard growing out of their dark complexions. I shall never forget the expression of anguish upon his face."

When she went back outside later that day, Hamilton advised her to head toward Lexington Avenue "as a safer retreat from the crowd." She followed his advice but accidentally made a turn that brought her right back into the mayhem. "Oh! my soul—what a sight presented itself!" she wrote. "Masses of infuriated women, tossing their arms wildly—weeping women and children, and pale desperate men—pools of blood—broken furniture burning ruins." Oakes Smith addressed the people in a low, calm voice, telling them that five thousand soldiers were on their way to the city and would open fire with grapeshot and without warning. She went from group to group, urging them to return to the safety of their homes. When she saw one boy, about thirteen years old, she told him, "My poor boy—go home—keep out of these dreadful scenes." The child burst into tears and sobbed, "I have'nt got any home." Another woman explained that his mother had been dead for some time, his father had been killed in the army, and the boy lived upon the kindness of others.

One "pale desperate looking man leaning against a wall" told Oakes Smith, "Madam, (he said in good accent) it may be easy to tell us what to do—but I *will* not obey this draft. I may as well be shot here as anywhere. Look here—(pointing to blood upon the walk)—the soldiers fired upon us—not a word—no warning—and I took a child up shot through the head—covered with blood—I looked at him—it was my own child—I *will* have revenge." A "great burly fellow" soon "eyed me with a savage frown" and muttered that she was "one of them aristocrats from the fifth Avenue" and "a Spy—sent here from the Black Republicans!"

Oakes Smith immediately recognized that she was in danger, "but I did not flinch—I do not think I turned pale—I repelled the charge in a calm, firm voice, and went on—he following and muttering—but I did not fear— a superhuman strength seemed mine. I knew better than to leave them—so I kept on talking in [a] low calm manner, advising him as seemed best."

As Elizabeth reached 33rd Street, the disorder continued to increase. She saw a dense crowd standing around a lamppost, upon which hung the body of Colonel Henry O'Brien, a New York resident and Irish officer of the Eleventh New York Volunteers, who had commanded his troops to fire above the crowd the previous day in order to disperse them. Sadly, O'Brien's men had killed a mother and her two-year-old child in the process, and when the mob saw him now, they exacted their revenge. Women, men, and children knocked O'Brien unconscious and then beat him and lit wads of paper under his head as he lay helpless on the ground.

Oakes Smith lamented, "It was a sickening sight—for four hours they tortured the unhappy man—prolonging his sufferings with a fiendish fury. I expressed compassion for him—but they justified their conduct on the ground that he was a *traitor* to his countrymen." Oakes Smith turned up 4th Avenue with "quite a group following me and thanking me for what I had done."[16]

For all the horrors she witnessed and the dangers she encountered in the streets, Oakes Smith was fortunate to have left the Hamilton home when she did. At about 10:15 p.m. that evening, a group of "men and boys" came down East 29th Street chanting his address: "68, 68, 68." One of Hamilton's neighbors recalled, "a large number of the rioters assailed neighbor Hamiltons with loud cries for the 'Nigger.'" When asked what they were doing, one of the rioters declared to a passerby, "There is a nigger living here with two white women, and we are going to bring him out, and hang him on the lamp-post, and you stop and see the fun."

One of the rioters rang the doorbell "violently." When no one answered they burst through the door that led down into the basement.

THE RIOTERS DRAGGING COL. O'BRIEN'S BODY THROUGH THE STREET. Page 196.

"*The Rioters Dragging Col. O'Brien's Body through the Street.*"
J. T. Headley, *The Great Riots of New York, 1712 to 1873* (New York: E. B. Treat, 1873).

Hamilton's forty-year-old white wife, Eliza Jane, "met them at the head of the stairs" as they came up to the ground floor from the basement. The crowd consisted of four or five men and seven or eight boys. Mrs. Hamilton asked them what they wanted. One man replied that "they were looking for Mr Hamilton as they wanted to kill him." "Why?" she asked. The man claimed that Hamilton "had injured his mother and he wanted to be revenged." Eliza had no idea what the man was talking about. She also assured them that "there were no colored persons" around. But none of this mattered. The intruders pushed past her and searched the home for her husband. She followed one of them, a thirteen-year-old boy named John Leary Jr., and caught him stealing clothes. She confronted him and got him to return the clothes since she knew his family.

Eventually the men came back downstairs and asked her for liquor and cigars. "I told them I had no liquor," Mrs. Hamilton later reported to the authorities, "but gave them cider and segars." As one historian describes the scene, "The men had made themselves comfortable on the ground floor drinking cider and smoking cigars while the boys roamed the house. They scattered things around and made a mess in a room on the third story, stealing $25 in cash and a few other items valued at about $40. Similarly, a few drawers had been tipped upside down in the basement, but nothing seemed to be missing."

While the men sat drinking in her parlor, Mrs. Hamilton caught young Leary in a back room, trying to steal a gun. She wrestled him for the weapon and was able to hold on to the pistol, but the boy told a large Irishman with "two murderous looking weapons in his hands" that she had a gun. He came and "took the gun from me in a forcible manner" and told her she "was damned lucky to escape so well." The men left back through the basement about forty-five minutes after they entered. Fortunately, Jeremiah "had already made his way over the fence into 28th St.," before the mob forcibly entered his home.[17]

The next morning, Wednesday, July 15, Oakes Smith finally made it to the trains that would carry her back to Long Island. "In the cars I found Mr Hamilton—looking haggard and internally excited, but outwardly calm, and determined," she wrote. Oakes Smith insisted that he come to her home. He remained with her family at "The Willows" for nearly a week and they all "anxiously . . . awaited returns from the great City." A few days later, Hamilton's family joined them. Having so many houseguests was exhausting for Elizabeth and Isotta. When the Hamiltons finally returned to Manhattan later in July, a neighbor reported, "the blinds are closed and not a face to be seen."[18]

The racial violence that enveloped New York City in mid-July 1863 is unparalleled in American history. Working-class men, women, and children—mostly Irish Democrats—lashed out against Lincoln's conscription and emancipation policies. These poor immigrant families did not want to send their menfolk off to fight in a war that might lead freed slaves to flood the labor markets of the North. At least 105 people died during the five days of rioting; most of the victims were black men who were beaten, lynched, burned, and mutilated. In one of the most stunning displays of inhumanity, the Irish mob burned the Colored Orphan Asylum, where, according to the asylum's records, "the children numbering 233, were quietly seated in their school rooms, playing in the nursery, or reclining on a sick bed in the Hospital, when an infuriated mob, consisting of several thousand men, women, and children, armed with clubs, brick bats, etc. advanced upon the Institution." The children and their teachers prayed to God for deliverance as the mob shouted, "Burn the niggers' nest!" "Murder the d—d monkeys," and "Wring the necks of the d—d Lincolnites." By some miracle, all the children survived.[19]

When recording her experiences in her diary, Oakes Smith blamed Lincoln and the Republicans. "The Radicals have done their utmost to exasperate all classes—in order to have martial law proclaimed in the City," she wrote. "God save us from such calamity—the streets of New York would run blood—and the prisons be filled with men and women suffered to be obnoxious to the powers that be."[20] This was a common refrain in Oakes Smith's diary—that the Lincoln administration was constantly contriving ways to increase its own power at the expense of others' liberty.

By the end of the summer, the conflagrations over Vallandigham's arrest and the draft had subsided. One friend of Elizabeth's consoled her, urging her not to despair. Appleton had been "one of the first martyrs of this administration," like Vallandigham "and a host of others." But vindication would eventually come, she hoped.[21]

Federal authorities, meanwhile, hoped for a different sort of vindication. Back in Boston, Sheriff John M. Clark and US Marshal John S. Keyes continued to brood over Oaksmith's escape. "I have not ceased to think of the matter you spoke about when last I saw you," Clark wrote to Keyes in September 1863. "I should be more rejoiced to accomplish the capture & return of Oaksmith than at any other earthly success I desire." Still, Clark would not "go upon a wild goose chase" just because somebody claimed to have spotted Oaksmith in New Orleans. "I am willing *to pay or do, or go* to get him & if the information can be made reasonably reliable, I shall be glad to act upon your suggestion to send some one to get him."[22]

14

LINCOLN

Eighteen sixty-two was a momentous year for the Lincoln administration when it came to its dealings with the slave trade. The convictions of Appleton Oaksmith and Samuel Skinner, the execution of Nathaniel Gordon, and the ratification of the Lyons-Seward Treaty all appeared like a massive culmination of Lincoln's life-long hatred of slavery and the slave trade. For Lincoln, the questions involved were deeply moral in nature. And extreme measures would be needed to ultimately rid the nation of this stain. To a British journalist, Lincoln said, "The slave-trade will never be put down till our laws are executed, and the penalty of death has once been enforced upon the offenders."[1] It is little wonder then, that Lincoln is remembered for holding firm when so many petitioners asked him to pardon Gordon. Many Northerners viewed the execution of "the wretched pirate" Gordon as evidence that Lincoln was moving with a firm resolve against slavery and the slave trade. "Mr Lincoln, in selecting his district attorneys and marshals, had an eye to their capacities for arresting the foreign slave trade," wrote one enthusiastic New Englander. "Under the energetic and sagacious action of his officers slave ships which, under former administrations, boldly entered our northern ports to fit out for their atrocious and inhuman voyages, are now suppressed. . . . Without the professions of a philanthropist, Mr L. has evinced a noble and generous nature, and should rank with the honored names of Clarkson and Wilberforce."

On the other side of the Atlantic, the London *Daily News* surmised that "Gordon would have had a better chance had his life depended on the decision of some impulsive negro–phile, instead of being at the disposal of the severe, deliberative, but inflexible tenant of the White House, a man who, amidst the severest trials has never swerved a hair's breadth from the policy which he professed when he was a candidate for office." Lincoln's closest associates, according to the *Daily News*, "said that he would not lose the precious opportunity to strike a blow at a system which costs hundreds of lives yearly and dooms the brave men of the two African squadrons to ruin their health on a pestilential coast." Moreover, Lincoln's refusal to intervene in Gordon's case "is an index of the quality of Mr. Lincoln's government, of its strength of principle, and the consistency of its policy, and *it marks the end of a system*."[2]

But was Gordon's case really an "index" of how Lincoln dealt with slave traders? The evidence suggests a more complicated story.

Congressman John B. Alley of Massachusetts recollected a conversation in which Lincoln stated that he was "kindly enough in nature, and can be moved to pity and to pardon the perpetrator of almost the worst crime that the mind of man can conceive or the arm of man can execute," but he concluded that he "never will pardon" any person "who, for paltry gain and stimulated only by avarice, can rob Africa of her children to sell into interminable bondage." Such a person, Lincoln said, may "rot in jail before he will ever get relief from me."

This alleged statement of Lincoln's had been made in connection with a sailor aboard the slaver *Orion*, which had been captured off the coast of Africa on October 3, 1859, after taking 1,023 Africans on board. According to Alley's recollection, a number of citizens of his district had sent Lincoln a petition asking for the release of a man in the Newburyport Jail who had been sentenced to several years' imprisonment and a $1,000 fine. The prisoner would not be released until he paid the fine. Since he was unable to do so, the unpaid fine was essentially turning his prison term into a life sentence.[3]

Three imprisoned sailors from the *Orion* petitioned Lincoln for pardon. William Dunham, the *Orion*'s second mate, had pleaded guilty at his trial in Boston in October 1860 and received a sentence of one year and nine months in prison at the Charles Street Jail. In September 1861, several prominent citizens wrote to Lincoln urging pardon, including Massachusetts governor John A. Andrew and Suffolk County sheriff John M. Clark. Dunham claimed that he had believed the *Orion*'s voyage had been lawful when he signed on to sail with her and that he only learned of her real intentions after more than two months at sea. Dunham also claimed that he was becoming quite ill as a result of his imprisonment. But US Attorney Richard Henry Dana Jr. was not convinced by this explanation, and he saw no reason to grant a pardon. Dana even went to the prison to ask the physician there about Dunham's health, learning that "there is nothing in the state of Dunham's health calling for the intervention of the Executive clemency." Following Dana's advice, Lincoln rejected Dunham's petition on October 26, 1861.[4]

Byron Chamberlain, first mate of the *Orion*, had been found guilty and sentenced to two years in prison at Salem, Massachusetts. On July 30, 1861, Chamberlain wrote to Lincoln claiming that he had not known the real intention of the voyage until it was too late and that he had been "decoyed into employment." He also told Lincoln that he would "gladly enlist in the naval service" of the United States if only Lincoln would pardon him. But Lincoln chose not to act.

A few months later, on October 20, Byron's father, A. C. Chamberlain wrote to Lincoln. This letter adopted a different tone, stating that Byron now accepted the full responsibility for his guilt. "I rejoice that he has suffered first, because the law is fully vindicated in his own person, secondly, because I am persuaded, he is cured of the avaricious wickedness which led him to comit [*sic*] the crime," wrote Byron's father. Moreover, he claimed that Byron "is now a Christian man" and like the prodigal son, he hoped he would soon "return to his father's house." Again, however, Lincoln refused to act.[5]

So far, the cases of the *Orion* seem to align with Congressman Alley's recollection—Lincoln refused to grant clemency. Yet the facts of the Dunham and Chamberlain cases do not align with one important detail in Alley's recollection. Only one slave trader—Thomas Morgan—was held at the Newburyport Jail. Morgan had been captain of the *Orion*, and he was the person who had allegedly duped both Dunham and Chamberlain (so they claimed in their petitions to Lincoln).

At his trial, Morgan had pleaded guilty and was sentenced to two years' imprisonment and a $2,000 fine. Morgan now claimed that up until the time of his involvement with the *Orion* he "had ever borne a[n] honourable and unblemished reputation" and that he had become "the dupe of others and was misled, without criminal intention on my own part." Between July 1861 and December 1862, Morgan submitted four petitions for pardon to Lincoln, as well as other documents attesting to his inability to pay his fine and his good behavior in jail. Yet the pardon attorney called Morgan's case "a very plain one," pointing out that Lincoln had refused to pardon Dunham and should do the same in this case.

On one of Morgan's petitions, Lincoln added a small notation, "The gentleman who brings me the letter says it is a 'Slave-trade' conviction, of a minor grade." This was hardly a "minor" case considering the large number of Africans found on board the *Orion*. Nevertheless, Lincoln remitted the sentence on March 11, 1863. Lincoln's public rationale was that Morgan's sentence had expired in October 1862 and that it was "endured by him in a humble and exemplary manner," and that he was unable to pay the fine.

In short, Lincoln showed mercy because Morgan's inability to pay the fine was turning his two-year imprisonment into a life sentence.[6] The very man Congressman Alley said Lincoln claimed he could never free from prison was the one Lincoln released.

And Morgan was not the only one. On July 2, 1862, Lincoln pardoned James Brayley, a British subject who had been master of the schooner *Alice Rogers*, and who had been convicted of bringing two black boys from Jamaica to Virginia in April 1860 to sell as slaves. Brayley was sentenced to three years at hard labor at the penitentiary in Washington and a $1,000 fine. James Buchanan had refused to pardon Brayley on February 28, 1861, and Lincoln had followed suit on October 11, 1861. But on July 2, 1862, Lincoln granted Brayley pardon, citing as his reasons that Brayley had "conducted himself in a humble, exemplary, and truly penitent manner" during the first two-thirds of his sentence, that he had a destitute wife and children "who are respected and beloved in the community where they reside," and because "many highly respectable citizens of Port Chester, New York, have urgently recommended . . . clemency."[7]

On May 21, 1863, Lincoln pardoned Albert Horn, who had been convicted in October 1862 of fitting out the *City of Norfolk* in New York City for the slave trade. Horn was sentenced to five years' imprisonment, but while in prison he became deathly ill with bronchitis or tuberculosis. Horn's attorney, James T. Brady—an old New York associate of Oaksmith's—wrote to Delafield Smith asking him "to cooperate in an application for a pardon or a remission of punishment." "I cannot do this," Smith replied, claiming that Horn's guilt "was clearly established. The crime is of a flagrant nature; and it deserves, in my judgment, a higher penalty than is affixed to it by the statute." But Smith conceded that Horn's health was essentially turning his prison term "into the penalty of death" and he admitted that "the law would not be infringed, but on the contrary protected, by executive clemency exercised in such manner as the President may determine."

Brady forwarded Smith's letter to Attorney General Edward Bates and simply asked for the pardon "on grounds of humanity" since "keeping him in prison will shorten his life." Brady maintained that "the execution of Gordon, and Horn's conviction & sentence have fully satisfied" the public's need for justice and would "forever" discourage any further slaving out of Manhattan. Even Robert Murray, the hardnosed US marshal, concurred in the request for pardon, writing, "He is very weak, afflicted in body and mind, and . . . that to continue his imprisonment will result in materially shortening his life." On account of Horn's ill health, Lincoln granted "a full and unconditional pardon." When Horn walked out of the prison his wife kissed Murray's hand. "The Marshal was much affected," reported the *New York Post*.[8]

A few weeks later, on July 25, 1863, Lincoln pardoned Rudolf Blumenberg, a New Yorker who had been convicted of perjury in a slave trading case. Blumenberg's crime was posting bond for an alleged slaver when he did not have the money. (After bond was posted, the ship was taken out of port to Africa.) Blumenberg had been tried twice by a prosecutor from James Buchanan's administration—on December 4, 1860, and March 6, 1861—but both trials led to hung juries. After Delafield Smith took office, however, Blumenberg was convicted, on May 14, 1861. Smith was convinced that corruption and bribery had caused the outcomes of the first two trials.

From Sing Sing Prison, Blumenberg passed information along to Robert Murray about the slave trade. Murray consequently urged the Lincoln administration to grant executive clemency on account of Blumenberg's "bad health," his "distress[ed]" wife, and the fact that "he has given much useful information against slave-dealers." According to Murray, Blumenberg had been "eminently useful in procuring information" from other prisoners. Several members of Lincoln's cabinet—including Secretary of the Interior Caleb B. Smith and Postmaster General Montgomery Blair—also became strong advocates for Blumenberg's release. Blair, a conservative Republican from Maryland, got involved because Blumenberg had two brothers serving in the Union army from Maryland, one of whom had been badly wounded at Antietam in September 1862.

But Delafield Smith was horrified, writing to Blair that "Blumenberg's perjury was of the most flagrant character" and that he had haughtily taunted Smith after the trial "that he *could* keep out of prison and *would*." Smith acknowledged that Blumenberg was a Republican, but called him "a loud-mouthed 'Republican' . . . and a hypocrite." Moreover, he stated that Murray was "much mistaken" about the usefulness of the information Blumenberg had given while in prison. In light of Smith's strenuous protest, Lincoln declined to grant a pardon on October 22, 1862. By the summer of 1863, however, Smith had a change of heart. He became convinced that Blumenberg had made a good faith effort to procure information for Murray, and he wrote to Lincoln that "executive interposition would be safe." Lincoln immediately began the process of issuing a pardon.[9]

One pardon, in particular, might have shocked and upset Oaksmith more than any other that summer. On June 27, 1863, Lincoln pardoned

Samuel P. Skinner, citing Skinner's age, "declining health," and that he "was not the main perpetrator of the offence for which he was convicted, but acted as accessory thereto; and whereas, on the trial of Appleton Oaksmith, the principal offender, the said Samuel P. Skinner was used as a witness by the Government, and gave free and full testimony in the case." Richard Henry Dana Jr. expressed his willingness to see Skinner pardoned, writing that his testimony had "blow[n] the defence sky high . . . by exposing the fabrication of [Oaksmith's] defence." With the US attorney's blessing, Lincoln was happy to set the poor "dupe" free.[10]

As these brief sketches reveal, Lincoln's record in dealing with slave traders is far more complicated than the famous Gordon case would indicate. Delafield Smith worried that pardoning slave traders "would make the execution of Gordon an idle and therefore a cruel ceremony."[11] And yet, even he and Murray supported the pardon and release of several men they had convicted. These instances of mercy should not be interpreted as evidence that the Lincoln administration waffled in its commitment to destroy the transatlantic slave trade. A high profile, internationally significant incident in 1864 captures the administration's commitment to ridding the world of this barbaric commerce. It would also have major implications for Appleton Oaksmith's future.

The slave trade into Cuba had been illegal since 1820, but corrupt seamen continued to bring cargos of Africans to Cuba's rocky shores. Unfortunately, the Cuban government often turned a blind eye; however, in mid-November 1863, Cuban authorities seized a cargo of 1,105 Africans who had been illegally imported to the island. The Spanish civil and military official responsible for the seizure, Jose Augustin Arguelles, collected a $15,000 reward as part of the prize money for his efforts. But Arguelles was no abolitionist. In fact, he schemed with a local priest who oversaw the recording of the region's vital records to claim that 141 of the Africans had died of smallpox and been burned. Arguelles then sold them for between $700–750 apiece, pocketing some $100,000—in addition to his government reward.

Before getting found out, Arguelles took his wife and newfound fortune to New York City. The Captain General of Cuba, an abolitionist and vigorous opponent of the slave trade named Domingo Dulce, called Arguelles "a scoundrel worse than [a] thief or highwayman" and requested Secretary of State Seward to extradite Arguelles to Cuba, for the 141 slaves could not be freed under Spanish law until Arguelles was returned.

Domingo Dulce.
Collection of Jonathan W. White.

The problem was that Spain and the United States did not have an extradition treaty, so there was no way for Seward to legally capture and return the fugitive. Dulce held several meetings with Thomas Savage, an American diplomat in Havana, while Gabriel Garcia y Tassara, the Spanish minister in Washington, met with Seward. Soon after these meetings, Seward ordered Robert Murray to arrest Arguelles and return him to Cuba. "So far as depends on me," Seward told a Spanish diplomat, "Spanish slave-dealers who have no immunity in Havana, will find none in New York."

Murray carried out Seward's order in mid-May 1864, and Arguelles arrived in Havana within a few days in the custody of Dulce's agent and two US deputy marshals. After one night in the common jail he was lodged in the Morro Castle, a Spanish fortress in Havana harbor that dated to 1589. Eventually Arguelles was tried in both military and civil courts. The court-martial sentenced him to loss of rank and two years' imprisonment, while the civil court sentenced him to nineteen years at hard labor. Captain General Dulce was pleased with all that had transpired. "I ask you to make known to Secretary Seward," he wrote to Spanish minister Tassara, "how much I thank him for his cooperation in this affair, because by it, he assists the exposure and punishment of a crime totally distinct from any political matter; the result of which will be that more than two hundred beings, who are groaning in slavery, will owe to his Excellency the recovery of their freedom."[12]

As humanitarian as Seward's intentions may have been, the kidnapping of Arguelles was carried out without the knowledge of Lincoln's cabinet. Secretary of the Navy Gideon Welles was "surprised at the proceeding" since there was no extradition treaty between the United States and Spain, writing that the "act shocks me." Secretary of the Treasury Salmon P. Chase believed the extradition was "devoid of policy and wanting law," although some newspaper editors speculated that Chase opposed this action in order to strengthen his own chances for defeating Lincoln at the upcoming Republican National Convention. Attorney General Edward Bates similarly thought it "strange that a step so important and delicate should have been taken without any Cabinet discussion."[13]

Following the kidnapping, Elizabeth Oakes Smith met with Mrs. Arguelles in New York, and the two women agreed that Marshal Murray was "a malignant falsifier—one who would rather lie than tell the truth." The nation had become "debased," concluded Oakes Smith, "under the masterly guidance of Abraham the Magnificent."[14]

15

KIDNAPPING

By the summer of 1864, Seward and Murray had become more audacious in their attempts to destroy the slave trade. With the war going badly for the Union—and the possibility that Lincoln might not be reelected—they needed to do everything they could to end the human traffic before the ascendance of a Democratic administration. Their successful abduction and rendition of Arguelles had been thrilling for Murray, who was "evidently proud of the adroitness with which he did the job." But Murray had to flee Manhattan because he had been indicted for kidnapping in a New York City court. When he reached Washington, however, Attorney General Bates noticed that he seemed "not much alarmed by the indictment."

The conservative members of Lincoln's cabinet were appalled by the Arguelles affair, believing that Seward had taken such action to boost his own image throughout the nation. Bates speculated that Seward "was led to the hazardous measure (of very doubtful policy, at least, if not clearly illegal) by his belief that it would be a capital hit, to win the favor of the extreme anti-slavery men."[1] Secretary of the Navy Welles similarly thought that "Seward sometimes does strange things, and I am inclined to believe he has committed one of those freaks which makes me constantly apprehensive of his acts. He knows that slavery is odious and all concerned in slave traffic are detested, and has improved the occasion to exercise arbitrary power, expecting to win popular applause by doing an illegal act." Welles worried that "Constitutional limitations are to him unnecessary restraints. . . . Could the abduction by any possibility be popular Mr. S. expects it to enure to his credit."

At a cabinet meeting in June 1864, Seward responded to criticism from Welles by stating that "a nation is never bound to furnish asylum to dangerous criminals who are offenders against the human race." Moreover, he claimed, the rendition "was an act of comity merely." Of course, Welles was not satisfied by these explanations, and he feared that the broad "hostility to the slave trade" that existed in the United States would permit "a great wrong . . . [to] be perpetrated with impunity and without scrutiny."[2] Welles's apprehension was precisely Seward's desire. Indeed, his recent success in the Arguelles case only emboldened him.

Nearly two years after his escape from the Charles Street Jail, Appleton Oaksmith was still on Seward's mind. Perhaps it irked Seward that Oaksmith had been "lurking" (Seward's word) about Havana since his escape.[3] He also received a reminder from US Marshal John S. Keyes in late May. In an official letter, Keyes reiterated the idea that he had proposed to Seward back in November 1862—that Seward ask Spanish authorities to "surrender" Oaksmith over to the federal government.[4]

On June 6—just a few weeks after the Arguelles affair—Seward sent a dispatch to the US consulate in Havana, instructing Vice Consul General Thomas Savage to "immediately . . . endeavor to learn if Oaksmith is now in the Island of Cuba." If Oaksmith was present, Savage was to inform Captain General Dulce of Oaksmith's "complicity . . . in the slave-trade" and "ascertain whether, if an officer of the United States be sent to Cuba, such measures will be taken by the Captain General as will lead to his apprehension and delivery" to federal authorities. Seward informed Savage that Oaksmith "possesses considerable property and has influential friends, both of which are used to promote the rebel interests." Finally, Seward cautioned Savage: "You will be careful to exercise in this matter your best judgment, and let all your enquiries be attended with due caution and secrecy."[5]

Seward could not have hoped for a better consular agent in Havana. Thomas Savage had grown up in the city and had been working tirelessly since the 1850s to destroy the illegal slave trade. Prior to the Civil War, several slaving captains denounced Savage's "tyranny" and "malice" toward them (when necessary, Savage would exercise extralegal authority to stop slavers from leaving the port at Havana). Upon receiving Seward's dispatch about Oaksmith in 1864, Savage replied, "This notorious person has been engaged during his residence here in favoring the interests of our rebels." He then explained that Oaksmith had departed for Galveston, Texas, but when he returned, "I shall have notice of his arrival immediately after it occurs and will carry out your wishes with due caution."[6]

Word that Seward wanted Oaksmith kidnapped began to circulate in the press. "We see it hinted that the Cuban government *may* deliver up one Appleton Oaksmith, who was once convicted in Boston as a slave trader, but who succeeded in making his escape to Cuba," wrote the editors of the *Daily Ohio Statesman* in June 1864. "Spain, it seems, granted him the right of asylum and refuge, though convicted in our courts, which, indeed, strikingly contrasts with Seward's and Lincoln's treacherous kidnapping and secret extradition of Col. Arguelles, who has never been even indicted or tried, and that without the least investigation into the facts." The Democratic editors continued: "It is indeed disgraceful and humiliating to our name as Americans, and no Administration but Lincoln's was ever base enough to do such a thing; but he not only does it with alacrity, but adds insult to injury in defending it."[7]

This theory also appeared in Republican papers. One editor surmised that the government had abducted Arguelles and sent him to Cuba "without warrant of law" because "the Spanish Government had intimated that if the United States authorities would arrest and deliver Col. Arguelles into their hands, they in turn would surrender Appleton Oaksmith. . . . If this be true, Oaksmith, who has been living in affluence in Cuba, may find himself a prisoner ere this, and ready to be delivered to this Government." Reporting on this story, the New York correspondent for the *San Francisco Bulletin* wondered, "Some of our people are puzzled to decide which of the two Governments have made the best bargain in this international exchange of two scoundrels."[8] The *Sacramento Daily Union* similarly reported

> that the Spanish Minister at Washington made a formal agreement with Secretary Seward that for the surrender of Arguelles to the Spanish Government he would engage to surrender to the United States Appleton Oaksmith, the Boston slave-trader, who three years since fled to Cuba and is now in Havana. No Eastern newspaper is permitted to print this fact; but as Oaksmith will be in our hands and probably serving his five-year term in State Prison long before this can reach the Pacific side, I venture to send it forward. The hanging of Gordon taught the slave-traders that we were in earnest, and the catching and imprisonment of Oaksmith will show them that we are still determined to break up their nefarious traffic.[9]

Throughout the war, the US government was also determined to break up another type of illicit maritime commerce—Confederate blockade running. By the summer of 1864, the Union blockade was strangling the Confederate coastline, and the port at Galveston, Texas, was one of the few places blockade-runners continued to operate. Blockade-runners who worked on the Gulf of Mexico had several advantages over those who operated on the Atlantic Ocean, including more hiding places and vastly more predictable waters. On average, two vessels attempted to run the blockade in the Gulf every day, and in 1864, 87 percent of the steamers were successful.[10]

Oaksmith left Havana on June 1, according to Savage, on the "Anglo-Rebel Steamer Caroline, Capt. McDonall, cleared ostensibly for Belize, with a general cargo of supplies for the South, but she went into Galveston, Texas." The *Caroline* had been a blockade-runner under several other names—including the *Union* and *Rosita*—but after having been captured and sold several times, she now sailed under British colors. One member of her crew remembered her as "a rattle-trap of a steamer, with a 'walking beam.'" In fact, her captain was Oaksmith sailing under the alias "John McDonald." As Oaksmith would later explain, "Driven from the North, I sought refuge in the South, and espoused the Confederate cause."[11]

After "a severe chase from the Blockaders," the *Caroline* made it safely from Havana to Galveston, then up Buffalo Bayou to Constitution Bend.[12] The crew discharged their cargo, took on a load of cotton, and prepared to return to Galveston. Oaksmith noticed a "big pile of sails" in the pilothouse and ordered a German sailor named Buis to "take 'em out and put 'em on deck out of the way." Buis angrily retorted, "I shipped as quartermaster on this boat, and don't do deckhand's work." "D—n you," replied Oaksmith, "take your things and go ashore." Buis then gathered up his belongings and went onto the beach, where he opened one of his bags and pulled out a pistol, which he pointed at Oaksmith, who was facing the other way. The crew shouted out a warning to their captain, who then went to his cabin to retrieve "a big six-shooter." Now Buis was frightened. Oaksmith yelled, "D—n you, leave here or I'll kill you!" But Buis was too frightened to move, so Oaksmith shot him in the leg. Buis "fell to the ground howling out that he was murdered," while Oaksmith ordered someone, "Haul that man up to Houston; he's only shot through the leg. I ought to have killed him, but he isn't worth it."[13]

After about a month in Texas, the *Caroline* left Galveston, under cover of darkness on Thursday, July 7, at about 11 p.m. Night, rain, or fog were the preferred conditions for blockade-runners leaving port. Nevertheless, Union blockaders almost immediately discovered the vessel, and three gunboats—the USS *Aroostook*, USS *Penguin*, and USS *Kanawha*—gave chase. "Some one in town must have given us away," recalled one member of the crew, "for by the time we had got a couple of miles down the coast, a signal was made to the blockading fleet, and [the] gunboats started after us."

The crew of the *Caroline* threw about a hundred bales of cotton overboard and stayed close to the island city to avoid capture. By morning light, the Union gunboats "were peppering us with shot and shell, which broke the walking beam and bored a couple of big holes through the ship," recalled a crewman. As the ship's machinery overheated and stopped functioning, Oaksmith decided "to beach her" about sixteen miles west of Galveston. As the men evacuated, one crewmember, Ed Farley, ran down to the fire room and threw a shovel full of hot coals onto the cargo of cotton. This instantly set the ship ablaze. Oaksmith, the crew, and three passengers then escaped to shore in lifeboats.

The Union blockaders sent sailors on several launches in pursuit of Oaksmith and his men, but scouts from the Thirty-fifth Texas Cavalry (Brown's Regiment) fired upon them from behind the sand dunes, killing several Yankees. The launches retreated, at which point the gunboats opened fire with shell and grapeshot, killing one of the crew—a fireman named John McCall, who was trying to return to the ship to save some money and horses. The gunboats "kept up their fire until the vessel was burnt to the waterline" at about 11 a.m. Oaksmith and the crew of the *Caroline* meanwhile made their escape by land, arriving at Galveston on July 8 at about 2 a.m., "some barefooted, having saved nothing, except what they carried on their backs." The city they encountered was "a most forsaken place; its streets covered with sand, its wharves rotting, its defenses in a most deplorable condition." Newspapers throughout the North celebrated the destruction of the *Caroline*, although they all erroneously called her the *Matagorda*. Texas papers purposefully concealed the name of the adventurous captain.[14]

By mid-July, Thomas Savage was hearing rumors that Oaksmith would return to Havana on the *Matagorda*.[15] His sources were fairly accurate, although it would take a little longer than Savage expected. In August, Oaksmith was still in Houston, where he published a patriotic Confederate poem titled "The Sunny South" in the *Houston Daily Telegraph* under the pseudonym "Captain J. McDonald."[16] Finally, in September, about two months after the *Caroline* debacle, Oaksmith sailed from Galveston for Havana on the *Matagorda*, an iron side-wheel steamer formerly known as the *Alice*. Built in Wilmington, Delaware, the *Matagorda* carried no firepower but was reputed to be "quite fast." In addition to her captain, she carried a small crew of fewer than twenty men, most of whom were foreigners, as well as the wife of a Confederate soldier and her three children and nurse. Her cargo consisted of about eight hundred bales of Texas-grown cotton.

Shortly after 3 p.m. on September 10, while cruising around the Gulf of Mexico, the lookout on the masthead of the USS *Magnolia* discovered black smoke to the southwest. The *Magnolia* immediately altered course and got close enough to see that her prey was a side-wheel steamer. "All steam and sail were made on the Magnolia, and off we went after her," recalled one of the men aboard the blockader.

Upon seeing that she was being pursued, the *Matagorda* "clapped on all canvas, frequently altering her course and making sail, all the time emitting from her chimney dense black smoke." The captain of the *Magnolia* described the *Matagorda* as "making and taking in sail, endeavoring all he knew how to get away from us." But the Union blockaders would not give up. Indeed, the excitement aboard the *Magnolia* was palpable as her captain ordered "pork, pitch, wood, &c." to be thrown into the ship's boiler to increase her speed.

After three hours the blockader pulled within six miles of the *Matagorda*. Near sunset the *Magnolia* fired her forward pivot gun toward the *Matagorda*, sending a shot and shell over her rigging. But Oaksmith and his crew ignored the warning and kept pressing on under both steam and sail. "We now began in earnest," recalled the blockader; "shot and shell were fired continually from all our guns, and the bursting of the shells over and all round her was awful to look on." Finally, at about 10:30 p.m., a shell burst close enough to the *Matagorda* that she finally capitulated, showing a lantern on her side to signal surrender. She hove to and the executive officer of the *Magnolia* prepared to board her. By now the vessels were about seventy-five miles northwest of Cape Saint Antonio, Cuba. Unbeknownst to the Union naval officer, he was on the verge of capturing one of the Union's most significant prizes—not the ship, although she was a beauty—but Appleton Oaksmith.

During the seven-hour, eighty-mile chase, the crew of the *Matagorda* threw about two hundred bales of cotton overboard in a futile attempt to increase speed. But she still had a great deal on board. In addition to the ship, the sailors aboard the *Magnolia* seized nearly six hundred bales of cotton, as well as the *Matagorda*'s tackle, apparel, furniture, and stores. After her capture, the *Matagorda* was sent to Key West, but because her cargo was so valuable, she was escorted to Boston by the US gunboat *Iuka*. One of the *Magnolia*'s officers believed she "can easily be converted into a vessel of war . . . and if such is the case would be of very efficient service." At Boston, however, she was condemned in the same federal court that had convicted Oaksmith in 1862. US Marshal John S. Keyes would have the honor of advertising the ship and cargo for sale. In early November, the vessel sold for $55,000, while the cargo of cotton commanded $333,500.65. Keyes himself would net $5,296.27 for his services as auctioneer.[17]

The *Matagorda* was one of only about two hundred blockade-runners to be captured on the Gulf of Mexico (roughly 10 to 15 percent of attempted runs ended in capture or destruction).[18] Miraculously, Oaksmith managed to escape on that calm, moonlit night out on the Gulf. One member of his crew later recalled the scene. As the Union blockaders were boarding the *Matagorda* on one side, Oaksmith and another sailor "pulled off in a small boat from the other side and got safe to shore. It was a narrow escape for him, as they would have hung him if they had got him." Not knowing where he had gone, the *Boston Traveler* reported, "It is probable that he was drowned." Meanwhile his brother Sidney wrote to their mother, "I have sad intelligence dear Mother, to communicate—I have just received information that leaves little doubt, that our dear——, who was on his way from Galveston in the Steamer thence to Havana, a Passenger, has been made a prisoner and carried into Key West, with the rest of the Passengers & crew. They were chased and captured by a Federal Steamer. He may not be recognized, and may be here in a few days—but I have little hope—God bless and help us all."[19]

Elizabeth was devastated but helpless. However, neither report proved true. Instead, Oaksmith somehow floated his way back to Cuba. As with his other major life events, his brief career as a blockade-runner inspired a poem: "Peal after peal awake the night, / Shrill scream the shell across our deck; / While, like a hunted deer, our flight . . . . / Right through the iron storm we press."[20]

Word that Oaksmith had returned to Havana reached Vice Consul General Thomas Savage. On September 21, Savage called on Captain General Dulce and explained Oaksmith's history. Savage then asked Dulce whether he would permit Cuban authorities to capture the fugitive and return him to the United States. Dulce "assented at once" without even asking for any evidence. "All he asked was my assurance that Oaksmith belonged to one of our Northern States, which assurance I gave him. His Excellency distinctly said that such rogues should find no assylum [*sic*] here," reported Savage. Fearing that Oaksmith might leave the island before a Union warship could come to take him, Savage asked whether Dulce "had any objection to arrest and deliver the culprit to me as soon as I could have a vessel of the United States here to convey him out of the Island—to this His Excellency also assented without hesitation, simply remarking that we should keep the matter very secret, and saying that he would have Oaksmith secured upon my advising him that I had a vessel in readiness to take him away."

Now Savage had only to patiently wait for the arrival of a vessel. As Oaksmith had "no means or business here," Savage worried that he might soon leave again for Galveston. For this reason, Savage was determined to arrest him and have him detained at Fort Jefferson on the Dry Tortugas until a Union vessel could take him North.[21] Meanwhile, back in Boston, John M. Clark—the sheriff of Suffolk County who had let Oaksmith slip through his fingers two years earlier—wrote privately that "the capture and return of Appleton Oaksmith . . . would be a source of much satisfaction to me, more than language can express." "God forbid that I should rejoice over the ignominy of any one, not even of so base a being as he," Clark continued, "yet I do want to see his familiar face in Suffolk County Jail."[22]

On September 28, the USS *Shenandoah* arrived at Havana with an order to take Oaksmith to Key West. Savage hurried to see the captain general, "who gave peremptory orders for the apprehension and delivery" of Oaksmith. Dulce then selected "the best police officers" for the covert operation.[23] At some point between 11 p.m. and midnight, a dozen policemen surrounded the home of Sidney Oaksmith, believing that they would find Appleton there. Three officers entered the house, lighted the gaslights, and ordered a "very sick man" to get out of bed and dress himself. When the unidentified man moved slowly, the officers shouted "useless and unnecessary threats of personal violence." The officers wielded canes and kept their hands on concealed weapons as they told the man to "get up and come along with [us]."

Not recognizing the men who hovered over his bed, "and feeling somewhat stupefied at being jerked suddenly out of a deep sleep into which he had been placed by order of the doctor attending him," the sick man protested their intrusion into his bedroom and demanded to know what right they had to be in his house at such a late hour of the night. They simply replied "for him to hurry up, and he would soon see the authority, and learn the particulars."

The sick man informed the officers that he had been bedridden for a week or more and asked to be able to call his doctor. "Gentlemen, 'tis impossible for me to go with you," he told them. "See in what condition I am in, unable to walk, am very weak, and am not entirely over the sweat the doctor ordered me." But it "made no difference" to the police what the doctor had ordered. They forced him to get up and dress. If he "thought he could not walk, they could very easily find a way to make him." At that point the police "commenced some more energetic pulling, sufficiently so to compel him to rise and attempt dressing with the aid of a servant." A carriage and more officers were waiting for them outside on the street.

Again the man protested, stating that he had broken no law of the country, that he had been living in Cuba for three years and that "all persons who knew him could testify to his good character." But the police looked at each other and said, "It is him, it is him!" "Oh, yes, I am positive!" "Why certainly. Without doubt it is the man we are in search of!"

The policemen walked around the house "with the air of those clothed in authority," although "they would not acknowledge their authority." The lowest ranked among them detained the prisoner while the other two searched the house in a "peculiar bungling way," upstairs and downstairs, looking in beds and under the stairs, "leaving no place unsearched." When the officers returned to the prisoner's bedroom, they found him "unable to walk far, and suffering from the great pain in his swollen face." They confiscated his penknife and pencil, telling him that prisoners could not have such items. As they led him toward the front door, however, they suddenly began to doubt that they had the right person, "noting his weakly condition, they told him to be seated till they returned, leaving him once more in charge of the policeman."

The two officers went off to another room and spoke with a servant, who showed them a portrait of Appleton. After ten or fifteen minutes the officers returned and "after another good look" at their prisoner, they "very coolly told [him] to go to—bed! that he was not the man they were in search of; that it was his brother they wanted." It turns out they were about to arrest Sidney Oaksmith, not Appleton! According to a correspondent of the New York *Express*, Appleton had learned of the impending abduction earlier in the day and had "left the city, and I presume is under the protection of a flag that respects the laws of its country, and the will of its people."

The police asked Sidney where his brother was, but Sidney claimed not to know. One local observed that Sidney's illness "did not weigh a feather with those charged with the duty of making the arrest," and that if their "dragging him uselessly and cruelly from his bed had been the cause of his death, it would have been equally a matter of no consequence to them." Another Havana resident opined that the police could have discovered their mistake "without giving him so much trouble."

The police kept a watch around the premises all night. The next morning at 7 a.m. they reentered Sidney's house and confiscated the photograph of Appleton, telling a servant that if Sidney wanted the picture back he "could address himself to the captain general, or chief of police." The *Shenandoah* also departed from Havana for Tampa. Meanwhile, Appleton managed to stay hidden somewhere in Havana until October 12, when he left for parts unknown.[24] The chief of police assured Vice Consul General

Sidney Oaksmith.
Courtesy of the David M. Rubenstein Rare Book and Manuscript Library, Duke University.

Savage that he "will have Oaksmith sooner or later, and then keep him con-fined in a dungeon until I can have a vessel that will carry him out of the Is-land." Savage, in turn, informed Seward that "I believe the Captain General is anxious to deliver him up."[25] Seward's reply does not appear to survive.

Word of the botched kidnapping attempt reached Elizabeth Oakes Smith two weeks later. "A terrible day," she wrote in her diary on October

13, "the mails brought me a letter from Sidney who is better, but still ill." On the page beneath this writing she pasted a newspaper clipping about Sidney's terrible ordeal. "Oh my God out of the depths I cry unto thee! Sidney writes tenderly and hopefully. Who could credit all this persecution—the case has been sustained wholly by perjury and corruption—the officials know perfectly well that Appleton was never engaged in the Slave Trade—they know he never received one penny for anything connected therewith and they know also, that he did not *aid or abet*, which is the only pretext upon which the trial was based." Elizabeth firmly believed "the whole matter is one of *revenge*—my family know so many of the secrets of this corrupt Administration that they are determined to put us out of the way of exposing them—they would kill Appleton if they had good opportunity. Dear Heaven, give me patience." Making matters all the worse, she reflected on the loneliness her family was facing: "In these horrible times people are afraid to show sympathy."[26]

A few days later Elizabeth returned to the subject. "When will this oppressive Government cease to persecute my family?" she wondered. "There is no doubt that Seward sent Arguilles back for the sake of wreaking his vengeance upon Mr. Oaksmith. Nobody of any penetration believes that he had been engaged in the Slave Trade—they tried to affix *Treason* upon him at first, but as they could do nothing in that line, and finding him engaged for a few months as a Ship Broker, they hit upon this ugly charge to ruin him."[27]

On October 22, Elizabeth wrote a long letter to Appleton. She had heard that Captain General Dulce was going to be removed from authority in Cuba because "the crown of Spain resents his taste for kidnapping." She also believed that the Lincoln administration's apparent policy of compelling "other governments to conform to this extradition system, [is] so repugnant to every humane and generous mind. Treaties are of no consequence to the Tyrants at Washington." A few days later, she received a "bright & hopeful" letter from Sidney. "Appleton has thus far eluded his persecutors," she learned. "Oh! how it goes to my heart to have my young hero, my bright young Poet, my beautiful boy thus hunted from place to place by these malignants! God deliver us from this national scourge. We are having a reign of terror, which must ultimate[ly end] in blood." Still, she was pleased to learn that Sidney's health was improving and that Appleton was safe.[28]

Brief notices of the attempted kidnapping appeared in newspapers throughout the nation.[29] A few Democratic papers offered critical commentary. "Mr. Seward's 'Bell,' . . . has been tinkling again," wrote the editors of the New York *Express*, "this time in Havana, for the arrest of an American citizen—*what for*, nobody as yet seems to know." The editors wondered if "the Washington despotism is not secretly seeking to strengthen itself by alliances with the monarchical despotisms of Europe, more effectively to annihilate our liberties at home." A "suspicious intimacy, or rather fellow feeling," seemed to exist between Lincoln and Captain General Dulce, which was "not agreeable for a lover of white man's liberty to contemplate."[30]

One widely circulated article, under the headline "The Why of It," proposed to explain why the kidnapping attempt had been made. According to the story, Dulce never "made application for the return of Arguelles. His abduction is therefore the work of Marshal Murray instigated or sanctioned by Seward, who wanted above all things to get hold of Appleton Oaksmith, on account of a scathing letter, published by that gentleman in the Tribune . . . dissecting Seward's 'little bell' operations and his infamous treatment of the prisoners confined in Fort Lafayette. He resorted to the desperate scheme of giving Arguelles in exchange for Oaksmith out of revenge for the terrible severity of that letter. The plot failed, however." Another writer in Havana, who signed his name "Veritas," informed American readers that Dulce had received "an autograph letter from President Lincoln asking as a personal favor the arrest and return of Mr. Appleton Oaksmith. These are plain, unvarnished facts, that are now public talk here, and should be made known to the people of the United States, that they may know in whose hands they trust their liberties."[31]

Some Democrats believed they could use reports of these illegal activities to their advantage in the upcoming presidential election. An anonymous correspondent in Havana who went by "Juan" surmised that the Spanish government had agreed to kidnap Oaksmith in exchange for the extradition of Arguelles—and "for the gratification of Messrs. Lincoln, Seward, etc." "These are a few of the many humiliating truths that should be whispered in the ears of the people during the Presidential campaign, that they may know and understand that the heads of government, who are continually crying out 'more fathers, more brothers, more sons, more blood,' to enforce the broken laws of a distracted nation, are themselves the greatest transgressors."

Indeed, with Lincoln about to stand before the people for a second term, Juan wanted American voters to think calmly and well before going to the polls, for the presidential election would be their last chance to save the republic from tyranny. "These acts, and worse are done at the bidding of the authorities at Washington," wrote Juan. "They are pulling down, with hands dyed in treachery and ambition, that grand and mighty fabric the American Republic!" Under Lincoln, the United States had become a land of "tyranny and corruption. . . . The happy and prosperous nation that was four years ago the envy, the admiration of the world, to-day excites its pity, its disgust!"

Juan wanted Lincoln's "evils and the many corruptions" proclaimed from coast to coast so that voters could "choose a leader who will prove himself worthy of their choice, by watching earnestly and following closely their beacon light—the Constitution!" He continued: "Let the mothers whose sons have found unknown and bloody graves upon the Potomac; let the sisters and the fathers, whose brothers and pride have been sacrificed upon this Moloch of human life, whose hearts still at the names of Vicksburg, Port Hudson and Atlanta; let the widows and the orphans, the desolated homes, send forth one wail to heaven and cry out—'Oh, God, how much more!'" Four more years of Lincoln's rule would crush "all national vitality" in the United States. Juan therefore called on the people to vote the Republicans out.[32]

Despite Juan's earnest attempts, the botched Oaksmith kidnapping attempt never gained traction as a national political issue. Instead, Democrats chose to highlight Arguelles in their party platform in August 1864. Buried in the middle of a long plank that castigated the Republicans' record on civil liberties—such as abridgment of free speech and press and the right to bear arms—the Democrats also criticized the Lincoln administration for its "denial of the right of asylum."[33]

There was a logical reason for the Democrats to defend one slave trader and not another. Oaksmith had been convicted through the normal processes of law (although his arrest and removal to Boston had been outside of normal judicial processes). Arguelles, by contrast, had been dealt with in what appeared to be an abnormal, extralegal manner. Even many of Lincoln's political supporters were alarmed by Seward's actions. Secretary of the Navy Gideon Welles complained that Seward "has queer fancies for a statesman," pointing out that Seward boasted that he did not read books about international law and that, "In administering the government he seems to have no idea of constitutional and legal restraints, but acts as if the ruler was omnipotent."[34]

Welles was a conservative Republican, but even some radicals expressed concern. Senator Charles Sumner of Massachusetts wrote privately, "The Arguelles case is as bad as can be. I told the Presdt, the moment I heard of it, that it was utterly indefensible." After recounting the nature of Arguelles's despicable crimes, Horace Greeley's *New York Tribune* concluded, "And yet—and yet—we should greatly prefer to see these matters regulated by law than by executive dictum." Other Republicans and abolitionists agreed. A group of Radicals who met at Cleveland in late May to nominate Union general John C. Fremont for president, stated in their platform, "That the right of asylum, except for crime subject to law, is a recognized principle of American liberty; that any violation of it cannot be overlooked and must not be unrebuked." In his letter accepting the nomination for president, Fremont remarked that Lincoln's administration was one "marked at home by disregard of constitutional rights, by its violation of personal liberty and the liberty of the press, and, as a crowning shame, by its abandonment of the right of asylum, a right especially dear to all free nations abroad."[35]

Peace Democratic leader Clement L. Vallandigham latched onto Fremont's letter of acceptance, quoting it in a stump speech in Ohio on June 15, 1864.[36] But with everything going on in the war during the summer of 1864—the bloody carnage of the Overland Campaign in Virginia and William T. Sherman's inability to capture Atlanta—why did the Democrats care about this issue enough to include it in stump speeches and their party platform? Because Arguelles's "extraordinary rendition" appeared to be one more instance of white men's rights being sacrificed in order to expand the rights of black men and women.

Ohio Democrat Samuel "Sunset" Cox decided to make an issue of the Arguelles affair on the floor of the House of Representatives that summer, introducing a resolution that called the rendition "a violation of the Constitution of the United States and of the law of nations."[37] When the Republican majority in the House referred Cox's resolution to "a hostile committee," Cox brought Arguelles up again during a heated debate over repeal of the infamous Fugitive Slave Act of 1850. Cox criticized his fellow members, saying that their position in favor of repeal was akin to saying, "All right, Mr. President, you can seize a white man and take him from the country in defiance of the great right of asylum, but when a black man, escaping from one State to another, and whom we are commanded by the Constitution to deliver up, and under sanction of our oath to make laws for such delivery, we break down the constitutional clause and the laws sanctioned by the judiciary in order to create in the North an asylum for the blacks of the South." In other words, at the very moment that Congress was repealing a law that commanded federal authorities to extradite fugitive slaves, it was ignoring the Lincoln administration's illegal rendition of a white man.

Cox maintained that he had seen no evidence against Arguelles. "He was not, then, in the legal sense, as Mr. Seward asserted, an enemy of the human race. He was not a pirate in any legal or moral sense, but a criminal under the laws of Spain. He could only be delivered to Spain under a treaty or a statute, and neither existed between this country and Spain. Yet gentlemen who are becoming so careful about the personal liberty of black men as to refuse to render them up in pursuance of the Constitution sustain the extradition of a white man without evidence, law, treaty, or constitutional authority."

For Cox, Arguelles's rendition was an international "humiliation, by which America is no longer the home of the oppressed or refuge of the foreigner, by which we are made the hissing and byword of the nations, we cast our mouths in the dust of abject degradation." In one of Cox's most extreme wartime utterances, he proclaimed, "Such refugees have the right to shoot down the officers who thus arrest them, and be entirely innocent of crime. Refugees under such circumstances would have the right to sue Mr. Lincoln, Mr. Seward, or the marshal of New York [Robert Murray] for false imprisonment, because of the absence of all law and all treaty in relation to that subject." Connecting this discussion to the topic of the debate—repeal of the Fugitive Slave Act of 1850—Cox concluded that in "all matters of rendition, whether of fugitives from service or justice, or of political refugees, there is always some law required to carry out in good faith the treaty or agreement upon those subjects." In other words, Congress should not repeal the Fugitive Slave Act and thus nullify the fugitive slave clause of the Constitution, and in like manner, it should not tacitly sanction the illegal rendition of a white man without any law to permit such action.[38]

Democratic newspapers agreed with Cox. "In the name of 'freedom to the slave,'" wrote the editors of the *Daily Eastern Argus* (Seba Smith's old paper in Portland), Seward "deliberately outraged the liberties of the free, made the commercial metropolis of America a ward of the proconsular city of Havana, and submitted the flag of the United States to the most intolerable shame which has been put in our time upon the banner of an independent people." Democrats also criticized the Republican National Convention, which met in June, for ignoring this issue. "Not a word does it contain respecting the freedom of the press, the right of asylum, or the right of white men to person and property," reported the New York *World*.[39]

As the election approached, Elizabeth Oakes Smith lamented the recent ordeals suffered by her sons in Cuba. In late October she had high hopes that the Democratic nominee, Major General George B. McClellan, would win the White House. But by the time the election rolled around on November 8, things had taken a far better turn for the Union than they had been throughout the summer. Major General William T. Sherman had captured Atlanta, Admiral David G. Farragut had captured Mobile Bay, and General Philip Sheridan ravaged the Shenandoah Valley. Lincoln easily won reelection, taking roughly 55 percent of the popular vote and a near sweep in the Electoral College.[40] The Democrats were able to make little hay of the Arguelles and Oaksmith incidents, other than occasional newspaper articles criticizing Lincoln. They tried to turn the Arguelles case into an issue about the rights of white people. But no voter cast a ballot in November 1864 based on his beliefs about the sacred right of asylum.

Only after his reelection did Lincoln publicly and explicitly defend his decision in the Arguelles case. "For myself, I have no doubt of the power and duty of the Executive, under the law of nations, to exclude enemies of the human race from an asylum in the United States," he wrote in his annual message to Congress in December 1864. "If Congress should think that proceedings in such cases lack the authority of law, or ought to be further regulated by it, I recommend that provision be made for effectually preventing foreign slave traders from acquiring domicile and facilities for their criminal occupation in our country." As historian Mark E. Neely Jr. concludes, Arguelles "was closer to being a pirate than a political refugee. Lincoln either saw the case that way or was willing to make the case look that way in order to insure freedom for the slaves and to send Arguelles back to the chain gang."[41]

16

DIVORCE

The botched kidnapping ordeal had been hard on the entire Oaksmith family. "Do not *grieve or* worry about me, dear Mother," Sidney wrote to Elizabeth on November 29, 1864. "I shall be patient and do the best I can, I seem born to vicissitudes myself, but it is a source of satisfaction to me to think that those I love are comparatively exempt from the privations which so many are now enduring. Your heart would *bleed* if you could see what I have seen."[1] Yet the family could feel some relief, for somehow Appleton had slipped through the grasp of federal authorities yet again. It is not clear exactly where he had gone, but he appears to have left Cuba about October 12, 1864. Some believed that either he or Sidney were traveling on a steamer between New York City and Havana with "a party of 13 men . . . pretending to be a Band of Minstrels."[2] By November, he appeared to be in New Orleans. Back in Havana, Thomas Savage seized a letter that he believed had been sent from Appleton to Sidney, thanking him for a photograph, and asking for "a thousand segars of good tobacco."[3] In early December, US Attorney Richard Henry Dana Jr. informed Seward that he had "trustworthy information" that Oaksmith was in New Orleans. Seward passed this information along to Lincoln's new attorney general, James Speed, adding that the fugitive was in hiding "perhaps under an assumed name." The secretary enclosed a warrant for Oaksmith's arrest and suggested that it "be sent to that city for execution."[4] By December, however, Savage believed that Oaksmith had moved on and was leading "a gang of pirates which captured lately one of our transport steamers off Matamoros," along the Texas-Mexico border.[5]

Savage's intelligence was mostly accurate. By February 1865 Oaksmith was back at Houston, Texas, where he obtained a letter of introduction from Confederate general John George Walker to General E. Kirby Smith, who was headquartered at Shreveport, Louisiana. "Permit me to introduce to your acquaintance the bearer of this, Capt John McDonald, who visits you on business that he will explain. Though personally unknown to me, Capt. McDonald has been represented to me as a very efficient seaman, and as an intelligent, bold & daring officer." Walker trusted that "the interview between yourself & Capt. McDonald may result in something beneficial to our Gov't & to Capt. McDonald."

Walker's suspicions appear to have been aroused by Oaksmith. A short while later he sent a second letter to Kirby Smith—one that Oaksmith would not have seen. "This morning I gave a letter to you, introducing Capt John McDonald—such is the name by which he is generally known here. It is proper to say to you however, I have been informed his real name is Oakes Smith—that he is a native of Philadelphia, & of a good family now resident there. He was formerly engaged in the Slave trade, and it is said, from that, or some other cause, has become highly obnoxious to the Yankees, from whom he would have little mercy to expect if captured—this may account for his assumed name." Walker concluded: "I have been reliably informed that he is a good seaman, & a bold & daring officer. His object in visiting you is to ask your assistance in procuring for himself & others commissions in the volunteer Confederate Navy, for the purpose of protecting them in privateering & running the blockade. He desires further to get permission to take out cotton sufficient to arm his ship. I do not know sufficient of Capt. McDonald to recommend your aiding him."[6]

Presumably Oaksmith made his way to Shreveport with the first letter to meet with Kirby Smith, although no record of the meeting—or whether Oaksmith received a commission or letter of marque to serve in the Confederate navy—has been located.[7] At any rate, the war would be over in a matter of weeks anyway.

Back in New York, Elizabeth Oakes Smith put on a happy face, publicly showing support for the Union war effort. In December 1864 she donated an autograph to be sold at the Sanitary Fair in Philadelphia—an effort by loyal Northerners to raise money to support Union soldiers.[8] But on the inside she was weary, worn down, and feeling isolated. She longed to know how Appleton was doing and whether he was even still alive. On February 27, 1865, she went into New York City and found herself "weighed by a profound desire to know something of the condition of my dear Appleton." She saw a book nearby and picked it up, closed her eyes, opened to a random place, and put her finger on the page, resolving "that the first words upon which I should open . . . should be to me an Oracle." The words she found were disheartening: "Then you would not be here to wish; you would not be alive now." Elizabeth was understandably troubled by this revelation. "I have my oracle, but how shall I interpret it?" she wrote in her diary. "Can the liberated spirit only know these things? Is he in the land of spirits? I wait—I think—I pray."[9]

Elizabeth's close friends could see how she was suffering, but they were powerless to change her circumstances. "The authorities seem inexorable—why, Heaven only knows," wrote one friend in Manhattan. "If martyrdom is the penalty of Republican hatred, surely a sufficient expiation has been made; if a doubtful offense is to be punished as the 'unpardonable sin,' then must the great Arbiter of events 'recompense' the suffering, 'in the Earth.'" Still, this correspondent hoped to offer Elizabeth some encouragement. "Whenever you find an opportunity to communicate with the absent one, assure him that he has many friends here—those who would gladly prove their fidelity by works rather than words."[10]

On March 22, 1865, Oakes Smith again returned to her diary: "Appleton's birth day. Edward and Eugenia embarked for Cuba. I am now quite alone—all my children gone—one in Texas, one in Cuba, one in Buenos Ayres, and one upon the sea." Two days later she felt "sick in heart." To keep unpleasant thoughts from her mind she busied herself reading and writing letters, recording her reminiscences, going to church, and teaching Appleton's children. Although she was "very low in spirits all day" on April 5, she delivered a lecture that night to the local lyceum upon "the progress of civilization which at length culminated in the great expression of modern ideas in the habeas corpus law," recounting the history of civil liberty in the West back to Magna Carta in AD 1215.[11]

On April 10, news thundered throughout the North that Confederate general Robert E. Lee had surrendered the Army of Northern Virginia at Appomattox Court House the day before. "The war is now most probably over," she wrote. "The people are everywhere wild with the hope of peace." Indeed, celebrations enveloped New York City, with flags and banners waving, orators pontificating, crowds surging, cannons booming, fireworks crackling, worshippers praising, revelers dancing, and newsboys hawking. Oakes Smith even consented to address a local group of joyous citizens on the evening of April 14. Later that evening she recorded the experience in her diary: "In the midst of my speech about ten o clock, without apparent cause I had a sharp pain through my heart—just one pang, like the thrust of a sword—I shall bear sad news: some catastrophe has occurred." Several members of the audience remarked that she suddenly looked pale, with one young woman stating "that as I stood perfectly calm, speaking with the banners in the background I looked like the pictures of Gen. Washington."[12]

April 14, it turns out, was one of the most tragic days in American history. Earlier that morning Lincoln had told his cabinet about a dream he'd had the night before in which he was on a boat heading toward an unknown shore. Lincoln believed this was a portentous dream—that "great news" would soon be coming from the front. But fate had something else in store. The actor John Wilkes Booth shot Lincoln just after 10 p.m. at Ford's Theatre—the very moment that Oakes Smith felt the chest pain and turned deathly pale. The next day, word of his assassination shocked the nation. Some newspapers reported that Oakes Smith "was glad of it" and that she thought "J. Wilkes Booth was a gentleman," going so far as to surmise "that possibly Edward Oaksmith was one of the conspirators who assassinated Lincoln."[13] These rumors, however, were unfounded. Edward was out of the country. (Sadly, he would die of yellow fever in Cuba a few months later, on August 31.) And on April 15, Oakes Smith took to her diary to vent her mixed emotions and grief: "Poor Lincoln! the tool and victim of party! seems hardly dealt with—vain and weak, and low-bred as he was . . . he was better than his party and the country will be the worse for his death." John Wilkes Booth's conspirators had also tried to kill Seward that night. The secretary was confined to his bed, having suffered terrible injuries from a carriage accident. One of Booth's cronies made it into Seward's bedroom and stabbed him viciously and in the process also wounded Seward's two sons. Oakes Smith wrote, "God knows that the crimes of Seward are very great, and he has persecuted thousands, with that 'little bell' of which he boasted, yet I was led to pray fervently that God would be merciful to him."[14]

Appleton was still in Texas as late as March 22, 1865. It is unknown how he reacted to Lincoln's death or the attempt on Seward's life. But one record left behind is a bit of a puzzle. Somehow, on August 23, 1864, he procured a divorce from Isotta in Adams County, Indiana. The divorce laws in Indiana were notoriously lax. If a petitioner could prove his or her residency in the state (something that could be easily done even if it was not actually the case), the laws permitted divorce for nearly any reason. In addition to the typical grounds for divorce—such as infidelity, impotency, abandonment, cruelty, or drunkenness—the Indiana law included this catch-all: "Any other cause for which the court shall deem it proper that a divorce should be granted." So easy was it to procure a divorce in Indiana that one writer called the state "the first divorce mill" in America. People traveled from throughout the country to obtain divorces in Indiana in the 1850s and 1860s (a concept now known as "migratory divorce"), leading one Indianapolis newspaper to observe, "We are overrun by a flock of ill-used, and ill-using, petulant, libidinous, extravagant, ill-fitting husbands and wives as a sink is overrun with the foul water of the whole house. . . . Nine out of every ten have no better cause of divorce than their own depraved appetites."[15]

It is unclear exactly how Oaksmith procured the divorce. It is unlikely that he made it to Indiana while he was in exile. It is possible that he had one of his brothers, perhaps Edward, travel to Indiana under the pretense that he was Appleton. But it seems more likely that Appleton hired a firm to procure the divorce for him. Lawyers advertised such services in New York papers. "Divorces obtained in New York, Connecticut, Indiana and Illinois. Legal everywhere. No charge in advance; Advice free," stated one such ad. Back in Indiana, some legislators complained, "Agencies are established in New York and other Eastern cities, which advertise to procure divorces for any parties desiring the same, whether cause exist therefor or not." These agencies worked with attorneys in Indiana who claimed to represent both sides, forging names and signatures, in order to earn a fee. Of course, this system lent itself to fraud. And like so many others, Appleton's petition contained clear deceptions, claiming that he and Isotta were married until November 12, 1861, "when they separated with the intention of final separation," and that he had "for more than one year . . . been a *bona fide* resident of Indiana—and is a resident of [Adams] county."[16]

Having obtained a divorce (the papers were probably waiting for him in New York), Oaksmith left Texas at some point in mid- to late 1865, reaching New York City by November. Although the war was over, he was still a fugitive from the law and continued to live under the alias "John McDonald." In New York, he relied on this deception to cover his tracks. On November 21, his brother Sidney signed a notarized letter of recommendation, certifying the dishonest statement "that Capt. John McDonald was employed by the former firm of S. Oaksmith & Co of Hayti W. I. [West Indies] and New York of which I was a member, as a Shipmaster from the year 1853 to 1860 a period of over six years, during which time he commanded the following vessels in which the said firm was interested." Sidney then listed six vessels, including the *Mary Adeline* and *Magnolia*. "It gives me pleasure to state that Capt. McDonald gave us entire satisfaction, and was noted for his sobriety and attention to business," continued Sidney with obvious relish. "We always reposed the greatest confidence in him, and I can confidently recommend him to any parties in want of a Master for any class of vessel."[17]

In January 1866 Oaksmith appeared in New Brunswick, Canada, where he married his cousin, Augusta Mason. Augusta—the daughter of Elizabeth's stepsister, Eleanor—had suffered many losses in her life. Her

Augusta Mason Oaksmith.
Courtesy of the Carteret County Historical Society.

father, a sea captain, had been "swept overboard at sea" in 1846, and she had lost two brothers—one to yellow fever in Havana and another who died of smallpox in 1864 while serving in the First Maine Cavalry. Now, perhaps, she might find happiness. The wedding appears to have been a small ceremony, with Appleton's mother and eldest daughter, Bessie, in attendance. Elizabeth hated Isotta so much that she was not bothered by what she had written about divorce in 1851: "A true man or woman must naturally have a sense of shame, when subject to divorce; more than all this, where children exist."[18]

About the time of his marriage to Augusta, Appleton wrote a short poem, titled "Our Trust," that captured how he felt about his new wife: "I need no vows, from her, to prove / She will be true, when I am far, / For well I know, to me her love / Turneth as constant as a star. / Seas may divide, and weary years / In distant lands may drag their chain / But still my spirit never fears / But what, in time, we'll meet again." In February 1866, Oaksmith took Bessie and his new wife to England, settling on a small farm in Chigwell, a community to the northeast of London. As he later explained, he "fled the country" because the "state of public opinion at that time" made it "impossible to establish my innocency." Almost immediately Bessie began calling Augusta "mama."[19]

On June 25, Oaksmith sent for Isotta to meet him in Liverpool, apparently instructing her to leave the two younger children, Corinne and Randolph, with Elizabeth. Isotta did not want to leave the children, but Elizabeth allegedly promised to bring them later. Elizabeth also suggested that Isotta take supplies necessary for housekeeping as well as toys that belonged to Bessie, who had been with Oaksmith since the previous Christmas. At this point Isotta did not know that her husband had filed for divorce in Indiana and married Augusta.

When Isotta arrived in Liverpool, Appleton took her to a lodging house on Chatsworth Street, telling her that it would be unsafe for them to stay at a hotel "as he feared to be rearrested." According to Isotta, Appleton said he could not live with her in public but that he would visit her every day and bring Bessie to see her. "But he never did so. He showed me to my room & left me there," Isotta later wrote. The next day Oaksmith arrived at her room with a letter. Drawing it from his pocket, he read it to her. "It seemed to be a letter from him to me," she wrote. "His mother had sent to him the said letter and had written in the back of it thus, Dear Appleton, I did not give Isotta the letter, as I feared her temper; you can best manage her, Your mother." After reading the letter he insisted that she sign some divorce papers, but she refused. According to Isotta, "He then told me that unless I did as he told me he never would let me see my children again. He said you have no means to return with & if you had, they would be removed before you get there. If you sign them, I will send for you again in a year. I was in his power entirely & saw that resistance was useless & signed the fatal papers. I had no idea such a thing was expected of me when I went to him." Isotta claimed that Appleton then told her to go to Smyrna, in Asia Minor, where she had family.[20]

While Appleton was beginning his life anew in England—and bringing utter heartache to Isotta—Elizabeth was working diligently to secure a pardon from Andrew Johnson, the Tennessee Democrat who had succeeded Lincoln as president. She received a letter of introduction from Orestes Brownson to Seward recommending her to the president's attention. The famous theologian stated that he "knew her son and her family intimately, and I do not believe that he was a man likely to engage in the slave trade, and I know enough of his affairs to be able to explain all the suspicious circumstances in the case without implicating him in the least in the crime for which he was convicted." Calling attention to Johnson's known leniency toward former Confederates, Brownson pointed out that "when we are daily pardoning, and very properly, hundreds and thousands of worse criminals . . . there is no necessity of enforcing the extreme rigor of the law against one who if pardoned & permitted to return to his country, will prove a useful and honorable citizen."[21]

In mid-September 1866, Oakes Smith met with Thurlow Weed, a close Albany associate of Seward's, "who has promised to use his influence to procure the return of Appleton." According to Oakes Smith, Weed relayed an "offer from Seward and others" that would guarantee her son's "return and the favor of the Administration." Appleton simply had to denounce Stewart L. Woodford, the Republican candidate for lieutenant governor of New York, as having "connived at the Slave Trade." (Woodford, it will be recalled, had been the assistant US attorney who had dined with Oaksmith when the *Augusta* was being appraised back in 1861). But this was something Appleton simply would not do. Oakes Smith informed Weed that this "was utterly impossible. He had always denied the charge himself; great offers of office and emolument had been made him by persons in power, as one side and then another gained the ascendancy, but he had from the first treated all such offers with contempt, saying, 'If they want a perjured scoundrel they must look somewhere else for it, I am not the man.'" Elizabeth told Weed that her son "preferred exile to dishonor." She recounted the Lincoln administration's treatment of Appleton, and informed Weed that "it was of no use to tempt [Appleton] with any dishonorable overtures—he would not listen to them—he valued his honor more than his life."

Weed replied that he "by no means approved the proposition" and that he'd "told those who made it, that it would be useless for from what he had learned of the character of the young man, he would not accede to it—still as it was insisted upon, he could do no less than state it." Oakes Smith stated, "I would rather he would remain in exile, than be corrupted in this way." "Certainly" Weed said, "and I am glad he is not the kind to be corrupted in any way." So ended the conversation.[22]

In mid-October Oakes Smith again met with Weed. At his suggestion, she called on Marshal Murray, who, amazingly, supplied a letter endorsing Oaksmith's release (unfortunately Murray's letter does not appear to survive). She then went to New York City municipal judge Abraham D. Russell, who told her, "Tell the President that the best method will be to order a nolle pros. [*nolle prosequi*, a formal notice that a prosecutor is abandoning a case] there never was any proof against him—he never was concerned in the Slave trade—his trial in Boston was a mere farce—a piece of political oppression—and private malignity—I am well aware of the infamous attempts which have been made to induce him to perjure himself—but Appleton is not the kind of man to do that, as I am glad to know it." Russell added that the "pretended trial was a disgrace to the judiciary. It would not have been tolerated in the New York Courts." When Oakes Smith repeated these words to several acquaintances, they told her that Seward's recalcitrance stemmed from Appleton's manifesto, which had appeared in the *New York Tribune* in 1862.

Oakes Smith took the train to Washington, riding with Weed and Abram Wakeman, the surveyor of the port of New York City. In Washington, however, Seward "positively refuse[d] to do anything in Appleton's case" until the United States concluded treaty negotiations with Spain. He allegedly promised, however, that once the treaty was ratified he would no longer oppose Appleton's pardon. Oakes Smith was "terribly disappointed" by this news, recording in her diary that "this blow made me quite ill, in fact." But Seward made this promise in the presence of Weed and Wakeman, so Oakes Smith hoped that it "was only a brief postponement—and that they regarded the final issue as certain." She returned home to New York disillusioned and exhausted.[23]

Back at home, Oakes Smith started writing letters to important politicians of both parties—Stewart L. Woodford, now the lieutenant governor-elect of New York; Erastus Brooks, a New York newspaper editor originally from Portland, Maine; and the Democratic ex-mayor of New York

City, Fernando Wood. "I shall try to create an outside pressure," she wrote in her diary, "which may neutralize the malignity of Mr. Seward."[24] In early December she received a "kind letter" from Weed informing her that he and Murray had both gone to Seward on Appleton's behalf but that Seward would not relent. She became very lonely, with no one in the "dreary" old house with her but Seba. Sitting in her home she remembered back to when she had met Seward in 1861 and he had assured her that Appleton would be released from Fort Lafayette. She had hastened to the barge to welcome him in her arms and was instead informed by an officer that he had been removed to Fort Warren. Reflecting on the broken promises over the past five years made her angry. Seward had lied to her in 1861. Now he promised that Appleton would be pardoned as soon as a treaty with Spain was negotiated. But she doubted whether that was really true. And how "it galls me to ask pardon for a man, who has committed no offence," she wrote. "God be merciful to a country where Rulers are without faith, mercy or principle!"[25]

Oakes Smith nevertheless continued her letter-writing campaign. In January 1867 she sent an appeal to Andrew Johnson's daughter, Maria Johnson Patterson, asking for an interview with the president. Patterson replied that Johnson would be happy to see her any day except for Tuesdays or Fridays, since the cabinet met on those days. "My God I thank thee for this ray of hope," Oakes Smith wrote in her journal. "The promptitude and tone of her reply fill me with the happiest auspices." Seba, too, hoped these efforts "may not end in disappointment."[26]

Sidney Oaksmith was now a law student at Columbia College of Law, and in early 1867 Elizabeth turned to him for legal advice. Sidney wrote her about the importance of securing a full presidential pardon as opposed to just a *nolle prosequi* (which would simply end the prosecution) since a pardon "would be a *final disposal of the whole thing for ever*, relieving him entirely from all disabilities or fears in the future." Sidney told his mother how he admired "the persistency & devotion you have for the past four years exhibited in 'A' case" but he also worried about the "many anxieties & so much fatigue" she endured. "I believe you will now be successful, still we must not build up *too many immediate* hopes," Sidney warned her. "Do not exert yourself too much or be too sanguine of success. Those in authority have so much to occupy their thoughts that the little heart historys [*sic*] of one family are but as passing clouds & also I fear as soon forgotten."[27]

Sidney's warnings proved prescient. A few days after receiving Sidney's letter, Elizabeth returned to Washington, only to be disappointed again. Again she was horrified by "the malignity of Mr. Seward" and "truly

I was shocked to see an old man, evidently in his dotage, filling the office of Secretary of State. I said so plainly to the Attorney General." Oakes Smith carried with her "documents that proved the *innocence* of *Appleton*," and she claimed to receive a promise from Attorney General Henry Stanbery that a *nolle prosequi* would be entered in the record in the federal court in Boston, to drop the case against Oaksmith. She called Stanbery "exceedingly kind— a wise, gentlemanly, sympathetic man, as I think a great Lawyer ought to be." Next, she met with President Johnson for a "pleasant" conversation. "He is a dignified, sensible, gentlemanly man—he talks well and to the purpose—no noise—no affectations—a self-poised man, not easily turned from his purpose," she wrote. "Far more intelligent and manly in appearance than Mr. Lincoln, who was a tool in the hands of others, with a touch of the mountebank." But a setback soon came. A few weeks later, Attorney General Stanbery informed her that Seward had again defeated her application for pardon. At the very moment she received this news from Stanbery, Oakes Smith claimed to hear an audible voice that said, "Wait and see the salvation of God."[28]

Letters from important persons arrived at Andrew Johnson's desk throughout the spring of 1867. In February, US senator William Pitt Fessenden, a Republican from Maine who had previously served as secretary of the treasury under Lincoln, urged Johnson to issue a pardon in Oaksmith's case. Having known Seba and Elizabeth Oakes Smith for many years, and feeling "an interest in their happiness," Fessenden wrote,

> I know that the absence of their son against whom I have heard no charge except that for which he was indicted, and on account of which he became a fugitive, has been to them a source of great distress. They firmly believe in his innocence. But whether guilty or not, I am of the opinion that considering the punishment he has endured by long absence from his native country, his family & friends, the fact that all necessity for further examples by way of punishment for such offences, has apparently ceased, and the previous respectable standing of the accused, no good can accrue by keeping the indictment longer hanging over him, compelling him longer to remain an exile and a wanderer.

Executive clemency "in his case will not, I think, be misplaced."[29]

But Sidney again warned his mother about the possible pitfalls that could cause her efforts to falter. "I think it is of the utmost importance that if you succeed in your present mission [to secure a *nolle prosequi*] the thing should be kept as *quiet as possible*, and the result made known to 'A' as soon as possible and that he should come back *without delay* and *procure a full pardon.*" Sidney's rationale made sense. He did not want Isotta to find out and interfere before a full pardon was granted. "Should Mad R [Re-becchini] for any cause come in here and undertake to '*make a fuss*' there are as you know always enough to be found to 'aid & abet,' and it might perhaps be used to his disadvantage in procuring a pardon. She belongs to a *treacherous race* and has given too many proofs of her nationality to be brutal, when *her money is gone*, you must not be surprised at anything."[30]

Again, Sidney's apprehensions proved prophetic. While Elizabeth was keeping busy doing everything she could for her son, word somehow reached Isotta all the way in Smyrna that Appleton had married Augusta and that Elizabeth was seeking a pardon for Appleton. Isotta immediately returned to Patchogue to claim her children, arriving on May 18, 1867. "A day of distress," wrote Elizabeth in her diary that night. "Isotta came, in a state of the most terrible fury." Elizabeth's perception of the previous year's events was far different from Isotta's:

> She went out of the house nearly a year ago and left her children in it. She deserted them in fact, although I warned her if she went to Apple-ton, he would never live with her. Her violence—her jealousy—her slanders of him—her connivance with his enemies had completely exasperated him. She persisted in going. When she left the children she never asked me to take care of her children—she never asked me advice or assistance in any way. The children were happier without her than with her, for I had done more for them than their Mother, and they loved me better. Her violence terrified them. I was grateful to God when they escaped her pernicious influence.

Isotta's view of their reunion, by contrast, placed Oakes Smith in a bad light. According to her, Elizabeth refused to reveal where her children were.[31]

Still in a rage, Isotta wrote a long letter to Andrew Johnson on May 24, informing him of how Appleton had deserted her and of his "illegal" marriage to Augusta. She asked the president to "consider my unhappy position and only award the pardon when he shall have manfully done as I request"—that is, return her children. She also traveled to the White House and met with Johnson in person, telling him of how Appleton "had wickedly and unjustly procured a divorce from her." Isotta's petition had nothing to do with her ex-husband's guilt or innocence but with how he had spurned her. Elizabeth would later see a copy of the letter, calling it "a weak, foolish tissue, some little truth with a mass of falsehood," and concluding, "I pity her from the bottom of my heart for *being what she is.*"[32]

Years of Oakes Smith's lobbying, letter writing, and prayer came to naught when Isotta met with Johnson at the White House, for upon hearing her sad story the president decided against a pardon. There was extraordinary irony in this moment, for here, Andrew Johnson, the man who pardoned every Confederate, refused to grant a pardon. Oakes Smith was "in utter despair of all but trust in God." She then filled her diary with spleen for her former daughter-in-law. "Isotta has done her wicked traitorous work." She had received "nothing but kindness and considerateness at our hands, but she is if not insane a dangerous person. I do not feel quite safe. Appleton lived with her longer than it was safe to do so, and finally paid her way home to her Father, dividing with her his little all, he agreeing to support the children." Oakes Smith claimed that Isotta had "consented to the arrangement, and they exchanged papers amicably." (This statement, of course, is contradicted by Isotta's telling of the story in which Appleton forced her to sign the papers when she arrived in Liverpool.) According to Oakes Smith, the plan had been that once the prosecution against Appleton was dropped, Isotta "would be at liberty to see her children, and live as a friend if possible." But now that plan was ruined. "She is naturally treacherous, deceitful and lieing. No one can rely upon her, or minister to her—such is her natural rage and jealousy. We are made miserably ill by this blow she has given us, and now she plays right into the hands of our deadly enemy, Mr. Seward, who will never forgive Appleton's 'letter to the Public,' in which he shows up the falsehood and oppression of Mr. Seward." Reflecting on how much trouble Isotta had caused for the family over the years, Oakes Smith wrote, "Alas! books might be written upon the cruelty and rage of Isotta from which we all suffered for more than ten years, and now when we have tried to hide these things from the public she comes down upon us as above." For weeks Oakes Smith felt "ill in body" when she thought about what had transpired, and she worried about what would happen to the children if Appleton should die, for she did not want them to be returned to "their ferocious mother."[33]

Oakes Smith pasted a short newspaper clipping entitled "Woman's Vindictiveness" in her diary. "Women will go very far in their vindictiveness—much further than most men," it began. "Appleton Oaksmith, who came so near being pardoned out of the penitentiary last week . . . will comprehend this fact extensively." The article recounted Isotta's visit to see Johnson, where she had explained how Appleton had obtained the divorce "by gross fraud" and how Isotta had implored the president not to show mercy "to a man so unprincipled." Despite all Elizabeth had done for her

son—pleading his case "so eloquently . . . that success seemed certain"—
Isotta was able to destroy his hopes and exact revenge. "Hell has no fury
like a woman scorned," the author reminded his or her readers, "and the
discarded wife, with her alleged injuries rankling in her bosom, paused at
no expense, hesitated at no difficulty, which promised to give her taste of
her 'great revenge.' Care, fatigue, outlay, bashfulness, all were forgotten in
her hope of keeping the man who had wronged her in a dungeon. And
she succeeded." There was a moral in this sad tale, which the author revealed with tongue firmly planted in cheek. "Never wrong a woman. 'Kill
her with kindness,' if you want to get rid of her, and let your poison be
purchased at the dry goods and jewelry stores. Do this, and she will never
pursue you to a prison cell and glory in robbing you of your liberty while
she enjoys her own."[34]

From England, Appleton wrote his father: "The worst enemy I have
had for years has been at our very hearth stone—no one can ever know all
I have undergone in that affair—and I am glad she is out of the household,
although I regret the scandal she has caused." At least now his family was in
"*peace*." Despite the disappointment, Appleton was determined to maintain
his resolve. "I have *no fears* for the future," he wrote his mother. "*Perhaps it
is all for the best that that woman has shown to the world what she is. I can wait.
I am working and the results will come.*"[35]

17

STORMS

Appleton Oaksmith would have to continue waiting. In fact, he may have given up hope of ever returning to the United States. On November 26, 1869—after living in England for almost four years—he applied to become a naturalized British subject. His petition was granted a week later, on December 2. He continued to work as a sailor, and he eventually took a position as an agent for a trading company, making business trips to mainland Europe. In 1869 he became associate editor of the *London Cosmopolitan*, and during the Franco-Prussian War (1870–1871) he served as a war correspondent for the London *Globe*. He used his pen to settle old scores, publishing one article called "William H. Seward—England's Devoted Enemy," which traced how Seward was responsible for all that had gone wrong in the United States during the Civil War era—including that Seward, "for objects of personal and party malignity, bade defiance to all human rights—trampling these Constitutional rights under his feet—and caused the arrest of a large number of loyal citizens, throwing them into those ever-to-be-remembered bastiles of the North—Forts Warren and Lafayette—without warrant, without law, and without cause."[1]

Despite his many efforts, Oaksmith could not pull himself out of debt. In 1867 he took his wife and three children on a three-month voyage around Cape Horn. At first the trip "was like a beautiful dream," wrote Augusta—a "fine vessel, fine weather . . . everything comfortable, with *the best husband* in the world to care for me and the most loving children. I was very happy." But the weather turned and for "two long *months* we were not outside the cabin, the windows all darkened. . . . It was most terrible times." The family and all their belongings were soaked, and Appleton worked day and night on the deck to keep the vessel going. For weeks on end, he was freezing and drenched, "utterly worn out for want of rest." During one three-day stretch he stayed above deck working without ever going belowdecks for sleep, and for the last three days of the voyage he had nothing to eat as he divvied up the rations between his wife and children. "It was a fearful time," Appleton later wrote. Augusta worried that "he would fail—would become utterly exhausted and perish." And yet, Augusta wrote, "notwithstanding all this he was always cheerful, more—considerate for the comfort of the lowest man on the ship than his own—Always a pleasant word for the children, and *so patient* through everything."

Appleton's children—Bessie, Corinne, and Randolph—grew to love their stepmother, and she in turn showered them with affection. One night, when Augusta went into their bedroom to check on them, Bessie woke up and lifted her head for a kiss. "Mama you dont know how much I love you," she whispered. The more time Augusta spent with her stepchildren the less she could understand how they were related to Isotta. "The wonder grows with me every day—how *such a woman* could give birth to such a child," Augusta wrote of Bessie. "From all accounts and *last particularly* one would as soon think of an angel & devil as parent and child." Appleton and Augusta both reported to Elizabeth that the children "despise" their birth mother. "They shall never again be *under that woman's influence*," wrote Appleton. "Little Bessie grieves sometimes (but only with a strange pity) while the others never speak of her and seem to have forgotten her existence." Randolph once asked his father "if Madame Isotta was *ever any relation to our family*." Far away in England, the children missed their grandparents, Elizabeth and Seba, very much.[2]

The Oaksmiths lived in a home called "The Marchins" in Essex County—a place that Bessie described as "sweet quiet country" with "plenty of trees and fields and a plenty of fresh air." Eventually Augusta's mother, Eleanor P. Mason, also moved in with the family. During their first three years in England, Augusta delivered two children, but both died in infancy. Then, on June 25, 1870, she gave birth to a third child—Mildred—who survived.[3]

Although they were settling into their new lives in England, a major rift was about to emerge in the family. In 1870, Appleton had a falling out with his uncle and former attorney, Benjamin F. Sawyer. Sawyer had served as an attorney for Eleanor P. Mason (Sawyer's half-sister and Appleton's aunt and mother-in-law) and had lost $5,000 that she was to receive as life insurance when one of her daughters died in 1867. When Sawyer was unable to pay Mason the money he owed her, Oaksmith told Sawyer that he wanted "all family ties & considerations . . . forever severed." Mason added that she no longer considered him her brother. Oaksmith called Sawyer a "scoundrel," writing to another associate, "There is something *dreadful* to me in the wickedness of that man."[4] All that Sawyer had done to help Oaksmith during his troubles in 1861 and 1862 was forgotten.

Back in the United States, Seba was becoming frail. "Some days I feel so weak that it is a great task for me to get through with my work," he wrote to Elizabeth in November 1865. For her part, Elizabeth found time with her husband increasingly frustrating. "Great God! how refreshing would be a little cheerful sympathy!" she wrote in her diary in July 1867. "Alone. No one to exchange one word with for nearly a week—no one in the house but Mr. Smith, always a taciturn man, always melancholly one, and now so deaf it is next to an impossibility to make him hear." The loneliness was becoming almost unbearable. "I am becoming quite the worse for this solitude," she continued. "The great house and empty rooms seem dreary and haunted. . . . Mr. Smith makes me half wild by his melancholly surmises about the children. I tremble and pray, and doubt and fear, but try to keep up a cheerful aspect." All Elizabeth wanted was "to rush out—leave this desolate house." During the days Seba sat reading newspapers; in the evenings he and Elizabeth played chess. Privately, she wrote a friend that her "invalid husband has much confined me." He finally died on July 28, 1868—in Elizabeth's words, "poor and neglected" and "a good and gifted man." Elizabeth was "too poor" to give Seba a proper headstone at the time. When she later did, it bore words that he had wanted: "Poet and Scholar."[5]

Tragedy would also strike with Sidney. Following his arrest and imprisonment with Appleton in 1861, Sidney's health had faltered.[6] In Cuba, he regained much of his energy, and now, in the postwar period, he was practicing law in New York City. Appleton and Sidney had been close since they were children. "The love of a brother is dearer and truer than all the friendships of the world," Appleton had once written of "Sid."[7] In 1869 Sidney purchased the decommissioned ironclad ram *Atlanta* from the federal government. His plan was to sell her to the Haitian government, which was then engaged in civil war. Among his crew were about one hundred black men who wished to go to Haiti "in aid of their own race."

Shortly before departing for Haiti on December 19, Sidney penned a brief letter to his wife, Fanny. He reflected on "how much I left behind," but trusted "that He who has seen fit to watch over and guard me through life amidst all my errors will not now forsake me, but direct me on the right path." Sidney also hastily scrawled a note in pencil to his mother. "Keep up good spirits & pray for me till we meet," he wrote, "for I *believe* my course will be acceptable in the eyes of God."

But the *Atlanta*—now re-commissioned the *Triumph*—never made it to Haiti. She likely foundered somewhere off the east coast of the United States, perhaps near Cape Hatteras, the Graveyard of the Atlantic. The wreck site has never been located. Rumors circulated in the papers that the black crewmembers had died but that at least some of the white officers had survived. As late as February 1870, Elizabeth clung to the hope that her son was still living, but she also feared that he may have been captured by the Spanish government. She implored the secretary of the navy as "an anxious and sorrowing Mother" to telegraph Cuban authorities in Havana or to send out a search vessel to see if Sidney was still alive. Secretary of State Hamilton Fish and Admiral David Dixon Porter both replied that they had no information to offer her. Eventually Elizabeth accepted the terrible reality, and she annotated Sidney's scrawled pencil note, "Darling Sidney's last words."[8] Elizabeth had now lost a fourth son. And like his long line of forebears, Sidney Oaksmith had breathed his last as he slipped beneath the waves.

Back in Patchogue, Alvin brought renewed shame on his family. About 1868 or 1869 he had moved to New York with his Uruguayan wife, Delfina. Alvin described her as "a girl of no talent and poorly educated but of fine feelings & sentiments and *good common sense*," as well as "ladylike in appearance & manners, affectionate, and a good mother & wife." But things apparently took a turn for the worse at almost the same moment that Sidney was lost at sea. As the *Brooklyn Daily Eagle* reported, Alvin and Delfina had been having difficulties for some time when, on Monday, January 24, 1870, "he assaulted her in a most brutal manner, beating her about the head and face, and inflicting such injuries as to cause her physician to fear for the safety of one of her eyes." The paper reported that for several days before this beating Delfina "had not been permitted to leave the house of her mother-in-law, where she had been subjected to the most heartless cruelties." Delfina only managed to escape one night at midnight with the help of a servant girl, and she made her way to a friend's house where she began to recuperate. Alvin was arrested, tried, and convicted in court. He was fined $50 and required to post bond that he would keep the peace. A week later the *Brooklyn Daily Eagle* dubbed him "the Patchogue wife beater."[9]

Isotta continued her quest to regain custody of her children—or at least to see them. She corresponded with Richard Henry Dana Jr. and William H. Seward, hoping they might use international law to go after her ex-husband. Dana replied that he was no longer US attorney "& can do nothing about the matter upon which you wrote me."[10] Heartbroken and destitute, Isotta ran an advertisement in the *New York Tribune* in the fall of 1869 stating, "Mrs. Appleton Oaksmith has resumed her teaching of Italian, French, and Music, in classes or private lessons."[11] In early 1871 she published a statement in the newspapers calling Appleton "a bigamist and a fugitive from justice" who had "cruelly abandoned her" while his mother, Elizabeth, had "stolen her children." Later that year she returned to Portland, Maine, where a sympathetic local newspaper urged readers to greet her with kindness in light of the cruelty she had received from Appleton. "It is hoped the friends of this injured woman, as well as all friends of human charity will give her a cordial welcome to the city that once held for her a happy home." While in Portland, Isotta performed a concert at Fluent Hall.[12]

Elizabeth Oakes Smith continued to resist Isotta's efforts, but she, too, was exhausted and suffering. Shortly after Isotta's meeting with Andrew Johnson in 1867, Elizabeth took to her diary: "June 11th. So ill and distressed that I feel as if my reason would desert me. Cry mightily unto God. I am unable to take in the malignity of Isotta in this last act of hers—it is more devilish than human." She was superstitious and alarmed by foreboding signs. One day, after bats flew into her house and she saw snakes at her feet near her garden, Elizabeth wrote in her diary, "Within a brief space two creatures of ill omen have come in my path." By 1870 she had fallen into hard economic times. She wrote to Horatio King, an old acquaintance from Maine who had been postmaster general under James Buchanan, seeking a postal appointment to earn supplemental income. She also wanted to sell an expensive Gilbert Stuart painting of George Washington's first secretary of war, Henry Knox, to Congress for display in the Capitol Rotunda. All the while, she kept writing to officials in Washington on behalf of her son.[13]

Unfortunately, Appleton's name and connection to the slave trade reappeared in newspapers throughout the nation, bringing renewed public contempt upon the family. In 1870 Appleton's former prosecutor, Stewart L. Woodford, ran for governor of New York as a Republican. The Democratic press—along with some Republicans who had wanted Horace Greeley to win the Republican nomination—resurrected the story that Woodford had colluded with Oaksmith to send the *Augusta* on a slaving voyage in 1861. Some of the fiercest articles appeared in the New York *Sun*, a paper edited by Greeley's former associate, Charles A. Dana. The articles quoted extensively from articles in the *New York Tribune* that Robert Murray had fed to Greeley in 1861. Murray also published an open letter claiming that Woodford had accepted a bribe from Oaksmith and that he (Murray) had met with Oaksmith at the Charles Street Jail and that Oaksmith had admitted his guilt.

Appleton read these reports in London and was furious. He swore two affidavits contradicting Murray; however, Democratic papers, in language dripping with sarcasm, doubted that Oaksmith could be trusted in this matter. "The Stars and Stripes and the pirate flag they kept sweetly intertwined," editorialized one. "Oh, the loving, pure minded, patriotic pair."[14] After reading the reports in the *Sun*, Elizabeth lamented, "It does seem as if the papers will never let us rest again."[15]

Some Republican papers came to Woodford's defense, pointing out that Judge Shipman and Secretary of the Interior Caleb B. Smith had exonerated him of any wrongdoing. One upstate New York paper argued that "Murray in this matter is moved by a spirit of revenge. He is not only angry with the Administration for having very properly turned him out of office, but he will never forget Gen. Woodford for having, as he believes, thwarted him in a cunning scheme by which he (Murray) expected to pocket two or three hundred thousand dollars in fines and forfeitures from the merchants and shippers of the city of New York." According to this report, Murray had instituted suits against several hundred parties, but Woodford discontinued the suits because he believed them unjust and based on a tortured understanding of the law. "This was a great disappointment to Murray, who expected that his share of the plunder would be at least $250,000; and, believing Woodford chiefly responsible . . . he then and there, in the most violent manner, vowed eternal vengeance against the young lawyer." The "Oaksmith libel" was "proof of the fact."[16]

Elizabeth was saddened by this "late infamous attack by Murray." She wrote her son in England, "The election will soon be over, and then I trust Woodford and you will come out and exhibit the whole system of perjury, and wickedness. . . . You must tell about Arguelles, and Seward, and the whole set of perjurers, bribers and scoundrels."[17]

Woodford lost the election, although he always maintained his innocence.[18] And despite the renewed notoriety in the press, Appleton became convinced that the new attacks on Murray had impugned the ex-marshal's character enough to make pardon feasible. Indeed, the increased press attention buoyed the family's hopes. Elizabeth spoke with one friend who said "that there was no slave trade about it . . . and people are just getting their eyes open to see it."[19] From England, Appleton wrote directly to President Ulysses S. Grant. "Recent events have revealed the true character of this man Murray," he explained, "and I believe your Excellency will now see that he is a person not worthy of the slightest belief." Accordingly, he asked the president to do him "*justice*."[20] The following month, Elizabeth sent another letter to Horatio King in Washington, DC. "My

Son Sidney is no more—Appleton still under the cloud—Do you think Mr Grant would do anything for him?"[21] Oaksmith hired King to serve as his attorney in pursuit of a pardon.

Letters and sworn affidavits poured into the office of the pardon attorney in Washington, DC, attesting to Oaksmith's innocence. Politicians, shipbrokers, railroad and bridge contractors, merchants, Civil War generals, and childhood friends all pleaded on Oaksmith's behalf. Seward's old associate Thurlow Weed wrote that Oaksmith "had been severely if not unjustly dealt with." A New York law firm that had done work for Robert Murray added that the arrest and imprisonment were "both unjustifiable and illegal" and that "the proof abundantly showed" that Oaksmith "acted as broker," not the owner, of the *Margaret Scott*. "We are satisfied of his innocence and that great wrong and injustice has been done him," they concluded. Horace Greeley added that if Oaksmith were "substantially innocent" then he deserved a pardon.[22]

Richard Henry Dana Jr.—now in private practice as an attorney—opposed Oaksmith's petition. "I have always said to the applicants that if Oaksmith would return to jail and apply personally for a pardon, his case would be considered but not otherwise. There is no doubt that he was guilty and that his guilt was of an aggravated character, he being a man of unusual cleverness and with no scruples." Based on Dana's recommendation, the attorney general declined the request on September 12, 1871. From his perspective, "The offender escaped from prison. . . . Under these circumstances, it is hardly proper to consider his application, much less to grant it."[23]

Elizabeth was devastated by this development. "It is nearly twelve years that I have greatly suffered," she wrote to Gerrit Smith. "I am wrecked in fortune, and doubly wrecked in good name." The news of the decision "drives me to despair," she told Horatio King. After securing letters in support from "powerful and high-toned men through the Country, Politicians of all parties, judges and lawyers and literary men, who know us and know we have been cruelly dealt by: after all our sufferings—nothing can be done? One little act of goodness, which we might claim is a right, rather than a mercy. Our enemies in Boston are bent upon crumbling us to the dust—bent upon our ruins." She knew that her son could not return to Boston and turn himself in. "If he goes there our name is to again ring through the Country with every opprobrium and epithet—we are to be branded with shame and fines and imprisonment. Better to die in exile, bitter as it will be. To go to Boston is to go to prison." She concluded her missive, "Can nothing be done? Oh my friend, this is indeed a blow," and she signed it, "Yours in distress."[24]

Though the details are murky, Oaksmith made a trip to the United States in mid-1871, while his pardon request was still under consideration at the Department of Justice. He wrote to Grant from Portland, Maine, on July 4, insisting on his innocence. "I don't know what more I can do or say," he wrote. "I came to this country because I had a firm belief that *this Administration would do me justice.* I have never seriously expected it before." He insisted that the people of Boston had been bloodthirsty for suspected slave traders in 1861, and that justice had not been their real motive. "At the time of my conviction in Boston—they would have convicted you—or [Attorney General Amos T.] Akerman—or *anybody else*—if they had been *only accused*—as long as Dana *said* that he, you, or they were guilty."[25]

By the fall of 1871 Oaksmith was in New York City. While walking down Cortlandt Street about halfway between Broadway and Greenwich in November, he ran into Benjamin F. Sawyer, who appeared "very pale, and evidently disturbed." Sawyer tried to shake Oaksmith's hand but was rebuffed. For forty-five minutes Sawyer strove to persuade his nephew that he was "very poor" and that he had meant Eleanor Mason no harm, but Appleton refused to accept his explanations.[26]

Appleton continued to pursue executive clemency from Grant. "I did not escape from justice—but I did from *injustice*; and from what I regarded as a prostitution of the legal power of the Government to objects of personal malignity," he informed the president. Appleton must have been feeling confident, for in 1872 he left England with Augusta and their four children aboard his ship *Troubadour.* The voyage was an exciting one, for at sea Augusta delivered a baby girl named Pauline. In July he disposed of a cargo at Galveston, Texas, and while there he signed an oath renouncing his British citizenship. According to two accounts, Oaksmith went directly to the White House to meet with Grant "representing himself as Counsel for Oaksmith." Appleton allegedly "personally so charmed Grant, that he obtained his own pardon." When, after granting the pardon, Grant asked him why he was so persistent on Oaksmith's behalf, Appleton is said to have responded, "Because I am Appleton Oaksmith." While this story may be apocryphal, Oaksmith did indeed secure pardon from Grant on October 7, 1872. Grant's rationale for issuing the pardon was that he had received a large numbers of petitions from prominent persons who believed Oaksmith was innocent. The case against him in Boston was finally discontinued on May 28, 1873. After more than a decade of exile—what his attorney called "twelve years of torture"—Appleton was finally a free man.[27] Some observers worried, however, that this pardon might portend leniency toward violent members of the Ku Klux Klan.[28]

In early 1873, Oaksmith sailed to Beaufort, North Carolina. According to one of his daughters, he had been forced to land there during a violent storm about a year earlier. While he was waiting for repairs to be completed on his ship, he stumbled upon a real estate auction near Morehead City. Hoping to "aid the auctioneer" by driving up the price, Oaksmith bid "an absurdly low price and walked away." The next day the auctioneer saw him on the street and informed him that his bid had been the only one. "Thus Appleton Oaksmith had inadvertently bought a home in North Carolina where he was to live for the rest of his life." Carteret County land records confirm the daughter's recollection. The land volumes held by the Register of Deeds reveal that Oaksmith bought "100 acres land more or less in Morehead Township" at a sheriff's sale in March 1872 for $11.25, a price that included the taxes and other costs. Appleton's daughter Corinne enjoyed their new home, which they called "Hollywood": "This house is a very pretty one it has upper and lower verandas and is very pleasantly situated and is close to the water and has a lot of trees in front of it."[29]

Appleton quickly became active in railroad development; however, his business schemes never panned out the way he hoped they would. In 1874 he ran for the state legislature as an independent candidate. Democrats in the area warned voters "not [to] be ensnared in Oaksmith's Radical trap." Some called him an "imposter" whose railroad schemes were frauds. Others claimed that he was ineligible for state office because he was not a

Hollywood.
Courtesy of the State Archives of North Carolina.

US citizen. The editors of the Goldsboro *Carolina Messenger* opined, "He is a humbug, a mere confidence man. His whole stock in trade consists in a brassy face, a promising tongue, deceit, impudence, a slick liar, ram goats and sheep, and two jackasses." Other insults leveled at him during the campaign included "rascal," "a man of doubtful character," "an oily gammon," a "vagabond," and "not only a hypocrite, but a traitor." One local stated that when he first met Oaksmith he was introduced as "McDonald"—the alias Oaksmith had used during the Civil War.[30]

Oaksmith won election to the state house of representatives, where he served with seventeen African American men.[31] In the election he

North Carolina legislature, ca. 1874. Oaksmith is standing toward the front right, behind a younger man.
Courtesy of the Library of Congress.

defeated "a regular Southern 'war horse,'" by which he meant an ex-Confederate who longed to maintain white supremacy in North Carolina. Oaksmith's time in state politics was largely unremarkable except that he was ardently anti-Klan and in favor of protecting the rights of ex-slaves. Although he had been a lifelong Democrat, he opposed the Southern men of that party who believed "*we will have but one party in the South—the white man's party*," and he longed for a new political coalition that eschewed racial violence and that sought to elevate African Americans. He supported the creation of a new "Reform Party," consisting of both conservative Republicans and Democrats. "Away with all talk about the white man's party," he proclaimed, "and let us run up the banner of the great party of the future, whose mission shall be not only to restore our Government and institutions to their pristine purity but also, while sacredly guarding the political rights of all, maintaining in a firm and kindly way those lines of race which God himself has made. Equality in all things political; distinctions, according to the personal rights of each, in all things social."[32]

While Oaksmith did not support social equality among the races, he delivered speeches in favor of "the inalienability of the rights of Southern citizens of African descent," and he called on white Southerners to abide by the Thirteenth, Fourteenth, and Fifteenth amendments to the US Constitution. "I here most emphatically declare that never so long as I have a voice to raise will I consent to the abridgement—no matter how small the degree—of a single right or liberty now enjoyed by that Race," he intoned. "And I say to them now, and I would that every colored citizen in this State could hear my voice . . . the rights which the Constitution of the United States have given you, can never be annulled or impaired by any human power. This question has long since been settled and can never be revived again."[33] Perhaps Oaksmith's years in prison and exile led him to appreciate the sanctity of constitutional rights for all citizens, regardless of race. Having been denied due process and other rights, he loathed seeing other people denied them as well.

Oaksmith became embroiled in a heated debate over the federal Civil Rights Act of 1875, which sought to guarantee equal treatment for African Americans in public accommodations. When two Republicans in the state legislature bolted from their party and proposed resolutions opposing the act—claiming that it overrode the "social rights of the Anglo Saxon race" and sought "the utter destruction of the white people of the South"—Oaksmith publicly opposed the resolutions. While he considered the Civil Rights Act "an unwise preponderance of social privileges to one race in opposition to the sentiments and feelings of the other," he nevertheless maintained that the "peace and prosperity" of North Carolina "depends upon maintaining in a just and equitable manner the rights of all citizens, without regard to race or previous condition" of servitude. One paper opined: "His efforts seem to have pleased the Radical members very much."[34]

By October 1874 it was clear that Appleton's aunt and mother-in-law, Eleanor P. Mason, was dying. Eleanor prayed for her estranged half-brother, but Appleton and Augusta were bitter and angry. Appleton informed Sawyer of her condition and angrily told him that if she did not live until the spring *"you will be her murderer."* He also intimated that he would institute legal proceedings against Sawyer in the spring. Sawyer replied with a harsh letter that may give insight into Oaksmith's earlier affairs. He wrote, "You rave like a madman (though you have not the slightest reason so to do) what else could I expect from a man like yourself who I believe never breathed an honest breath since your childhood and whose whole life has been marked with a series of swindling and crime that falls to the lot of a very few convicts. To hear you talk of Honesty & Honor is about as great a farce as I ever witnessed." Sawyer then threatened his nephew: "Of one thing be assured in a contest with me blows will be given as well as received. I have 'The Sun' articles and when you move I will forward them to North Carolina for republication." He signed off, "Yours with contempt." Eleanor died at Hollywood a few days later, on November 13. Appleton penned a poem "In Memoriam," lamenting that she had crossed "the Eternal Sea."[35]

By the mid-1870s, Elizabeth Oakes Smith was dividing her time between Patchogue and Hollywood. She did her best to keep occupied "lest the dear faces of Sidney and Edward should too violently weigh me with a sense of bereavement."[36] In September 1875, Appleton traveled to Long Island to collect his mother's belongings and bring them back to North Carolina. On September 7, two vessels, the schooner *Minnie*, which he commanded, and another vessel, the *Elizabeth*, departed Patchogue. For days the ships encountered a "heavy gale" that Oaksmith described as a cyclone. On September 19, he scrawled in his ship's log: "This is a fearful night and morning. This may be the last log I shall ever write. Shall put this little book in a bottle with a line to my dear wife and throw it overboard if we are like[ly] to founder." Oaksmith and his crew worked at the pumps day and night to keep the ships afloat. All the while he had "my little bottle ready" should the ship begin to sink, adding, "We can barely keep up with the leak and our strength is failing. Unless there is a change for the better within 6 hours we are lost." The *Minnie* survived but the *Elizabeth* did not, and Oakes Smith lost much of what she owned—uninsured property that was worth about $5,000. "I suppose that you have heard that Appleton was wrecked in the terrible gale," she wrote. "One vessel was a total loss, the other nearly so—barely escaping with life. Most of my old furniture is at the bottom of the sea."[37]

When in Patchogue, Elizabeth raised produce and eggs, and did writing and speaking to stay out of debt. Appleton's only surviving brother, Alvin, reported: "Mother . . . is very well and having a grand time. She has had splendid receptions wherever she has been. Her lectures are crowded, and the press speaks in terms of admiration. She is certainly a remarkable woman."[38] When in North Carolina, she got to enjoy her growing flock of grandchildren. Bessie and Corinne took after their father and paternal grandparents, writing poetry that appeared in newspapers throughout the United States. Bessie, now eighteen years old in 1876, had grown into an admirable young woman, with one local newspaper describing her as "very tender, gentle and refined, shrinking and sensitive, cultivated to an unusual degree and yet firing up with quick resentment at any injustice to her father, whom she loved with a devotion and attachment paralleled only by that of Theodosia Burr to her father." (This was a striking comparison, as Aaron Burr is one of the most notorious scoundrels in American history.) Corinne, two years younger than Bessie, was more attractive than her older sister—"brilliant, fearless, earnest, impassioned, a fine horsewoman and bold rider, a fine musician, a beautiful songstress, and earnest student with a mind that constantly hungered for knowledge." Elizabeth thought Corinne "a girl to be proud of[,] full of Genius, and fine generous feelings." But Corinne's poetry could be dark and contemplative. She wrote of growing older, and of death. In one poem, entitled, "When I'm Cremated," she mused, "Will they cremate me when I die? / Will they cremate me? / Will my smoke rise to the sky / When my fate begins to fry? . . . / I wonder if my friends will cry / When I['m] cremated." In another, about a shipwreck, she imagined herself drowning: "Those waves so bright / As they gaily tossed / Now blacker than night / As they beat and brake / With my own hearts ache / And I am lost."[39]

The Oaksmith family continued to grow in North Carolina. Augusta delivered a boy, Stanley, in May 1873. Augusta's older sister, Ellen Mason, also lived next door. It was a busy household.[40] At one point Appleton garnered national attention for discovering the Mecklenburg Resolutions—an alleged declaration of independence before *the* Declaration of Independence.[41] Amid the busyness of life, Appleton took some time on his birthday in 1876 to send a short and deferential letter to President Grant opposing

Grant's appointment of Richard Henry Dana Jr. as minister to England. "I have reason to consider him a dishonest cold hearted and bad man," Oaksmith wrote the president, who "was engaged in the conspiracy which sought my ruin."[42] The Senate ultimately rejected Dana's nomination.[43]

In North Carolina, Elizabeth took seemingly incongruent positions on matters of race. On the one hand, she claimed that African Americans were "disinclined to work unless driven by necessity. Their tropical blood is naturally lazy." On the other hand, she was open to admitting "colored people" into a fraternal organization to which she belonged, and she attended black religious camp meetings. In 1876 she even wrote to the Democratic candidate for president, Samuel J. Tilden, urging that if the Democrats would show "a very little sympathy" toward the "colored people" of the South, that they would win black votes.[44] Appleton, meanwhile, took a public stance on race that must have shocked anyone who was following the news. In October 1877, he returned to New York City to participate in a mass meeting of the American Foreign Anti-Slavery Society at the Cooper Institute—the venue where he had offered pro-slavery, pro-Union resolutions during the secession crisis in January 1861. This time, Appleton shared the stage with the great black preacher Henry Highland Garnet, who, presiding over the meeting, intoned, "The time has come when slavery shall be banished from the face of the earth." Oaksmith was one of several figures to make a brief address, and toward the end of the meeting he introduced resolutions calling upon the US government "to interfere in behalf of the Cuban slaves." These resolutions were unanimously adopted, reported the *New York Herald*.[45] It is not entirely clear why or how Oaksmith came to develop more enlightened views on matters of race in the years following his exile. Perhaps his work with African American legislators in Raleigh transformed his thinking. In the South, he also interacted with African Americans in ways he would not have at other times and places earlier in his life. His mother claimed that "the negroes in this vicinity . . . are very fond of my son Appleton, and come to him frequently for advice."[46] Or, perhaps he was doing penance for past wrongs.

Appleton continued to face personal and financial hardships. He was so severely ill in 1876 that several newspapers reported on his ailments. Augusta delivered a baby girl named Katharine on July 5, 1877, but she died just three months later, on October 14. The grieving father published a short, eight-stanza poem about his beloved child. "Only a little grave / That few will ever see, / In sound of the mourning wave / And the music of the sea."[47] That same year Appleton again filed for bankruptcy.[48]

His brother Alvin sent him a long letter, trying to persuade him to move to Kansas. "I am truly sorry to hear from you as well as Mother of your continual illness of body and mind," he wrote. "I have heard repeatedly of the illness of yourself or some member of your family; and it must be more than discouraging." But of even greater concern, Alvin was

> pained that you are wasting your life and consequent happiness of your family in a place where there is so little prospect in the near future. Life is passing away, your children are growing up, and if things go as they have been what is there in the future for them in Hollywood. . . . The people among you appear to be broken, dead, dispirited, and want life and energy. If you are willing to sacrifice your own health and talents, do you think it best for the children—What could the girls do if you are taken away—*I am sure you think of these things.*

Alvin closed with a stern admonition: "Rouse yourself my Brother, consider your affairs and determine to make a change. *Let, lease,* or, *sacrifice if must be,* your places North and South and make a break for new fields."[49]

Appleton chose not to heed this advice—he was a man of the water, not an overland pioneer. But even his mother was beginning to worry about his life at sea. In December 1878, she warned Augusta, "Tell Appleton, to be sure that he is doing the best thing for himself by thus trying so often these dangerous, unproductive voyages."[50] Elizabeth was more prescient than she knew. For all the tragedy that Appleton had endured thus far, 1879 would be the most devastating year of his life.

In January, rumors circulated that Appleton had fathered a child by a local woman. "A matter has come to my knowledge of such an infamous nature that painful as it is I feel it should be settled at once," he wrote indignantly. "I have heard that Ida Pelletier had a child previous to her last one, and that *she* had stated that *I* was its father. I do not believe that she could in her right mind make such a statement: to whoever asserts—be they man, woman, or child—that I have ever had improper relations with *any woman* since my residence in this State is an infamous liar." As far as he was concerned, if Ida had really said such a thing, then "she is either *insane or one of the basest women I ever knew*—she cannot even say that I ever even kissed her *when she was supposed to be pure and good,* for I never trifle in that way—and never permit it."[51]

In March, Augusta wrote to her mother-in-law in Patchogue, "Our lives here are dull and uneventful as usual but as always fully occupied." She remarked that Bessie, now twenty-one, "has a good deal of the

Bohemian—thinks she had rather board than ever have a home of her own." Little Mildred, now nine, had jokingly named one of her hens "Bessie," and Mildred and Pauline enjoyed driving calves around the yard. Mildred could milk a cow as well as any adult, but if she had her way, would rather be indoors reading. "You used to think her too grave," Augusta wrote. "She is now always bright and companionable." Augusta closed, "I am afraid I have wearied you with our home affairs and childrens talk—but it makes up our life."[52]

In late April, Appleton and others gathered around the bedside of John Jones, a sixty-nine-year-old Methodist circuit rider who was dying from some sort of painful malady. A neighbor, who remarked that Oaksmith was "an agnostic," wrote that Appleton was so moved by the dying scene that he "underwent a marvelous change of mind and heart and returned to his home back up in the country rejoicing in his new found faith and hope of heaven." Shortly before he died, Reverend Jones called for Oaksmith to come to him. Jones's daughter recalled the scene: "Pa asked him what he thought was the meaning of being a Christian. With tears streaming down his eyes he told it was the resigning of all our purposes and everything to God. . . . Papa put his dear hands over Mr. Oaksmith and pronounced a beautiful blessing. God grant that he may be a Christian." Jones died on May 1. The next day, a minister in Beaufort preached the funeral sermon out of 1 Kings 8:57–58: "The Lord our God be with us, as he was with our fathers: let him not leave us, nor forsake us."[53]

In early June, Bessie received a six-page letter from her grandmother. "Do write, my dear Child, and do not doubt my love for you all, and everyone," Oakes Smith closed, "Tenderly your Grandam."[54] Bessie and Corinne were in a contemplative mood that June. Perhaps the death of Reverend Jones had shaken them. Both girls wrote poems that reflected on mortality. Bessie's poem "My Life" likened herself to things that disappear quickly—"a single gem, of the crystal dew," a drop of rain, a star, a flake of snow, a rainbow, or a "ripple in all of the rippling seas."

> Such, such is life and though lowly, these
> Have each their mission and part,
> The dew and the rain, the flowers and the trees,
> The ocean—the human heart.
>
> And like all of these in life's surging throng,
> There's a simple place for me,—
> A note or a chord in dear nature's song,
> To swell her great harmony.

That same month Corinne wrote a poem titled "*Sic Itur Ad Astra*," a Latin phrase which means, "Such is the way to immortality." Steeped in allusions to the Bible as well as images from nature, Corinne wrote of "crosses that are carried," the place "where Lethe's waters flow"; of "idols crushed and broken" and "patient faith unshaken, / Through years of misery!"

> We know in the great supernal,
>   God watches us one and all,
> And gathers with love eternal,
>   Our treasures as they fall.
>
> He garners them in His keeping,
>   However we faint and die,
> And the end of earth's sorrow and weeping,
>   Is immortality.

July 4 started out as a beautiful day, and Appleton took four of his daughters and two of his sons on a boat ride across the Bogue Sound for Beaufort. Appleton was the only one in the boat who could swim and was also the only one "who had ever confronted peril and death" before. While they were sailing about halfway between Fort Macon and Beaufort, the boom swung overhead but the sail got caught on something and the "boat yawed and capsized," turning completely upside down. It all happened "in a moment." Appleton yelled, "Look out for the little children—each take one and cling to the boat!" Bessie grabbed Mildred (9), Corinne took Pauline (7), and Randolph grabbed six-year-old Stanley. The boat began to fill with water and sink, but Appleton cried, "*Stick to the boat.*" Appleton worked with all his might to right the vessel but he just did not have the strength. "I was clinging to the stern to get a breath for my task when Bessie and Corinne turned round and saw their little sisters being swept away." The two older girls "uttered one shriek and threw themselves off and struggled to get to them." At this moment Appleton realized that the anchor had gone to the bottom and was holding the vessel down. He quickly passed boat gratings and oars to the older girls to hang onto. He told the little children to cling to the gratings and instructed Bessie and Corinne to put the oars under their arms and "keep heads up and arms down." Corinne answered him, "all right papa" and shouted to the others, "Keep your heads up and arms down, and keep quiet."

Oaksmith dove six feet under water, fighting against a strong current, and tried desperately to free the boat from her anchor, but without a knife he could not do it. Upon resurfacing he urged Randolph to continue clinging to Stanley and the boat. He saw his daughters "drifting away, but apparently safe." By now his strength was waning. He called to a nearby fishing boat. The men aboard looked but did not come to his assistance. Appleton later wrote,

> Could I have got the boat clear from her cable in time, I believe I could have saved my daughters. I wasted much strength in that vain endeavor. Had I not done so I might possibly have got one of them to the shore, but after they drifted twenty feet by the stern, it was impossible for me to get either back to the boat. It required all my strength to swim to the bow against the current when I made my vain effort to set the boat adrift for their rescue. My agony was so great that I could not endure it, and I started to swim to my daughters—where we doubtless should have all perished together, which would have been better for me were it not for the living—when I saw the boat which rescued us coming round the point of marsh. My reason told me the chances for saving my daughters were greater with my help in that boat than out of it, and I waited in agony till she came, and directed the kind friends who were in her where to search.

The search would only end in heartache. Appleton found Corinne, Mildred, and Pauline floating lifelessly in the water. Mildred's little arms still clung to an oar. "The truth was very plain to me," wrote Appleton in utter despair, "—the poor child had lost her hold upon the grating, and Bessie, my noble eldest daughter, had deliberately given up her only support, put her drowning young sister across the oar, and died as she had lived, from devotion to those she loved." Corinne had done the same thing. The second grating was gone, and Pauline's lifeless body floated near the other oar. Appleton lifted his three daughters into the rescue boat. Bessie was never found. The boat then returned to Randolph and Stanley who were still desperately clinging to the capsized vessel. Appleton scooped them into the boat, next to their dead sisters. Appleton blamed himself for what happened and bore it in "agony and sorrow." Bessie was twenty-one, Corinne, nineteen, Mildred, nine, and Pauline, seven. "Baptized unto death," wrote one North Carolina newspaper, "these children were sung to sleep by the ceaseless hymn of the waves."[55] For a man who had survived so many perilous voyages around the world, he never could have imagined such a tragic ending to a joyride in the waters near his home.

18

DEATH

Words cannot describe how Appleton felt as he made the sad journey home to inform Augusta of what had happened. For days Augusta—who was six months pregnant—could not leave her room. Appleton did not dare leave her alone. "Since that dreadful disaster I have been at deaths door," wrote Augusta a few months later, "and my husband was so broken down that he has been confined to the house ever since and unable to attend to any business." Condolence letters poured in from relatives, friends, and even strangers. "*These have not been fruitless,*" wrote Appleton. The "first tears" that Augusta was able to shed "were awakened by these tender missives." The local newspaper tried to encourage the surviving Oaksmiths—as well as their readers—by reminding them that the four sweet girls who had drowned were now in a place where they "are better with Him, than with them." The paper praised the literary talents of Bessie and Corinne, remarking, "Poets will sing of them, and their sad story will be told many and many a year after we shall have passed away." But the newspaper editors anticipated what might become of the survivors. "The fear among his friends is, that this terrible bereavement may break Mr. Oaksmith down, and his usefulness be lost."[1]

Elizabeth hurried to Hollywood to be with her son, making it just in time to experience a hurricane in August 1879 that killed several people in the area.[2] Back in Patchogue, old neighbors remarked on what exceptional girls Bessie and Corinne had been. Alvin's eldest daughter, Elizabeth, wrote to her namesake grandmother, "Poor little Stanley so young and so much sadness to begin life with." In August, while still in North Carolina, Elizabeth wrote a long poem entitled "In Memoriam." Crying out helplessly, she wondered, "Oh! rushing wild, untutored breeze; / Oh! ye remorseless, heaving seas, / Could ye not pity such as these?"[3]

Oaksmith gathered his daughters' belongings and moved them into an upstairs bedroom—their toys and clothes and anything else of theirs that survived. Over the ensuing years he would spend hours in that room mourning their loss. As late as 1951 that bedroom still appeared as Oaksmith had left it in 1879. He told one friend in August, "I am *sick in body and mind* and cannot attend to business." And to prominent politician Zebulon Vance, he wrote, "Since that dreadful day I have never left my home, and have well nigh broken down under the weight of my affliction." For her part, Augusta told a friend, "Only the exceeding Mercy of God has enabled my husband and myself to cling to life."[4]

At some point in the 1880s Appleton moved to a home in New Bern and Hollywood fell into disrepair. The old house, which once had exhibited "luxury and pride" now showed "the ravages of time that poverty and sheer neglect had not stayed." The roof was rotten and covered in moss, the shutters were battered, some hanging in place by a single hinge. The stone steps leading into the house were askew and the fence around the yard was broken and dilapidated. Weeds and tall grass had grown up throughout the yard, and the outbuildings looked as though they might fall in a strong wind. The appearance of the place was "uncanny" and "ghostly," wrote one visitor in the late 1880s.[5]

Up in New York City, Isotta had fallen on hard times. In December 1878, her brother, who had been her primary means of support, had fallen from an elevated railway platform and fractured his skull. Isotta made it to his side moments before he died. Now, in July 1879, she was living in a boardinghouse in the city. While at the dinner table one of her fellow boarders, who happened to be a telegraph operator, announced that he had learned that morning of a disaster near Beaufort, North Carolina—that a boat had capsized and four sisters had drowned. "Did you learn their names?" asked someone at the table. "Yes," he replied, "it was—let me see—Oak-Smith, yes, Capt. Appleton Oak Smith and family." Isotta fell from her chair in a "dead faint." She had not seen her three children for almost fifteen years, but the thought of her daughters' bloated corpses floating lifelessly in the water was more than she could bear. The next day she gave an interview to a reporter from the *New York Sunday News*. The interview does not appear to survive, but the import of it was repeated in newspapers throughout the country. The *Cincinnati Daily Gazette* called Appleton "one of the worst scoundrels who ever escaped the gallows" and, after recounting his story along with that of Nathaniel Gordon's, concluded, "It is rare that so great a rascal contrives to avoid his deserts." The *Philadelphia Inquirer* erroneously reported, "He and Captain Gordon were captured off Long Island in a slave ship and were condemned to death for piracy." Some even wondered if Sheriff Clark up in Boston might now try to rearrest him.[6]

Isotta also propagated the rumor that her ex-husband had drowned their children on purpose.

Upon seeing these accounts, Appleton was livid. Sidney's widow, Fanny, wrote to him, regretting that "Isotta has been venting her malice through the papers." Appleton wrote to several newspaper editors asking whether they would publish a rejoinder.[7] In September he published a short rebuttal in the Boston *Herald*, and in December, he finally worked up the resolve to offer a full response to Isotta. He let readers know that Isotta had come to North Carolina to try to take Randolph home with her, but she was unsuccessful. Appleton was quick to point out that while in Hollywood she did not even visit Corinne's grave (Bessie's body was never found). Oaksmith denied having ever been a slave trader or that he "was arrested with Capt. Gordon, or ever had any connection, directly or indirectly, with him." And he denied what he saw as slanderous attacks about their marriage and divorce, and his remarriage to Augusta. The *Herald* also printed statements by Elizabeth Oakes Smith and Randolph. Elizabeth said there was "not a word of truth in any of the scandalous stories that Isotta Rebecchini has told," and Randolph recounted Isotta's temper. "My recollection of her is not pleasant," he wrote. "I can remember how she used to beat and abuse us children, always quarreling with some one. I remember the last time she beat me. She had dragged me up the back stairs, and was holding one hand over my mouth and beating me with the other, when my Grandmother Oakes Smith came up and took me away from her. . . . The time has come for me to take my stand, and I now publicly declare that I will never acknowledge this person as my mother, or hold any communication with her, until she drops the name Oaksmith, and retracts the misstatements she has told and published about my father and his family."[8]

Despite these three statements, Isotta's accusations had a lasting effect. According to one visitor to North Carolina in the late 1880s, Oaksmith became a pariah after his daughters' death. "Loud was the talk that he had deliberately taken them out and drowned them, as times were getting too hard with him, to support them. He was regarded with so much aversion and horror now by his neighbors, that he moved to Newburne." In the 1950s, some residents of Carteret County claimed that "rumors are still prevalent in the Morehead City area that Oaksmith had drowned his daughters intentionally."[9]

If Appleton thought he could find comfort in his only surviving brother, he was wrong. Alvin was too preoccupied with his own family problems to be much of an encouragement. In 1879, his oldest daughter, Elizabeth, "abandoned" him "and joined forces with her mother." She left the house while Alvin was out and left his three other little children in the home, alone. When Alvin returned, the children were afraid to tell him what had happened, and when they finally did "it nearly drove me crazy." In words that must have seemed insensitive to Appleton, Alvin wrote, "One of the flock is gone & it is not the hand of God that has taken it from us. How much can a man stand and contain himself? I am tempted all the time to put a finish to it all but I go to work at something and ask God to strengthen us."[10]

To help make ends meet, Augusta sent her jewelry to a pawnshop in New York, and Appleton sold his family's two pianos since Bessie and Corinne were no longer there to play them. He also wrote to Zebulon Vance in Washington, DC, seeking "some change of scene and occupation," but there were no vacancies and a long line of other applicants anyway.[11] But there was at least one shining moment in this dark period. On September 27, 1879, Augusta gave birth to a beautiful baby girl, Theodora. It was a miracle that she did not lose the baby considering all the stress, pain, and heartache she'd endured. Augusta remarked privately, "She is my greatest comfort."[12]

But the emotional effects of the drowning continued to tear the family asunder. Randolph, now almost twenty years old, ran away from home about 1880. It is unknown whether he communicated with his father or stepmother ever again. His life to this point had been one of turmoil—born during Appleton's incarceration in Boston, he likely didn't meet his father until he was four or five years old, when he was taken away from Isotta. Such a traumatic upbringing, in conjunction with the drowning of his sisters, must have been more than he could bear. He traveled far, far away, to North Dakota. About the time of Appleton's death, Randolph's mother, Isotta, moved to North Dakota to live with him and she became a US citizen the following year. That Randolph took her into his home leads one to wonder whether Appleton or Elizabeth had written the statement attributed to him that appeared in the newspapers in 1879. In 1889 Randolph married and had three or four children, one of whom he named after the grandfather who had helped raise him—Seba Bryan Oaksmith. Randolph moved to Louisiana at some point between 1897 and 1900, where he had another child. Isotta died in his home on July 1, 1901. Eventually he settled in Arkansas, where he died in 1948.[13]

Throughout the 1880s the Oaksmiths struggled to survive. Appleton spent years unsuccessfully trying to recover money from the federal government for his losses during the filibustering schemes of the 1850s. He also continued to travel for work and for court cases, leaving Augusta at home with the surviving children.[14] When Augusta was home alone, she found storms to be quite upsetting. "I have felt more nervous in gales ever since the dreadful hurricane of '79," she wrote to her mother-in-law, who had also experienced the storm. At night, after the children were in bed and the house was covered in shadows, Augusta ruminated on the past. "I miss the dear loved ones so much I almost despair," she wrote. "They were all so dear and each filled a different place in my heart." Theadora, who went by Dora and Thea (and as an adult, Dorothy), was now a toddler in 1881. She often reminded Augusta of Corinne—sympathetic, appreciative, intuitive, and cheerful. "She grows like a flower, and is a perpetual delight," Augusta told Elizabeth. "She is delighted with the birds and flowers." Two other children would be born to Appleton and Augusta—Vincent in 1882, and Geraldine in 1884.[15]

By the 1880s Elizabeth had become a bitter, frustrated, angry old woman. She had been defeated by life, by the Civil War, by the power of government, and by the forces of nature. As a child growing up in Maine, she had loved the outdoors and especially the water. She had always sought to live in "harmony with nature."[16] But the elements had devastated her family. Having lost the talented granddaughters that she had raised during the Civil War, she exhibited bitterness toward her youngest grandchildren because they did not show sufficient interest in reading and education. In fact, she seemed to resent children and adolescents in general. "It is an age of crime," she wrote in her diary. "Children are pampered and indulged and grow up without responsibility; with no sense of duty. Passion rules the hour. God only knows whither our own country is drifting."[17]

Like many adult children of aging parents, Appleton began to worry about his mother's moods. "I feel very anxious about mother," he wrote to Augusta in 1883. "She don't know what to do about those girls"—referring to his young daughters. Moreover, he noted that she seemed "broken down" and did not treat him fairly. "I have had a hard time with poor mother," he continued. "She has been *too hard* with me—she ought to have paid more attention to my advice and wishes—poor mother."[18] In her loneliness, Elizabeth burned most of the journals she had kept since she was eight years old, as well as much of her correspondence and unpublished writings.[19]

Throughout the 1880s, Appleton's health and financial situation increasingly worsened. He and his mother planned to write a book together, but they never found the time to do it.[20] About 1885, Appleton suffered some sort of severe malady that brought about paralysis. He traveled to New York City for medical care, but the doctors there could not agree on a diagnosis. Appleton had great difficulty writing and kept a bottle of chloroform under his pillow for when the pain became unbearable. For weeks on end, he could stomach nothing but oatmeal and milk. Eventually Augusta joined him in Manhattan while Elizabeth stayed back in North Carolina with the children. In 1886 he wrote to his mother that he hoped he could still win his claims against the government. "How I should like to give you all the money you could spend," he told her. And he asked her to "kiss the dear children for their loving but afflicted Papa."[21]

The children missed their parents dearly and hoped that their father would recover so that he could come home. But by 1887, recovery and return were becoming less and less likely. One of the last times Elizabeth saw her son, he struggled to say, "Dear Mother—I—not long—I—not long."[22] She understood. Now, alone in North Carolina caring for Appleton's children—just as she had for his older children during the Civil War—Elizabeth began to fall into despair. Her 1887 diary records her disillusionment with life. In January she mourned, "Appleton sick, Alvin unsettled—the world is receding from me—I should die it seems to me—but despite of disheartenment neglect and poverty I desire to live—feel that I might do more." Anniversaries were particularly hard for her. On Sidney's birthday, February 14, she recounted her lost son's sweet smile. "Oh life is a terrible struggle, and yet I hold on to it with a grasp despite of this solitude and depression. Somehow the eternal world seems near but I do not want to go." A month later, on Appleton's birthday, she wrote, "Poor disabled boy." When she learned that her daughters-in-law had traveled to New York City together, she groused, "No good will come of it to me. God is my witness I never wronged them. I have been patient beyond human endurance. An Italian, a Spaniard, a French girl—a Yankee. All quarrelsome—all malignant—jealous." Only Augusta received Elizabeth's praise, for she was "the devoted wife . . . with Appleton in New York."[23]

Throughout the spring and summer of 1887 Elizabeth professed to be in good physical health, but emotionally she was suffering. "This climate is unfriendly to me," she wrote to a friend in September, as she suffered from "Lion sickness" and a fever. "Miserably depressed," she jotted in her diary on September 2. "Try to throw it off but in vain. My life has come to an end of purpose." Indeed, she was isolated and lonely, with no adult to converse with except Augusta's sister. Much of her time was spent reading in the library. When one publisher wrote to her about republishing her work, she replied, "I have no desire to be resuscitated by Syndicate."[24]

Finally, in late October, word reached Elizabeth in North Carolina that her favorite son had died. On October 26, after a life of adventure, crime, risk, failure, and heartache, Appleton breathed his last. He was sixty-two years old. "This is the date of the departure of my beloved son Appleton to the unseen world—a great and exceeding grief to me," Elizabeth wrote in her diary. "Crushed to the earth, I could not rise to the comfortings of the divine Spirit and the Hopes of the spiritual and eternal. Alas! I could barely see the dear beautiful face in its narrow recepticle. Ah how manly—how lovely it looked! too lovely to be hid in the cold earth." Now she felt "as if half of my life were extinct. He was a poet in the high sense, and we could understand each other with no need of words."[25]

Appleton's body was sent by train to North Carolina, where it was buried with Masonic honors on October 30. Upon reporting these events, the *New Berne Weekly Journal* opined: "In many respects Capt. Oaksmith was a remarkable man. A true history of his life would doubtless be an interesting little volume." Oaksmith's enemies claimed that he "was not mourned" and that "he was such a weird fearful character that the neighbors seemed mighty glad he was gone." This does not seem likely, however. "Do not dispair Uncle lived a good life and has suffered much," wrote one of Alvin's daughters. "He will have his reward in heaven."[26]

Those who had known Appleton struggled to make sense of his life. How could a man from such a highly cultivated literary family have turned to slave trading, wondered New York City artist David Edward Cronin, an old acquaintance. "The parents being of a highly superior order, morally and intellectually, and the training of the sons, up to a certain period, almost perfect—whence did the dark strand in their otherwise noble compositions come?" Cronin speculated that American society had corrupted Oaksmith and his brothers. "The faculty for excellence in literature or art is almost invariably accompanied with a dominating love of approbation," and Oaksmith "possessed this love of approbation to the degree of criminal weakness." According to Cronin, Oaksmith also believed that "society scoffs at merit unless aligned with material prosperity," so Oaksmith was "determined to win it at whatever hazard."[27]

Elizabeth would have been horrified by this analysis of her family. In November she wrote a sonnet about Appleton called "The Sorrowful Gate," and she prayed God "to lift me out of this sad, sad sense of bereavement." Letters of condolence were of little comfort. "Oh! how cold how dead the world is to me!" she wrote in her diary. "My world seems to come to an end by this great bereavement. Four noble boys—all strong—manly, beautiful—one only left me. I am nearly blind from weeping." She poured out her grief and sorrow in correspondence, telling one friend that "now that my Son Appleton has gone . . . I am inexpressibly lonely."[28] Two years later, on March 22, 1889, Elizabeth opened one of her scrapbooks to the page that contained an article about the July 4 disaster. "Dear Appleton's birthday," she wrote. "Was ever sorrow like my sorrow! Behold the record here adjoined, and think of the dear Father's heart wrung with agony—the mother's grief—the pitiless waves that submerged all. Appleton was never afterwards the same."[29]

Looking back over her life, Elizabeth could trace all of her heartache to her wedding day. "Despite my seeming public career," she wrote, "I have been essentially a household woman."[30] If she had not been married, she could have pursued a vocation as a teacher. She would not have had sons to lose, nor suffered through Appleton's absence over the course of a decade. She would not have lost four granddaughters in a boating accident. She would not have seen her sons wind up in unhappy marriages of their own. Indeed, the *sine qua non* of all her suffering was her wedding day. And now, as an elderly woman, sitting alone with her pen in hand, she recalled only dark memories of her earlier years.

Relying on her unpublished autobiography, scholars have portrayed the marriage between Seba and Elizabeth as unhappy from the start. In it, Elizabeth had written that the "girl who has sacrificed this by a premature Marriage will carry in her breast, to the end of her life, the sense of a loss— the sense of desecration."[31] Yet real affection had existed between Seba and Elizabeth early in their marriage. "Do you not feel if you and I were to live fifty, or even a hundred years, and not see each other during the whole of the time, that our affection would remain as vivid to the last as it is now?" Seba had written her in 1833. Elizabeth returned with a gesture of affection. In one letter, she circled a spot on the page and wrote, "I can only say kiss this place because I have kissed it for you." And in another letter urging him to come home soon, she wrote, "I am putting my mouth into the prettiest pucker by the time you come, and I begin to hope another ten years or longer may elapse before it will be necessary for you to leave me again."[32] It was the financial hardships that began in the late 1830s and Seba's obsession with geometry in the 1840s and 1850s that sowed the seeds of strife in their marriage. By the time of the Civil War, things had crumbled beyond repair. In November 1861, she wrote in her diary of how deeply "unfit" she was to be a mother and how "sad" her "conjugal relation" had been—"not from vice or imbecility, or evil passion but simply from lack of sympathy between Mon Mari [her name for Seba] and myself."[33] Then, the emotional strains engendered by the Civil War led Elizabeth to hate her marriage, and to believe she had felt that way since she said her vows in 1823.

Like most nineteenth-century Americans, Elizabeth Oakes Smith had thought a lot about death over the course of her life. When her mother had died in 1851, she wrote a grief-stricken letter to her sons of her "deep . . . desire to fold you all in my arms."[34] But, of course, now her sons were gone, and no one was there to offer comfort in her affliction. She had out-lived her husband, five of her six sons, and at least nine grandchildren. Her favorite granddaughters had gone down in the boat that fateful July 4, Randolph was estranged from the family, and she did not enjoy the company of her youngest grandchildren. She turned yet again to her thoughts, writing essays on the suffering of Job, on shipwrecks, and on "Overcoming the Darkness." In her final decade she continued to fight for women's rights. When a woman was sentenced to hang for the murder of her husband, Oakes Smith wrote to the governor of New York asking that the punishment be commuted to imprisonment for life "on the ground that she was driven to wild, malignant frenzy by the twenty years of cruel treatment she had endured from her husband." When the woman was hanged anyway, Oakes Smith protested in a public letter against the execution of women "on the ground, that as woman had no voice in the making of the laws, and had given no consent to them, they ought not to suffer the extreme penalty of any law."[35] In quiet moments alone, she reminisced about earlier times, like when she had known Robert E. Lee before the Civil War, when he had been stationed at Fort Hamilton in New York. She had conversed with him about the meaning of dreams.[36] But the memories of loved ones lost were never far from her mind. News of the Johnstown Flood in Pennsylvania in 1889—which killed more than two thousand people—led her to imagine the shouts and cries and hopelessness of the dying. And that grief and despair caused her mind to flood with memories of her four dead granddaughters—and her lost sons.[37]

On March 12, 1893, she scrawled a note. "My Mother's birthday. I am putting my house in order as I can. Much to do." She looked around her study and saw piles of manuscripts—unfinished writings of hers as well as pieces by her sons—"my gifted, beautiful boys. Alas! alas! much is incomplete—but Oh how full of lovely thought and divine inspiration—but they, and I will go, and leave no just record of what we were." She concluded, "But life has been such a struggle at the best."[38]

The struggle was nearly over; she would not outlive the year. Elizabeth Oakes Smith died on November 16, 1893, at the age of eighty-seven. Her body was transported from North Carolina back to Patchogue, where she was buried next to Seba. According to her obituary in the local newspaper, she was laid to rest "unattended by a single mourner." A friend wrote to Augusta urging her not to grieve because Elizabeth "was ready to go" and now "has joined your other dear ones who have gone before." Another correspondent sent perhaps the most fitting tribute. "Soon the earth will close over our own heads, and the world will go on as though we had not lived, the only consolation to our sorrowing souls being the prospect of meeting with loved ones gone before, 'watching & waiting for us.'" She continued, "Life is a complex problem to be solved by each individual influenced by the surrounding conditions of existence—some with fair tides & wind, others with almost constant adversity. I trust the Madame has anchored safe in heaven—where all of her remaining family may finally meet her."[39] No metaphor could have been more apt. Since girlhood, the sea had brought Elizabeth nothing but heartache and loss. Earthly storms would trouble her no more.

Appendix 1

OAKSMITH FAMILY TREE

PARENTS

Seba Smith Jr. (September 14, 1792–July 28, 1868). Son of Seba Smith Sr. (1767–1831) and Apphia Stevens Smith (1770–1853). Born at Buckfield, Maine. Married Elizabeth Oakes Prince on March 6, 1823.

Elizabeth Oakes (Prince) Smith (August 12, 1806–November 16, 1893). Daughter of David Prince (1782–1809) and Sophia Blanchard Prince (1787–1851). Stepdaughter of Lemuel Sawyer Sr. (1779–1835). Half-sister of Benjamin Franklin Sawyer (1813–1888) and stepsister of Eleanor P. Mason (1806–1874).

CHILDREN OF SEBA AND ELIZABETH OAKES SMITH

Benjamin (1824)
Rolvin (June 16, 1825–May 6, 1832)
Appleton (March 22, 1828–October 26, 1887)
Sidney (February 14, 1830–January 1869)
Alvin (January 1833–1902)
Edward (1834–August 31, 1865)

CHILDREN OF APPLETON OAKSMITH AND ISOTTA REBECCHINI OAKSMITH

Buchanan (1857)
Bessie (February 26, 1858–July 4, 1879)
Corinne (March 30, 1860–July 4, 1879)
Peyton Randolph (March 18, 1862–May 30, 1948)

CHILDREN OF APPLETON OAKSMITH AND
SOPHRANA AUGUSTA (MASON) OAKSMITH
(JUNE 11, 1843–MAY 4, 1912)

Unknown child who died in infancy in England
Eleanor (September 25, 1868–August 16, 1869)
Mildred (June 25, 1870–July 4, 1879)
Pauline (February 29, 1872–July 4, 1879)
Stanley (May 11, 1873–December 12, 1938)
Katharine (July 5, 1877–October 14, 1877)
Theadora "Dorothy" (September 1879–July 24, 1960)
Vincent (January 29, 1882–May 27, 1951)
Geraldine (April 22, 1884–July 29, 1965)

Appendix 2

THE *WELLS* AND *MANUEL ORTIZ*

On February 18, 1862, US Attorney E. Delafield Smith filed an indictment in the US Circuit Court for the Southern District of New York against Oaksmith for fitting out the schooner *Wells* for the slave trade. The vessel had been seized by federal authorities at Greenport, Long Island, in April 1861, but Oaksmith was able to secure her release, just as he later did with the *Augusta*. One sailor later swore an affidavit describing how he joined the crew of the *Wells* in late March 1861 and then traveled with her to the Congo River, where the crew built a slave deck and then picked up a cargo of six hundred Africans. During the forty-five-day passage from Africa to Cuba, 160 of the Africans died—as did the ship's captain, J. Calvin Wells. This sailor testified regarding Oaksmith's involvement in the voyage, including that Oaksmith promised to pay him for his work.

Oaksmith later claimed that he had merely served as the agent for the firm that purchased the vessel and that he had no other interest in her or knowledge of her work. Copies of five letters, all dated March 30, 1861, and all in Oaksmith's handwriting, are in his papers at Duke University, although these letters do not give any special insight into the situation. Oaksmith later said that he was a broker for Jose Pietra-hita. Oaksmith included several dozen pages of documentation related to the *Wells* with his petitions to Ulysses S. Grant. In a document dated July 4, 1871, and written at Portland, Maine, Oaksmith wrote: "I never had any interest in this vessel whatever, or knowledge of her or her business except making that charter as Broker." He recounted how Captain Wells had died on the ship's voyage and speculated that some of the passengers and crew had conspired together, "murdered the Captain, . . . [and] ran away with the vessel and turned her into a Slaver."[1]

Some news reports also connected Oaksmith to the slaver *Manuel Ortiz*, although very little documentation connecting him to this vessel appears to survive. Ambrose Landre briefly mentioned it in his deposition in the *Margaret Scott* case.[2]

ABBREVIATIONS IN NOTES

Agard	Anonymous oral history, May 30, 1897, Agard Collection, Box 2, New Bedford Whaling Museum, New Bedford, MA.
AMO	Augusta Mason Oaksmith (AO's second wife).
AO	Appleton Oaksmith.
AO Collection	Appleton Oaksmith Collection, Southern Historical Collection, University of North Carolina, Chapel Hill.
AO journal	Journal of Appleton Oaksmith, 1851–1852, Appleton Oaksmith Papers, David M. Rubenstein Rare Book and Manuscript Library, Duke University, Durham, NC.
AO Papers	Appleton Oaksmith Papers, David M. Rubenstein Rare Book and Manuscript Library, Duke University, Durham, NC.
Augusta Case File	*United States v. Bark Augusta*, Record Group 21 (Records of the US District and Circuit Courts for the Southern District of New York), National Archives at New York.
Augusta Report	Senate Ex. Doc. No. 40, 37th Cong., 2nd sess., *Congressional Serial Set*.
Boston Case File	*United States v. Appleton Oaksmith*, Case No. 73 (May 1873 Term), RG 21 (Records of the US District and Circuit Courts for the District of Massachusetts), National Archives at Boston. (A smaller *Oaksmith* case file [Case No. 15, March 1862 Term], is also held in RG 21 at the National Archives at Boston.)
Brownson Papers	Orestes Augustus Brownson Papers, University of Notre Dame Archives, Notre Dame, IN.
CBS	Caleb Blood Smith (secretary of the interior).
CWL	Roy P. Basler et al., eds., *The Collected Works of Abraham Lincoln*. 9 vols. New Brunswick, NJ: Rutgers University Press, 1953.

Disloyalty File   Appleton Oaksmith treason file, RG 59 (General Records
                         of the Department of State), Entry 963 (Correspondence
                         Regarding Prisoners of War, 1861–1862), Box 8, Na-
                         tional Archives at College Park, MD.

EDS   E. Delafield Smith (federal prosecutor in New York City).

Elmore Collection   William E. Elmore Collection, 1821–2007, Special Collec-
                         tions, East Carolina University, Greenville, NC.

EOS   Elizabeth Oakes Smith (mother of AO).

EOS Autobiography   Leigh Kirkland, "'A Human Life: Being the Autobiogra-
                         phy of Elizabeth Oakes Smith': A Critical Edition and
                         Introduction." PhD diss., Georgia State University,
                         1994. (The original manuscript is held at the New
                         York Public Library.)

EOS diary   Diary of Elizabeth Oakes Smith, Elizabeth Oakes Smith
                         Papers, Small Special Collections Library, University of
                         Virginia, Charlottesville, VA.

EOS Letters   Autograph Letters Signed from Elizabeth Oakes Smith to
                         Various Recipients, Folger Shakespeare Library, Wash-
                         ington, DC.

EOS Mss   Elizabeth Oakes Smith Papers, New York Public Library.

EOS Papers   Elizabeth Oakes Smith Papers, Small Special Collections
                         Library, University of Virginia, Charlottesville, VA.

FO   Records of the Foreign Office, National Archives of the
                         United Kingdom, Kew, UK.

GSP   Gerrit Smith Papers, Special Collections Research Center,
                         Syracuse University Libraries, Syracuse, NY.

Hanging Gordon   Ron Soodalter, *Hanging Captain Gordon: The Life and Trial
                         of an American Slave Trader.* New York: Atria, 2006.

Keyes Papers   John Shepard Keyes Papers, Concord Free Public Library,
                         William Munroe Special Collections, Concord, MA.

LC   Manuscript Division, Library of Congress, Washington, DC.

Lincoln Papers   Abraham Lincoln Papers, Manuscript Division, Library of
                         Congress, Washington, DC.

M160   Records of the Office of the Secretary of the Interior
                         Relating to the Suppression of The African Slave Trade
                         and Negro Colonization, 1854–1872, National Archives
                         microfilm publication M160.

M179   Miscellaneous Letters of the Department of State, 1789–
                         1906, National Archives microfilm publication M179.

M899   Dispatches from US Consuls in Havana, Cuba, 1783–1906,
                         National Archives microfilm publication M899.

MdHS   Maryland History Center, Baltimore, MD.

NARA   National Archives and Records Administration.

NARA-CP   National Archives at College Park, MD.

NARA-NY   National Archives at New York.

NYHS	New-York Historical Society.
NYPL	New York Public Library.
O.R.	*War of the Rebellion: A Compilation of the Official Records of the Union and Confederate Armies.* 128 vols. Washington, DC: Government Printing Office, 1880–1901.
Pardon File	RG 204 (Records of the Office of the Pardon Attorney), Entry 1a (Pardon Case Files, 1853–1946), National Archives at College Park. (Each citation is followed by an alpha-numeric case file number.)
Pardons and Remissions	RG 59 (General Records of the Department of State), Entry 897 (Presidential Pardons and Remissions, 1794–1893), National Archives at College Park, MD.
RG 21	Record Group 21, Records of the District and Circuit Courts of the United States (the appropriate judicial district and branch of the National Archives are given in each citation).
RG 59	Record Group 59, General Records of the Department of State, National Archives at College Park, MD.
RG 60	Record Group 60, General Records of the Department of Justice, National Archives at College Park, MD.
RM	Robert Murray (federal marshal in New York City).
Secret Correspondence	RG 59 (General Records of the Department of State), Entry 955 (Secret Correspondence, 1861–1863), National Archives at College Park, MD.
SS	Seba Smith Jr. (father of AO, husband of EOS).
TePaske	John Jay TePaske, "The Life of Appleton Oaksmith: Its Latin American Aspects." MA thesis, Duke University, 1953.
WHS	William Henry Seward (secretary of state).

NOTES

PROLOGUE

1. Joseph McMaster, *Charles Street Jail* (Charleston, SC: Arcadia, 2015). Thanks to Joe McMaster for helping me confirm the location of AO's cell.

2. EOS Autobiography, 72–74, 80, 86, 105, 114, 117, 120; Boston *Repertory*, March 28, 1809; Boston *Columbian Centinel*, March 29, 1809; Portland *Freeman's Friend*, January 14, 1809; EOS to Caroline May, ca. 1847, Rufus W. Griswold Papers, Boston Public Library; EOS to Edward C. Stedman, March 1, 1888, EOS Letters. EOS's Autobiography can be a problematic source as it was written in old age after her life had been utterly devastated. I rely on it out of necessity, but with caution, as one of the few sources capable of giving insights into her early life.

3. "The Drowned Mariner," *The Poetical Writings of Elizabeth Oakes Smith* (New York: J. S. Redfield, 1845), 186–89. One of her finest poems, "The Acorn," traces the life of an oak tree that becomes part of a proud ship that sinks in a gale. Ibid., 126–37.

4. EOS Autobiography, 120, 127, 159; Portland *Gazette*, June 19, 1809; Eleanor P. Mason to Benjamin Franklin Sawyer, April 6, 1871, AO Papers.

5. EOS Autobiography, 75–80, 86–87; pension record of Seth and Lydia Blanchard, in NARA microfilm M804 (Revolutionary War Pension and Bounty-Land Warrant Application Files), reel 264.

6. EOS Autobiography, 138–40, 144; David Hanna, *Knights of the Sea: The True Story of the Boxer and Enterprise and the War of 1812* (New York: NAL Caliber, 2012), 175–99.

7. EOS diary, November 28, 1864. One member of the Oaksmith family claims to have a memoir written by AO but would not permit me to see it.

8. *Passages from the Correspondence and Other Papers of Rufus W. Griswold* (Cambridge, MA: W. M. Griswold, 1898), 132.

9. Timothy H. Scherman, "Oakes Smith Returns to Maine: 'The Defeated Life,' Katahdin, and the Dangers of Biographical Criticism," Gorman Lecture Series, Yarmouth History Center, June 10, 2014; Jeanne Winston Adler, *The Affair of the Veiled Murderess: An Antebellum Scandal and Mystery* (Albany: State University of New York Press, 2011), 177.

CHAPTER 1. FAMILY

1. EOS Autobiography, 164, 167.

2. EOS Autobiography, 168, 177–79, 182. Sophia had also been married at age sixteen, as had Elizabeth's older sister, Hepzibah. See Scherman, "Defeated Life."

3. Portland *Eastern Argus*, March 12, 1822, March 21, 1826, September 21, 1827, October 26, 1829; Portland *Christian Mirror*, October 15, 1829; EOS Autobiography, 177, 181, 220; SS to N. Cleveland, February 6, 1854, Seba Smith Papers, George J. Mitchell Department of Special Collections and Archives, Bowdoin College Library, Brunswick, ME; SS to Rev. Dr. Nichols, September 12, 1850, Seba Smith Papers, NYPL; Mary Alice Wyman, *Two American Pioneers: Seba Smith and Elizabeth Oakes Smith* (New York: Columbia University Press, 1924), 1–15; Cameron C. Nickels, "Seba Smith Embattled," *Maine Historical Society Quarterly* 13 (1973): 7–27. Copies of an autobiography by SS are available in the collections of his papers at both Bowdoin College and NYPL.

4. Keene, *New Hampshire Sentinel*, June 3, 1840.

5. EOS Autobiography, 179–80, 184; EOS to AMO, December 3, 1878, EOS Papers.

6. EOS Autobiography, 186, 201–7; EOS to May, n.d.; David E. Cronin, *The Evolution of a Life Described in the Memoirs of Major Seth Eyland* (New York: S. W. Green's Son, 1884), 49.

7. EOS diary, March 22, 1864; SS Autobiography; TePaske, 2–3; AO journal, December 25, 1851; Beaufort *Weekly Record*, November 18, 1887.

8. EOS Autobiography, 216; Wyman, *Two American Pioneers*, 30; Milton and Patricia Rickels, *Seba Smith* (Boston: Twayne Publishers, 1977), 24–71.

9. Robert E. Johannesen, ed., *The Letters of Stephen A. Douglas* (Urbana: University of Illinois Press, 1961), 2; Christopher Looby, ed., *The Complete Civil War Journal and Selected Letters of Thomas Wentworth Higginson* (Chicago: University of Chicago Press, 2000), 137; Howard K. Beale, ed., *Diary of Gideon Welles: Secretary of the Navy under Lincoln and Johnson*, 3 vols. (New York: W. W. Norton, 1960), 2:345, and 3:336–37; David Crockett, *A Narrative of the Life of David Crockett of the State of Tennessee*, sixth edition (Philadelphia: E. L. Carey and A. Hart, 1834), 17; Francis P. Blair to Andrew Jackson, December 23, 1838, Andrew Jackson Papers, LC.

10. Rickels, *Seba Smith*, 54; Francis Lieber, ed., *Letters to a Gentleman in Germany, Written after a Trip from Philadelphia to Niagara* (Philadelphia: Carey, Lea & Blanchard, 1834), 153–55; Richard Henry Dana Jr., *Two Years Before the Mast: A Personal Narrative* (1840; new edition, Boston: Fields, Osgood, & Co., 1869), 362.

11. Douglas L. Wilson and Rodney O. Davis, eds., *Herndon's Informants: Letters, Interviews, and Statements about Abraham Lincoln* (Urbana: University of Illinois Press, 1998), 427; Todd Nathan Thompson, *The National Joker: Abraham Lincoln and the Politics of Satire* (Carbondale: Southern Illinois University Press, 2015), 15; William Henry Herndon to Jesse W. Weik, November 17, 1885, in Douglas L.

Wilson and Rodney O. Davis, eds., *Herndon on Lincoln: Letters* (Urbana: University of Illinois Press, 2016), 166.

12. Sylvanus Cobb to Lincoln, December 27, 1862, Lincoln Papers.

13. EOS Autobiography, 220; SS, *The Life and Writings of Major Jack Downing of Downingville, Away Down East in the State of Maine* (Boston: Lilly, Wait, Colman and Holden, 1834); Rickels, *Seba Smith*, 70, 139.

14. SS to EOS, October 29, 30, 31, November 1, 2, 5, 7, 9, 10, 1833, and EOS to SS, November 11, 13, 14, 15, 16, 17, 1833, all in EOS Papers.

15. Adam Tuchinsky, "'Woman and Her Needs': Elizabeth Oakes Smith and the Divorce Question," *Journal of Women's History* 28 (Spring 2016): 39. For the best work on this point, see Scherman, "Oakes Smith Returns to Maine."

16. EOS to SS, May 30, 1837, EOS Papers.

17. AO journal, January 1, 1852, December 25, 1851.

18. EOS Autobiography, 220–21; SS to EOS, June 3 [1837], EOS Papers; Rickels, *Seba Smith*, 72. Much of the correspondence from 1836–1837 in the EOS Papers deals with their investments and hard financial times.

19. EOS Autobiography, 230, 244–50. In his autobiography, SS stated that they went to Charleston in the fall of 1838 and returned to New York in January 1839.

20. EOS diary, October 26, 1861; EOS Autobiography, 251–54, 290; Michael Sappol, *A Traffic of Dead Bodies: Anatomy and Embodied Social Identity in Nineteenth-Century America* (Princeton, NJ: Princeton University Press, 2002), 125, 350.

21. EOS Autobiography, 252, 256–60; Beaufort *Weekly Record*, November 18, 1887; EOS to B. F. Underwood, December 7, 1887, EOS Letters.

22. AO journal, December 25, 1851.

23. SS to Rufus W. Griswold, August 11, 1842, Miscellaneous Personal Papers, NYPL; Alice E. Smith, ed., "Letters of Thomas B. Read," *Ohio State Archaeological and Historical Quarterly* 46 (January 1937): 68–80; Thomas B. Read, "Sonnet," *Southern Literary Messenger* 7 (July 1841): 473.

24. EOS diary, October 26, 1861; EOS Autobiography, 237–39, 302, 304; Alfred Bendixen, "The Emergence of Romantic Traditions," and Virginia Jackson, "Longfellow in His Time," both in Alfred Bendixen and Stephen Burt, eds., *The Cambridge History of American Poetry* (New York: Cambridge University Press, 2014), 181, 253; AO journal, December 25, 1851.

25. SS to Griswold, August 11, 1842; EOS, *The Western Captive and Other Indian Stories*, ed. Caroline M. Woidat (Tonawanda, NY: Broadview, 2015), 10; Leigh Kirkland, "Elizabeth Oakes Smith," in Denise D. Knight, ed., *Nineteenth-Century American Women Writers: A Bio-Bibliographical Critical Sourcebook* (Westport, CT: Greenwood, 1997), 324–30; Rickels, *Seba Smith*, 72–96, 124–31.

26. Scherman, "Oakes Smith Returns to Maine"; "Eyes," *United States Magazine* 3 (August 1856): 164; Charles Hoffman to Rufus Griswold, July 12, 1843, quoted in Timothy H. Scherman, "Looking for Liz, or, On Being Haunted by Elizabeth Oakes Smith," *The Researcher* 14 (Spring/Summer 1998): 5.

27. Anne Marie Dolan, "The Literary Salon in New York, 1830–1860" (PhD diss., Columbia University, 1957), 82–100; James A. Harrison, ed., *The Complete Works of Edgar Allan Poe, Vol. 15: Literati—Autography* (New York: Thomas Y. Crowell, 1902), 117–18.

28. EOS Autobiography, 263, 270; Dolan, "Literary Salon in New York," 89–91.

29. Charles Hemstreet, *Literary New York: Its Landmarks and Associations* (New York: G. P. Putnam's Sons, 1903), 200–201. Poe's published criticism of "The Sinless Child" was more critical. See Poe, "Literary Criticism," *Godey's Lady's Book* 31 (December 1845): 263.

30. Cronin, *Evolution of a Life*, 48.

31. Beaufort *Weekly Record*, November 18, 1887; TePaske, 6; AO journal, December 25, 1851; Seaman's Protection Certificate Abstracts, New York, 1814–1869, second quarter, 1844, National Archive microfilm M2003 (Quarterly Abstracts of Seamen's Protection Certificates, New York City, NY, 1815–1869), reel 2.

32. *Journal of the Assembly of the State of New-York; at their Seventy-Second Session*, 2 vols. (Albany, NY: Weed, Parsons, and Co., 1849), 2:185, 344; EOS to Rufus W. Griswold, ca. 1849, Griswold Papers.

CHAPTER 2. CALIFORNIA

1. AO journal, April 18, 1851; Leonard L. Richards, *The California Gold Rush and the Coming of the Civil War* (New York: Knopf, 2007), 21.

2. AO journal, May 16, 1851.

3. AO journal, April 18, 1851; Louis J. Rasmussen, *San Francisco Ship Passenger Lists*, 4 vols. (1966; reprint, Baltimore: Genealogical Publishing Co., 2002), 2:109.

4. Enos L. Christman, *One Man's Gold: The Letters and Journal of a Forty-Niner*, comp. by Florence Morrow Christman (New York: McGraw-Hill, 1930), 109–10; Malcolm E. Barker, ed., *San Francisco Memoirs, 1835–1851: Eyewitness Accounts of the Birth of a City* (San Francisco, CA: Londonborn, 1994), 254.

5. AO to Sidney Oaksmith, March 9, 1851, Miscellaneous Personal Papers, NYPL.

6. AO journal, April 18, 1851; *Panama Star*, May 6, 1851; J. T. Mote to purser [AO], April 11, 1851, AO Papers; finding aid for the Captain William T. Thompson Papers, San Francisco Maritime National Historical Park; AO to Sidney Oaksmith, March 9, 1851, Miscellaneous Personal Papers, NYPL.

7. AO journal, April 21, 24, 28, 29; May 1, 5, 7, 11, 16, 1851.

8. AO journal, May 19, 22, 25, 1851.

9. George R. Stewart, *Committee of Vigilance: Revolution in San Francisco, 1851* (Boston: Houghton Mifflin, 1964), 72–76; AO journal, May 19, 22, 25, 30, June

4, 13, 1851; San Francisco *Daily Alta California*, June 13, 1851; Barker, *San Francisco Memoirs*, 279–87.

10. AO journal, June 4, 1851.

11. AO journal, June 13, 1851; AO to Sidney Oaksmith, September 15, 1851, EOS Papers.

12. AO journal, June 15, 1851; *San Francisco Daily Herald*, July 7, 12, 30, 1851.

13. Stewart, *Committee of Vigilance*, 135–36; AO journal, June 23, 1851; Mary Floyd Williams, ed., *Papers of the San Francisco Committee of Vigilance of 1851, Vol. 3: Minutes and Miscellaneous Papers, Financial Accounts and Vouchers* (Berkeley: University of California, 1919), 160; Barker, *San Francisco Memoirs*, 256, 270, 287–93.

14. AO journal, June 23, July 1, 1851; Stewart, *Committee of Vigilance*, 132.

15. AO journal, July 12, 1851; Stewart, *Committee of Vigilance*, 143–53, 163–201.

16. Admiralty Case Nos. 49, 51, 59, 60, and 61, all in M1249 (Admiralty Case Files of the US District Court for the Northern District of California, 1850–1900), reels 3–4; AO journal, July 1, 12, 1851; SS to EOS, December 12, 1851, AO Papers; AO to Chairman of the Executive Committee, August 2, 1851, in Williams, *Papers of the San Francisco Committee of Vigilance of 1851*, 407–8; John Bartlett Goodman III, *The Key to the Goodman Encyclopedia of the California Gold Rush Fleet* (Los Angeles: Zamorano Club, 1992), 11.

17. AO to Sidney Oaksmith, September 15, 1851, and AO to Messrs. Tallant and Wilde, August 2, 1851, both in EOS Papers; AO journal, August 12, 1851; Nereus [AO], "Lines on Leaving San Francisco, Aug. 6th, 1851," AO Scrapbook, 1870–1874, AO Papers.

18. AO journal, August 12, 1851.

19. EOS to My Dearly beloved Children, August 10, 1851, EOS Papers.

20. AO journal, August 17, 24, 1851.

21. AO journal, September 3, 7, 13, 21, 1851.

22. AO journal, September 25, 1851.

23. AO journal, September 25, October 5, 20, 22, 23, 27, November 12, 18, 1851.

24. Dana, *Two Years Before the Mast*, 56.

25. AO journal, November 30, December 3, 7, 17, 1851. Eventually word of the mutiny reached New York through the newspapers, which made SS "feel very anxious about Appleton." See SS to Sidney Oaksmith, May 19, 1852, Miscellaneous Personal Papers, NYPL.

26. AO journal, December 17, 1851.

27. AO journal, December 25, 1851.

28. AO journal, January 11, 1852.

29. AO journal, January 15, 28, 31, 1852.

30. AO journal, March 9, 1852.

31. AO journal, April 4, 18, 1852; Alexander E. Allinson to AO, April 9, 1852, AO Papers.

32. Master's Log of the *Mary Adeline*, AO Papers; Laurin Penland, "Diary Fore-shadows Conviction for Involvement in Slave Trade" (posted on the blog of the Rubenstein Library at Duke University, June 23, 2020); *New York Times*, March 8, 1855; Philadelphia *Daily Pennsylvanian*, May 7, 1855; Leonardo Marques, *The United States and the Transatlantic Slave Trade to the Americas, 1776–1867* (New Haven, CT: Yale University Press, 2016), 170; EOS to SS, April 10, 1852, EOS Papers.

CHAPTER 3. AFRICA

1. AO journal, April 26, 1852.
2. This may have been Marsden, or it may have been a Portuguese firm. About this time the British were quite suspicious of the Portuguese. "The Spirit of Slave Traffic is broken but by no means subdued," wrote one British sailor; "the very excitement of the horrid system appears to possess a charm among these Portu-guese, who impress upon the Negro Chiefs that they must have it again." See H. W. Bruce to the Duke of Northumberland, April 30, 1852, FO 84/895; Marques, *United States and the Transatlantic Slave Trade*, 177.
3. Dale T. Graden, *Disease, Resistance, and Lies: The Demise of the Transatlantic Slave Trade to Brazil and Cuba* (Baton Rouge: Louisiana State University Press, 2014), 184–87; Edward Kent to Daniel Webster, April 10, 1852 (postscript dated April 26), in *Slave and Coolie Trade*, House Exec. Doc. No. 105, 34th Cong., 1st sess., pp. 55–56.
4. *An act to prohibit the importation of slaves into any port or place within the jurisdic-tion of the United States, from and after the first day of January, in the year of our Lord one thousand eight hundred and eight*, act of March 2, 1807, in 2 Stat. 426; *An Act in addition to the Acts prohibiting the slave trade*, act of March 3, 1819, in 3 Stat. 532; *An Act to continue in force "An act to protect the commerce of the United States, and to punish the crime of piracy," and also to make further provisions for punishing the crime of piracy*, act of May 15, 1820, in 3 Stat. 600.
5. Bernard H. Nelson, "The Slave Trade as a Factor in British Foreign Policy, 1815–1862," *Journal of Negro History* 27 (April 1942): 192–203; Christopher Dickey, *Our Man in Charleston: Britain's Secret Agent in the Civil War South* (New York: Crown, 2015), 16, 26.
6. John Harris, "Yankee 'Blackbirding': The United States and the Illegal Trans-atlantic Slave Trade, 1850–1867," (PhD diss., Johns Hopkins University, 2017), 8; Warren S. Howard, *American Slavers and the Federal Law, 1837–1862* (Berkeley: University of California Press, 1963), 27; Marques, *United States and the Transatlan-tic Slave Trade*, 181; John Harris, *The Last Slave Ships: New York and the End of the Middle Passage* (New Haven, CT: Yale University Press, 2021).
7. *Hanging Gordon*, 7–8; Matthew Karp, *This Vast Southern Empire: Slaveholders at the Helm of American Foreign Policy* (Cambridge, MA: Harvard University Press, 2016), 12, 25–27, 41–42, 51–57.

8. *A Treaty To settle and define the boundaries between the territories of the United States and the possessions of Her Britannic Majesty in North America; for the final suppression of the African slave trade; and for the giving up of criminals, fugitive from justice, in certain cases,* ratified August 22, 1842, in 8 Stat. 576; Karp, *This Vast Southern Empire,* 74; William McBlair to wife, August 20, 1857, William McBlair Papers, The Mariners' Museum, Newport News, VA.

9. McBlair to wife, October 29, 1857, McBlair Papers.

10. AO journal, May 9, 16, 1852.

11. George E. Brooks Jr., *Yankee Traders, Old Coasters, and African Middlemen: A History of American Legitimate Trade with West Africa in the Nineteenth Century* (Boston: Boston University Press, 1970), 225; Christopher Lloyd, *The Navy and the Slave Trade: The Suppression of the African Slave Trade in the Nineteenth Century* (London: Frank Cass, 1968), 127; AO journal, June 6, 1852; Roger Anstey, *Britain and the Congo in the Nineteenth Century* (Oxford, UK: Oxford University Press, 1962), 19–23.

12. George A. Seymour to H. W. Bruce, May 30, 1852, FO 84/895. In addition to suppressing the slave trade, British warships also played a role in promoting "legitimate" commerce. See Anstey, *Britain and the Congo,* 19.

13. AO journal, June 8, 10, 1852.

14. C. Herbert Gilliland, ed., *USS* Constellation *on the Dismal Coast: Willie Leonard's Journal, 1859–1861* (Columbia: University of South Carolina Press, 2013), 48, 55–57, 65–66, 76–77.

15. Lloyd, *Navy and the Slave Trade,* 125, 127; AO journal, June 17, 1852.

16. Garner W. Allen, ed., *The Papers of Francis Gregory Dallas, United States Navy Correspondence and Journal, 1837–1859* (New York: Naval History Society, 1917), 230; Andrew H. Foote, *Africa and the American Flag* (New York: D. Appleton, 1854), 282, 345–47; Brooks, *Yankee Traders,* 285.

17. AO journal, June 18, 1852. For more on the suspicious activities of the Portuguese near Shark's Point, see Charles A. Wise to Sir, April 9, 1852, FO 84/895.

18. AO journal, June 24, 1852; AO to John S. Gillmer, July 26, 1852, enclosed in Gillmer to Daniel Webster, August 17, 1852, in NARA microfilm T331 (Dispatches from US Consuls in Bahia, Brazil, 1850–1906), reel 1. AO originally estimated fifteen hundred African attackers, but the British thought it was about three thousand, and AO came to accept that number. See *New York Times,* April 19, 1853.

19. AO to Kiddle, June 23, 1852, copy in RG 76 (Records of Boundary and Claims Commissions and Arbitrations), Entry 434 (Miscellaneous Claims, ca. 1812–1874), box 2.

20. AO journal, June 27, 1852. On June 24, the officers of the *Dolphin* gave AO a letter expressing "our high admiration of the daring and intrepid conduct displayed by you on the late occasion of your vessel getting on shore on Sharks Point." The officers contrasted AO's "intrepid conduct . . . with that of the dastardly Portuguese on board your vessel, who were parties concerned in the cargo," but

who had acted cowardly and selfishly. A copy of the letter is enclosed in Gillmer to Webster, August 17, 1852; the original is in AO Papers.

21. Extract of letter of Lieutenant Wood to unnamed relative, July 2, 1852, and AO, "Farewell Lines: Addressed to the Officers and Crew of her Britannic Majesty's brigantine Dolphin, River Congo, June 29, 1852," and "Farewell Lines: Addressed to Lieut. W. Wood, Commander of her Britannic Majesty's brigantine 'Dolphin,' River Congo, June 29, 1852," all as a newspaper clipping in AO Papers (the first two items appeared in *New York Times*, April 19, 1853, but the second poem did not).

22. AO journal, July 4, 1852.

23. *New York Times*, October 7, 1852; London *Nautical Magazine and Naval Chronicle* (January 1853): 55–56.

24. St. Louis *Globe-Democrat*, quoted in *Fort Wayne Daily Gazette*, August 2, 1885.

25. TePaske, 14. For others who have presumed his guilt in this expedition, see Gerald Horne, *The Deepest South: The United States, Brazil, and the African Slave Trade* (New York: New York University Press, 2007), 44–45; Dale Torston Graden, *From Slavery to Freedom in Brazil: Bahia, 1835–1900* (Albuquerque: University of New Mexico Press, 2006), 7–8; Graden, *Disease, Resistance, and Lies*, 184–85; Dale T. Graden, "'This City Has Too Many Slaves Joined Together': The Abolitionist Crisis in Salvador, Bahia, Brazil, 1848–1856," in Alusine Jalloh and Stephen E. Maizlish, eds., *The African Diaspora* (College Station: Texas A&M University Press, 1996), 147–48.

26. SS to EOS, December 12, 1851, AO Papers.

27. SS to Sidney Oaksmith, May 19, 1852, Miscellaneous Personal Papers, NYPL.

28. *Commerce and Navigation: Report of the Secretary of the Treasury, Transmitting a Report from the Register of the Treasury of the Commerce and Navigation of the United States, for the Year Ending June 30, 1852* (n.p., 1853), 4–40; Donald L. Canney, *Africa Squadron: The U.S. Navy and the Slave Trade, 1842–1861* (Washington, DC: Potomac Books, 2006), 39–40; Anstey, *Britain and the Congo*, 21; Phyllis M. Martin, *The External Trade of the Loango Coast, 1576–1870* (New York: Oxford University Press, 1972), 150–54. During the fiscal year ending on June 30, 1852, American merchants carried $1,211,360 worth of exports to Africa—0.63 percent of the total exports from the United States, which was valued at $192,368,984. While the cargo in Oaksmith's case was from Brazil, this Treasury Department report does reveal that American merchants were participating in small but legitimate commercial voyages to Africa.

29. Foote, *Africa and the American Flag*, 292–94; Marques, *United States and the Transatlantic Slave Trade*, 235.

30. Foote, *Africa and the American Flag*, 347.

31. AO journal, July 14, 1852.

32. AO to Gillmer, July 26, 1852; Gillmer to Daniel Webster, August 17, 1852; *New York Times*, April 19, 1853; John James Dyer to Sir, November 8, 1852, RG 76, Entry 434.

33. AO journal, October 31, 1852.

34. AO journal, November 25, 1852; *New York Times*, December 11, 1852.

35. AO to EOS, April 1, 1854, pasted in EOS diary, p. 251.

36. AO journal, December 6, 1852.

CHAPTER 4. DIPLOMACY

1. SS to AO, December 8, 1852, AO Papers.

2. "A Literary Gathering," *Ohio Cultivator* 14 (May 1, 1858): 143; Agard; EOS to Gerrit Smith, January 19, 1853, GSP.

3. *Portland Daily Advertiser*, September 12, 1849; *Boston Evening Transcript*, August 31, 1849.

4. EOS's editorials were gathered together as a book titled *Woman and Her Needs* (New York: Fowlers and Wells, 1851), quotations from pp. 22, 38, 41–42, 72, 78, 90.

5. EOS Autobiography, 266; Harriet Lupton to Maria Weston Chapman, June 6, 1852, Anti-Slavery Collection, Boston Public Library; EOS to Elizabeth Cady Stanton, March 2, 1852, Papers of Elizabeth Cady Stanton and Susan B. Anthony, reel 7.

6. Paulina Davis to Elizabeth Cady Stanton, February 9, 1852, EOS to Elizabeth Cady Stanton, February 17, 1852, Papers of Stanton and Anthony, reel 7.

7. EOS to Horace Greeley, n.d. [October 31, 1851], Horace Greeley Papers, NYPL. A copy of EOS's prospectus for the *Egeria* is available in EOS to Wendell Phillips, January 22, 1852, Wendell Phillips Papers, Houghton Library, Harvard University, Cambridge, MA; EOS to Gerrit Smith, October 2, 1852, January 19, May 26, 1853, all in GSP.

8. Horace Greeley to EOS, November 1, 1851 (GLC00496.026), Gilder Lehrman Collection, Gilder Lehrman Institute of American History, New York, NY. Greeley apparently still spoke highly of her public lectures. See *Salem* (MA) *Register*, November 27, 1851. EOS professed not to want to get rich off reform work, but to help support herself. See EOS to Wendell Phillips, October 23, December 21, 1851, both in Phillips Papers.

9. Angela G. Ray, "Performing Womanhood: The Lyceum Lectures of Elizabeth Oakes Smith," paper delivered at the Society for the Study of American Women Writers, November 2006; SS to Sidney Oaksmith, May 19, 1852, Miscellaneous Personal Papers, NYPL; *Diary of Rev. Moses How* (New Bedford, MA: Reynolds, 1932), 26; Philadelphia *Pennsylvania Freeman*, April 1, 1852; *Cleveland Leader*, June 1, 1852. For a critical response, see Bradford Torrey, ed., *The Writings of Henry David Thoreau, vol. 3, Journal, September 16, 1851–April 30, 1852* (Boston: Houghton Mifflin, 1906), 168.

10. *The Proceedings of the Woman's Rights Convention, Held at Syracuse, September 8th, 9th & 10th, 1852* (Syracuse: J. E. Masters, 1852), 12, 15–19; Ray, "Performing Womanhood"; EOS to Elizabeth Cady Stanton, February 17, 1852, Papers of

Stanton and Anthony, reel 7. For her speech at the Syracuse Convention, white Southerners dubbed EOS one of the "progressive women of the north." See Mobile *Alabama Planter*, September 18, 1852. For some of the newspaper criticism of the Syracuse Convention, see Elizabeth R. Varon, *We Mean to be Counted: White Women and Politics in Antebellum Virginia* (Chapel Hill: University of North Carolina Press, 1998), 101.

11. William J. Mahar, *Behind the Burnt Cork Mask: Early Blackface Minstrelsy and Antebellum American Popular Culture* (Urbana: University of Illinois Press, 1999), 94–95; Danny O. Crew, *Suffragist Sheet Music: An Illustrated Catalog of Published Music Associated with the Women's Rights and Suffrage Movement in America, 1795–1921, with Complete Lyrics* (Jefferson, NC: McFarland, 2002), 37; M. C. Campbell, *Wood's New Plantation Melodies* (New York: Garrett, 1859), 33. EOS had some trepidation about how she appeared at the lectern. See EOS to Wendell Phillips, November 3, December 21, 1851, both in Phillips Papers.

12. Boston *Liberator*, May 18, 1833; EOS Autobiography, 244–49; EOS to Wendell Phillips, December 21, 1851, Phillips Papers; EOS to Gerrit Smith, October 2, 1852, GSP; EOS to William Lloyd Garrison, June 27, 1852, Anti-Slavery Collection, Boston Public Library.

13. In 1855, SS published a short story titled "Billie Huggin's Wife" that ridiculed women's rights advocates. See Fred Lewis Pattee, *The Feminine Fifties* (New York: D. Appleton-Century Co., 1940), 100–101. One anthologist says SS "was bitter about her popularity." See Cheryl Walker, ed., *American Women Poets of the Nineteenth Century: An Anthology* (New Brunswick, NJ: Rutgers University Press, 1992), 66.

14. SS to EOS, December 12, 1851, AO Papers. EOS suffered "a severe pain down the back of the neck, and right arm, so that I have at times been in the greatest agony after a Lecture, though unconscious of it at the time." See EOS to Elizabeth Cady Stanton, June 11, 1852, Papers of Stanton and Anthony, reel 7.

15. SS, *New Elements of Geometry* (New York: George P. Putnam, and London: Richard Bentley, 1850); SS autobiography, Seba Smith Papers, Bowdoin College. The Seba Smith Papers at NYPL is overflowing with correspondence with professors and college presidents promoting his work.

16. EOS to My Dearly beloved Children, August 10, 1851, EOS Papers.

17. EOS to SS, June 14, 1852, EOS Papers.

18. Sidney Oaksmith to Daniel Webster, August 11, 1852, SS to Daniel Webster, August 27, 1852, in NARA microfilm T330 (Dispatches from US Consuls in Aux Cayes, Haiti, 1797–1874), reel 3; EOS to Daniel Webster, August 25, 1852, both in NARA microfilm M873 (Letters of Application and Recommendation during the Administrations of James Polk, Zachary Taylor, and Millard Fillmore, 1845–1853), reel 64; Sidney Oaksmith to Daniel Webster, August 17, 1852, undated letter by AO, and EOS to W. B. Sayles, April 21, 1853, all in NARA microfilm M967 (Letters of Application and Recommendation during the Administrations of Franklin Pierce and James Buchanan, 1853–1861), reel 33; SS to AO,

December 8, 1852, AO Papers; passport applications of Sidney Oaksmith, January 31, 1861, and October 15, 1869, NARA microfilm M1372 (Passport Applications, 1795–1905), reels 94, 163. SS had spoken complimentarily of Webster in *Life and Writings of Major Jack Downing*, 224–30.

19. Alvin Oaksmith, "My Dream," *Potter's American Monthly* 5 (September 1875): 692–96, and (October 1875): 767–70; "Disasters," *Sailor's Magazine* 27 (February 1855): 180–81. Alvin's recollection offers much more detail of the harrowing journey, although he mistakenly remembered the shipwreck as the *Royal Southard* when it was actually the *Royal Southwick.*

20. EOS Autobiography, 264–65; TePaske, 46–50.

21. *New York Times*, January 26, 29, 30, February 5, 19, March 8, 9, 10, 1855.

22. EOS Autobiography, 264, 267; AO journal, October 9, 1851; TePaske, 46–53; Robert E. May, *The Southern Dream of a Caribbean Empire, 1854–1861* (Baton Rouge: Louisiana State University Press, 1973), 46–51.

23. TePaske, 53–55; May, *Southern Dream*, 52, 64–76; AO to Sidney Oaksmith, March 5, 1855, and AO to Charles P. Marsden, March 5, 1855, both in *United States v. Barque Magnolia*, RG 21 (Southern District of Alabama), Mixed Case Files, Case #2524 (April 1855 Term), National Archives at Atlanta.

24. Philadelphia *Daily Pennsylvanian*, May 2, 3, 4, 5, 7, 8, 9, 10, 11, 12 15, 1855; *United States v. Darnaud* (1855), in *Federal Cases*, 30 vols. (St. Paul, MN: West, 1894–1897), 25:757; Marques, *United States and the Transatlantic Slave Trade*, 176–82, 195–96.

25. AO trial journal, June 17–July 1, 1855, AO Collection; *New Orleans Daily Crescent*, July 2, 1856; *New York Tribune*, June 20, 1857.

26. AO trial journal, July 1–August 13, 1855. AO's reading of the Neutrality Act was plausible, as it refers to ships of war and armed vessels, not merchant vessels. See *An Act in addition to the "Act for the punishment of certain crimes against the United States," and to repeal the acts therein mentioned*, act of April 20, 1818, in 3 Stat. 447.

27. *United States v. Magnolia*; AO trial journal, July 1–August 10, 1855.

28. AO trial journal, August 13–October 6, 1855; *Portland Daily Press*, September 14, 1871; *New York Sunday News*, December 28, 1879; US Naturalization Records Index, 1791–1992, and US Passport Application, October 15, 1869, both on Ancestry.com. Some records on Ancestry.com indicate that they were married in Portland, Maine, on September 24, 1855, while others say they had a marriage ceremony in New York City on September 27, 1855. Their divorce record states that the wedding was on September 24 in Portland. It seems likely they were married in Maine and then registered their marriage in New York three days later.

29. AO trial journal, October 5–15, 1855; House Report No. 420, 44th Cong., 1st sess.; Guthrie to AO, October 6, 1855, RG 56 (General Records of the Department of the Treasury), Entry 27 (Miscellaneous Letters Sent, 1789–1878), vol. 23, NARA-CP.

30. TePaske, 64–67; *United States v. 1735 Boxes, 76 Kegs Containing Ball Cartridges, 16 Kegs Containing Fine Powder, and Two Boxes of Common Powder part of the*

Armament of the Amelia, RG 21 (Southern District of New York), Admiralty Case File #A13–305, NARA-NY (the original case file does not appear to survive, so I used the information in the court's docket book); John N. Lewis to William L. Marcy, December 22, 1855 (plus enclosures), in T346 (Dispatches from US Consuls in Port-au-Prince, Haiti, 1835–1906), reel 3.

31. SS, *My Thirty Years Out of the Senate* (New York: Oaksmith, 1859), 428, 436, 444–46.

32. Ibid., 449–54.

33. Richards, *California Gold Rush*, 139–43; TePaske, 68–69.

34. As late as 1879, Oaksmith would still try to make claims against the federal government for his financial losses in 1856. In fact, his daughters were still trying to recover their father's lost money in the early 1950s. TePaske, 70–99, 108–21; Robert E. May, *Manifest Destiny's Underworld: Filibustering in Antebellum America* (Chapel Hill: University of North Carolina Press, 2002), 97; AO to John A. Quitman, September 4, 1856, John A. Quitman Papers, Houghton Library, Harvard University.

35. May, *Southern Dream*, 80–81, 106–10; AO to Horatio King, September 8, 1871, Pardon File C-610; Robert E. May, *John A. Quitman: Old South Crusader* (Baton Rouge: Louisiana State University Press, 1985), 335–38, 445.

36. Julia Deane Freeman to Sarah H. Whitman, September 26, 1856, in Catherine Kunce, ed., *The Correspondence of Sarah Helen Whitman to Julia Deane Freeman: Writer to Writer, Woman to Woman* (Wilmington: University of Delaware Press, 2013), 36.

37. Whitman to Freeman, September 15, 1857, in Kunce, *Correspondence*, 54; *Emerson's Magazine and Putnam's Monthly* 5 (November 1857): 576–77, (December 1857): 686–87. He may also have written a poem titled "Lines on the Death of an Infant" in the November issue, pp. 648–49.

38. EOS diary, October 30, November 3, 14, 1861; *New York Sunday News*, December 28, 1879. In the 1960s, one of AO's daughters claimed that Isotta "was quite unfaithful to my late father" and that multiple men "had her favors." See Corrections to TePaske by Geraldine Oaksmith, ca. 1962, AO Papers. Isotta, for her part, claimed that AO was unfaithful to her and had a child with a Brooklyn widow named Mrs. E. V. White. Isotta also said that EOS acted "violently" toward her within days of their wedding. As one paper reported an interview with Isotta: "From that day commenced a series of persecutions against the young wife which have been continued with steadily increasing violence until the present time. The mother-in-law refused to treat the young wife as a daughter; forbade her the service of the domestics; refused to allow her linen to be washed in the house; treated her with indignity at the table; and in every way sought to humiliate and degrade her." Isotta also claimed that Mrs. White tried "to cut her throat with a carving knife." See Paris, ME, *Oxford Democrat*, September 9, 1870.

39. Prospectus and other documents related to *The Great Republic*, in AO Scrapbook, 1858–1881, AO Papers; Oaksmith and Co. to Our Creditors, March 20, 1860, EOS Papers; *Brooklyn Daily Eagle*, August 8, 1860.

40. *New York Daily Herald*, October 13, 1858, January 22, 1859; *Buffalo Courier*, January 25, 1859.

41. EOS diary, May 19, 1867; Whitman to Freeman, February 19, 1860, in Kunce, *Correspondence*, 128; EOS Autobiography, 263, 269.

42. SS to Horatio King, March 4, 1861, Horatio King Papers, LC; a considerable number of letters in AO Papers pertain to the paper factory in Virginia.

43. Freeman to Whitman, November 6, 1859, in Kunce, *Correspondence*, 108; AO statement dated May 29, 1862, Boston Case File.

CHAPTER 5. SECESSION

1. EOS diary, June 27, 1863.

2. Walter Stahr, *Seward: Lincoln's Indispensable Man* (New York: Simon & Schuster, 2012), 174.

3. On compromise efforts, see David M. Potter, *The Impending Crisis, 1848–1861* (New York: Harper & Row, 1976), 522–54.

4. Terry Golway, *Machine Made: Tammany Hall and the Creation of Modern American Politics* (New York: Liveright, 2014), 64–81.

5. AO to WHS, January 4, 1861, WHS Papers, University of Rochester.

6. Lincoln to Lyman Trumbull, December 10, 1860, in *CWL*, 4:149–50; Dana quoted in Eric Foner, *Free Soil, Free Labor, Free Men: The Ideology of the Republican Party before the Civil War* (New York: Oxford University Press, 1970), 220.

7. AO to WHS, January 4, 1861, WHS Papers.

8. AO to WHS, January 10, 1861, WHS Papers.

9. Stahr, *Seward*, 211–27.

10. James T. Brady, Elijah F. Purdy, S. B. Cushing, and AO to Dear Sir (printed invitation), January 14, 1861, EOS Papers; *New York Tribune*, January 17, 1861. Wilson would go on to become colonel of the Sixth New York Zouaves and the Sixty-Ninth New York Volunteers during the Civil War.

11. AO to Dear Sir (printed invitation), January 16, 1861, EOS Papers.

12. *New York Tribune*, January 23, 1861; Robert E. Cray, *A Notable Bully: Colonel Billy Wilson, Masculinity, and the Pursuit of Violence in the Civil War Era* (Kent, OH: Kent State University Press, 2021), 128–29. A draft of AO's resolutions is held in AO Papers.

13. Records and correspondence related to fundraising and the call for the mass meeting are held in the AO Papers.

14. *New York Times*, January 29, 1861.

15. J. B. Devoe to AO, January 29, 1861, AO Papers; AO to Robert Newman Gourdin, January 29, 1861, and Gourdin to AO, January 29, 1861, both in Philip N. Racine, ed., *Gentleman Merchants: A Charleston Family's Odyssey, 1828–1870* (Knoxville: University of Tennessee Press, 2008), 434; William L. Barney, *Rebels in*

the Making: The Secession Crisis and the Birth of the Confederacy (New York: Oxford University Press, 2020), 100–102, 142, 184–85, 208–9, 237.

16. "To the People of Mississippi," and "To the People of Georgia," both in AO Papers; "To the People of Louisiana," War Letters, 1861–1865, NYHS; *Brooklyn Evening Star*, January 29, 1861; AO to Gourdin, February 1, 7, 1861, AO Papers.

17. "The Union Marseillaise," April 1861, enclosed in EOS to Lincoln, December 9, 1861, Lincoln Papers.

18. Jonathan W. White, *Abraham Lincoln and Treason during the Civil War: The Trials of John Merryman* (Baton Rouge: Louisiana State University Press, 2011).

19. WHS quoted in Harris, *Last Slave Ships*, 222.

CHAPTER 6. THE *AUGUSTA*

1. *Proceedings of the First Three Republican National Conventions of 1856, 1860 and 1864* (Minneapolis, MN: Charles W. Johnson, 1893), 132.

2. Karp, *This Vast Southern Empire*, 76–77.

3. Sen. Exec. Doc. No. 1, 37th Cong., 2nd sess., pp. 453–54; New York *Commercial Advertiser*, August 8, 1861; New York *World*, August 16, 1861; Auburn, New York *Northern Christian Advocate*, August 21, 1861; George C. Whiting to CBS, August 29, 1861, M160, reel 8; CBS to RM, August 3, 1861, reel 6. The marshals from Maryland, Delaware, the Eastern District of Pennsylvania, New Jersey, Connecticut, Rhode Island, Massachusetts, and Maine all attended.

4. *African Repository* 38 (December 1862): 373; *Hanging Gordon*, 77, 89–91.

5. John G. Grinnell to John P. Usher, June 25, 1864, M160, reel 4; RM to Whiting, November 8, 1861, and February 1, June 2, 1862, M160, reel 6.

6. RM to Edward Bates, January 25, 1862, RG 60, Entry 9-A (Letters Received by the Attorney General, 1809–1870); RM to CBS, January 15, 25, 1862, M160, reel 6 (includes a copy of RM's bill).

7. RM to CBS, June 8, 1861, January 10, 1862, M160, reel 6.

8. CBS, "Decision of the Secretary of the Interior on the Evidence Taken in the Recent Investigation at New York City," January 8, 1862, "Correspondence, Testimony, and Exhibits, Relating to the Slave Bark *Augusta*, 1861–1862," M160, reel 5; Benjamin Quarles, *Lincoln and the Negro* (New York: Oxford University Press, 1962), 94; Virginia Mason, ed., *The Public Life and Diplomatic Correspondence of James M. Mason* (1903; reprint, New York: Neale, 1906), 228.

9. *Sketches of Men of Progress* (New York: New York and Hartford Publishing Co., 1870–1871), 117–23, 127–28.

10. Jonathan W. White, "Freedom by Hatchet," *Civil War Times* 57 (August 2018): 50–57.

11. AO's lawyer, Benjamin F. Sawyer, later testified that AO was "wholly insolvent and in great need of money." In May 1861 Sawyer commenced proceedings on behalf of AO to "have him discharged from his debts which at this time were

large that his assets were of little or no value." On July 22, 1861, AO was "duly discharged from his debts being at that time utterly bankrupt & insolvent." Sawyer went on to say that at no time in the last two years "would it have been possible for the said Oaksmith to have raised any considerable sum of money for his own purposes" and that he "has had great difficulty in supporting his family" and that Sawyer often loaned him "small sums of money for that purpose." See affidavit of Benjamin F. Sawyer, sworn January 2, 1862, Boston Case File.

12. Jacob Appley treason file, AO treason file, RG 59, Entry 963 (Correspondence Regarding Prisoners of War, 1861–1862), Box 1, NARA-CP.

13. Testimony of Gilbert H. Cooper, John O. Ireland, and Isaac M. Case, *Augusta* Case File.

14. Testimony of RM, December 20, 1861, *Augusta* Report; Kevin S. Reilly, "Slavers in Disguise: American Whaling and the African Slave Trade, 1845–1862," *American Neptune* 53 (June 1993): 177–89.

15. Libel against the *Augusta*, filed June 19, 1861, and testimony of Luther Horton, Ezekiel E. D. Skinner, and AO, all in *Augusta* Case File.

16. *New York Tribune*, June 27, 1861; New York *Evening Post*, June 25, 1861.

17. Affidavit of Jacob Appley, sworn July 2, 1861, *Augusta* Case File.

18. RM to CBS, July 3, 1861, *Augusta* Report.

19. Howard, *American Slavers*, 99, 155–69, 188–89 (quotations from p. 99).

20. *Proceedings, December 9, 1929, Being on the Occasion of the Presentation to the United States District Court for the District of Connecticut of a Portrait of William Davis Shipman, a Judge of Said Court 1860 to 1873* (n.p., n.d.), 15–16; EDS to CBS, December 6, 1861, "Correspondence, Testimony, and Exhibits, Relating to the Slave Bark *Augusta*, 1861–1862," M160, reel 5; Jonathan W. White and Daniel Glenn, eds., "The Politics of Judging: The Civil War Letters of William D. Shipman," *Connecticut History Review* 59 (Spring 2020): 80–100.

21. Testimony of EDS, *Augusta* Report; S. R. Harlow and H. H. Boone, *Life Sketches of the State Officers, Senators, and Members of the Assembly of the State of New York, in 1867* (Albany: Weed, Parsons and Co., 1867), 18–22.

22. Testimony of John O. Ireland, *Augusta* Case File.

23. Testimony of AO, *Augusta* Case File.

24. Testimony of Isaac M. Case, *Augusta* Case File.

25. Testimony of Stewart L. Woodford, *Augusta* Report.

26. *United States v. Augusta* (1861), 24 *Federal Cases* 892. Although Shipman was not persuaded by AO's arguments, he appears to have been at least moderately impressed by his demeanor in court. Shipman later wrote that AO "appeared to be a person of education and intelligence, and I supposed him at the time to be acting as associate counsel in the cause." See Report of William D. Shipman, *Augusta* Report.

27. Testimony of EDS, *Augusta* Report; New York *Evening Post*, September 20, 1861.

28. Testimony of Woodford, *Augusta* Report. Shipman later concluded that Woodford's decision to dine with AO was an "indiscretion," but he did not think

it had been done with "improper motives." See Report of William D. Shipman, *Augusta* Report.

29. Notice of appeal, October 2, 1861, petition for appeal, October 3, 1861, testimony of Woodford, all in *Augusta* Case File.

30. Testimony of RM, Woodford, Henry F. Capen, Benjamin F. Sawyer, Thomas P. Stanton, and Thomas Stack; AO to Capen, October 8, 9, 1861, all in *Augusta* Report. Woodford recollected AO saying that the stores should be valued at $500; Capen recalled AO saying that the ship's value should be dropped to $1,700 and the stores at $500, so that the entire appraisal would be $2,200. For other discussion of the value of the ship on the open market, see the testimony of Gilbert H. Cooper, ibid.

31. "Mr. Oaksmith to the Public," January 31, 1862, in *New York Tribune*, February 5, 1862.

32. EOS diary, October 27, 28, 1861.

33. EOS diary, November 10, 15, 1861.

34. EOS diary, November 2, 9, 10, 1861; EOS, "Hymn for Our Country: Inscribed to President Lincoln," in Frank Moore, ed., *Rebellion Record: A Diary of American Events*, 12 vols. (New York: G. P. Putnam, 1861–1868), vol. 3, poetry section p. 59; Lincoln to EOS, November 14, 1861, in Roy P. Basler and Christian O. Basler, eds., *The Collected Works of Abraham Lincoln: Second Supplement, 1848– 1865* (New Brunswick, NJ: Rutgers University Press, 1990), 37. EOS gave Lincoln's letter to Sidney for his autograph book. See EOS diary, November 16, 1861.

EOS's youngest son, Edward, apparently joined the Union army for six months in the summer of 1861 but, according to EOS, "refused to register his name, saying 'it was a man's highest duty to serve his Country.'" During the Battle of Bull Run on July 21, 1861, the Confederates routed the Union troops, and one of the casualties was Colonel James Cameron, brother of Lincoln's secretary of war, Simon Cameron. One of the soldiers detailed with recovering the dead officer's body was Edward Oaksmith. See EOS to Editor Literary Leaves Syndicate, n.d., Miscellaneous Personal Papers, NYPL; EOS to Simon Cameron, March 15, 1876, February 22, 1876, Letter Book of EOS and AMO, 1876, AO Papers; AO to Horatio King, September 8, 1871, Pardon File C-610.

35. Quoted in EOS diary, December 29, 1864. Alvin told his mother, "I think you will love Delfina—she is not particularly smart or talkative—but so gentle—so affectionate—so thoughtful and womanly—she loves you very dearly, and says she feels as if she had always known you."

36. RM to George C. Whiting, January 13, 1862, M160, reel 6.

37. Testimony of Woodford, RM, John H. Smith, and Ely Devoe, *Augusta* Report. RM dated this meeting to November 16, but it was almost certainly November 6.

38. See chapter 17.

39. RM to CBS, November 6, 26, 1861, and CBS to RM, November 7, 1861; testimony of RM, Joseph Thompson, and John H. Smith, all in *Augusta* Report.

40. W. G. King to RM, n.d., and November 15, 1861, and E. C. D. Skinner to RM, November 15, 1861, all in *Augusta* Report.

41. *Brooklyn Daily Eagle*, November 19, 1861; New York *World*, March 3, 1865; *Boston Daily Advertiser*, March 13, 1865; RM to George Whiting, January 10, 1862, M160, reel 6.

CHAPTER 7. FORT LAFAYETTE

1. RM to WHS, November 30, 1861, M179, reel 185.

2. Testimony of RM, *Augusta* Report; RM to WHS, November 18, 1861, Disloyalty File; RM to CBS, April 3, 1862, M160, reel 6. For the State Department's role, see Mark E. Neely Jr., *The Fate of Liberty: Abraham Lincoln and Civil Liberties* (New York: Oxford University Press, 1991).

3. RM to WHS, December 11, 1861, Disloyalty File.

4. Testimony of George P. Andrews and EDS, *Augusta* Report; *New York Times*, November 21, 1861. At least a dozen of the men would not be released until February or March 1862. See the treason files of James Brady, A. C. Harris, and Jacob Appley, all in RG 59, Entry 963 (Correspondence Regarding Prisoners of War, 1861–1862), Boxes 1 and 5, NARA-CP.

5. *O.R.*, ser. 2, vol. 2, pp. 229, 671; testimony of James Lee, *Augusta* Report.

6. John Strausbaugh, *City of Sedition: The History of New York City during the Civil War* (New York: Twelve, 2016), 198; John A. Marshall, *American Bastile: A History of the Illegal Arrests and Imprisonment of American Citizens during the Late Civil War*, twenty-second edition (Philadelphia: Thomas W. Hartley, 1876), 652–53.

7. AO to EOS, November 29, 1861, Disloyalty File; Lately Thomas, *Between Two Empires: The Life Story of California's First Senator, William McKendree Gwin* (Boston: Houghton Mifflin, 1969), 258–79; *O.R.*, ser. 2, vol. 2, pp. 322–23, 1041–76. Later in the war, Casemate No. 2 would be home to a number of Confederate prisoners of war, as well as two Southern desperados—John Yates Beall and Robert Cobb Kennedy—both of whom were executed by the Lincoln administration in 1865. See *Harper's Weekly*, April 15, 1865.

8. Charles J. Faulkner and others to Lincoln, October 8, 1861, WHS Papers, University of Rochester.

9. Martin Burke to RM, October 24, 1861, and RM to WHS, October 25, 1861, both in WHS Papers. See also RM's letter of August 30, 1861.

10. "Mr. Oaksmith to the Public," January 31, 1862, in *New York Tribune*, February 5, 1862.

11. AO, "A Dream of the Bastile," December 12, 1861, in *Southern Magazine* 10 (January 1872): 65–68.

12. RM to Martin Burke, December 13, 1861, Disloyalty File. RM would eventually coerce CBS to initiate an investigation into possible fraud and collusion in the *Augusta* case. CBS instructed Judge Shipman to conduct the investigation,

but Shipman ultimately found no collusion to exist, and CBS concurred in his assessment. See Report of Judge Shipman, and CBS to Shipman, January 8, 1862, both in *Augusta* Report.

13. *Albany Evening Journal*, November 30, 1861; RM to WHS, November 30, 1861, M179, reel 185.

14. "Mr. Oaksmith to the Public"; EOS diary for 1861–1864, n.d. (p. 78).

15. *Brooklyn Daily Eagle*, November 19, 1861; San Francisco *Evening Bulletin*, December 21, 1861.

16. AO to WHS, November 25, 1861, Disloyalty File.

17. AO to EOS, November 29, 1861, Disloyalty File (letter never delivered).

18. "Mr. Oaksmith to the Public."

19. *O.R.*, ser. 2, vol. 2, p. 156; EOS diary, p. 71.

20. Affidavit of AO, January 4, 1862, Boston Case File; Algernon S. Sullivan to AO, December 11, 1861, enclosed in Martin Burke, commander of Fort Lafayette, to E. D. Townsend, adjutant general of the army in DC, December 12, 1861, Disloyalty File. On Sullivan's arrest, see Mark A. Weitz, *The Confederacy on Trial: The Piracy and Sequestration Cases of 1861* (Lawrence: University Press of Kansas, 2005), 80. WHS's papers contain correspondence from Hawley dating back to 1839. For more on Hawley, see Charles D. Ross, *Breaking the Blockade: The Bahamas during the Civil War* (Jackson: University Press of Mississippi, 2021).

21. Quoted in Neely, *Fate of Liberty*, 23.

22. Burke to WHS, December 13, 1861, AO to Burke, December 13, 1861, RM to Burke, December 13, 1861, all in Disloyalty File; affidavit of AO, January 4, 1862, Boston Case File. WHS approved of this seizure. See WHS to Burke, December 16, 1861, Secret Correspondence.

23. Isotta Oaksmith to Lincoln, December 9, 1861, Disloyalty File; EOS to Lincoln, December 9, 1861, Lincoln Papers.

24. EOS to John P. Hale, December 9, 1861, and EOS to WHS, December 9, 1861, both in Disloyalty File. Word of EOS's "touching letter" to WHS made it into the press. See *Springfield* (MA) *Republican*, December 12, 1861.

25. Edward Oaksmith to EOS, December 14, 1861, EOS Papers.

26. EOS diary for 1861–1864, n.d. (pp. 60–68); EOS to James Cephas Derby, December 19, 1861, WHS Papers; "Mr. Oaksmith to the Public." On Derby and his brother's admiration for AO's work, see Cephas L. Derby to SS, August 20, 1857, J. C. Derby to AO, April 29 and July 16, 1879, all in AO Papers.

27. EOS diary, March 25, 1864; *The Washington Despotism Dissected in Articles from the Metropolitan Record* (New York: Metropolitan Record, 1863), 124; Neely, *Fate of Liberty*, 19.

28. EOS to Derby, December 19, 1861, WHS Papers.

29. Hawley to Frederick W. Seward, December 14, 1861, Disloyalty File.

30. AO to WHS, December 17 and 18, 1861, Disloyalty File; Jacob Appley treason file, RG 59, Entry 963, Box 1.

31. Hartford *Daily Courant*, January 10, 1862; Report of William D. Shipman, *Augusta* Report.

32. Frederick W. Seward to Martin Burke, December 16, 1861, Secret Correspondence.

33. *Passages from the Correspondence of Griswold*, 131–32.

CHAPTER 8. FORT WARREN

1. Indictment of AO, Boston Case File; RM to WHS, December 11, 1861, Disloyalty File; Frederick W. Seward to RM, December 13, 1861, Secret Correspondence.

2. Keyes to WHS, December 14, 1861, Disloyalty File. The *Margaret Scott* had been seized by a vessel in the US Revenue Cutter Service on September 8, 1861. See Thomas Sands to CBS, February 1862, M160, reel 4.

3. Frederick W. Seward to Keyes, December 17, 1861, WHS to RM, December 17, 1861, both in Secret Correspondence.

4. "Mr. Oaksmith to the Public," January 31, 1862, in *New York Tribune*, February 5, 1862; affidavit of AO, January 4, 1862, Boston Case File; AO to Ulysses S. Grant, September 25, 1869, AO Letters, NYHS.

5. RM to Keyes, December 19, 1861, Keyes Papers.

6. Lawrence Sangston, *The Bastiles of the North* (Baltimore: Kelly, Hedian & Piet, 1863), 65; Keyes to WHS, December 20, 1861, and Richard Henry Dana Jr. to WHS, December 21, 1861, both in Disloyalty File.

7. AO, "The Void," published in the *Boston Post*, January 22, 1862, in AO Collection; AO to WHS, December 23, 1861, Disloyalty File.

8. Minor Horne McLain, "Prison Conditions in Fort Warren, Boston, during the Civil War," (PhD diss., Boston University, 1955), 62–63, 95–134; Thomas John Claggett to Thomas Maddox, n.d. (MS1860), MdHS.

9. B. F. Hallett to Charles J. Faulkner, November 14, 1861, James Alph. Mac-Master to Charles J. Faulkner, November 28, 1861, and Adolpho Wolfe to Charles J. Faulkner, December 3, 1861, all in Faulkner Family Papers, Virginia Museum of History and Culture, Richmond, VA; Charles Macgill to daughters, January 7, 1862, Charles Macgill Papers, David M. Rubenstein Rare Book and Manuscript Library, Duke University; George William Brown, *Baltimore and the Nineteenth of April, 1861: A Study of the War* (Baltimore: Johns Hopkins University, 1887), 111–12; McLain, "Prison Conditions," 79–94; Roger W. Hanson to wife, May 23, 1861, Roger W. Hanson Papers, LC.

10. Seth C. Hawley to WHS, November 24, 1861, in *O.R.*, ser. 2, vol. 2, p. 147. Dimick was subsequently ordered to keep better guard over the prisoners. See Lorenzo Thomas to Dimick, December 7, 1861, in ibid., 174.

11. A number of these postdate AO's time at Fort Warren. See, for example, Maggie R. Douglas Autograph Album, 1862–1886, Virginia Museum of History and Culture; Frank M. Harris Autograph Book, 1862, Rubenstein Library, Duke University. Several are held at MdHS.

12. AO, "Fort Warren Aphorisms," *Southern Magazine* 9 (November 1871): 639.

13. Macgill to wife, December 20, 1861, Macgill Papers; Sangston, *Bastiles of the North,* 121.

14. McLain, "Prison Conditions," 140–43; Thomas W. Hall Jr. to Mother, December 25, 1861, Thomas W. Hall Correspondence (MS 2390), MdHS; J. Hanson Thomas to Annie (wife), December 24, 26, 1861, Dr. J. Hanson Thomas Collection (MS 3091), MdHS.

15. AO, "Footprints," *Southern Magazine* 9 (December 1871): 660–61.

16. Sangston, *Bastiles of the North,* 120–21; Charles W. Mitchell, ed., *Maryland Voices of the Civil War* (Baltimore: Johns Hopkins University Press, 2007), 279; Thomas W. Hall Jr. to Mother, January 1, 1862, Hall Correspondence.

17. Frederick W. Seward to Dana, December 23, 1861, Frederick W. Seward to Keyes, December 23, 1861, and WHS to Dimick, December 23, 1861, all in Secret Correspondence.

18. US Army Autograph Book (1861), Rubenstein Library.

19. AO affidavit, January 4, 1862, in Boston Case File; San Francisco *Evening Bulletin,* January 27, 1862; *O.R.,* ser. 2, vol. 2, pp. 231, 234.

20. *Boston Herald,* December 30, 1861, reproduced in *New York Herald,* December 31, 1861; San Francisco *Evening Bulletin,* January 27, 1861; indictment of AO, affidavits of EOS, Benjamin F. Sawyer, Edwin G. Reynolds, John S. Kelso, and Raniero Rebecchini, January 2, 1862, and affidavits of AO, January 4, 18, 1862, all in Boston Case File.

CHAPTER 9. CHARLES STREET JAIL

1. Robert B. MacKay, "The Charles Street Jail: Hegemony of a Design" (PhD diss., Boston University, 1980), 36–37, 48–49, 64–65, 75, 98–99, 105; *Twenty-Seventh Annual Report of the Board of Managers of the Prison Discipline Society, Boston, May, 1852* (Boston: T. R. Marvin, 1852), 140.

2. *Twenty-Fourth Annual Report of the Board of Managers of the Prison Discipline Society, Boston, May, 1849* (Boston: T. R. Marvin, 1849), 10; MacKay, "Charles Street Jail," 98–99.

3. *Twenty-Fourth Annual Report,* 8, 12; *Twenty-Seventh Annual Report,* 139.

4. *Twenty-Fourth Annual Report,* 11.

5. *Twenty-Seventh Annual Report,* 139–40.

6. MacKay, "Charles Street Jail," 106–8.

7. MacKay, "Charles Street Jail," 104–5, 115–17; *Twenty-Fourth Annual Report,* 10; *Twenty-Seventh Annual Report,* 140.

8. Testimony before the grand jury in the US Circuit Court for the District of Massachusetts, October 13, 1862, M160, reel 6; Cronin, *Evolution of a Life,* 52.

9. Affidavit of AO, January 18, 1862, Boston Case File.

10. "Mr. Oaksmith to the Public," January 31, 1862, in *New York Tribune*, February 5, 1862.

11. John White Scott Papers, LC.

12. "Unrecognized," *The Friend: A Religious and Literary Journal* 37 (October 31, 1863): 68; "Deserted," February 1862, in Scrapbook, 1870–1874, AO Papers. "Unrecognized" appears to have first appeared in the New York *Anglo-African*, a black newspaper, on October 7, 1862, but AO published it again above the date "February 1, 1862, Boston" in *The Friend* in 1863.

13. Death certificate on ancestry.com/.

14. E. Reynolds to AO, April 1, 1862, and Ruston Maury to AO, March 8, 1862, both in Elmore Collection.

15. AO to Horace Greeley, March 29, 1862, Horace Greeley Papers, NYPL.

16. EOS diary, June 13, 1863.

17. EOS, "A Plain Statement," October 6, 1870, EOS Papers.

18. Mack to AO, March 1, 1862, AO Papers.

19. EOS to Orestes Brownson, August 25, 1862, Brownson Papers.

20. Sarah H. Whitman to CBS, March 1, 1862 (enclosed in letter from US senator H. B. Anthony, March 3, 1862), "Correspondence, Testimony, and Exhibits, Relating to the Slave Bark *Augusta*, 1861–1862," M160, reel 5; Whitman to Julia Deane Freeman, February 23, 1862, in Kunce, *Correspondence*, 160–61; EOS Autobiography, 311–15; Sen. Ex. Doc. 40, 37th Cong., 2nd sess., p. 13.

21. EOS diary for 1861–1864, no date (p. 60).

CHAPTER 10. EXECUTION

1. *Hanging Gordon*, 53–57, 60–61, 127–28; Marques, *United States and the Trans-atlantic Slave Trade*, 237.

2. *Hanging Gordon*, 58, 128.

3. *Hanging Gordon*, 15, 30–31, 53; Pardon File A-367.

4. *Hanging Gordon*, 58–59, 66–67, 73; James A. Rawley, "Captain Nathaniel Gordon, the Only American Executed for Violating the Slave Trade Laws," *Civil War History* 39 (September 1993): 221.

5. *Hanging Gordon*, 61–65.

6. *United States v. Nathaniel Gordon*, RG 21 (Southern District of New York), Criminal Case Files, 1790–1912, NARA-NY; *Hanging Gordon*, 67, 75–77, 79, 88.

7. Indictments of Thomas Nelson et al., filed in the October 1860 term and the May 1861 term, both in RG 21 (District of New Hampshire), Criminal Case Files, National Archives at Boston.

8. Thomas Savage, Thomas Nelson, Samuel Sleeper, and John McCafferty to Abraham Lincoln, May 11, 1861, Pardon File A-367.

9. *African Repository* 38 (December 1862): 373; CBS, "Decision of the Secretary of the Interior on the Evidence Taken in the Recent Investigation at New York

City," January 8, 1862, "Correspondence, Testimony, and Exhibits, Relating to the Slave Bark *Augusta*, 1861–1862," M160; *Hanging Gordon*, 77, 89–91; *Lloyd's Pocket Companion and Guide through New York City, for 1866–67* (New York: Thomas Lloyd, 1865), 70; Benson J. Lossing, *History of New York City*, 2 vols. (New York: Perine, 1884), 1:397.

10. *Hanging Gordon*, 92.

11. Thomas W. Clerke to Abraham Lincoln, March 30, 1861, RG 60, Entry 350 (Records Relating to the Appointment of Federal Judges, Marshals, and Attorneys, 1853–1901), NARA-CP; recess appointment of EDS as US Attorney for the Southern District of New York, April 4, 1861, RG 59, Entry 789 (Temporary Attorneys' Commissions, 1829–1887), NARA-CP; appointment of EDS, RG 59, Entry 788 (Permanent Attorneys' Commissions, 1825–1888), NARA-CP.

12. *Hanging Gordon*, 107–14.

13. *Hanging Gordon*, 115.

14. *Hanging Gordon*, 118–33.

15. *Hanging Gordon*, 133–34; EDS to CBS, November 22, 1861, in "Communications Received from E. Delafield Smith," M160, reel 5.

16. *Hanging Gordon*, 144–46; John R. Spears, *The American Slave-Trade: An Account of Its Origin, Growth and Suppression* (New York: Charles Scribner's Sons, 1900), 220.

17. *Hanging Gordon*, 146–47.

18. *Hanging Gordon*, 149; *New York Examiner*, February 13, 1862; Charles Sumner to Orestes Brownson, February 2, 1862, in Beverly Wilson Palmer, ed., *The Selected Letters of Charles Sumner*, 2 vols. (Boston: Northeastern University Press, 1990), 2:100.

19. *Hanging Gordon*, 172; A. H. Merryman et al. to Lincoln, n.d., Isaac Dayton to Lincoln, January 23, 1862, and Edward P. Cowles to Lincoln, January 27, 1862, all in Pardon File A-391; Michael Burlingame, *Abraham Lincoln: A Life*, 2 vols. (Baltimore: Johns Hopkins University Press, 2008), 2:352.

20. *Hanging Gordon*, 166–67, 173; WHS to Lincoln, February 3, 1862, Lincoln Papers.

21. *Hanging Gordon*, 168; Burlingame, *Abraham Lincoln*, 2:351–52.

22. *Hanging Gordon*, 150, 168–69, 194–95.

23. Ralph Waldo Emerson, journal entry for January 31, 1862, in Edward W. Emerson, ed., "Washington in Wartime: From the Journal of Ralph Waldo Emerson," *Atlantic Monthly* 94 (July 1904): 1; Burlingame, *Abraham Lincoln*, 2:352.

24. Edward Bates to Lincoln, February 4, 1862, Lincoln Papers; Edward Bates, diary entry for February 5, 1862, in Howard K. Beale, ed., *The Diary of Edward Bates, 1859–1866* (Washington, DC: Government Printing Office, 1933), 229. Bates would later say that he verbally warned Lincoln not to grant the respite because it would "be taken as an implied promise of pardon or commutation, however strongly he might asseverate to the contrary." See ibid., 233. Bates would prove to be right.

25. Lincoln, "Stay of Execution for Nathaniel Gordon," February 4, 1862, in *CWL*, 5:128–29.

26. Lincoln had long believed that the principles of the Declaration of Independence applied to "all people of all colors everywhere." See *CWL*, 2:406, 3:301.

27. *Brooklyn Daily Eagle*, February 21, 1862; *Ex parte Gordon*, 66 US 503 (1862); Carl Brent Swisher, *The Oliver Wendell Holmes Devise History of the Supreme Court of the United States, Vol. V: The Taney Period, 1836–64* (New York: Macmillan, 1974), 706.

28. Bates, diary entry for February 18, 1862, in Beale, *Diary of Edward Bates*, 233; Elizabeth Keckley, *Behind the Scenes: Thirty Years a Slave and Four Years in the Lincoln White House* (1868; reprint, New York: Fall River Press, 2014), 59–60.

29. Rhoda E. White to Lincoln, February 17, 1862, Lincoln Papers; Bates, diary entry for February 18, 1862, in Beale, *Diary of Edward Bates*, 233; *Hanging Gordon*, 197–99.

30. Gilbert Dean to Lincoln, February 18, 1862, and Bates to Lincoln, February 18, 1862, both in Lincoln Papers; *Hanging Gordon*, 200.

31. Edwin D. Morgan to Lincoln, February 20, 1862, RG 59, Entry 113 (Miscellaneous Correspondence, 1784–1906), NARA-CP; *Hanging Gordon*, 206.

32. *Brooklyn Daily Eagle*, February 21, 1862; Theodore E. Tomlinson, David C. Aitken, and George W. Wiley to Lincoln, February 20, 1862, RG 59, Entry 113, NARA-CP; Don E. Fehrenbacher and Virginia Fehrenbacher, eds., *Recollected Words of Abraham Lincoln* (Stanford: Stanford University Press, 1996), 40–41.

33. New York *Journal of Commerce*, quoted in Pittsfield, MA, *Berkshire County Eagle*, February 27, 1862; *Brooklyn Daily Eagle*, February 21, 1862; New York *Journal of Commerce* quoted in Baltimore *Sun*, February 24, 1862; *New York Times*, February 22, 1862; *Brooklyn Daily Eagle*, December 26, 1897.

34. *Hanging Gordon*, 224.

35. *Brooklyn Daily Eagle*, April 24, 1877.

36. *New York Times*, February 22, 1862; "Autobiography of John S. Keyes," Keyes Papers.

37. *New York Times*, February 22, 1862; New York *Anglo-African*, March 1, 1862; *Hartford Courant*, February 22, 1862; *New York Examiner*, February 27, 1862; Huntington *Indiana Herald*, February 26, 1862.

38. Quarles, *Lincoln and the Negro*, 95; George Templeton Strong, diary entry for February 22, 1862, in Allan Nevins and Milton Halsey Thomas, eds., *The Diary of George Templeton Strong*, 4 vols. (New York: Macmillan, 1952), 3:209.

CHAPTER 11. TRIAL

1. W. A. Clarke to AO, March 31, 1862, and Charles L. Woodbury to AO, May 30, 1862, both in AO Papers.

2. Benjamin F. Sawyer to AO, May 20, 1862, Elmore Collection. The *Augusta* case was finally settled in November 1863. See the docket book for the US District

Court for the Southern District of New York, p. 348, in RG 21 (Southern District of New York), NARA-NY.

3. Affidavit of Benjamin F. Sawyer, filed January 17, 1862, Boston Case File.

4. *United States v. Appleton Oaksmith*, RG 21 (Southern District of New York), Criminal Case Files, 1790–1912, NARA-NY; RM to WHS, December 11, 1861, Disloyalty File. See also appendix 2.

5. Seth C. Hawley to Frederick W. Seward, December 14, 1861, Disloyalty File.

6. *United States v. Samuel P. Skinner*, RG 21 (District of Massachusetts), National Archives at Boston; Richard Henry Dana Jr. to Edward Bates, March 21, 1863, in Pardon File A-455; *Boston Daily Advertiser*, November 15, 1861; Keyes to George C. Whiting, September 11, 1861, M160, reel 6; *Boston Morning Journal*, November 21, 1861. Landre's sworn statements are in *United States v. Margaret Scott*, RG 21 (District of Massachusetts), National Archives at Boston.

7. Thornton K. Lothrop to CBS, July 2, 1862, M160, reel 5.

8. Keyes to WHS, November 18, 1862, Keyes Papers.

9. Earl F. Mulderink III, *New Bedford's Civil War* (New York: Fordham University Press, 2012), 2–5, 10–16, 32–41, 45–52, 138–39, 142–47.

10. Indictment of AO, and petitions for continuance to next term, May 29 and 31, 1862, all in Boston Case File.

11. Charles Warren, *The Supreme Court in United States History*, revised edition, 2 vols. (Boston: Little, Brown, and Co., 1926), 2:323; Swisher, *Taney Period*, 247; EOS diary, November 17, 1864.

12. EOS to Horace Greeley, June 3, 1862, Horace Greeley Papers, NYPL. In this letter, EOS asked Greeley to explain the *Tribune*'s hostility to her family. After insisting on her sons' innocence, she concluded bitingly, "It is probably all a business trifle to you."

13. *New York Herald*, June 12, 1862; *Brooklyn Evening Star*, June 25, 1862.

14. *Boston Herald*, June 10, 1862; *Brooklyn Evening Star*, June 25, 1862.

15. Docket book of the US District Court for the District of Massachusetts, September 1861 and March 1862 Terms, pp. 387–90, National Archives at Boston.

16. *New York Herald*, June 12, 1862; *Brooklyn Evening Star*, June 25, 1862.

17. Thornton L. Lothrop to CBS, July 2, 1862, M160, reel 5; *New York Herald*, June 13, 1862.

18. *Boston Evening Transcript*, June 9, 12, 14, 16, 1862; *Boston Herald*, June 10, 11, 12, 13, 16, 1862; *Boston Traveler*, June 14, 15, 1862; *Springfield* (MA) *Republican*, June 10, 14, 1862; New York *Evening Post*, June 11, 14, 16, 1862.

19. *Brooklyn Evening Star*, June 25, 1862.

20. RM to George C. Whiting, June 16, 1862, M160, reel 6.

21. *Brooklyn Evening Star*, June 25, 1862.

22. *New York Herald*, June 15, 1862.

23. RM to George C. Whiting, June 16, 1862, M160, reel 6. RM used the word "shrewd" in a letter to George Whiting, January 10, 1862, M160, reel 5.

24. *New York Herald*, June 15, 1862; RM to George C. Whiting, June 16, 1862, M160, reel 6.

25. Whiting to RM, June 18, 1862, M160, reel 6.

26. *New York Independent*, quoted in Honolulu *Friend*, September 1, 1862.

27. Francis Lousada to Lord John Russell, June 24, 1862, in *Accounts and Papers of the House of Commons, Session 5 February–28 July 1863* (London, 1863), 71:314.

28. RM to George C. Whiting, June 16, 1862, M160, reel 6.

29. Whiting to RM, June 20, 1862, M160, reel 6. In a letter of June 18, 1862, Whiting told RM that the department "congratulate[s] you upon your success in the case of Oaksmith, for after all it is your case."

30. "Autobiography of John S. Keyes," Keyes Papers; A. Taylor Milne, "The Lyons-Seward Treaty of 1862," *American Historical Review* 38 (April 1933): 511–25; WHS to Lincoln, April 24, 1862, Lincoln Papers; Isaac Dayton to Lincoln, January 23, 1862, Pardon File A-391; *CWL*, 5:46–47, 7:36.

31. Horatio King to Amos T. Akerman, July 20, 1871, Pardon File C-610; *O.R.*, ser. 1, vol. 12, p. 511; *New York Times*, December 11, 1861; ORN, ser. 2, vol. 1, p. 135; Mulderink, *New Bedford's Civil War*, 139–42.

32. Motions for a new trial, June 14, 21, 26, 1862, all in Boston Case File.

CHAPTER 12. ESCAPE

1. EOS to Orestes Brownson, August 25, 1862, Brownson Papers; AO, "My Little Daughter's Prayer," September 7, 1862, published in the *New York Atlas*, in vol. of AO Poems, 1861–1862, AO Papers; AO's letter does not survive, but EOS quoted it in EOS diary, September 8, 1862, and April 17, 1863.

2. Philadelphia *Inquirer*, September 16, 1862; *Boston Transcript* quoted in *Albany Evening Journal*, September 15, 1862. AO is the first escapee listed in the prison logbooks, although the record only dates to 1862, so it is possible that other prisoners escaped in the previous decade. See Charles Street Jail Records, ser. 4 (Log Books), Occurrence Log, vol. 1, Boston City Archives.

3. AO to John S. Keyes, September 10, 1862, M160, reel 6.

4. TePaske, 26.

5. Grand jury testimony, October 13, 1862, and John S. Keyes to George C. Whiting, September 13, 1862, both in M160, reel 6; Suffolk County Criminal Calendar for 1862, Massachusetts State Archives.

6. AO to John S. Keyes, September 10, 1862, M160, reel 6.

7. *Boston Post*, September 18 and October 2, 1862. The *Post* mistakenly announced the reward as $500.

8. John S. Keyes to George C. Whiting, September 13, 1862, M160, reel 6.

9. Stephen Fuller (foreman), grand jury findings, M160, reel 6.

10. Isotta believed that AMO helped him escape from jail. See Paris, ME, *Oxford Democrat*, September 9, 1870.

11. *Boston Evening Transcript*, October 18, 1862; *Boston Herald*, October 18, 1862; Cronin, *Evolution of a Life*, 46–51; EOS diary, November 29, 1864. When

Edward died in Cuba in 1865, he was mistakenly identified as "the notorious fitter out of slavers." See Boston *New England Farmer*, October 28, 1865; *Philadelphia Inquirer*, November 1, 1865; *New Orleans Times*, November 5, 1865.

CHAPTER 13. EXILE

1. TePaske, 26–28. Isotta believed that AO spent six months "with his mistress, Mrs. White, in Brooklyn, where his mother visited him." See Paris, ME, *Oxford Democrat*, September 9, 1870.

2. *New York Sunday News*, December 28, 1879.

3. *Boston Evening Transcript*, October 30, 1862; *Boston Traveler*, October 30, 1862; Philadelphia *Inquirer*, October 31, 1862; EOS diary, February 8, 1865. In another diary entry, EOS wrote that AO "did not join his brother till Dec. 1863. He was very ill for a long time." See EOS diary, November 29, 1864. It is unclear whether this means that AO was in Cuba but did not join Sidney in Havana for that first year in Cuba. It seems more likely that she simply miswrote the date and meant to write 1862.

4. *Lowell Daily Citizen and News*, October 31, 1862; John S. Keyes to CBS, November 18, 1862, M160, reel 6; Keyes to WHS, November 18, 1862, Keyes Papers.

5. EOS diary, May 24, July 1, 1863. The affidavits and other records are in Pardon File C-610.

6. *Harper's Weekly*, February 27, 1864. See also Frank A. Daniel to AO, January 15, 1877, AO Papers.

7. EOS diary, April 16, 1863.

8. EOS diary, November 1, 1861, February 1, 1865; "The Willows," in Corinne Oaksmith copybook, 1877–1878, AO Papers.

9. EOS diary, June 5, 1863. During AO's exile, EOS sent a curious letter to WHS asking for "a copy of the foreign correspondence of the Secretary of State to add to the historic treasures of my little Library. I am told it can only be procured by application to yourself." A few months later she thanked him for the volume, saying it contained "important links in the history of the present eventful period." See EOS to WHS, February 2, 1864, WHS Papers; EOS to WHS, July 21, 1864, M179, reel 214. It is unclear what her motives were in making this request, as AO would not be embroiled in international controversy until later that year (see chapter 15).

10. EOS diary, November 5, 1864.

11. See Neely, *Fate of Liberty*; White, *Abraham Lincoln and Treason*.

12. Frank L. Klement, *The Limits of Dissent: Clement L. Vallandigham & the Civil War* (Lexington: University Press of Kentucky, 1970), 139–72.

13. EOS diary, May 21, 1863.

14. EOS diary, June 27, July 1, 4, 5, 1863.

15. EDS to Lincoln, July 8, 1863, Lincoln Papers.

16. EOS diary, July 20, 1863; Harold Holzer, *Lincoln and the Power of the Press: The War for Public Opinion* (New York: Simon & Schuster, 2014), 443–45; Adrian Cook, *The Armies of the Streets: The New York City Draft Riots of 1863* (Lexington: University Press of Kentucky, 1974), 101, 118–19; Iver Bernstein, *The New York City Draft Riots: Their Significance for American Society and Politics in the Age of the Civil War* (New York: Oxford University Press, 1990), 36–37.

17. Shane White, *Prince of Darkness: The Untold Story of Jeremiah G. Hamilton, Wall Street's First Black Millionaire* (New York: St. Martin's Press, 2015), 296–303.

18. EOS diary, July 20, 22, 24, 25, 1863; White, *Prince of Darkness*, 302.

19. Bernstein, *New York City Draft Riots*, 4–5, 21, 27, 288; Harold Holzer, *The Civil War in 50 Objects* (New York: Penguin, 2013), 208–14.

20. EOS diary, July 20, 1863.

21. Quoted in EOS diary, February 8, 1865.

22. John M. Clark to Keyes, September 24, 1863, Keyes Papers.

CHAPTER 14. LINCOLN

1. Edward Dicey, "Lincolniana," *MacMillan's Magazine* 12 (June 1865): 190.

2. Burlingame, *Abraham Lincoln*, 2:353.

3. John B. Alley, in Allen Thorndike Rice, ed., *Reminiscences of Abraham Lincoln by Distinguished Men of His Time*, sixth edition (New York: North American Review, 1888), 583. On the capture of the *Orion*, see Gilliland, *USS Constellation on the Dismal Coast*, 48, 55–57, 65–66, 76–77.

4. Pardon File A-338.

5. Pardon File A-381.

6. Pardon File A-358; Pardons and Remissions, vol. 7, p. 434. To be precise, Lincoln's action in Morgan's case was a remission of sentence and not a full pardon. It is possible that Lincoln may have made these remarks to Alley during one of Morgan's earlier petitions and that the president later chose to turn against his earlier emphatic language.

7. Pardon File A-323; *United States v. Alice Rodgers*, RG 21 (Eastern District of Virginia), Entry 51 (Norfolk Division, Admiralty Case Files, 1801–1966), box 18, National Archives at Philadelphia; Pardons and Remissions, vol. 7, pp. 370–71.

8. Pardon File A-472; *United States v. Albert Horn*, RG 21 (Southern District of New York), Criminal Case Files, 1790–1912, NARA-NY; James T. Brady to Lincoln, May 13, 1863, Lincoln Papers; Pardons and Remissions, vol. 7, pp. 450–51; Marques, *United States and the Transatlantic Slave Trade*, 246–50.

9. Pardon File A-413; RM to George C. Whiting, June 16, 1862, M160, reel 6; Pardons and Remissions, vol. 7, pp. 470–71.

10. Pardon File A-455; Pardons and Remissions, vol. 7, pp. 463–64.

11. EDS to Montgomery Blair, November 19, 1862, Lincoln Papers.

12. Frederick W. Seward, *Seward at Washington, as Senator and Secretary of State* (New York: Derby and Miller, 1891), 215; Mark E. Neely Jr., *Lincoln and the Democrats: The Politics of Opposition in the Civil War* (New York: Cambridge University Press, 2017), 192–205; Thomas Savage to WHS, November 20, 1863 (two dispatches of that date), March 27, April 22, May 23, June 10, 28, and July 19, 1864, all in M899, reel 46. Spanish authorities began asking for the rendition of Arguelles as early as March 1864. See *Papers Relating to Foreign Affairs, Accompanying the Annual Message of the President to the Second Session Thirty-Eighth Congress* (Washington, DC: G.P.O., 1865), part 4, pp. 59–60, 69–70. On Dulce's anti-slave trade activities, see John V. Crawford to Lord John Russell, September 30, 1863, and Jos. T. Crawford to Lord John Russell, November 6, 16, December 12, 1863, all in FO 84/1197. Tassara and WHS had been acquaintances since the 1850s. See Kinley J. Brauer, "Gabriel Garcia y Tassara and the American Civil War: A Spanish Perspective," *Civil War History* 21 (March 1975): 7–8.

13. Gideon Welles, diary entries for May 20 and June 6, 1864, in William E. Gienapp and Erica L. Gienapp, eds., *The Civil War Diary of Gideon Welles, Lincoln's Secretary of the Navy: The Original Manuscript Edition* (Urbana: University of Illinois Press, 2014), 413–14, 423; *Philadelphia Age*, May 26, 1864; Edward Bates, diary entry for June 9, 1864, in Beale, *Diary of Edward Bates*, 374.

14. EOS diary, November 30, 1864. Thomas Savage claimed that this woman was not Arguelles's wife. See Savage to WHS, June 10, 1864. Historian Mark E. Neely Jr. rightly notes that Lincoln wielded extraordinary power in this incident even though the use of this power had nothing to do with winning the war. "The rendition of Arguelles had nothing to do with war and everything to do with humanitarianism," observes Neely. In this moment, Lincoln "was beginning to usher in the new era of human rights." Neely, *Lincoln and the Democrats*, 203–4.

CHAPTER 15. KIDNAPPING

1. Edward Bates, diary entry for June 9, 1864, in Beale, *Diary of Edward Bates*, 374.

2. Gideon Welles, diary entries for May 20 and June 6, 1864, in Gienapp and Gienapp, *Civil War Diary of Gideon Welles*, 413–14, 423; Neely, *Lincoln and the Democrats*, 195–96. WHS's argument may have been influenced by a memorandum he received from P. J. Joachimsen, May 31, 1864, WHS Papers.

3. WHS to James Speed, December 27, 1864, RG 60, Entry 9-A (Letters Received, 1809–1870), Box 12.

4. John S. Keyes to WHS, May 25, 1864, M179, reel 212.

5. WHS to Thomas Savage, June 6, 1864, RG 59, Entry 59 (Consular Instructions), vol. 37.

6. Howard, *American Slavers*, 113–23; Savage to WHS, June 22, 1864, M899, reel 46.

7. Columbus *Daily Ohio Statesman*, June 21, 1864; London *Daily Telegraph*, October 28, 1864; Springfield *Daily Illinois State Register*, June 19, 1864.

8. *Portland Daily Advertiser*, quoted in *New York Tribune*, May 30, 1864 (and a number of other papers); *San Francisco Bulletin*, June 25, 1864; *Boston Morning Journal*, May 31, 1864.

9. *Sacramento Daily Union*, June 15, 1864.

10. Edward T. Cotham Jr., *Battle on the Bay: The Civil War Struggle for Galveston* (Austin: University of Texas Press, 1998), 168–75; James W. Daddysman, *The Matamoros Trade: Confederate Commerce, Diplomacy, and Intrigue* (Newark: University of Delaware Press, 1984), 159–61; Michael Brem Bonner and Peter McCord, *The Union Blockade in the American Civil War: A Reassessment* (Knoxville: University of Tennessee Press, 2021), 108.

11. Marcus W. Price, "Ships that Tested the Blockade of the Gulf Ports, 1861–1865," *American Neptune* 11 (October 1951): 262, 271; Savage to WHS, June 22, 1864, M899, reel 46; St. Louis *Globe-Democrat*, quoted in *Fort Wayne Daily Gazette*, August 2, 1885; AO to Ulysses S. Grant, September 25, 1869, NYHS. Isotta claimed that AO went by other aliases as well, including Robert Maxwell and Mr. Rebecchini. See Paris, ME, *Oxford Democrat*, September 9, 1870.

12. G. Holland to Clinton McClarty, June 9, 1864, M909 (Papers Pertaining to Vessels of or Involved with the Confederate States of America: "Vessel Papers"), reel 7.

13. St. Louis *Globe-Democrat*, quoted in *Fort Wayne Daily Gazette*, August 2, 1885.

14. *Houston Daily Telegraph*, July 11, 1864; St. Louis *Globe-Democrat*, quoted in *Fort Wayne Daily Gazette*, August 2, 1885; Savage to WHS, July 19, 1864, M899, reel 46; L. Tuffly Ellis, "Maritime Commerce on the Far Western Gulf, 1861–1865," *Southwestern Historical Quarterly* 77 (October 1973): 194; Thomas E. Taylor, *Running the Blockade: A Personal Narrative of Adventures, Risks, and Escapes during the American Civil War*, third edition (London: John Murray, 1897), 157. For one of the Northern reports, see *Cincinnati Daily Enquirer*, July 28, 1864. Secretary of the Navy Gideon Welles said that blockaders were "justified in firing" into blockade-runners because "the blockade must be enforced." See Bonner and McCord, *Union Blockade*, 67.

15. Savage to WHS, July 19, 1864, M899, reel 46.

16. *Houston Daily Telegraph*, August 16, 1864.

17. Portland, ME, *Daily Eastern Argus*, September 30, 1864; New York *World*, September 22, 1864; Washington, DC, *Evening Star*, October 3, 1864; Washington, DC, *National Republican*, October 3, 1864; London *Guardian*, October 19, 1864; *United States v. Matagorda*, RG 21 (District of Massachusetts), Case File #174 (September Term, 1864). The total sale price for everything sold was $389,367.35. For an account of the *Matagorda*'s trip to Boston, see "Logs of the Prize Steamer *Matagorda*, September 20–29, 1864," 2 vols., RG 45 (Naval Records Collection of

the Office of Naval Records and Library), Entry 608 (Logs and Journals Kept by US Naval Officers, March 1776–June 1908), item 118.

18. Ellis, "Maritime Commerce," 197.

19. St. Louis *Globe-Democrat*, quoted in *Fort Wayne Daily Gazette*, August 2, 1885; *United States v. Matagorda*; *Boston Traveler*, October 14, 1864; Sidney Oaksmith to EOS, September 17, 1864, quoted in EOS diary, November 28, 1864.

20. "The Blockade-runner's Song," in Book of Verse by AO (1865), EOS Papers.

21. Savage to WHS, September 23, 1864, M899, reel 46.

22. John M. Clark to John S. Keyes, September 26, 1864, Keyes Papers.

23. Savage to WHS, October 1, 1864, M899, reel 46.

24. Newspaper clippings from the New York *Express*, pasted in EOS diary, pp. 190–92; EOS diary, October 19, 1864.

25. Savage to WHS, October 1, 1864, M899, reel 46.

26. EOS diary, October 13, 1864.

27. EOS diary, October 18, 1864.

28. EOS diary, October 22, 28–29, 1864.

29. See, for example, New Orleans *Daily True Delta*, October 23, 1864; *Springfield (MA) Republican*, October 20, 1864; *Hartford Daily Courant*, October 15, 1864.

30. Newspaper clippings from the New York *Express*, pasted in EOS diary, pp. 190–92. These articles were reprinted throughout the United States. See, for example, *Daily Milwaukee News*, October 26, 1864.

31. *Greenport* (NY) *Watchman*, quoted in *Plymouth* (IN) *Weekly Democrat*, August 3, 1865; clippings from the *Express*.

32. Clippings from the *Express*. Ironically, by this time, Richard Henry Dana Jr. considered Lincoln "a shapeless mass of writhing ugliness" who "lacks administrative power" and "is not up to the office." See Burlingame, *Abraham Lincoln*, 2:610.

33. *Official Proceedings of the Democratic National Convention, Held in 1864 at Chicago* (Chicago: Times, 1864), 27. Historian Mark Neely recently rediscovered this clause.

34. Welles, diary entry for January 30, 1865, in Gienapp and Gienapp, *Civil War Diary of Gideon Welles*, 581.

35. Charles Sumner to Francis Lieber, June 12, 1864, in Palmer, *Selected Letters of Charles Sumner*, 2:244; Neely, *Lincoln and the Democrats*, 195–96; *The American Annual Cyclopaedia and Register of Important Events of the Year 1864* (New York: D. Appleton, 1865), 787.

36. *O.R.*, ser. 2, vol. 7, p. 330.

37. WHS responded to the resolution, and Cox's request for information, on June 24, 1864. See *Papers Relating to Foreign Affairs, Accompanying the Annual Message of the President to the Second Session Thirty-Eighth Congress* (Washington, DC: G.P.O., 1865), part 4, pp. 35–56

38. *Congressional Globe*, 38th Cong., 1st sess., pp. 2772, 2910–20.

39. Columbus *Daily Ohio Statesman*, June 24, 1864; New York *World*, June 9, 1864.

40. EOS diary, October 23, 27, 1864; *Tribune Almanac and Political Register for 1865* (New York: Tribune Association, 1865), 46–68.

41. *CWL*, 8:140; Neely, *Lincoln and the Democrats*, 202.

CHAPTER 16. DIVORCE

1. Quoted in EOS diary, December 26, 1864.

2. Abram Wakeman to John A. Dix, January 18, 1865, and William T. Minor to RM, January 9, 1865, both in NARA microfilm M416 (Union Provost Marshal's File of Papers Relating to Two or More Civilians), reel 51.

3. AO to Sidney Oaksmith, November 18, 1864, enclosed in RM to WHS, November 29, 1864, M179, reel 218.

4. EOS diary, November 28, 1864; Richard Henry Dana Jr. to WHS, December 8, 1864, and Thornton K. Lothrop to Frederick W. Seward, December 23, 1864, both in M179, reel 219; WHS to James Speed, December 27, 1864, RG 60, Entry 9-A (Letters Received by the Attorney General, 1809–1870); Speed to Cuthbert Bullitt, December 28, 1864 (enclosing warrant), in NARA microfilm M345 (Union Provost Marshals' File of Paper Relating to Individual Civilians). The federal court in Boston issued bench warrants for AO's arrest on both December 23, 1864, and March 9, 1865, but neither was returned. See John Bassett Moore, *A Treatise on Extradition and Rendition*, 2 vols. (Boston: Boston Book Co., 1891), 2:857–58.

5. Savage to WHS, December 14, 1864, M899, reel 46.

6. John George Walker to E. Kirby Smith, February 12, 1865 (two letters of the same date), both in RG 109 (War Department Collection of Confederate Records), Entry 3 (Collected Record Books of Various Executive, Legislative, and Judicial Offices), chap. 2, vol. 123, pp. 137–38.

7. I searched Kirby Smith's papers at UNC as well as several volumes of Confederate correspondence in RG 109 but was unable to locate any evidence of a meeting between AO and Kirby Smith or AO receiving a Confederate commission.

8. Thomas Birch and Son, *Sanitary Fair Sale. Catalogue of Valuable Illustrated German Books, Needle Work, Autographs, Relics, and Curiosities, Guns, etc. etc. To Be Sold for the Benefit of the Great Central Fair, on Wednesday Morning, Dec. 21, 1864, at 11'clock, at the Auction Store, No. 1110 Chestnut Street, Philad. Thomas Birch & Son, Auctioneers* (Philadelphia: Sherman & Co., 1864), 8.

9. EOS diary, March 6, 1865. These words come from Elizabeth Sheppard, *Counterparts, Or the Cross of Love* (1854; reprint, Boston: T. O. H. P. Burnham, 1869), 152. EOS misremembered "now" and wrote it as "to know" when she wrote it in her diary a week later.

10. John R. Reid to EOS, January 11, 1865, EOS Mss.

11. *Potter's American Monthly* 14 (June 1880): 469; EOS diary, March 22, 24, 25, 27, 28, 30, 31, April 2, 5, 1865.

12. EOS diary, April 10, 13, 14, 1865; Nevins and Thomas, *Diary of George Templeton Strong*, 3:574–82.

13. Jonathan W. White, *Midnight in America: Darkness, Sleep and Dreams during the Civil War* (Chapel Hill: University of North Carolina Press, 2017), chap. 7; *Passages from the Correspondence of Griswold*, 132.

14. EOS diary, April 15, 16, 1865. Some newspapers confused Edward with his brother, calling him "the notorious fitter-out of slavers." See, for example, *Wilmington* (NC) *Herald*, November 1, 1865. Privately EOS expressed gladness that slavery had been destroyed, but she also believed that Southern leaders should be treated leniently. She was also horrified when the Lincoln assassination conspirators were executed after a military trial. See EOS to Gerrit Smith, June 27, July 10, 1865, both in GSP.

15. *Appleton Oaksmith v. Isotta Oaksmith*, Decree of Divorce, August 23, 1864, AO Papers; Val Nolan Jr., "Indiana: Birthplace of Migratory Divorce," *Indiana Law Journal* 26 (Summer 1951): 515–23; Richard Wires, *The Divorce Issue and Reform in Nineteenth-Century Indiana* (Muncie: Ball State University, 1967), 1–25. Horace Greeley opposed these laws, calling Indiana "the paradise of free lovers." But the laws became universally famous, even finding a place in the fiction of William Dean Howells. Isotta believed that either Sidney or a man named Charles S. Larrabee "went to Indiana, and personifying Appleton, obtained for him a divorce." See Paris, ME, *Oxford Democrat*, September 9, 1870.

16. Nolan, "Indiana," 524; Wires, *Divorce Issue and Reform*, 10–17; *Divorce of Appleton Oaksmith v. Isotta Oaksmith*, filed August 23, 1864, Roll No. 28, Packet No. 63, Metal Box No. 38, Adams County Circuit Court, Decatur, IN.

17. Affidavit of Sidney Oaksmith, November 21, 1865, notarized November 25, 1865, Elmore Collection.

18. Eleanor P. Mason to Benjamin F. Sawyer, April 6, 1871, AO Papers; pension record of Jonas W. Mason, RG 94 (Records of the Adjutant General's Office), NARA; EOS, *Woman and Her Needs* (New York: Fowlers & Wells, 1851), 76. Isotta later claimed that AO tried to get married under the name "John Mc-Donald" but that AMO refused to wed him unless he went by his real name. See Paris, ME, *Oxford Democrat*, September 9, 1870. While AO was making his way toward Canada, Isotta was suffering from a sore throat and rheumatism. See SS to EOS, November 30, 1865, EOS Papers. AMO would lose her sister to disease within two years.

19. "Our Trust," in Book of Verse by AO (1865), Bessie Oaksmith to AO, June 19, 1866, both in EOS Papers; naturalization record for AO, HO 1 160/6377, National Archives of the United Kingdom at Kew; Isotta Oaksmith to Andrew Johnson, May 24, 1867, copy in AO Papers; AO, "An Anniversary," January 9, 1878, AO Papers; AO to Ulysses S. Grant, October 24, 1870, Miscellaneous Personal Papers, NYPL.

20. Isotta Oaksmith to Andrew Johnson, May 24, 1867, copy in AO Papers. Under the terms of their agreement, AO paid Isotta $450 in six quarterly pay-

ments of $75/each over the next two years. See receipt signed by Isotta Rebecchini, July 27, 1866, AO Papers. Isotta later claimed that AO made her sign this while threatening her with a revolver, but he denied the allegation. See *New York Sunday News*, December 28, 1879. AO also appears to have insisted that she resume use of her maiden name and give up the surname Oaksmith. AO's daughters later claimed that in England "Isotta bribed a man to take her out there to kidnap the children. . . . Later, she almost knocked father down, with her large handbag, in a hotel lobby in London." See Corrections to TePaske by Geraldine Oaksmith, ca. 1962, AO Papers.

21. Orestes Brownson to WHS, March 23, 1866, NYHS. EOS and Sidney Oaksmith were both extraordinarily grateful for Brownson's letter. See EOS to Sidney, March 31, 1866, and Sidney to EOS, April 8, 1866, EOS Papers; EOS to Orestes Brownson, March 19 and 26, 1866, Brownson Papers.

22. EOS diary, September 29, 1866; EOS, "A Plain Statement," October 6, 1870, EOS Papers. EOS's recollection is corroborated by other documentary evidence. Weed wrote to her, "I talked with the Secretary of State about the case" and "a favorable effort in behalf of your son can be made now." Weed to EOS, September 14, 1866, AO Papers.

23. EOS diary, October 17, 18, 1866.

24. EOS diary, November 17, 1866.

25. EOS diary, December 3, 4, 5, 18, 1866.

26. EOS diary, January 14, 16, 1867; SS to EOS, February 5, 1867, EOS Papers.

27. Sidney Oaksmith to EOS, February 4, 1867, EOS Papers; EOS to Le Baron Bradford Prince, December 17, 1866, The Huntington, San Marino, CA.

28. EOS diary, February 11, 28, 1867. About this same time EOS also instructed SS to send copies of various poems to Stanbery. See EOS to SS, February 5, 1867, EOS Papers.

29. William Pitt Fessenden to Andrew Johnson, February 7, 1867, in Paul H. Bergeron et al., eds., *The Papers of Andrew Johnson: Vol. 12, February–August 1867* (Knoxville: University of Tennessee Press, 1995), 13. AO's 1867 pardon file (Pardon File B-312) does not appear to survive; however scattered letters are extant and his pardon file at NARA-CP lists RM as a correspondent, presumably in favor of pardon.

30. Sidney Oaksmith to EOS, February 7, 1867, EOS Papers.

31. Isotta Oaksmith to Andrew Johnson, May 24, 1867, copy in AO Papers; EOS diary, May 18, 1867.

32. Isotta Oaksmith to Andrew Johnson, May 24, 1867; EOS diary, June 14, 1867; *Boston Journal*, June 1, 1867.

33. EOS diary, May 19, June 8, 1867; Sidney Oaksmith to EOS, June 2, 1867, EOS Papers.

34. *Times and Messenger*, June 2, 1867, in EOS diary.

35. AO to SS, January 28, 1868, AO to EOS, November 29, 1867, EOS Papers.

CHAPTER 17. STORMS

1. AO Naturalization Record, HO 1 160/6377, National Archives of the United Kingdom at Kew; TePaske, 31–32; AO Scrapbook, 1870–1874 (5805), pp. 46–47, AO to Frederick A. Lane, May 10, 1870, both in AO Papers.

2. AMO to EOS, December 27, 1867, AO to Sidney, EOS, and SS, October 22, 1867, AO to EOS, November 29, 1867, all in EOS Papers. For accounts of the children's activities, see Bessie to AO, June 19, 1866, April 18, 1870, August 13, 1871, and Corinne to AO, April 20, 1870, all in EOS Papers.

3. AO Naturalization Record; photographs of Eleanor's gravestone are available in both the AO Papers and the EOS Papers; London *Cosmopolitan*, June 30, 1870 (clipping in scrapbook in EOS Papers).

4. See Eleanor P. Mason to Benjamin F. Sawyer, April 6, May 29, 1871, AO to Sawyer, May 29, 1871, Sawyer to AO, July 1, 1871, AO to E. H. Birbeck, April 3, 1875, all in AO Papers; AMO to EOS, December 27, 1867, EOS Papers. AO claimed that he had proof that Sawyer secretly opposed his return to the United States. See AO to Sawyer, May 29, 1871, AO Papers.

5. EOS diary, July 25, 26, 1867; SS to EOS, November 30, 1865, Alvin Oaksmith to EOS, October 2, 1868, both in EOS Papers; EOS to Editor Literary Leaves Syndicate, n.d., Miscellaneous Personal Papers, NYPL; EOS to Gerrit Smith, July 5, 1867, GSP; EOS Autobiography, 177; Rickels, *Seba Smith*, 136.

6. EOS to J. C. Derby, December 19, 1861, WHS Papers; EOS to John P. Hale, December 9, 1861, Disloyalty File; EOS to WHS, December 9, 1861, Disloyalty File.

7. AO journal, January 1, 1852.

8. *Portsmouth* (NH) *Journal of Literature and Politics*, January 1, 1870; New York *Herald*, March 28, February 3, 1870; Sidney Oaksmith to EOS, December 19, 1869, EOS to Secretary of the Navy, February 1, 1870, Hamilton Fish to EOS, February 14, 1870, David Dixon Porter to EOS, February 15, 1870, all in EOS Papers; Fanny Oaksmith to AO, October 7, 1879, AO Papers. Sidney had just gone into bankruptcy in January 1869. See New York *Commercial Advertiser*, January 8, 15, 1869.

9. Alvin Oaksmith to EOS, October 20, 1868, EOS Papers; *Brooklyn Daily Eagle*, January 29, February 9, 1870.

10. Richard Henry Dana Jr. to Isotta Oaksmith, March 28, 1868; Dana Family Papers, Massachusetts Historical Society, Boston, MA; Isotta Oaksmith to WHS, August 21, 1868, M179, reel 285; WHS to Isotta Oaksmith, September 14, 1868, WHS Papers.

11. This ad ran over several issues. See, for example, *New York Tribune*, September 8, 1869.

12. *Chicago Evening Mail*, January 28, 1871; *Portland Daily Press*, September 14, 26, 27, 1871.

13. EOS diary, June 11, 14, July 25, 1867; EOS to Horatio King, March 23, 25, 1870, Horatio King Papers, LC; Pardon File C-610.

14. Benjamin F. Sawyer to AO, September 19, 1870, AO Papers; *Albany Argus*, October 1, 20, 1870; New York *World*, October 3, 1870; *New York Times*, October

12, 1870; *New York Herald*, October 13, 1870; *Schenectady Reflector*, October 13, 1870; *Brooklyn Daily Eagle*, October 13, 17, 20, 22, 1870; New Orleans *Times-Picayune*, October 16, 1870; *Norwich Aurora*, October 19, 1870; *Albany Evening Journal*, October 22, 1870; James B. Mix, *The Biter Bit; or The Robert Macaire of Journalism. Being a Narrative of Some of the Black-Mailing Operations of Charles A. Dana's "Sun"* (Washington, DC, 1870), 56–69. According to some news reports, Greeley defended Woodford. See Wilmington *Delaware Tribune*, October 27, 1870.

15. EOS to AO, November 2, 1870, EOS Papers. In August 1870 AO wrote a poem entitled "Slander," in which he mused, "I know that the time will come when I / Shall little care what the world may say." See "Slander," in poetry book, AO Papers.

16. *Albany Journal*, quoted in *Buffalo Morning Express and Illustrated Buffalo Express*, October 18, 1870; *Troy Times*, October 22, 1870.

17. EOS to AO, November 2, 1870, EOS Papers.

18. In a private letter Woodford thanked Hannibal Hamlin for standing by him: "Nor have I forgotten the almost paternal kindness with which you . . . stood by me when I was unjustly assailed in my official relations here in 1861 & 62." See Stewart L. Woodford to Hannibal Hamlin, February 1, 1869, Hannibal Hamlin Papers, Maine Historical Society. Following the election, AO also published a letter calling the accusations against him lies. See *New York Tribune*, December 26, 1870. Isotta responded in the *New York Tribune* on January 25, 1871.

19. EOS to AO, November 2, 1870, EOS Papers.

20. AO to Ulysses S. Grant, October 24, 1870, Miscellaneous Personal Papers, NYPL. AO had also written to Grant a year earlier but the president did not appear to respond. See AO to Grant, September 25, 1869, AO Letters, NYHS.

21. EOS to Horatio King, December 8, 1870, Horatio King Papers.

22. Pardon File C-610 (quotations from statements by Weed, October 10, 1871, and Beebe, Donahue, and Cooke, August 26, September 25, 1871; Greeley quoted in AO to King, August 29, 1871).

23. Pardon File C-610 (quotation from Dana, August 3, 1871).

24. EOS to Gerrit Smith, August 12, 19, 1872, both in GSP; EOS to Horatio King, April 23, 1872, in Pardon File C-610.

25. AO to U.S. Grant, July 4, 1871, Pardon File C-610.

26. AO to Eleanor P. Mason, November 13, 1871, AO Papers.

27. TePaske, 32–34; Pardon File C-610; oath subscribed to by AO, July 8, 1872, Elmore Collection; Agard; Indictment of AO, Boston Case File; Pardons and Remissions, vol. 11, p. 189. There is some question of the timing of this trip. TePaske states that AO left England in June; however, Pauline's obituary says that she was born aboard the ship on February 29, 1872. It is possible that she was born on an earlier voyage before the family left England. See Newbern *Newbernian*, July 19, 1879.

28. Keene *New Hampshire Sentinel*, November 21, 1872; *Daily Memphis Avalanche*, November 18, 1872.

29. TePaske, 33; Land Records, vol. FF, p. 458, Office of the Register of Deeds, Carteret County, Beaufort, NC; Corinne Oaksmith to Coker, January 15, 1873, EOS Papers.

30. Goldsboro *Carolina Messenger*, June 25, July 20, 30, 1874; *Wilmington Journal*, July 31, 1874. Once elected, his opponents challenged his qualifications for office, but the house committee ruled in his favor and seated him. *Charlotte Democrat*, November 23, 1874.

31. Four black men served in the state senate, and thirteen in the lower house with AO. See J. G. De Roulhac Hamilton, *Reconstruction in North Carolina* (New York: Columbia University, 1914), 604.

32. TePaske, 34–39; AO to Benjamin F. Butler, September 16, 1874, in James A. Padgett, ed., "Reconstruction Letters from North Carolina, Part IX: Letters of Benjamin Franklin Butler," *North Carolina Historical Review* 21 (January 1944): 52–54; Paul D. Yandle, "'The Relapse of Reconstruction': Railroad-Building, Party Warfare and White Supremacy in Blue Ridge North Carolina, 1854–1888" (PhD diss., West Virginia University, 2006).

33. *Newbernian*, January 17, 1875; Raleigh *Weekly Sentinel*, January 26, 1875.

34. *Raleigh News*, February 9, 21, 1875; *Charlotte Observer*, February 20, 1875; Goldsboro *Messenger*, February 25, 1875; Alan Friedlander and Richard Allen Gerber, *Welcoming Ruin: The Civil Rights Act of 1875* (Boston: Brill, 2020), 582–83.

35. Sawyer to AO, October 26, November 2, 1874, AO to Sawyer, October 26, 1874, AMO to AO, October 28, 1874, Ellen Mason to Sawyer, November 13, 1874, AO, "In Memoriam," all in AO Papers.

36. EOS to Orestes Brownson, October 18, 1875, Brownson Papers; William Cullen Bryant to EOS, December 15, 1874, in William Cullen Bryant II and Thomas G. Vos, eds., *The Letters of William Cullen Bryant: Vol. VI, 1872–1878* (New York: Fordham University Press, 1992), 195.

37. Logbook of the *Minnie*, AO Collection; Charles O. Pitts, "Voyage of the *Minnie*: Appleton Oaksmith and the Hurricane of September 1875," *The Mailboat* 1 (Fall 1990); *New York Herald*, September 28, 1875; Raleigh *Biblical Recorder*, October 1, 1875. In some records the *Elizabeth* was called the *Elizabeth A.*

38. EOS to Bessie Oaksmith, May 29, 1879, EOS to AMO, November 29, 1878, both in EOS Papers; Alvin to AO, January 10, 1877, AO Papers.

39. Newbern, NC, *Newbernian*, July 19, 1879; EOS to AMO, December 3, 1878, EOS Papers; Corinne Oaksmith copybook, 1877–1878, AO Papers.

40. Bessie to AO, June 19, August 12, 1873, Corinne to AO, February 5, 1875, all in Ellmore Collection; 1900 United States census.

41. William B. Hesseltine, ed., *Dr. J. G. M. Ramsey: Autobiography and Letters* (Nashville: Tennessee Historical Commission, 1954), 311–17. There is also a significant amount of correspondence regarding this discovery in AO Papers.

42. AO to Ulysses S. Grant, March 22, 1876, Letter Book, 1874–1880, AO Papers.

43. Jeffrey L. Amestoy, *Slavish Shore: The Odyssey of Richard Henry Dana Jr.* (Cambridge, MA: Harvard University Press, 2015), 289–96.

44. EOS to Stanley Spence, December 3 and 10, 1875, EOS Papers; EOS to Samuel J. Tilden, February 22, 1876, Letter Book of EOS and AMO, 1876, AO Papers; *Boston Evening Transcript*, May 26, 1894. For a story that reveals EOS's views of anti-abolitionists, see *New York Times*, July 22, 1884.

45. Clippings from the *New York Tribune* and *New York Herald* in a scrapbook in AO Papers.

46. EOS to C. B. Stout, September 3, 1874, quoted in *Boston Evening Transcript*, May 26, 1894.

47. *Beaufort Eagle*, May 17, 1876; *Goldsboro Messenger*, May 22, 1876; AO, "Katharine," Newbern, NC, *Newbernian*, October 20, 1877.

48. Bankruptcy Docket of Appleton Oaksmith, Case #1640, Bankruptcy Act of 1867, RG 21 (Eastern District of North Carolina, Eastern Division [New Bern]), National Archives at Atlanta; A. W. Shaffer to AO, November 30, December 1, 1877, AO Papers; AO bankruptcy records, Romulus A. Nunn Papers, State Archives of North Carolina.

49. Alvin Oaksmith to AO, June 18, 1877, AO Papers.

50. EOS to AMO, December 3, 1878.

51. AO to John Pelletier, January 28, 1879.

52. AMO to EOS, March 13, 1879, EOS Papers.

53. Lewis J. Hardee Jr., *Three Southern Families: A History of Connecting Hardee, Jones and Davis Families of Coastal North Carolina* (Southport, NC: Southport Historical Society, 1994), 133–40, 324.

54. EOS to Bessie Oaksmith, May 29, 1879, EOS Papers.

55. Hardee, *Three Southern Families*, 158; EOS scrapbook, March 22, 1889, EOS Mss; Raleigh *Observer*, July 6, 1879. Two local yacht owners searched for Bessie's body but never found it. They charged Appleton $20 for their services, but said that if that was too much $15 would suffice. See George W. Glasier and A. P. Smith to AO, August 8, 1879, AO Papers.

CHAPTER 18. DEATH

1. AMO to Robert Simpson, December 8, 1879, AO Papers; Newbern, NC, *Newbernian*, July 19, 1879. A few condolence letters survive in AO Papers.

2. Hardee, *Three Southern Families*, 199.

3. Elizabeth Oaksmith to EOS, July 31, 1879, and Alvin Oaksmith to EOS, July 31, 1879, both in EOS Papers; EOS, "In Memoriam," August 12, 1879, published in the *Baltimorean*, September 27, 1879. Friends also published poems. See J. W. Lang, "Lines to Appleton Oaksmith," *Newbernian*, October 18, 1879.

4. TePaske, 42–43; AO to Daniel Bell, August 12, 1879, AO to Zebulon Vance, December 9, 1879, AMO to Mary McK. Nash, September 18, 1879, all in AO Papers.

5. Agard. This recollection notwithstanding, accounts survive of AO making great improvements to the property in the early 1880s. See AMO to EOS, March 31, 1881, EOS Papers.

6. *New York Herald*, December 26, 1878; *St. Louis Post Dispatch*, October 11, 1891; *New York Sunday News*, December 28, 1879; *Cincinnati Daily Gazette*, July 11, 1879; *Philadelphia Inquirer*, July 7, 1879; newspaper clipping dated July 1879 in SS, *Life and Writings of Major Jack Downing* on GoogleBooks. I have been unable to locate a copy of the issue of the *New York Sunday News* that contains Isotta's interview.

7. Fanny Oaksmith to AO, October 7, 1879, R. M. Pulsifer to AO, July 30, 1879, AO to Editors of the *New York Sunday News*, August 28, 1879; AO to the editor of the Raleigh *News*, September 27, 1829; George C. Jordan to AO, September 30, 1879, all in AO Papers.

8. Boston *Herald*, September 24, 1879; *New York Sunday News*, December 28, 1879.

9. Agard; TePaske, 42.

10. Alvin to AO, November 4, 1879, AO Papers. In 1887, EOS wrote in her diary of Alvin—"deserted by his selfish children who are in traits like their artful Spanish mother. Oh! these terrible mistakes in marriage are beyond expression dreadful. . . . My husband myself & my children were deficient in worldly wisdom—the generation that follows are likely to make amends. Self—self is a strong feature." Diary of EOS, January 3, 1887, EOS Mss. However, Alvin somehow reconciled to Delfina in Maryland in the 1890s. See 1890 US Census and Alvin Oaksmith to EOS, July 5, 1892, EOS Papers; *Passages from the Correspondence of Griswold*, 131.

11. AMO to Robert Simpson, December 8, 1879, AO to Alfred Williams, December 9, 1879, AO to Zebulon Vance, December 9, 1879, Vance to AO, December 11, 1879, all in AO Papers.

12. Raleigh *Observer*, October 19, 1879; AMO to Harriet V. Adams, November 29, 1879, AO Papers.

13. AMO to EOS, March 31, 1881, EOS Papers; St. Louis *Post-Dispatch*, October 11, 1891; Belfast, ME, *Republican Journal*, August 8, 1901; records at Ancestry.com/. Stories survived that after the drowning Randolph ran to tell the authorities that his father had purposefully drowned the girls. TePaske, 41–42.

14. See the series of letters from AO to AMO from 1883 in EOS Papers.

15. AMO to EOS, March 31, May 3, 1881, EOS Papers.

16. Diary of EOS, April 4, 1887, EOS Mss. She privately admitted, "I feel something like shame when I am writing on my Autobiography." Diary of EOS, April 29, 1887, EOS Mss.

17. EOS to AMO, April 15, 1886, EOS Papers; Diary of EOS, February 28, 1887, EOS Mss.

18. AO to AMO, March 12, 1883, EOS Papers.

19. EOS Autobiography, 181; Diary of EOS, February 1, 1887, EOS Mss.

20. AMO to EOS, March 31, 1881, EOS Papers; EOS to Edward C. Stedman, March 1, 1888, EOS Letters.

21. AO to EOS, August 15, 1886, AO Collection; Diary of EOS, February 1, March 30, 1887, EOS Mss.

22. Stanley Oaksmith to AO and AMO, September 5, 1887, EOS Papers; EOS scrapbook, March 22, 1889, EOS Mss.

23. Diary of EOS, January 13, February 14, March 22, April 13, 1887, EOS Mss.

24. EOS to Sarah A. Underwood, September 23, 1887, EOS letters; Diary of EOS, March 22, August 12, September 2, 1887, EOS Mss.

25. Diary of EOS, October 25, 1887, EOS Mss.

26. EOS to Edward C. Stedman, April 7, 1888, EOS Letters; Beaufort *Weekly Record*, November 18, 1887; TePaske, i; Agard; Aurora [Oaksmith Piper] and

Lewis [Piper] to AMO, October 29, 1887, AO Collection. Condolence letters are in AO Collection and EOS Papers.

27. Cronin, *Evolution of a Life*, 54–55.

28. Diary of EOS, November 9, December 3, 1887, EOS Mss; EOS to B. F. Underwood, December 7, 1887, and EOS to Edward C. Stedman, March 1, 1888, both in EOS Letters.

29. EOS scrapbook, March 22, 1889, EOS Mss.

30. EOS to Edward C. Stedman, March 1, 1888, EOS Letters.

31. EOS Autobiography, 174. See, for example, Emily Stipes Watts, *The Poetry of American Women from 1632 to 1945* (Austin: University of Texas Press, 1977), 97; Jeanne Winston Adler, *The Affair of the Veiled Murderess: An Antebellum Scandal and Mystery* (Albany: State University of New York Press, 2011), 178; Nicholas L. Syrett, *American Child Bride: A History of Minors and Marriage in the United States* (Chapel Hill: University of North Carolina Press, 2016), 98–102. Timothy Scherman has challenged the idea that EOS was unhappy in her marriage from the start.

32. SS to EOS, November 6, 1833, and EOS to SS, November 11, 16, 1833, all in EOS Papers. Kissing the paper reflected true affection, as EOS did the same thing in a letter to one of her granddaughters twenty-five years later. See EOS to Eva Oaksmith, June 9, 1858, NYHS.

33. EOS diary, November 1, 1861.

34. EOS to My Dearly beloved Children, August 10, 1851, EOS Papers.

35. Diary of EOS, January 1, 20, 1887, EOS Mss.

36. Undated newspaper clippings in EOS scrapbook, EOS Mss.

37. Loose diary page of EOS, June 16, [1889], EOS Mss.

38. Loose diary page of EOS, March 12, 1893, EOS Mss.

39. *Passages from the Correspondence of Griswold*, 131–32; S. F. Fales to AMO, November 18, 1893, EOS Papers; Inola Sanders to AMO, November 18, 1893, AO Papers.

APPENDIX 2: THE *WELLS* AND *MANUEL ORTIZ*

1. *United States v. Appleton Oaksmith*, RG 21 (Southern District of New York), NARA-NY; testimony of Richard Hall, January 22, 1862, Boston Case File; Pardon File C-610; Marques, *United States and the Transatlantic Slave Trade*, 246. A British agent in New York believed that the *Wells* and *Augusta* were "fitted out by the same parties." See FO 84/1138, page 160.

2. *United States v. Margaret Scott*, RG 21 (District of Massachusetts), National Archives at Boston. The British consul in New York reported that the *Manuel Ortiz* had been sold by Samuel P. Skinner to a Liverpool man about August 1861, and that "there appeared to be nothing suspicious" in the transaction, but that it may have been a "fraudulent one" to hide their true purpose. See Edward M. Archibald to My Lord, September 17, 1861, FO 84/1138. For a news report, see *Boston Morning Journal*, November 21, 1861, which mistakenly called the vessel the *Manuel Cortez*.

SELECTED BIBLIOGRAPHY

MANUSCRIPTS

Boston, MA

    Boston City Archives

        Charles Street Jail Records

    Boston Public Library

        Anti-Slavery Collection
        Rufus W. Griswold Papers

    Massachusetts Historical Society

        Dana Family Papers

    Massachusetts State Archives

        Suffolk County Criminal Calendar for 1862

    National Archives at Boston

        RG 21 (Records of the US District and Circuit Courts for the District of Massachusetts)
        RG 21 (Records of the US District and Circuit Courts for the District of New Hampshire)

Cambridge, MA

    Houghton Library, Harvard University

        John A. Quitman Papers
        Wendell Phillips Papers

Chapel Hill, NC

Southern Historical Collection, University of North Carolina

Appleton Oaksmith Collection
Edmund Kirby-Smith Papers

Charlottesville, VA

Albert and Shirley Small Special Collections Library, University of Virginia

Elizabeth Oakes Smith Papers

College Park, MD

National Archives at College Park

Record Group 56 (General Records of the Department of the Treasury)

Entry 27 (Miscellaneous Letters Sent, 1789–1878)

Record Group 59 (General Records of the Department of State)

Entry 59 (Consular Instructions)
Entry 113 (Miscellaneous Correspondence, 1784–1906)
Entry 788 (Permanent Attorneys' Commissions, 1825–1888)
Entry 789 (Temporary Attorneys' Commissions, 1829–1887)
Entry 897 (Presidential Pardons and Remissions, 1794–1893)
Entry 955 (Secret Correspondence, 1861–1863)
Entry 963 (Correspondence Regarding Prisoners of War, 1861–1862)

RG 60 (General Records of the Department of Justice)

Entry 9-A (Letters Received by the Attorney General, 1809–1870)
Entry 350 (Records Relating to the Appointment of Federal Judges, Marshals, and Attorneys, 1853–1901)

RG 76 (Records of Boundary and Claims Commissions and Arbitrations)

Entry 434 (Miscellaneous Claims, ca. 1812–1874)

RG 204 (Records of the Office of the Pardon Attorney)

Entry 1a (Pardon Case Files, 1853–1946)

Concord, MA

Concord Free Public Library

John Shepard Keyes Papers

Durham, NC

    David M. Rubenstein Rare Book and Manuscript Library, Duke University

        Appleton Oaksmith Papers
        Charles Macgill Papers
        Frank M. Harris Autograph Book
        US Army Autograph Book

Greenville, NC

    Special Collections, East Carolina University

        William E. Elmore Collection

Kew, UK

    National Archives of the United Kingdom

        Records of the Foreign Office (FO)
        Records of the Home Office (HO)

New Bedford, MA

    New Bedford Whaling Museum

        Agard Collection

New York, NY

    Gilder Lehrman Institute of American History

        Gilder Lehrman Collection

    National Archives at New York

        RG 21 (Records of the US District and Circuit Courts for the Southern District of New York)

    New-York Historical Society

        Appleton Oaksmith Letters

    New York Public Library

        Elizabeth Oakes Smith Papers
        Horace Greeley Papers
        Miscellaneous Personal Papers
        Seba Smith Papers

Notre Dame, IN

    University of Notre Dame Archives

        Orestes Augustus Brownson Papers

Rochester, NY

    University of Rochester

        William Henry Seward Papers

Syracuse, NY

    Special Collections Research Center, Syracuse University Libraries

        Gerrit Smith Papers

Washington, DC

    Folger Shakespeare Library

        Autograph Letters Signed from Elizabeth Oakes Smith

    Manuscript Division, Library of Congress

        Abraham Lincoln Papers
        Horatio King Papers
        John White Scott Papers
        Roger W. Hanson Papers

    National Archives and Records Administration

        RG 45 (Naval Records Collection of the Office of Naval Records and Library)

            Entry 608 (Logs and Journals Kept by US Naval Officers, March 1776–June 1908)

        RG 94 (Records of the Adjutant General's Office)
        RG 109 (War Department Collection of Confederate Records)

DIGITIZED DATABASES

Ancestry.com
Gale
JSTOR
Newspapers.com
ProQuest
Readex

PUBLISHED PRIMARY SOURCES

Basler, Roy P., and Christian O. Basler, eds. *The Collected Works of Abraham Lincoln: Second Supplement, 1848–1865.* New Brunswick, NJ: Rutgers University Press, 1990.

Basler, Roy P. et al., eds. *The Collected Works of Abraham Lincoln.* 9 vols. New Brunswick, NJ: Rutgers University Press, 1953.

Beale, Howard K., ed., *The Diary of Edward Bates, 1859–1866.* Washington, DC: Government Printing Office, 1933.

Congressional Globe.

Cronin, David E. *The Evolution of a Life Described in the Memoirs of Major Seth Eyland.* New York: S. W. Green's Son, 1884.

Dana, Richard Henry Jr. *Two Years Before the Mast: A Personal Narrative.* 1840; new edition, Boston: Fields, Osgood, & Co., 1869.

Foote, Andrew H. *Africa and the American Flag.* New York: D. Appleton, 1854.

Gienapp, William E., and Erica L. Gienapp, eds. *The Civil War Diary of Gideon Welles, Lincoln's Secretary of the Navy: The Original Manuscript Edition.* Urbana: University of Illinois Press, 2014.

Gilliland, C. Herbert, ed. *USS* Constellation *on the Dismal Coast: Willie Leonard's Journal, 1859–1861.* Columbia: University of South Carolina Press, 2013.

Kirkland, Leigh. "'A Human Life: Being the Autobiography of Elizabeth Oakes Smith': A Critical Edition and Introduction." PhD diss., Georgia State University, 1994.

Kunce, Catherine, ed. *The Correspondence of Sarah Helen Whitman to Julia Deane Freeman: Writer to Writer, Woman to Woman.* Wilmington: University of Delaware Press, 2013.

Nevins, Allan, and Milton Halsey Thomas, eds. *The Diary of George Templeton Strong.* 4 vols. New York: Macmillan, 1952.

Oakes Smith, Elizabeth. *The Poetical Writings of Elizabeth Oakes Smith.* New York: J. S. Redfield, 1845.

———. *The Western Captive and Other Indian Stories.* Edited by Caroline M. Woidat. Tonawanda, NY: Broadview, 2015.

———. *Woman and Her Needs.* New York: Fowlers & Wells, 1851.

Palmer, Beverly Wilson, ed. *The Selected Letters of Charles Sumner.* 2 vols. Boston: Northeastern University Press, 1990.

Papers Relating to Foreign Affairs, Accompanying the Annual Message of the President to the Second Session Thirty-Eighth Congress. Washington, DC: G.P.O., 1865.

Passages from the Correspondence and Other Papers of Rufus W. Griswold. Cambridge, MA: W. M. Griswold, 1898.

The Proceedings of the Woman's Rights Convention, Held at Syracuse, September 8th, 9th & 10th, 1852. Syracuse: J. E. Masters, 1852.

Smith, Seba. *The Life and Writings of Major Jack Downing of Downingville, Away Down Eastin the State of Maine.* Boston: Lilly, Wait, Colman & Holden, 1834.

————. *My Thirty Years Out of the Senate*. New York: Oaksmith, 1859.

————. *New Elements of Geometry*. New York: George P. Putnam, 1850.

US Reports.

US Statutes at Large.

War of the Rebellion: A Compilation of the Official Records of the Union and Confederate Armies. 128 vols. Washington, DC: Government Printing Office, 1880–1901.

White, Jonathan W., and Daniel Glenn, eds. "The Politics of Judging: The Civil War Letters of William D. Shipman." *Connecticut History Review* 59 (Spring 2020): 80–100.

SECONDARY SOURCES

Amestoy, Jeffrey L. *Slavish Shore: The Odyssey of Richard Henry Dana Jr.* Cambridge, MA: Harvard University Press, 2015.

Anstey, Roger. *Britain and the Congo in the Nineteenth Century*. Oxford, UK: Oxford University Press, 1962.

Bonner, Michael Brem, and Peter McCord. *The Union Blockade in the American Civil War: A Reassessment*. Knoxville: University of Tennessee Press, 2021.

Brooks, George E. Jr. *Yankee Traders, Old Coasters, and African Middlemen: A History of American Legitimate Trade with West Africa in the Nineteenth Century*. Boston, MA: Boston University Press, 1970.

Burlingame, Michael. *Abraham Lincoln: A Life*. 2 vols. Baltimore: Johns Hopkins University Press, 2008.

Canney, Donald L. *Africa Squadron: The US Navy and the Slave Trade, 1842–1861*. Washington, DC: Potomac Books, 2006.

Dickey, Christopher. *Our Man in Charleston: Britain's Secret Agent in the Civil War South*. New York: Crown, 2015.

Ellis, L. Tuffly. "Maritime Commerce on the Far Western Gulf, 1861–1865." *Southwestern Historical Quarterly* 77 (October 1973): 167–226.

Graden, Dale T. *Disease, Resistance, and Lies: The Demise of the Transatlantic Slave Trade to Brazil and Cuba*. Baton Rouge: Louisiana State University Press, 2014.

————. *From Slavery to Freedom in Brazil: Bahia, 1835–1900*. Albuquerque: University of New Mexico Press, 2006.

Harris, John. *The Last Slave Ships: New York and the End of the Middle Passage*. New Haven, CT: Yale University Press, 2021.

————. "Yankee 'Blackbirding': The United States and the Illegal Transatlantic Slave Trade, 1850–1867." PhD diss., Johns Hopkins University, 2017.

Horne, Gerald. *The Deepest South: The United States, Brazil, and the African Slave Trade*. New York: New York University Press, 2007.

Howard, Warren S. *American Slavers and the Federal Law, 1837–1862*. Berkeley: University of California Press, 1963.

Karp, Matthew. *This Vast Southern Empire: Slaveholders at the Helm of American Foreign Policy.* Cambridge, MA: Harvard University Press, 2016.

Kirkland, Leigh. "Elizabeth Oakes Smith." In Denise D. Knight, ed., *Nineteenth-Century American Women Writers: A Bio-Bibliographical Critical Sourcebook.* Westport, CT: Greenwood, 1997, 324–30.

Lloyd, Christopher. *The Navy and the Slave Trade: The Suppression of the African Slave Trade in the Nineteenth Century.* London: Frank Cass, 1968.

Marques, Leonardo. *The United States and the Transatlantic Slave Trade to the Americas, 1776–1867.* New Haven, CT: Yale University Press, 2016.

Martin, Phyllis M. *The External Trade of the Loango Coast, 1576–1870.* New York: Oxford University Press, 1972.

May, Robert E. *John A. Quitman: Old South Crusader.* Baton Rouge: Louisiana State University Press, 1985.

———. *Manifest Destiny's Underworld: Filibustering in Antebellum America.* Chapel Hill: University of North Carolina Press, 2002.

———. *The Southern Dream of a Caribbean Empire, 1854–1861.* Baton Rouge: Louisiana State University Press, 1973.

Milne, A. Taylor. "The Lyons-Seward Treaty of 1862." *American Historical Review* 38 (April 1933): 511–25.

Neely, Mark E., Jr. *The Fate of Liberty: Abraham Lincoln and Civil Liberties.* New York: Oxford University Press, 1991.

———. *Lincoln and the Democrats: The Politics of Opposition in the Civil War.* New York: Cambridge University Press, 2017.

Nickels, Cameron C. "Seba Smith Embattled." *Maine Historical Society Quarterly* 13 (1973): 7–27.

Ray, Angela G. "Performing Womanhood: The Lyceum Lectures of Elizabeth Oakes Smith." Paper delivered at the Society for the Study of American Women Writers, November 2006.

Reilly, Kevin S. "Slavers in Disguise: American Whaling and the African Slave Trade, 1845–1862." *American Neptune* 53 (June 1993): 177–89.

Richards, Leonard L. *The California Gold Rush and the Coming of the Civil War.* New York: Knopf, 2007.

Rickels, Milton, and Patricia Rickels. *Seba Smith.* Boston: Twayne Publishers, 1977.

Scherman, Timothy H. "Looking for Liz, or, On Being Haunted by Elizabeth Oakes Smith." *The Researcher* 14 (Spring/Summer 1998): 4–13.

———. "Oakes Smith Returns to Maine: 'The Defeated Life,' Katahdin, and the Dangers of Biographical Criticism." Gorman Lecture Series, Yarmouth History Center, June 10, 2014.

Seward, Frederick W. *Seward at Washington, as Senator and Secretary of State.* New York: Derby and Miller, 1891.

Soodalter, Ron. *Hanging Captain Gordon: The Life and Trial of an American Slave Trader.* New York: Atria, 2006.

Spears, John R. *The American Slave-Trade: An Account of Its Origin, Growth and Suppression.* New York: Charles Scribner's Sons, 1900.

Stahr, Walter. *Seward: Lincoln's Indispensable Man.* New York: Simon & Schuster, 2012.

Swisher, Carl Brent. *The Oliver Wendell Holmes Devise History of the Supreme Court of the United States, Vol. V: The Taney Period, 1836–64.* New York: Macmillan, 1974.

Syrett, Nicholas L. *American Child Bride: A History of Minors and Marriage in the United States.* Chapel Hill: University of North Carolina Press, 2016.

TePaske, John Jay. "The Life of Appleton Oaksmith: Its Latin American Aspects." MA thesis, Duke University, 1953.

Tuchinsky, Adam. "'Woman and Her Needs': Elizabeth Oakes Smith and the Divorce Question." *Journal of Women's History* 28 (Spring 2016): 38–59.

Varon, Elizabeth R. *We Mean to be Counted: White Women and Politics in Antebellum Virginia.* Chapel Hill: University of North Carolina Press, 1998.

Watts, Emily Stipes. *The Poetry of American Women from 1632 to 1945.* Austin: University of Texas Press, 1977.

White, Jonathan W. *Abraham Lincoln and Treason during the Civil War: The Trials of John Merryman.* Baton Rouge: Louisiana State University Press, 2011.

Wyman, Mary Alice. *Two American Pioneers: Seba Smith and Elizabeth Oakes Smith.* New York: Columbia University Press, 1924.

INDEX

ABOUT THE AUTHOR

Jonathan W. White is professor of American studies at Christopher Newport University and is the author or editor of sixteen books that cover a variety of topics related to the Civil War. He serves as vice chair of The Lincoln Forum, on the Ford's Theatre Advisory Council, and on the boards of directors of the Abraham Lincoln Association and the Abraham Lincoln Institute. In 2019 he won the State Council of Higher Education for Virginia's Outstanding Faculty Award—the highest honor bestowed upon college faculty by the Commonwealth of Virginia. Last year he published *A House Built by Slaves: African American Visitors to the Lincoln White House*, winner of the 2023 Gilder Lehrman Lincoln Prize.